Boats and Boating in the Adirondacks

Hallie E. Bond

Boats and

Introduction by Philip G. Terrie

Boating

IN THE

Adirondacks

The Adirondack Museum / Syracuse University Press

EDITOR: Alice Wolf Gilborn
PHOTOGRAPHY: Boat hulls, Erik Borg; Artifacts and ephemera,
Lemon and Lemon, unless specified.
CONTRUCTION DRAWINGS: Samuel F. Manning, unless specified.
MAP: Jon Luoma.

Composed in Adobe Garamond types.
Printed by Thompson-Shore, Inc.
Book design by Christopher Kuntze.

The paper used in this publication meets the minimum requirements
of American National Standard for Information Sciences—Permanence of
Paper for Printed Library Materials, ANSI Z39.48-1984.

Research and publication of *Boats and Boating in the Adirondacks* were
funded in part by the National Endowment for the Humanities.

Jacket illustrations
FRONT: *Past and Present*, ca. 1890. Painting by Seneca Ray Stoddard.
BACK: Guideboats crossing an Adirondack carry on a wagon instead of on
the shoulders of guides. Hand-tinted glass lantern slide, ca. 1890.

Printed in the United States of America

FIRST PAPERBACK EDITION 1998
98 99 00 01 02 03   6 5 4 3 2 1

Library of Congress Cataloging-in-Publication Data:

Bond, Hallie E.
    Boats and boating in the Adirondacks / Hallie E. Bond ; with an
introduction by Philip G. Terrie. — 1st ed.
        p.   cm.
    Includes bibliographical references (p. 325) and index.

    ISBN 0-8156-0373-8 (alk. paper)
    ISBN 0-8156-0374-6 (pbk.: alk. paper)

    1. Boats and boating—New York (State)—Adirondack Mountains
Region—History. 2. Boatbuilding—New York (State)—Adirondack
Mountains Region—History. 3. Adirondack Mountains Region
(N.Y.)—History. 4. Adirondack Museum—Catalogs. I. Adirondack
Museum. II. Title.

VM351.B596   1995   95-8603
797'.09747'5—dc20

NOTE TO THE READER

A few definitions of words that have peculiar meanings in the Adirondacks,
or that are used in their nineteenth-century sense in this book are in order
here:

North Country: that region of New York State north of the Mohawk and
    south of the St. Lawrence rivers, east of Lake Ontario, and west of Lake
    Champlain.

Sport: a sportsman or sportswoman, referred to as such by the guides and
    periodicals of the nineteenth century.

Yacht: used here in its technical sense: a boat built or used primarily for
    pleasure.

Camp: any overnight accommodation in the Adirondacks, from a tent or
    bark lean-to to a summer estate with many buildings.

Contents

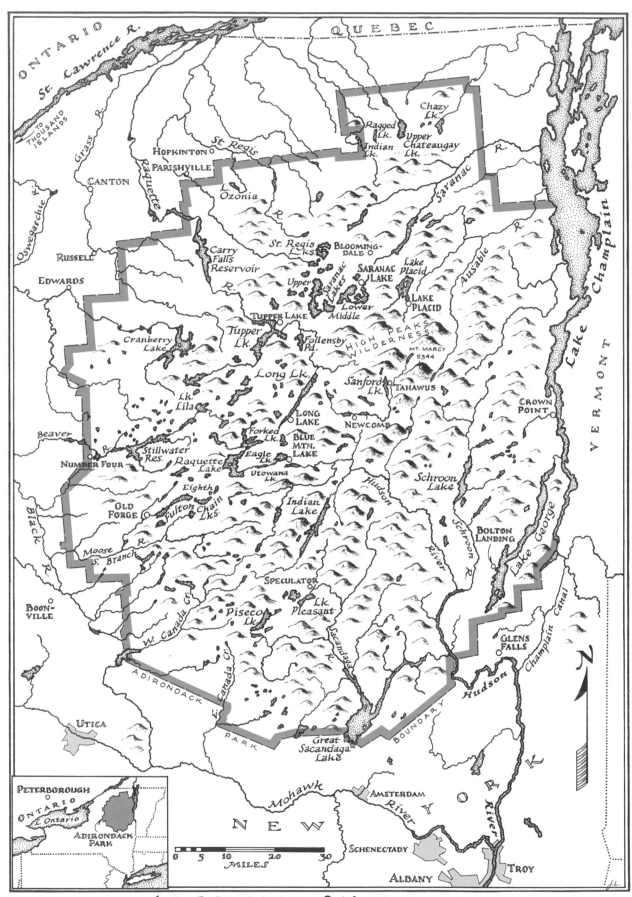

ADIRONDACK WATERWAYS

Foreword

The Adirondack Museum opened to the public in 1957 as an institution devoted to exploring and presenting the history of the Adirondack region, the place and its people. The museum's exhibitions and publications document the complex interaction between people and the land over time that has shaped the nature of work, commerce, recreation, and the creative imagination in the Adirondacks.

The Adirondack Museum is located at the center of the Adirondack Park, a mixture of private and state-owned lands, the largest park of any kind in the lower forty-eight states. Six million acres and equal in size to the state of Vermont, the Park contains 1,500 miles of rivers and more than 2,800 lakes and ponds. Throughout the history of the exploration and settlement of the region, the use of water has been key. The story of boats and boating in the Adirondacks crosscuts that history at every turn.

In 1991 the museum opened a newly renovated and interpreted exhibition on boats and boating, based on major research efforts by Curator Hallie Bond and staff. Inevitably, the exhibition was a synthesis of that research, and much valuable scholarship entered the museum's research files, inaccessible to a broader public. The museum decided in 1992 to expand the project and bring the story of boats and boating in the Adirondacks to new audiences. A major grant from the National Endowment for the Humanities made possible continued research. The grant, which brought humanities scholars and boat experts together with museum staff, resulted in a cross fertilization of new ideas and analysis that built on earlier research efforts.

This publication is a result of that collaboration. We thank the National Endowment for the Humanities for providing essential support for the research, writing, and production of *Boats and Boating in the Adirondacks*. Syracuse University Press is our publishing partner, and we thank them for a long and collegial relationship. Finally, I want to thank the project consultants, volunteers, and especially the staff of the Adirondack Museum for their ideas, energy, and continuing commitment to this project.

Jacqueline F. Day
DIRECTOR

Acknowledgments

"More than just boats," a recent brochure advertising the Adirondack Museum reminded the public. It is certainly that, with collections of fine art and rustic furniture that could stand on their own as specialized museums, and hundreds of other types of objects, from carriages to sugaring equipment to industrial equipment, which document the history of life in the Adirondacks. But it cannot be denied that the museum has one of the major maritime collections on the continent, renowned not only for its size and quality, but for its thorough documentation of the boats of a particular region. It consists not only of boat hulls, but paddles, oars and rigs, photographs, catalogs, manuscripts and printed material illustrating and documenting the use of boats in the Adirondacks. Nearly all the research for this book was done in the museum's collections, and all the boats, objects, photographs, ephemera and works of art used as illustrations are in its collections unless otherwise stated.

The first director of the museum, Robert Bruce Inverarity, recognized the importance of small craft in the region, particularly the guideboat, and laid the foundations for the collection. Acting on the advice of then Smithsonian curator Howard I. Chapelle, he initially collected broadly, envisioning a small craft museum of the world. He quickly narrowed his focus to that of the museum as a whole and concentrated on boats made or used in the Adirondacks. That collecting policy has been maintained to the present.

It has been my privilege to work with this collection for the past eight years. It was while curating the revision of the boat exhibit that I conceived the idea for a book which would not only enable me to interpret the boats in greater depth than was possible in an exhibit, interweaving the story of boating in the region with detailed information about the individual watercraft, but make the collection available to a much broader audience. The result was this combination of a narrative history and catalog. The two parts are meant to be read together, and the hope is that each section will enrich the reader's understanding of the other.

In a very real sense, this book could not have been written without the help of a man who died before I ever began work on it. The painstaking research of Kenneth Durant, now housed on two ten-foot-high shelves in the manuscript vault of the Adirondack Museum library and exhaustively indexed by Helen Durant, was as good as a doctoral advisor in directing me to sources to check and questions to ask.

I had another set of advisors, as well, who were more available for questioning. Readers James West Davidson, Michael T. Marsden, Philip G. Terrie, and Paul Jamieson all made extensive and invaluable comments on the narrative history from their perspectives as historians and writers. Small-craft historians Maynard Bray and Benjamin A. G. Fuller reviewed the catalog entries in addition to the narrative. My husband Mason Smith was untiring in explaining technical details of small-boat construction and performance and working out their ramifications with me. He also wrote five of the six construction notes and the glossary. My parents Robert F. and Mary J. Bond laid the groundwork for this book by teaching me how exciting and interesting history can be. In addition, they commented extensively on the manuscript in an effort to get me to write it as clearly as possible.

Photography of the collection for the catalog entries was made possible by the efforts—sometimes verging on the heroic—of a small corps of volunteers. In groups of two per day during three week-long sessions they hauled the boats out of their storage racks, cleaned them, positioned them for photography, and replaced them. Undaunted by heights, bad lighting, dust, crawling into cramped spaces, and my "cracking the whip," they even managed to keep *my* spirits up: Jim Amodio, Todd Burley, Al Lowe, Bill McPeak, Tom Malone, Larry Manion, Victor Pennes, Clara Rainis, Carl Stearns, and Fred Vanacore. In a class by herself was Jennifer Sundheim, who volunteered for two months, pitching in on boat-moving days as needed, as well as locating photographs for illustrations and checking footnotes.

The photos of the boats themselves were taken by Erik Borg, who not only delivered a superb visual record of the collection under sometimes trying conditions, but who is a true professional with whom it is a pleasure to work.

Throughout the eight years leading up to publication, I had the help of two energetic research assistants. Jennifer Johnson spent the summer of 1989 at the museum as an intern in the Hagley Program and recataloged most of the boats, establishing consistent measurements on them. She was assisted by volunteers Michael Anderson, Judy Damkoehler, Jane Jenks, Larry Manion, Victor Pennes, Walter Valliancourt, and Sidney Whelan. For three summers, I had the assistance of Neil Poppensiek, who checked endless details, filled in the story of the outboard motor in the Adirondacks, selected words for the glossary, and assembled the builders' list.

Adirondack Museum staff were generous with help in their areas of responsibility. The maintenance crew moved and removed boats and equipment to facilitate research and photography; Scott Chartier deserves special thanks for his cheerful assistance. Librarian Jerold Pepper is a resource himself, in addition to attending promptly to my numerous interlibrary loan requests. The curatorial staff all helped take care of my normal curatorial duties while I was preoccupied with the book. Registrar Tracy Meehan and Jim Meehan assisted by locating and pulling material for illustrations. Curatorial assistant Karen Joyce dealt ably with the clerical details. Even other departments pitched in; Michelle Pierson and Helen Schaeffer of Education and Development, respectively, gave far more than was required. I owe a particularly large debt of gratitude to the museum's editor of books and publications, Alice Gilborn. She not only brought her experience and professionalism to initial editorial work on the book, but helped me maintain my faith in the project from the beginning.

It was shortly after I joined the Adirondack Museum curatorial staff that I was given the opportunity to revise the boat exhibit, one of the oldest and best-loved exhibits on campus. That work fed my interest in the subject of small boats and their place in Adirondack history, and ultimately resulted in this book. I thank the director at the time, Craig Gilborn, for trusting me with this tremendous opportunity. I also thank his successor, Jacqueline Day, for encouraging me to continue with the project. And finally, in a very tangible sense, this book would not have been possible without the support of the National Endowment for the Humanities. That assistance is gratefully acknowledged.

INTRODUCTION   PHILIP G. TERRIE

This Venice of America

Adirondack history is a tale written on the water. In the Adirondacks, people have traveled, conducted warfare, hunted and fished, gone to church, proposed marriage, driven logs—in short, done just about everything that people can do in a mountainous, forested country—in, on, from, or by water. And it all required boats. Without boats, small and large, Adirondack history—social, recreational, commercial, and environmental—would be an affair entirely different from what we have come to know.

The first white man to see the Adirondacks, French explorer Jacques Cartier, did so on October 3, 1535; a few days earlier he had ascended the St. Lawrence to near the site of the modern city of Montreal in *L'Émerillon*, a pinnace of 40 tuns, the smallest of the ships with which he had sailed from France the previous May and the only one capable of sailing up the shoally and rapid St. Lawrence above Quebec. *L'Émerillon*, according to marine historian Samuel Eliot Morison, was a "small maneuverable vessel which carried oars as well as sails." Above Lac Saint-Pierre, even *L'Émerillon* encountered tough going, and Cartier and his crew proceeded from there in longboats, manned by six oarsmen—three to a side—and a coxswain. In three strenuous days they rowed up to Hochelaga, a Huron village located on the site of the modern Montreal.

Once at Hochelaga, Cartier, who hoped to follow the St. Lawrence if not quite to China then at least to a western sea, realized that the longboats could go no further (though he was conducted by his Huron hosts to the top of a hill, whence he got that first glimpse of the Adirondacks). The rapids at Lachine, which Cartier named in ironic recognition of the fact that they put an end to his search for a route to the Orient, prevented the passage of any boat larger than a canoe. Cartier thus found himself confronting just the circumstances that many an Adirondack explorer, sportsman, guide, or tourist would face repeatedly several centuries later: the condition of the waterways—including depth, rapidity of flow, and location of obstacles—determines the facility or even the possibility of movement. To get where you want to go in the Adirondacks, you need specialized craft, boats that are small and sturdy. Cartier apparently did not trust the Huron canoes at Hochelaga and so descended the river back to Quebec, passing along the way the mouth of the Richelieu River, which led, though he of course did not realize it, to Lake Champlain and the eastern foothills of the Adirondacks.[1]

Even though the Adirondack region was thus sighted, however distantly, at a point relatively early in the long saga of the European exploration, conquest, and settlement of North America, precisely those factors that frustrated Cartier kept the Adirondacks virtually unknown to whites for almost three centuries after that initial voyage up the St. Lawrence. In the middle of the eighteenth century, British cartographers knew more about the sources of the Ohio River than they did about the Adirondack fountains of the Hudson (Lake Tear of the

Clouds, the highest lake source of the Hudson, remained unknown until 1872). Explorer and map maker Lewis Evans, writing in 1755, could say of the country lying between the St. Lawrence and Mohawk rivers only that it "is entirely impassable by Reason of Ridges and Hills, not yet being broken, to drain the vast drowned Land and Swamps."[2] In 1784 the statesman and geographer Thomas Pownall confessed near total ignorance of the region: "It is said to be a broken unpracticable Tract; I own I could never learn any Thing about it."[3]

The difficulty of traveling through the North Woods by land and the preferability of watercraft were noted in fictional accounts of the eighteenth-century wars between the French and English. In James Fenimore Cooper's *The Last of the Mohicans,* Hawkeye and his Mohican comrades, hoping to rescue Alice and Cora Monroe, who had been kidnapped by hostile Hurons, conduct a lengthy debate on how most efficiently to prosecute the pursuit. The Mohicans argue for a rapid march through the forest, while Hawkeye insists that they take to their canoes and the waters of Lake George. Hawkeye, who knows the region well, finally prevails when he describes the "long and painful path" they must follow if they leave the water and compares it to "the light and graceful movements of a canoe." The next day, they set out in their canoe, but near the outlet, while negotiating "crooked and intricate channels," they are set upon by a Huron war party. The result is a dramatic canoe chase, punctuated by the rifle shots, war whoops, and hair-breadth escapes that made Cooper the best-selling novelist of his day.[4]

Even though Hawkeye and his little band are eventually forced into the forest to elude yet another war party, their experience illustrates fictionally what Cartier may have suspected and what a century and a half of Adirondack history have shown to be the case in fact: this is a region where geography and topography resist easy exploration. The uncut forest of the late eighteenth century, the same dense and dark forest that confronted both the first settlers and the first sportsmen in the following century, was roadless, nearly pathless, and often close to absolute impenetrability. Where men, horses, mules, or oxen had to work slavishly and excruciatingly slowly to move

themselves and their burdens even a short distance through this tangled matrix of old growth mixed with fallen trees and scattered new growth, small boats could glide relatively effortlessly across and along the region's many lakes, ponds, and rivers. Writing in 1849, the Reverend Joel T. Headley described clearly the superiority of boats when compared with travel by land:

To wander among the [Adirondacks] is the hardest toil that a forest life presents. Without roads, your only reliance the guide and compass, you are compelled to wade streams, cross marshes, and climb over vast tracts of fallen timber, and at last, when night comes on, pull your own couch from the fir trees around. If it were not that a chain of lakes extends the entire length of the wilderness, cutting it in two, it would be impenetrable. Along these sheets of water—from one to another, and around rapids and cataracts, the adventurer rows his boat or carries it on his head.[5]

From Lake George in the southeast to Cranberry Lake in the northwest, from the Chateaugay Lakes in the northeast to the Moose River in the southwest, and especially in the case of the magnificent lakes of the central plateau, the Adirondack region is a land of waterways. Often interconnected, these streams and lakes offer a transportation network unavailable (throughout most of Adirondack history) on *terra firma.* Before the arrival of the railroad, which began pushing into the region after the Civil War, getting from place to place in the Adirondacks was immeasurably easier along waterways than on land.

And even when railroads began to be constructed, the same factors that had always made getting about on land difficult made it hard to lay tracks. Serious land transport in the Adirondacks did not truly arrive until well into the present century (the last Adirondack river drive of logs occurred after World War II).[6] Once railroads (and, later, highways) were built, of course, they became more or less established and permanent, and the primacy of the waterway— except for the case of recreation—was a thing of the past.

Early in the nineteenth century, long before road or rail transportation was available, the first white settlers in the central Adirondacks began immigrating in small family groups. Actual dates for homesteads are difficult to set with precision, but we know that a family was struggling to establish a farm near Newcomb before 1820, and about a decade after that settlers were doing the same as deep in the wilderness as the shore of Long Lake.[7] With no roads and only primitive paths, these hardy pioneers relied on boats.

Explorers, too, depended on small boats in this largely uncharted wilderness. One of the most interesting of the early expeditions of exploration was undertaken by geologist Ebenezer Emmons, who, beginning in 1836 and for the following five summers, worked for the New York Natural History Survey and pursued his research in northern New York (among other things, he led the first recorded ascent of Mount Marcy, which he named, in August, 1837; he also proposed the name "Adirondack" for the entire mountainous region).[8] The Natural History Survey was an ambitious attempt to examine, catalog, and encourage the exploitation of all of New York's geological, botanical, and zoological resources. Emmons, a professor at both Williams College and the Albany Medical College, was assigned the task of describing the geology of most of the Adirondacks.

In June of 1840, Emmons met zoologist James DeKay, also employed by the Natural History Survey, at Lake Pleasant, where they began a lengthy and mostly water-borne tour of the Adirondacks. They trekked by foot to Lewey Lake near Indian Lake, where they rendezvoused with Elijah Benedict (also known as Lewis Elijah), the Abenaki Indian for whose early cabin and clearing Indian Lake is named. From Emmons's account of their subsequent adventures, it is hard to tell whether Benedict's skills as woodsman or his trusty canoe were more vital to the success of their mission, which eventually carried them all the way to the Saranac lakes, with a side trip to Old Forge. Emmons was impressed with Benedict's

birch canoe [which] gave us a safe transport through the wilderness for at least one hundred miles, together with our camp equipment, as tents, pork, bread, fish, guns, traps, hammers, and various objects caught by the way, making, in the whole, a tolerable load for so frail a bark, considering that it must necessarily pass over stones and sandbars and against rocks and logs, and overcome the various obstructions incident to a wild and unfrequented country.[9]

Emmons and DeKay did not know it, but they were helping to establish what would become a major element in the story of the Adirondacks in the nineteenth century: they were outsiders who came to the Adirondacks to see the wilderness, and they needed both the woodcraft and the small boat of a local man to get them from place to place and to keep them fed and healthy. The men (and a few women) who followed Emmons to the wilderness were usually not scientists; they came just to fish, hunt, and restore body and soul amid the scenic and recreational glories of the Adirondacks, but Emmons and DeKay helped to establish the pattern for these increasingly popular camping trips.

After several strenuous portages—or, as these often necessary interruptions of water-borne travel are universally called in the Adirondacks, after several carries—Emmons and his party reached Raquette Lake. Perhaps because their guide's canoe was indispensable to their expedition, Emmons had boats on his mind and remarked of the many tamarack trees along the Marion River that "the smaller trees are suitable for spars, while the larger, together with the principal roots[,] are adapted in all respects to form the substantial parts of vessels or boats."[10] Though this particular species did not in fact figure prominently in local boat building, Emmons was prescient in predicting that Adirondack timber would support such an industry.

At Raquette Lake Emmons visited the rough compound established by that lake's first settlers, a pair of rugged men named, amazingly, Beach and Wood. After admiring their vegetable garden, Emmons went on to display again his intuitive grasp of the region's future and the vital role to be played by small boats. He described Raquette Lake in detail:

The waters are clear but generally ruffled with the breeze. It is well supplied with lake trout which often weigh twenty pounds. The neighboring forests abound also in deer and other game. Hence it is finely suited for the temporary residence of those who are troubled with *ennui*, or who wish to escape for a time during the months of July and August from the cares of business or the heat and bustle of the city. To enable the traveller or invalid to make the most of the situation, a supply of light boats are [sic] always on hand for fishing or hunting, or for exploring the inlets and neighboring lakes which are connected with the Racket [sic].[11]

Emmons thus predicted what would become a prominent feature of the Adirondack story. As he so eloquently announced, here was a region whose recreational opportunities appeared limitless. The tourist seeking an escape from the drudgeries and distractions of modern life would find solace and rest amidst the scenic lakes of the central Adirondacks. All the tourist needed was a boat and a guide, preferably one as "safe and intelligent" as Elijah Benedict.[12]

Emmons was writing at a time when a variety of cultural factors were coming together that would encourage just the sort of recreational use of the Adirondacks he predicted. The romantic temperament, with its faith in the redemptive powers of nature, exercised enormous power among the American middle and upper classes. Emerging in Europe during the last decades of the eighteenth century, romanticism promoted the idea that modern (especially urban) life was inherently stressful, corrupting, debilitating, and spiritually enervating. The antidote to these commonly perceived evils of modernity was a retreat to the putative beneficence of nature. Where the modern city was considered a pit of iniquity and woe, nature was seen as a fount of divine virtue and regenerative power.

Obviously, in antebellum America, the people most in need of an escape from the miseries of overwork, the wage slaves of the North and the actual slaves of the South, were denied access to the sort of bourgeois vacation that Emmons envisioned on Raquette Lake. Likewise, those Americans who lived and worked in the countryside—farmers and loggers, for example—were unlikely to be reading Ralph Waldo Emerson's "Nature" and meditating on the salutary influences of a life in the wilderness.[13] But to the growing managerial and professional class, that is, to those Americans profiting from the new economy and culture developing around the nation's rapidly expanding cities, a retreat to the seacoast or the mountains became increasingly appealing and available. The loci of these vacations ranged from the opulent and cosmopolitan, as at Newport or Saratoga Springs, to the rustic and isolated, as at Maine's Moosehead Lake or the central Adirondacks.[14]

By the 1840s ministers, doctors, and businessmen from urban centers throughout the northeastern United States were beginning to take a few weeks away from work during the summer and head for the Adirondacks, where they hunted, fished, and generally lounged about, while their guides did most of the work.[15] Joel Headley, a Protestant minister in search of mental and physical health, was representative of the bourgeois, romantic travelers who began appearing in the central Adirondacks during the decades before the Civil War. Genteel camping trips quickly generated their own descriptive literature: Headley's *The Adirondack; or Life in the Woods*, first published in 1849 and republished, plagiarized, and expanded in numerous editions over the next thirty years, is an excellent example of the genre.[16] Headley's effusive appreciation for the Adirondack wilderness typified the tenets of popular American romanticism:

I love nature and all things as God has made them. I love the freedom of the wilderness and the absence of conventional forms there. I love the long stretch through the forest on foot, and the thrilling, glorious prospect from some hoary mountain top. I love it, and I know it is better for me than the thronged city, aye, better for soul and body both. . . . I believe that every man degenerates without frequent communication with nature. It is one of the open books of God, and even more replete with instructions than anything ever penned by man. A single tree standing alone, and waving all day its green crown in the summer wind, is to me fuller of meaning and instruction than the crowded mart or gorgeously built town.[17]

Here we see most of the characteristic features of the romantic faith in the power of nature to redeem the modern soul: the divinity of the natural landscape, the healthfulness of living close to nature, and anti-urbanism. Such romantic convictions have sent wave after wave of tourists, sportsmen, and invalids to the Adirondacks. While the florid style of Headley's account may seem a bit antique to the modern reader, similar sentiments have been repeated endlessly ever since.

Headley was but one of many writers to describe

the classic Adirondack camping trip. Sportsmen generally made their own way to a town or hotel on the edge of the central wilderness—Martin's Hotel on Lower Saranac Lake, for example, an early and eventually famous hostelry owned and operated by a remarkable family of guides, woodsmen, and raconteurs.[18] Other popular hotels could be found at all well-frequented gateways to the wilderness. Once arrived at these points, the sportsman would hire a guide; groups of sportsmen traveling together usually hired a guide apiece. In addition to furnishing camping gear and dogs for hunting deer, the guide provided the single most important item for an Adirondack sporting expedition—the guideboat.

With the sportsmen in the stern, the guide rowing from the bow, and blankets, overcoats, guns, fishing poles, pots and pans, supplies of salt pork and flour, and perhaps a deer hound stowed amidships, these guideboats would set out from Martin's or a similar establishment to tour the central Adirondacks. In 1858, no less a literary figure than Ralph Waldo Emerson himself embarked on an Adirondack camping trip. In "The Adirondacs," a poem he wrote to celebrate his only excursion into the American wilderness, he described the trip's beginning:

> At Martin's beach
> We chose our boats; each man a boat and guide—
> Ten men, ten guides, our company all told.

Once their camp was established on remote and untouched Follensby Pond, Emerson had ample opportunity to admire the prowess of the guides, especially their skill with boats:

> In Adirondac lakes,
> At morn or noon, the guide rows bareheaded . . .
> Their sinewy arms pull at the oar untired
> Three times ten thousand strokes, from morn to eve.[19]

After the Civil War the image of the Adirondacks as a recreational paradise was given one of its most forceful expressions in an 1869 best seller, *Adventures in the Wilderness; or, Camp-Life in the Adirondacks.* William H. H. Murray, minister at the Park Street Congregational Church in Boston, repeated, in an especially eloquent and appealing style, all the claims advanced by Headley and his generation.[20] Murray particularly emphasized recreation in his book. Like his predecessors, he subscribed to the facile romantic

faith in nature as a holy and redemptive place, but this appeared less important to him than the opportunities for wholesome sport and exercise. *Adventures in the Wilderness* recounts story after story of exciting exploits with the rod and gun and bracing, sometimes perilous, boat trips on the network of Adirondack rivers and lakes. So many eager campers and sportsmen were lured to the Adirondacks by Murray's tales of idylls in the woods and arrived there so utterly unequipped, psychologically or materially, for the realities of insects, damp bedding, and uncooperative weather that the popular press began calling them "Murray's Fools," and for the rest of his life Murray himself was known as "Adirondack Murray."[21]

In its emphasis on sport and recreation, *Adventures in the Wilderness* represents a significant development in the evolving image of the Adirondack region. Before the Civil War the Adirondack camping trip was largely an experience of the soul: pantheistic romantic travelers looked for, and found, divinity in the landscape, and they worshipped the wilderness for the immanence of God. They hunted and fished, of course, and they traveled by boat and occasionally by foot through the northern wilderness, but these activities were, to a large extent, part of the ceremonies of the religion of nature.

After, and to a certain extent because of, Murray we see increasing attention to the importance of recreation and exercise in developing and maintaining vigor and health. The Adirondacks—and similar wilderness retreats throughout the United States—moved from being the home of God to being the place where, the dominant culture declared, men from the elite and middle classes developed the muscles, self-reliance, and independence needed for success in the competitive world of industry and commerce. In this sense, Murray and his disciples anticipated the obsession with rugged exercise and the promotion of manly attributes that characterized Theodore Roosevelt (some of whose earliest camping experiences occurred in the Adirondacks) and his generation.[22]

This concern with putative masculine attributes became even more important when social commentators believed they perceived a decline in American masculinity itself. Throughout the final decades of the nineteenth century, various theorists on American culture routinely observed that American manhood was in a state of precipitous decline, that the masculine ruggedness displayed so heroically at Valley Forge and the Alamo had somehow been eroded by the combined forces of urbanization, over-civilization, and an extremely vague articulated notion that women had achieved a questionable hegemony in white, bourgeois culture. Americans feared their young men were becoming effete, refined, and delicate.[23]

The answer to this threat to national security, wrote a host of cultural critics, was to have America's youth return to the wilderness, where healthy sports and vigorous exercise would restore the national will. The prominent New Yorkers charged by the legislature in 1872 to investigate the possibility of establishing an Adirondack Park, for example, believed that wilderness recreation could address the alarming decline in masculinity, fatuously declaring,

The field sports of the wilderness are remarkably exhilarating, and strengthen and revive the human frame. The boating, tramping, hunting and fishing expeditions afford that physical training which modern Americans . . . stand sadly in need of, and which we must hope will, with the fashionable young men of the period, yet replace the vicious, enervating, debasing pleasures of the cities. It is to their eager pursuit of field sports that metropolitan Englishmen owe their superiority in physical power, with that skillful use of fire-arms, independence, fearlessness, cool presence of mind, and ability which they possess to bear the fatigues of war and exigencies of military service.[24]

American girls, though to a lesser extent, were also subject to this fear of declining vitality. Just as the boys who were supposed to furnish the nation's military and business leaders were accused of a loss of vigor, so too young women, whose destiny was to be healthy wives and productive mothers, were said to be but fragile shadows of their sturdy grandmothers. Neurasthenia, the stylish malady of the nervous system that afflicted upper- and middle-class women of the end of the nineteenth century, was evidence of the crisis of health.[25] For both boys and girls, the answer was the hearty life of the wilderness. Wealthy families found a new reason for an Adirondack vaca-

tion: where the father's hunting and fishing had been an initial rationale, now the whole family could improve body and soul by paddling a canoe across an Adirondack lake.

The larger context of this faith in the wilderness to revive the nation's vitality was a renewed and widely shared American compulsion to get back to nature. Murray was thus an early exponent of what a decade or two later became a national craze. Intellectually, this movement was a logical extension and descendant of the romanticism that had pervaded American culture since antebellum days; by the end of the nineteenth century, it had acquired a remarkably recharged authority. Middle-class Americans sent their children to summer camps, spent Sunday afternoons promenading in their cities' recently redesigned public parks, traveled on family vacations to newly established national parks like Yosemite and Mount Rainier, and read assiduously in the works of nature writers like John Burroughs and John Muir.[26] As before, opportunities to experience the restorative powers of nature were limited to the relatively well-to-do: the millions of inhabitants of the nation's slums, either unemployed or working for starvation wages in horribly unsafe and unsanitary factories and sweatshops, had virtually no access to the rural or wild corners of their country.

To middle-class Americans, the existence of just this teeming proletariat was but one more reason to abandon, at least for a few weeks, the filthy and slum-ridden cities. For the managerial and professional classes, moreover, despite their relative affluence, work was often tedious and alienating. And conventional religion, which in an earlier age might have provided a relief to a life that sometimes seemed sterile, was circumscribed by science and apparently surrendering to secularization. For those who could afford it, a retreat to nature supplied the antidote to, or at least an escape from, the travails of a society struggling toward the twentieth century. Adirondack lakes and rivers, now within a day's journey of a large, urban population, especially appealed to the back-to-nature cult and became a popular destination for Americans searching for healthy recreation far from the pressures of everyday routine.

A further development, which both resulted from

and promoted this growing interest in the Adirondacks, was improved transportation, making it easier for the denizens of eastern cities to reach the North Woods. A railroad had penetrated as far as North Creek by 1871, and stagecoach connections from there opened up the beautiful country around Raquette Lake. Stagecoach access to jumping-off points like Old Forge and Saranac Lake also improved after the Civil War. Along with transportation, and often financially interrelated, was a rapid expansion of the local hotel industry. From the Chateaugay lakes to the Moose River, hotels and boarding houses popped up along Adirondack waters. Some were humble affairs with straw-tick beds and indifferent food; others were opulent, modern hostels, like the Prospect House (the first hotel in the world to provide electric lights in every guest room) at Blue Mountain Lake, which opened its doors in 1882.[27]

Another consequence of the region's popularity was the establishment of large private clubs. Wealthy sportsmen, eager to enjoy the benefits of the wilderness without rubbing shoulders with Murray's Fools and others lured to the Adirondacks by the hope of landing a trout or shooting a deer, banded together to purchase huge parcels of the wilderness. At these clubs—the Adirondack League Club near Old Forge is one of the best examples—men (and some women) from prosperous families pursued the rituals of the outdoors. They hunted deer, angled for trout, and plied their boats across lakes and rivers they owned and protected for their exclusive use.[28]

All of these factors—the back-to-nature movement, the search for the strenuous life, and increased facility of access—combined to make the Adirondacks one of the nation's "sacred places."[29] For those who could afford it, the Adirondacks was a retreat from everything that appeared negative about modern American life. By the end of the nineteenth century the Adirondacks was known throughout the nation as a vacation mecca. The popularity of the region's splendid system of lakes and rivers led guidebook author Edwin R. Wallace to call the Adirondacks "this Venice of America."[30]

But at precisely the time that American millionaires, along with their middle-class contemporaries, were savoring the glories of Adirondack forests and lakes, the logging industry was threatening the continued existence of their new-found paradise. One feature of the economic expansion (the phenomenon behind the emergence of the new moneyed classes) during the Civil War and Reconstruction was an apparently insatiable appetite for lumber. Loggers slowly worked their way into the previously inaccessible Adirondacks and by the last decades of the nineteenth century were to be found throughout the region, although some places were harder hit than others. New Yorkers feared that logging and, perhaps more important, the disastrous fires that often succeeded logging operations, would lead to denuded hillsides. And the consequence of denuded hillsides, believed many people, was a threatened watershed. By watershed, they meant the capacity of Adirondack slopes, so long as they supported a healthy forest, to regulate the flow of water into the Hudson River, the Erie Canal, and other waterways vital to the state's economy. If the forests of the Adirondacks were destroyed, so went the reasoning of the day, the valleys below, especially to the south, would be subject to endless cycles of drought and flood, rather than the relatively stable flow of water they enjoyed before intensive logging began.

By the 1880s the Adirondacks, which only a half century before had been barely acknowledged as a part of New York State, was looming large in the public mind—or at least in that part of the public mind that could influence state policy. The future of the region both as a recreational retreat and as guardian of the watershed appeared to be in doubt. A few Adirondack enthusiasts, especially Verplanck Colvin, had been warning of disaster for years, but the political establishment did not begin to see the situation as serious until 1883, when it took the first of several steps designed to protect the Adirondacks. That year the legislature decreed that state lands in the Adirondack counties, which hitherto had been for sale and easily available to any party that bid for them, were no longer on the market.

Two years later the state created the Forest Preserve, made up of all state land in designated Adirondack and Catskill counties. The state declared its intent to keep it "forever … as wild forest lands." This meant that the land could never be alienated from the state, although logging was still permitted. In 1892, realizing that the state domain was too small and too scattered, the legislature, responding to the exhortations of a succession of governors, created the Adirondack Park, delineating a large, contiguous area in the central and southern Adirondacks in which the state had a pressing interest and which it intended to protect or even acquire.

Finally, in 1894, as the previous conservation measures appeared inadequate to accomplish the necessary job of protecting the public interest, rigid protection for the Forest Preserve was inscribed in a new state constitution. According to an extraordinary provision in the constitution approved by New York voters in November of that year, "The lands of the State, now owned or hereafter acquired, constituting the Forest Preserve as now fixed by law, shall be forever kept as wild forest lands. They shall not be leased, sold or exchanged, or be taken by any corporation, public or private, nor shall the timber thereon be sold, removed or destroyed."[31]

Although the primary motive behind this decade of conservation activity appears to have been utilitarian, a concern for recreation was always part of the drama. Besides their fears about a damaged watershed, New Yorkers wanted the Adirondacks protected for hunting and fishing, hiking, and boating. And within a few years the utilitarian arguments for protection faded away, while recreation, with an ever-expanding list of sports and outdoor activities, came increasingly to define the Adirondacks in the twentieth century.[32] The law- and constitution-writing of the 1880s and '90s, responding to anxieties about watershed and commerce, created the recreational retreat of today.

The twin threads of watershed and recreation come together in the need to protect the rivers and lakes of the Adirondacks. A century ago conservationists feared denuded hillsides and cataclysmic disruptions of the state's canals and riverine transportation corridors. Their response was a series of legislative and constitutional maneuvers that saved these waterways for twentieth-century canoeists and other boaters. Today's conservationists are equally concerned about Adirondack waters. From outside the Park comes the air-borne plague of acid precipita-

tion. From within (but largely supported by outside capital) comes the threat of inappropriate development on lake and river shores, while another important issue is the closing of traditional recreational water routes by private land owners. Waterways that were enjoyed by Headley and Emerson had been posted with no-trespassing signs.

The issue of the public's access to rivers for recreation is well illustrated in a case currently working its way through the New York courts. In June, 1991, a party of five canoeists attempted to paddle down the South Branch of the Moose River. Their route took them to the 53,000 acres owned by the exclusive and private Adirondack League Club. The canoeists believed that the Club had illegally prevented public passage on a river owned by the State of New York, while the Club argued that since the lands on either side of the river were private, the channel of the river was equally subject to the rights of ownership. The Club sued the paddlers for trespass. By the time the case reached the courts, the five canoeists had been joined by the Sierra Club, the Adirondack Mountain Club, and the New York State Department of Environmental Conservation, all of whom believed this test of New York law could be used to open up vital recreational waterways to the public.[33] Meanwhile, a bill was introduced in the New York State Assembly to guarantee public access to just these streams.[34]

The point of law involved whether or not the river is "navigable," with the Club insisting that its rocky, rapid channel is unnavigable and the canoeists maintaining the contrary, that the river is navigable and that common law permits public passage. In September, 1993, a judge on the New York State Supreme Court ruled that if a small motorboat or a rowed boat could make it down the river, then it is in fact navigable.[35] The Club appealed, but the original decision was upheld by the Appellate Division of the State Supreme Court in 1994.[36] While the ruling does not instantly open up all previously posted waterways to recreational use, it appears to be heading in a liberal direction. Canoes and guideboats may soon be plying rivers and streams that have been closed to the public for a century or more.

However this case is finally resolved, it shows the continuing importance of boats, boating, and water in the Adirondacks. It brings together issues that have been critical to Adirondack history: the rights (or obligations) of private property owners, the public's right of access to the state's recreational assets, and the centrality of small boats to Adirondack recreation and law. Just as conservationists of the late nineteenth century aimed to protect Adirondack rivers from what they perceived as the abuses of ruthless logging, today's activists are trying to return those rivers to the public domain. As much today as at any time over the last century and a half, the small boat with its human paddler or rower remains one of the most emblematic and symbolically charged figures on the Adirondack scene.

Realizing the small prospect there was of getting our shallop past the rapid, I was distressed, and I was particularly sorry to return without seeing a very large lake. . . . Having thought it over well, I decided to proceed thither . . . and I embarked with the Indians in their canoes.

—Samuel de Champlain, 1609[1]

CHAPTER I

Of Bark and Bateaux

In the spring of 1609 a delegation of Algonquin Indians met with the French explorer Samuel de Champlain, who had just weathered his second Canadian winter on the shores of the St. Lawrence River. They suggested to him, in a manner he could not refuse, that he join them in a campaign against their traditional enemies the Iroquois, who lived up the St. Lawrence and to the south. Champlain agreed, for in addition to the political advantages to the French, he was eager to view the Iroquois territory which included "a very large lake, filled with beautiful islands, and a large, beautiful region near the lake."[2] The lake would become known by his name. The beautiful region he could see from the water included the Adirondack mountains.

The party set off from Tadoussac, at the mouth of the Saguenay River, on June 28. The natives paddled birchbark canoes. Champlain and his twelve men traveled in a shallop, one of the ship's boats. The shallop was a two-masted vessel probably around twenty-five feet long which was rowed or sailed as conditions allowed. In addition to the men, the boat carried "all that was needed," in Champlain's words, including the captain's steel helmet with its brave white plume, and three or four arquebuses. These heavy matchlock guns were probably the main reason the Algonquin were so eager for Champlain's company.

After a month's travel, during which they paddled up the St. Lawrence for about three hundred and twenty-five miles, the allies turned south into a beautiful, broad-mouthed river which Champlain named "The River of the Iroquois," after the enemy, and which later became known as the Richelieu. About forty miles upriver, they encountered rapids impassable even for canoes, and Champlain realized unhappily that further travel in the shallop would be impossible. Rather than turn back, he decided to proceed with the natives "in order to carry out my promise and also to fulfil my desire." He sent most of the French back to Tadoussac in the shallop, and with two eager volunteers he carried his armor and guns around the falls and embarked in the canoes for the territory of the Iroquois.

Champlain was one of the first people on record to appreciate the importance of

Thomas Davies, A View Near Point Levy Opposite Quebec with an Indian Encampment taken in 1788.

Images of birchbarks from Champlain's time are rare and not very accurate. Thomas Davies's depictions of birchbarks are later but probably represent Algonquin birchbarks as they were at the time of European contact. Davies (1737[?]–1812) was a soldier in the British army who sketched and painted in watercolors in his spare time. Courtesy National Gallery of Canada.

the right boat to travel in the Adirondacks. Champlain did not venture into the interior of the mountains, but the boats he and other Europeans used in the years before settlement were prototypes for the craft which made life possible in the region for the next three hundred years.

The natives' boats must have seemed strange and risky alternatives to Champlain's shallop. The birchbark canoes were twenty to twenty-three feet long and forty to fifty inches in beam—not much shorter than the ship's boat but considerably lighter and more fragile. When he first saw the canoes of the St. Lawrence, Champlain noted that they were ". . . so light that a man can carry one of them easily; . . . [though] very liable to overturn, if one know not how to manage them rightly."[3] They could carry around a half-ton of cargo and were fast; the summer before, two had passed Champlain in his fully-manned ship's boat in an impromptu race on the river.

At the northern end of the lake which came to bear his name, Champlain found a rich land growing fine trees and vines and supporting an abundance of game and fish. The countryside was deserted, however, because of fighting among the native inhabitants. Champlain's allies traditionally lived in the regions to the north, and the Iroquois, their enemies, regarded the Mohawk valley and the valleys of Vermont as their territory. The two nations had been at war for more than a generation by the time of Champlain's visit. Part of their dispute was use of the Adirondacks.[4]

The Algonquin and the three Frenchmen paddled farther into the interior, mountains on either side of them. At the end of July, paddling by night to avoid detection, they approached the cape now occupied by Fort Ticonderoga. At ten o'clock they were discovered by a party of about two hundred Mohawks, one of the Five Nations of the Iroquois confederacy. After some initial shouting and insults, the two parties agreed to postpone the battle until daylight. Champlain and his allies lashed their canoes together with long poles. They awaited the dawn on the water, returning the singing and threats from their enemies on the shore. At first light Champlain donned his armor, loaded his arquebus and went ashore with the war party. As soon as he saw the enemy draw their bows, he shot, killing three Mohawks. The ensuing battle was short, and the Mohawks fled after a second shot from one of Champlain's compatriots.

The Iroquois were not only overmastered in the matter of weapons, but they also had the inferior boats. Champlain noted that they used canoes of "oak bark" (probably elm), boats which had flatter bottoms amidships and harder bilges than the sleek birchbarks. Elm and spruce (the latter used as a substitute for birchbark at higher elevations than elm typically grows) could not be formed to the fine shapes of the more pliable birchbark. Elm and spruce boats were "clumsy craft unsuited to long voyages, dangerous for crossing lakes, and suicide in white water."[5] Elm bark canoes were traditionally used only as temporary boats, probably built for a single campaign or at best for a season or two. The Iroquois had no tradition of birchbark construction because white birch trees large enough for adequate canoes were rare in their traditional territory.[6]

The superior birchbarks were regarded as important spoils of war among the Iroquois; had Champlain's battle turned out differently, his enemies would have made a valuable haul.

Defeat of the Iroquois at Lake Champlain, July 30, 1609.

This representation of the encounter between Champlain and his allies and the Iroquois appeared in the published account of Champlain's voyages in 1613. It has been thought to have come from the hand of Champlain himself, but the incongruity of some of the details, the birchbark canoes in particular, suggests that it was drawn by an illustrator in France who had never been to the New World. Public Archives of Canada, Neg. C–5750.

Elm and Birch Bark Canoes

Canoes of birch, elm, and spruce bark are all built in basically the same way, though more steps are taken with the finer birch bark canoes.* (See the drawing for the abbreviated elm bark process.) The builder peels a sheet of bark from a large tree. Ideally it is large enough to cover the entire hull of the canoe, but typically additional pieces must be added. If it is elm or spruce bark, the rough outer surface is scraped away. Then the bark is laid on the smoothed earth building bed, with the inside down.

The area of the bark which will form the double-ended shape of the bottom is weighted down, and the sides are bent up, the bark being gored and sewn or folded as necessary. A frame consisting of gunwales and thwarts is lashed on. Thin ribs of split wood are heated in water and bent, then fitted so that when their upper ends are caught between the inwales and the bark on each side and they are pushed into alignment, they stretch the bark almost to the desired shape.

These ribs are then removed, planks laid inside the bark, and the ribs progressively driven back in over the planking, from one end to the other. Typically there is more planking and ribbing in a birchbark canoe than in a spruce or elm bark canoe, since birchbark, though very tough, is thinner. The boat is held together by the lashing or sewing of bark and thwarts to gunwales, and given strength and shape by the tension in the ribs.

Elm and spruce bark canoes are much rougher craft than birchbark canoes. Their cruder shape is chiefly a result of folding the bark to lift the ends, rather than cutting gores and stitching the bark back together.

*For a discussion of constuction and use of elm bark canoes see Fenton and Dodge, "An Elm Bark Canoe," 159–206.

Elm Bark Canoe Model.

This model shows the simple construction of an Elm bark canoe. It is four feet long, with a beam of 9½".
Courtesy Peabody Essex Museum, Salem, Mass.

For millennia before Champlain first gazed on the Adirondacks, Indians had been hunting and fishing in the mountains. Very little remains to tell the story of exactly how or when they lived in the region. Archaeological evidence suggests that people occupied the mountains as far back as 5,000 years ago. Reports from more recent historians and travelers have corroborated those Champlain heard about Algonquin and Iroquois use of the Adirondacks and help explain how the native peoples may have built and used bark boats. As observed by the great scholar of native craft, Howard I. Chapelle, bark canoes when first seen by Europeans were highly developed and must have been the product of a long period of existence and improvement before Champlain traveled in one.[7]

Bark canoes were durable and carried great loads. Ebenezer Emmons was a naturalist and geologist who first surveyed the Adirondacks for New York State in 1837. It

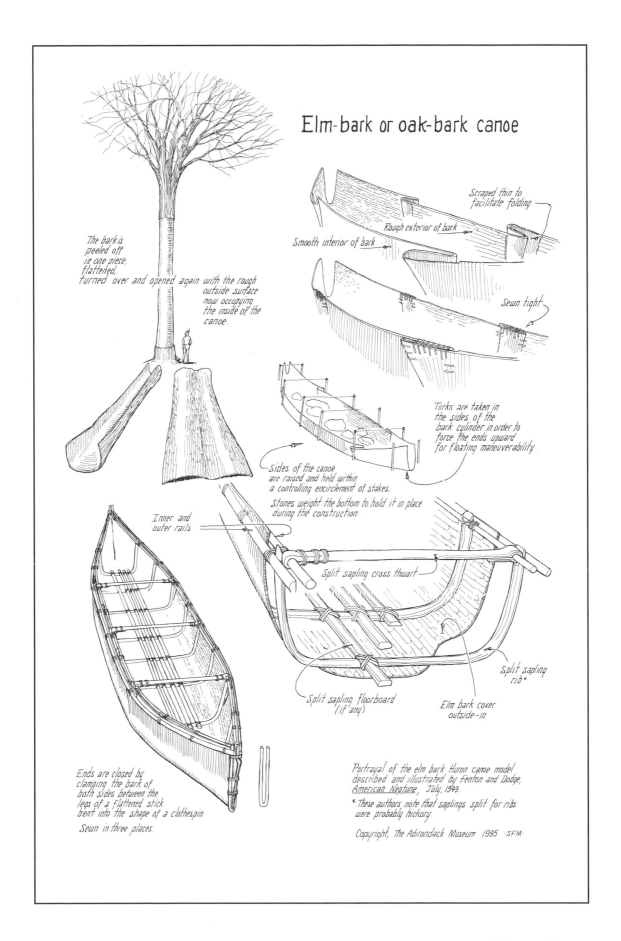

Elm-bark or oak-bark canoe

Scraped thin to facilitate folding

Rough exterior of bark

Smooth interior of bark

Sewn tight

The bark is peeled off in one piece, flattened, turned over and opened again with the rough outside surface now occupying the inside of the canoe.

Tucks are taken in the sides of the bark cylinder in order to force the ends upward for floating maneuverability.

Sides of the canoe are raised and held within a controlling encirclement of stakes.

Stones weight the bottom to hold it in place during the construction.

Inner and outer rails

Split sapling cross thwart

Split sapling rib*

Split sapling floorboard (if any)

Elm bark cover outside-in

Ends are closed by clamping the bark of both sides between the legs of a flattened stick bent into the shape of a clothespin.

Sewn in three places.

Portrayal of the elm bark Huron canoe model described and illustrated by Fenton and Dodge, _American Neptune_, July, 1949.

* These authors note that saplings split for ribs were probably hickory.

Copyright, The Adirondack Museum 1995 ·SFM·

was he who named the mountain mass "Adirondack," supposedly an Iroquois name for the Algonquin, and who named the state's highest peak for Marcy, the governor who authorized his survey. Emmons had high praise for his guide, an Indian from what is now Indian Lake, "who with his birch canoe gave us a safe transport through the wilderness for at least one hundred miles, together with our camp equipage, as tents, pork, bread, fish, meat, guns, nets, traps, hammers, making in the whole, a tolerable load for so frail a bark."[8]

A few years after Emmons's trip, a young Abenaki demonstrated the construction of an emergency boat in saving the vacation of a couple of inexperienced "sports" he found on the Raquette River just below Raquette Falls. The Indian was probably Mitchell Sabattis. He was then just nineteen but impressed the sports as the most intelligent of the party of five Indians with whom he was traveling. In time he was to become one of the most famous Adirondack guides, a woods-wise Indian who had qualities which particularly appealed to nineteenth-century sensibilities—he was in later years a pillar of the Methodist church and a teetotaler. The sports he rescued were John MacMullen, a teacher, and his student, "Jim R."[9]

MacMullen and Jim R. had set out from home to navigate the full length of the Raquette, intending to procure a boat in Long Lake. Arriving there in the summer of 1843, they indeed found one of the "light, cedar boats" they had heard about, but it was not for sale; the only available craft was a heavy double-ended rowboat. Mac-Mullen and his student rowed north in this "sloop's yawl" but got only as far as Raquette Falls, six miles downriver from the outlet of Long Lake. They were quickly discouraged on the long carry around the falls and attempted to let the boat down the rapids with ropes. But the force of the water tore the boat from their hands and wrecked it on the rocks. The two then cobbled together a raft, only to run the unwieldy craft onto a mass of deadfall in one of many sprawling loops of the river. They were hacking away at the encumbering branches when they were surprised to hear voices, and they looked up to see Sabattis and four companions come around a bend in a birchbark canoe. After some discussion with his companions, Sabattis crowded the men on board and continued on down the Raquette to a farmhouse on Tupper Lake where they could eat and the Indians could find a spruce tree suitable for a boat for the rest of MacMullen's journey. Sabattis's birchbark canoe carried quite a load; when the two tyros and their gear joined the four Indians, the freeboard decreased from six inches to three.

Sabattis took two days to build the canoe. Almost everything used in the project was found on the spot. "To good woodsmen like these," wrote MacMullen, "trees are as closets from which they take whatever they may need."[10] The hull was made of one piece of unblemished bark fifteen feet long and three feet wide. Two gores on each side gave rocker to the hull. It was sewn together with spruce roots and sealed with spruce gum. Hand-split cedar boards provided ribs, gunwales, thwarts, and planking.

MacMullen wisely decided to hire Sabattis as guide for the rest of the trip. One morning he was intrigued to observe Sabattis apparently kissing the boat. Was this some strange native ritual? MacMullen was reluctant to question the guide, but when

Arthur Fitzwilliam Tait,
Going Out: Deer Hunting
in the Adirondacks, *1862.*

*A. F. Tait almost always put
his Adirondack sports into
birchbark canoes, even
though he himself probably
traveled in a guideboat. Tait
(1819–1905) was one of the
most prolific and well-known
artists to publicize the
Adirondacks. Many of his
paintings were reproduced by
Currier and Ives. In depict-
ing birchbarks, Tait was no
doubt catering to the public's
idea of the appropriate boat
for an adventure in the
wilderness. 73.36.1.*

his curiosity overcame him he learned that Sabattis was merely "sucking for holes."
The Indian used a rag, a smoldering stick from the fire, and a mouthful of masticated
spruce gum. Any holes he found were patched by placing a bit of rag over the hole
and melting gum into the weave.

Lewis Bellows, a pioneer in the Chateaugay Lake region, was an early white settler
who adopted the bark canoe. In the 1850s he took sports into Ragged Lake in crude
spruce canoes which had small branches for ribs.[11] Samuel H. Hammond, one of the
earliest writers about sporting in the Adirondacks, rode in one, keeping his "chew of
tobacco precisely in the middle of the mouth. . . . So long as we remained seated on
the bottom, it was steady enough, but when, from our cramped position, it became
necessary to change our posture, it required the skill of a rope dancer to preserve our
equilibrium, and prevent one's self from being plumped into the cold waters of the
lake."[12]

The resourceful white settlers of the nineteenth century who built their own
spruce bark canoes for emergency or temporary expeditions may have learned the art
from Indians, or they may have studied rough and ready boatbuilding from books.
At the close of the Civil War, Sewell Newhouse, a member of the Oneida Community and designer of widely-used traps, wrote *The Trapper's Guide,* a volume with instructions for "capturing all kinds of fur-bearing animals" as well as "hints on life in
the woods" including boatbuilding. Construction of birchbark canoes is described at
length; dugouts and bateaux are explained more briefly. "Rough, temporary canoes,"

the book states, "may be made of spruce or basswood bark, by simply folding the ends and sewing or nailing them together, adding gunwales and lining, putting in a few knees and cross-pieces, and smearing all the joints with pitch."[13]

By the middle of the nineteenth century, as boats built with European technology by builders of European heritage became more common in the Adirondacks, working bark canoes became rarer. However, birchbark canoes in particular survive as romantic relics, paddled by people who see themselves as part of an historic continuum of paddlers in the Adirondacks.

Bark canoes are ephemeral. In use they last only a few decades at most, and the materials from which they are made return readily to the soil. There is more solid evidence documenting the use of the dugout, the other type of aboriginal canoe used in the region in pre-contact times.

While the Iroquois paddled birchbark canoes when they could get them and spruce or elm bark canoes when they couldn't, they traditionally built dugouts to use on large bodies of water.[14] These boats were much heavier than birchbarks and were typically left on the lake where they were built. Archaeological surveys in the Adirondacks have unearthed tools suitable for carving dugouts out of logs. These stone celts and bone and copper gouges date from as early as 3,000 to 1,000 B.C.[15] Several dugout canoes from the historic period have been found in lakes in the region. Radiocarbon dating has established a construction date around 1584 of one such boat that was found submerged in Lake Ozonia.[16]

Like birchbarks, use of dugouts continued into the nineteenth century. Romantics paddled some; others were "in practical use" in the words of J. H. Rushton. Rushton, who was one of the best-known canoe builders in the country at the end of the nineteenth century, then remembered using dugout canoes in the northern Adirondacks as a boy in the 1840s and 1850s. "It was not a make-shift," he defended the craft, "but was highly cherished by its owner."[17]

The most "practical use" of a heavy dugout in the nineteenth century was to save the labor of "backing in" a boat to a remote pond. In 1830, for example, the guides for the owners of the Adirondack Iron Works, a remote mine not far from the southern slopes of Mt. Marcy and forty miles over rough road from Crown Point, made a canoe out of a pine tree to carry their party up Lake Sanford.[18] The naturalist John Burroughs used one on an 1866 hunting expedition. Burroughs and his guide found the dugout at Nate's Pond, "under the top of a fallen hemlock, but in a sorry condition. . . . Freed from the treetop, however, and calked with a little moss, it floated with two aboard, which was quite enough for our purpose," which was jacking deer, or shooting the animals at night after mesmerizing them with a light.[19] Guides for the surveyor Verplanck Colvin built him a serviceable dugout from a cedar log to aid in the study of Lake Colden a decade later. Colvin named it *Discovery*. "Though narrow," he wrote, the canoe "carried three men with ease—and more when balanced

Verplanck Colvin, Dug-out on Beaver Lk., *ca. 1890.*

The surveyor Colvin photographed Frank "Pico" Johnson and William H. Ballard fishing in a crude dugout on Beaver Lake in the town of Watson. P. 7751.

with out-riggers. . . . The canoe remains at Avalanche Lake and will render the Avalanche Pass more convenient to travelers."[20]

When Champlain abandoned his shallop for a birchbark canoe at the falls on the Richelieu, he acknowledged the superiority of native craft for travel in the Adirondacks and the surrounding region. As the period of exploration blended into the period of settlement, however, Europeans began experimenting with their own boat-building traditions to serve better their styles of warfare and commerce.

In 1671 governor Courcelles of New France made a "promenade" up the St. Lawrence from Montreal to Lake Ontario to demonstrate that a European-style boat could transport more furs than the native canoe—even over the river's notorious rapids. His "flat batteau" was a double-ended, flat-bottomed boat descended from Old World models.[21] For more than a century after Courcelles's expedition, bateaux dominated both military and commercial transportation for Europeans settling the regions surrounding the Adirondacks.

The military bateau, as developed by the English and the French, literally determined the course of history in the New World. The struggle for control of the all-important waterways of the St. Lawrence and Lake Champlain–Lake George corridor depended on bateaux for moving men and materiel, from the first of the colonial wars until the American war of independence.[22] While the bateau first appeared in the part of North America held by the French, it was the British who mounted the most massive bateau effort on record. Bradstreet's "Battoe Service," formed at Schenectady in 1756, represents the scope of the British bateau fleet at its height.

Lt. Col. John Bradstreet was an American-born regular officer already in charge of building bateaux and whaleboats in Albany when William Shirley, commanding general of the British forces in North America, ordered a greatly increased bateau fleet for expeditions against the French. Bradstreet was given 2,000 "battoemen" and several hundred carpenters, whom he installed in shops along the waterfront in Schenectady. The impact on the little village at the foot of navigation on the Mohawk River must have been enormous; at the close of the colonial wars forty years later, the entire township contained only 500 families.

Bradstreet gained bloody, firsthand experience of the use of bateaux in warfare when he led the bateau fleet for General Abercromby's assault two years later on the French Ft. Carillon on Lake Champlain. Bradstreet's carpenters had built most of the boats in Schenectady; after that, his bateaumen rowed and carried them to the foot of Lake George. Bradstreet then took charge of the 900 bateaux which carried 6,367 British regulars and 9,024 provincial troops—the largest army assembled to that day in North America. The armada stretched for six miles as it rowed up the lake in columns. In addition to the bateaux, there were rafts, 135 whaleboats, and three small radeaux. In spite of the magnificent show and the fact that his army numbered four times as many men as the French, Abercromby met disaster when he arrived at the fort the English called Ticonderoga, and Bradstreet and his bateaux hastily had to evacuate the army to the southern end of Lake George.[23]

Almost immediately after the defeat, Bradstreet received permission to attempt to redeem British fortunes and the reputation of the bateau by an assault on Fort Frontenac, one of the strongest, most important French forts in North America. The fort stood on the site of present-day Kingston, Ontario, at the outlet of Lake Ontario, and

Admiralty archives in London contain this "draught" of a thirty-foot bateau from the eighteenth century. Courtesy National Maritime Museum, London.

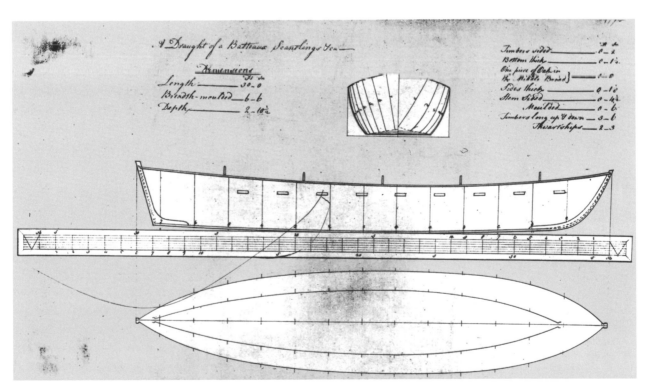

to get there Bradstreet had to pull or pole his bateaux up the Mohawk with its numerous rapids and "rifts," carry them around its Little Falls, then carry overland from what is now Rome to Wood Creek, row across Oneida Lake, then, after running the Oneida River, confront over fifty miles of open water on Lake Ontario. He pulled off what was a lightning raid by eighteenth-century standards. Within fifteen days his 300 bateaumen had moved the 2,600 troops stealthily up to the fort, and on August 27 the surprised and ill-defended fort fell to the British.

The eminent small-craft historian John Gardner has stated that the total of all the bateaux used in the colonial wars has never been reckoned, "but it would be a staggering figure."[24] Bradstreet reported two years after his victorious raid on Frontenac that there were 1,954 bateaux stored for the winter at Lake George and along the Hudson, and that the previous spring 1,200 had been built at Albany and 300 at Schenectady.[25] Thousands went up the Mohawk and thousands went up the Hudson to Lakes George and Champlain.

Remains of several of these colonial bateaux survive. The British typically sank their vessels between campaign seasons to protect them from the weather and the French. When Abercromby's tattered army arrived at the foot of Lake George in 1758, they sank the fleet. In the summer of 1960 amateur divers located a group of bateaux from this campaign in the shallow waters off Lake George village. A cooperative effort between the Adirondack Museum and the State of New York was mounted to raise parts of three bateaux so that actual colonial vessels could be studied.

John Gardner examined the bateau remains and determined that though rough, their designs were clearly American and not importations from Europe. They blend

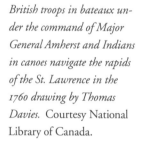

British troops in bateaux under the command of Major General Amherst and Indians in canoes navigate the rapids of the St. Lawrence in the 1760 drawing by Thomas Davies. Courtesy National Library of Canada.

John Gardner built this model of a colonial bateau on a scale of 1½ inches to 1 foot after studying the remains of the bateau found in Lake George in 1960. 68.147.11

lightweight construction and carrying capacity with surprisingly fine lines—essential for military use in an area with shallow, rocky streams. The most complete bateau had a thirty-two-foot-long, lengthwise-planked bottom made of four one-foot-wide boards. The frames were natural crooks of oak. The lapstrake sides were thinner and therefore lighter than carvel-planked sides would be, and produced a flexible, springy hull suitable for use in rapids.[26]

When the wars were over, many of the military boatbuilders went back home to New England with their knowledge of bateau construction. Other builders settled on the frontier and put their boatbuilding knowledge to service of the peacetime economy. Up and down the Atlantic coast there are boats related to the colonial bateau— various wherries and the Jersey sea skiff, among others.[27] On the edges of the Adirondacks smaller, more refined versions of the military bateau were already important commercial vessels by the end of the wars. Within two generations the bateau ancestor had inspired an even more refined boat, the Adirondack guideboat, which became essential to life in the interior of the mountains.

Indians had used the Mohawk River, tributaries of which drain the southern Adirondacks, for transportation long before the French and British moved in. Light bark canoes were the best craft for the trip, easily carried around the rifts, rapids, and falls in the river. In some places these rifts were twelve or eighteen inches deep during much of the year—occasionally even less. In the seventeenth and eighteenth centuries the river was essential to the travels of soldiers like Bradstreet, as well as to commerce. But as had French governor Courcelles, the soldiers and commercial travelers found that they needed a boat with more capacity than the bark canoe. The bateau gave this while still being light enough to carry around obstructions (providing, of

A View of the Boats & manner of navigating on the Mohawk River, *1807*.

The Schenectady bateau in the foreground waits its turn to pass through one of the wing dams built on the Mohawk to raise the water level over one of the many rifts. New York State Library.

course, plenty of men or a team of horses were available). Schenectady was the terminal for all commercial transport westward and the greatest bateau-building center in the region. The "Schenectady bateau" was the main vessel on the river until construction of the Erie Canal in 1825 made the small boat obsolete.[28]

The commercial bateaux which served the farmers and industries along the Mohawk were smaller and finer than the standard military bateaux which preceded them. They were generally between twenty and thirty feet long and four to five feet wide on the bottom. The sides were quite low, about twenty-four inches, and flared outwards. Regardless of size, these Schenectady bateaux were all characterized by flat bottoms of pine boards laid lengthwise with battens nailed across to hold them together. The frames were oak crooks and the sides were pine. Unlike the relatively plumb stems of the military bateaux, the stems of the Mohawk River bateaux were moderately raked, a result of the greater flare they had to their sides. The bateaux were equipped with oars, paddles, and a sail, but the standard method of propulsion was by poles wielded by two, three, or four men, depending on the size of the boat. Another bateauman steered with a long sweep lashed to the sternpost.

*   *   *

In 1763 Sir William Johnson, an Irish immigrant who had been titled for his services leading soldiers and dealing with Indians, built himself a suitably lordly home in the southern foothills of the Adirondacks. Johnson Hall stood on a hill near Canada Creek. A Palladian window lighted a grand formal staircase with mahogany railings, and the rooms were filled with furnishings from the best cabinetmakers and craftsmen in New York City. But even as crates of Chippendale chairs, flocked wallpapers, carpets, decanters, and glasses were poled up the Mohawk in the bateaux of the freight "forwarders" of Schenectady, the lands within sight to the north of this modern, civilized mansion were virtually unknown to all but a handful of white and native trappers. Cognizance of the region by the government and the general population was summed up by Thomas Pownall, colonial administrator, political theorist, and friend of Johnson's, who wrote in his 1784 *Topographical Description of the Dominions of the United States*, "the Country . . . called by the Indians Couxsachrage, which signifies the Dismal Wilderness or Habitation of Winter, is . . . very little known to the Europeans; and although a hunting Ground of the Indians, yet either not much known to them, or, if known, very wisely by them kept from the Knowledge of the Europeans. It is said to be a broken unpracticable Tract; . . . I own I could never learn any Thing about it."[29]

In the expansive decades following American independence, the Adirondack region became gradually better known. Official knowledge increased with the surveys and expeditions of Pownall's successors, and folk knowledge grew as farmers and entrepreneurs settled on the fringes of the region. Some settlers adopted Indian canoes and dugouts for navigation, as had Champlain, and some adapted European boat-building technology, as had the French and British generals. Nearly everyone, however, found that having the right boat was essential to success, and sometimes even to life itself, in the Adirondacks.

They were here alone, shut out from the world. . . .
They lived in their little log-houses and their little boats
were their horses, and the lake their only path.

—John Todd, 1845[1]

CHAPTER 2

The Lake Their Only Path

Although the mountainous region to the north was unsettled when Sir William Johnson built his country home, the neighborhood around Johnson Hall had been populated by Europeans since the beginning of the eighteenth century. The Mohawk valley was settled early with the aid of comparatively easy transportation afforded by the Mohawk River. By 1800 craftsmen, business people, speculators, farmers, and homemakers had established villages on the western and northern edges of the Adirondacks as well.

People settled on the eastern edge of the mountains, at Elizabethtown, not far from Lake Champlain, in the last decade of the eighteenth century. In the western Adirondacks, near the Black River, Lowville was a civilized enough village to support a co-educational academy by 1808 (although the only such institution in the North Country for nearly thirty years). To the north, Hopkinton, near the St. Regis River, could boast a library by 1810, subscribed to by forty-five citizens. These villagers of the periphery hunted and fished in the mountains seasonally, as had the native inhabitants before them, but few attempted to settle there. As late as 1849, Joel Tyler Headley observed that "settlements and civilization have advanced from five to twenty-five miles up the valleys and slopes of this elevated table, where they are met by the nearly uninterrupted wilderness of the interior."[2]

Headley, a prolific and successful writer of popular histories, who had suffered an "attack on the brain" in consequence of his labors, toured the Adirondacks in the 1840s to regain his health. His descriptions of the settlements of the region are some of the earliest. Most of the scattered inhabitants were too busy scratching a living from the unproductive soil to record the details of their everyday lives, so accounts of outsiders like Headley are the only ones we have. Headley introduced his *The Adirondack; or Life in the Woods*, which appeared in 1849, with a "general description of the country" so that his readers would "not regard it mere child's play to penetrate it." In this description he clearly identified the outstanding feature of the country from the point of view of settlers—and generations to come of travelers through the region—

as a "broad valley" extending from Plattsburgh in the northeast to Boonville in the southwest which afforded an "almost unparalleled line of natural navigation." He was describing the watersheds of the Saranac River and Lakes, the upper Raquette, and the Fulton Chain of Lakes, all of which are separated only by low, relatively short divides. In Headley's opinion, if it were not for this central valley, the region would be impenetrable. For the next half-century most travel and settlement occurred in this valley, and in consequence it was here that the Adirondack guideboat evolved, the region's most highly developed and most famous boat.[3]

Abenaki Indians, who traditionally lived in parts of present-day Vermont and Quebec, regarding the Richelieu River and Lake Champlain as the western limits of their territory,[4] were among the first settlers in the interior. Sabael Benedict moved to Indian Lake in what is now Hamilton County about the time of the American Revolution. Not long afterwards a few families of European descent moved to the present town of Newcomb, and by 1819 one Pliny Miller had built a home on the site of the future Saranac Lake. Around 1830 the Abenaki Peter Sabattis, grandfather of the guide Mitchell Sabattis, moved from his home in Parishville, in the northwestern foothills of the mountains, to Long Lake, becoming the first permanent settler there.[5] By 1842 four men and three women had formed a temperance society in Long Lake, which a visiting preacher, John Todd, turned into the First Congregational Church of Long Lake later that year. Todd, possibly wondering why anyone would want to live in such a desolate, isolated spot, reported that the settlers had fled to the mountains because they were afraid they were becoming alcoholics.[6]

Floating bridges and cable ferries patched together the rudimentary roads of the interior mountains. This ferry, photographed about 1890, crossed the Cedar River near Indian Lake in Hamilton County. P. 7202.

Harvey Moody's boat
Upper Saranac Lake. N.Y.
Sep. 13. 1853

Thomas Addison Richards,
Harvey Moody's Boat, Up-
per Saranac Lake, N.Y.,
Sep. 13. 1853. 74.223.76.

More likely, these early Long Lakers were attracted by abundant game and cheap land, in spite of a short growing season and poor soils. Other people moved into the region to exploit the great stands of merchantable timber and to look for minerals abundant enough to pay for their extraction. A surprisingly large number of people failed to appreciate the challenges of transportation in "the North Woods" as they made plans to extract the region's resources. They soon learned (often to their ruin) that transportation was essential to their schemes. Those who succeeded in thriving in the Adirondacks often did so by developing unique boats to take advantage of the region's tangled and broken waterways.

Because the Adirondack region is such poor farmland, most nineteenth-century settlers had to extract products from the woods to supplement the produce of mea-ger hill farms. Game, fish, maple sugar, and berries added to the farmer's diet; these and other products like spruce gum, furs, and saddles of venison for the market in-creased the farmer's income. A special type of boat was essential to life in the woods for the early settlers, to enable them to gather the produce of the woods, to get their products to market, and to visit their neighbors. Early observers of the Adirondack scene called the distinctive boat used there by the 1820s the "Adirondack skiff," or simply a "light skiff"; later, after further evolution, the craft became known as the Adirondack guideboat.

Early sporting tourists who described the guideboat were accustomed to naviga-tion along the coast or on large rivers like the Connecticut and the lower Hudson. To

people like Champlain in his shallop, or MacMullen in his yawl, the waterways of the
region were only barely navigable.[7] Waterfalls and rapids frequently obstructed the
rivers. The mountains broke up the watersheds, so that travelers often had to carry
boats and duffel from one river system to another. Even on the main routes through
the mountains there were "carries" a mile or two long. (The word "portage" is seldom
used in the Adirondacks.)

The requirements for the ideal Adirondack boat were complex and contradictory.
The settlers in the central valley needed a boat light enough to carry from waterway
to waterway and to move swiftly and easily over the long distances to market or between neighbors. At the same time, the boat had to be capacious enough to carry a
deer or traps and camping gear. Light weight and large carrying capacity are usually
incompatible in small boats, but early Adirondack boatbuilders had a model for construction techniques in the colonial bateau which gave great strength for light weight.
The flat bottom, sawn frames, and clinker construction of the colonial bateau were
highly refined by the 1820s in a distinctive regional boat.

According to his biographer, the Fulton Chain trapper Nat Foster could still easily carry his skiff upon his head and shoulders at the age of sixty. This was in 1827,
the earliest reference to the distinctive light boats of the Adirondacks.[8] It was not until 1857, however, that their construction and use was clearly described. Samuel H.
Hammond, a New York State judge whose books about his sporting adventures were
some of the first to draw attention to the region, wrote in 1857:

Frederick B. Allen, Boat on Shore, 1871. 61.50.17

[The] boats are constructed of spruce or cedar boards of a quarter of an inch in thickness, "clap-boarded," as the expression is, upon "knees" of the natural crook, and weigh from ninety to one hundred and ten pounds each. They are carried around rapids, or from river to river, on the back of the boatman in this wise: A "yoke" is provided, such as every man in the country, especially all who have visited a "sugar bush" at the season of sugar making, has seen. At the end of this yoke is a round iron projection, made to fit into a socket in the upper rave of the boat. The craft is turned bottom upwards, the yoke adjusted to the shoulders, the iron projections fitted into the sockets, and the boatman marches off, with his boat, like a turtle with his shell upon his back.[9]

The skin of the early Adirondack skiff did indeed look like a clapboard house, as Hammond had reported. This type of construction, called by boatbuilders

Adirondack Guideboats

The guideboat builders relied on patterns rather than a mold or molds. The essential patterns were those for ribs and stems. Some builders also used patterns for the bottom board and planks.

The builder fastened the rabbetted stems to his elliptically tapered bottom board and set it up on a "stock" which put the prescribed rocker in the ends. Next, the ribs, sawn from the naturally-curving roots of red spruce, were screwed to the bottom board. Their upper ends were aligned and fastened to temporary stringers, and their edges faired and beveled to receive the planking. The lower edges of the bottom board were beveled to receive the garboard plank. The builder then had the basic shape of the boat without any other forms.

The planks were put on, with great care in their spiling and fit. After the garboards, each plank had to be beveled on both edges, from its full thickness (typically 3/16") out to a feather edge (some builders used a beveled ship-lap) along its entire length, so as to mate perfectly with the bevels on the edges of the adjacent planks. Moreover, in areas of greatest curvature, the planks might have to be milled to a greater thickness, then backed out (hollowed) on the inside, and rounded on the outside, to give a 3/16" skin that was molded to the ribs.

Most strakes of planking were of two pieces, with short scarf joints landing on ribs. The planking was screwed to the ribs. Between the ribs, the seams were fastened with thousands of tiny clinched tacks, from the outside in and from the inside out, through the feather edge of each plank.

The hull was finished with short triangular decks, hardwood outwales (no inwales), fixed caned seats fore and aft, and a removable caned seat amidships. There were no floorboards in a working guideboat, only thin brass "kickplates" over one pair of rib-feet for each rowing position. There were always yoke cleats and a yoke, metal bangstrips on the stems and iron "shoes" on the bottom, and the standard "pinned" guideboat oars.

*This is a brief, generalized synopsis of information given in the definitive work on the guideboat, Kenneth and Helen Durant's *The Adirondack Guide-Boat.*

"lapstrake" or "clinker," was refined within a generation of Hammond's visit. By the 1870s most Adirondack skiffs had smooth skins inside and out. In effect, the boat-builders had removed the overlapping wood at each lengthwise seam by beveling to a feather edge the long edge of each plank and then making a corresponding bevel on the edge of the plank below it. The seam was then fastened by a double row of clenched copper tacks, half from the inside of the boat and half from the outside, through the matching bevels. Nowhere on the boat is its skin thicker than a single board.

Smooth-skin construction was primarily a result of the quest for a lighter boat to make "backing" over the carries as easy as possible, but it also resulted in a quieter boat, and, some felt, a faster one as well, compared to conventional lapstrake planking. The boats of Hammond's day were heavier than later ones, but still they amazed observers with their light weight. For one man to carry a sixteen-foot boat on his shoulders "seemed to be as impossible as carrying a man-o'-war," in the words of a writer for *Harper's* magazine in 1859.[10]

The extraordinarily light construction of the guideboat was made possible in part by the development of finer fastenings. Pointed, self-tapping wood screws were available by the mid-1840s and enabled builders to fasten thin planks efficiently with less worry about splitting. Machine-cut clenchable tacks were available by the 1870s, replacing more expensive and cruder hand-forged clinch nails.[11]

This smooth skin was fastened to a flat bottom and sawn ribs, the technique of framing used in bateau construction. Sawn ribs give excellent strength for their weight, and the guideboat builders were, above all, aiming for light weight. When placed

Adirondack guide boat

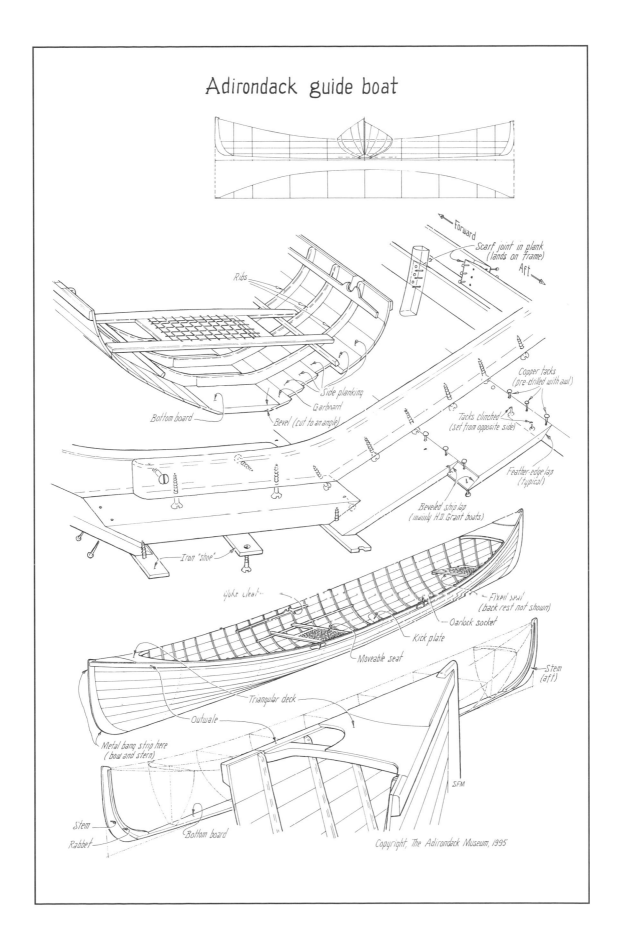

Forward

Scarf joint in plank
(lands on frame)

Aft

Ribs

Copper tacks
(pre-drilled with awl)

Side planking

Tacks clinched
(set from opposite side)

Gardboard

Bottom board

Bevel (cut to an angle)

Feather edge lap
(typical)

Beveled ship lap
(mainly H.D. Grant boats)

Iron "shoe"

Yoke cleat

Fixed seat
(back rest not shown)

Oarlock socket

Kick plate

Moveable seat

Stem
(aft)

Triangular deck

Outwale

Metal bang strip here
(bow and stern)

SFM

Stem

Rabbet

Bottom board

Copyright, The Adirondack Museum, 1995

2ᵈ Camp.
Roger's Brook.
Aug. 1869.

Frederick B. Allen, 2d
Camp. Roger's Brook.
Aug. 1869.

*The square inboard end of
the bow deck is characteristic
of early boats. The transom
fits smoothly into the stem in
this guideboat as it does in
the museum's Reuben Cary
boat (entry 60), in contrast to
the awkward stern of entry
107. 61.50.*

close together (generally on four- to six-inch centers) and cut so that they are wider in the side-to-side dimension of the boat than in the fore-and-aft direction, they form such a stiff structure that no thwarts, or cross-members, are needed to hold the boat in shape.

Guideboats have a great deal of "sheer," a term which describes the difference in height between the ends and the middle of a boat. The high ends enable the boat to keep dry in rough water, and the low center puts the rower close to the water. This distinctive shape is primarily a result of the boat's bateau-type construction in which planks sawn from wide boards are bent around a relatively wide, double-ended flat bottom.[12] The bottom of a guideboat is a single board cut to an elliptical shape and generally around eight inches wide amidships, narrowing to an inch at the ends. The shape and edge bevel of the bottom board in a guideboat also results in greatly flaring sides. The boat is quite tippy when lightly loaded, but it is also fast. It gets progressively more stable (and rows harder) as it is loaded and sinks into the water, acquiring more wetted surface.

Although Hammond did not mention it, the boats he saw were probably not double-ended, as most guideboats became by the 1870s. Originally, many (if not all) had tiny wineglass-shaped transoms, probably holdovers from another type of boat with which the early builders were familiar, the New York harbor gig.[13] The transom was abandoned probably because the boat was easier to build without it, and it served no useful purpose in a guideboat.

Many settlers in the practically untouched wilderness of the early nineteenth-century Adirondacks helped support themselves with trapping and market hunting. In 1835 Farrand Benedict, an engineer who worked with geologist Ebenezer Emmons on the geological survey of the region, noted that "It has long been known that hunters have transported in small boats their treasures of fish, game and fur through these waters, from the vicinity . . . of Lake Champlain to the valley of the Black River."[14] Four years later Emmons heard about two men from Saranac Lake who had rowed to Raquette Lake with a good supply of salt. They returned over the same route with seven barrels of lake trout in their two boats.[15] There are six carries on this route, one over a mile in length. One wonders how they crossed them with all their baggage.

The Adirondack boat was essential to life around an Adirondack farm. On Lower Saranac Lake Headley accompanied a young man on an expedition to get butter. It turned out that the dairy was located across two lakes and a stretch of woods, and Headley and the farmer reached it by a few short tramps and two boat trips. Later Headley heard that another settler on Lower Saranac Lake was off after milk, inquired whither, and learned that the intrepid farmer had a piece of cleared land half a mile down the lake where he pastured his cow. "So," he concluded, "you travel in boats, go on pleasure excursions in boats, get all your meat, and fish, and vegetables in boats, and finally your milk and butter in boats. Well, a boat with you is a great institution."[16]

The hamlet of Long Lake was typical of Adirondack settlements of the time. It was well situated in terms of water navigation, since Long Lake is actually only a

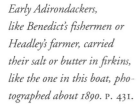

Early Adirondackers, like Benedict's fishermen or Headley's farmer, carried their salt or butter in firkins, like the one in this boat, photographed about 1890. P. 431.

widening of the Raquette River, which flows northwards to the St. Lawrence. Thirty
miles downriver from Long Lake one could carry over a divide and put into the watershed of the Saranac River, which flows into Lake Champlain; two lakes upriver one
could cross another low divide and be on the Fulton Chain of the Moose River, which
leads out to the Black River and the Mohawk. John Todd, the first of many well-
known clergy to visit the Adirondacks, described the settlement of Long Lake in 1841:

> Scattered along towards the head of the lake, we found a little community of eight or
> nine families. . . . It was Saturday when we arrived, and as soon as it was known that a
> minister had come, two of the young ladies sprang into a little boat, and rowed round
> to let the families know of the event. The ladies there can row and manage a boat as
> well as they can a horse in other places. In thus calling on their neighbors, they must
> have rowed twelve or fourteen miles. The Sabbath morning came and we met the little
> boats coming up, some rowed by a father with all his family in it, some by the sisters,
> and some by the little brothers; and one huge bark canoe, with an old hunter who lived
> alone many miles further in the wilderness.[17]

With their "light skiffs" early Adirondack settlers were able to stay in touch with
what passed for neighbors in the sparsely settled region. Headley related the story of
a woman who so longed for feminine conversation that she took her six-month-old
infant and fourteen-year-old daughter on a trip from their home on Raquette Lake
to visit a friend who lived thirty miles away.

> Now carrying the boat on her head around the rapids—in one place two miles on a
> stretch while the girl lugged along the infant and oars—now stemming the swift cur-
> rent, and anon floating over the bosom of a calm lake, she pursued her toilsome way—
> accomplishing the *thirty miles by night*. What think you of that? . . . To make a visit of

thirty miles through an unbroken forest, with a babe six months old, and a girl only fourteen years of age, and carry and row her own boat the whole distance. . . . I hope she had a glorious gossip to pay her for her trouble.[18]

The Adirondack guideboat was ideal for traveling through much of the central mountains because it was swift and capacious yet easily carried. These qualities came at the expense of others, however. In their quest for lightness builders often thinned the planking down to an improbable 3/16 inch; rowers had to use great care to avoid punching holes in their boats on rocks and deadfalls. Guideboats are fast in part because of their narrow bottoms, but this construction also makes them tippy. In particular, a person sitting in the stern of a guideboat, where the passenger usually sits, is perched on the top of an inverted pyramid and can easily rock the boat.[19] And while rowing is probably the most efficient way for a single person to propel a boat, rowers cannot see where they are going without constantly craning their necks—an annoyance generally and a danger in rapids or meanders where the boatman must constantly make adjustments.

Settlement and travel were concentrated along the easiest route through the mountains, Headley's central valley, and travel along that route and its branches was most commonly in guideboats. The Adirondack upland to the west and north presents a gentler aspect than to the northeast. In the nineteenth century this region was not considered part of the Adirondacks; the name of the ancient Indian tribe was associated by most with what is now known as the High Peaks. Trappers, hunters, and intrepid sports who did venture into the north and west, traveled overland to find lakes and streams to explore. These travelers sometimes brought guideboats with them, but more often, at least in the years before the Civil War, they used other watercraft such as the dugouts and bark canoes of the Indians or other small boats with a European heritage.

J. H. Rushton, who grew up in the Adirondack foothills south of Russell, remembered the boat woodsmen used in his childhood in the 1850s and 1860s as "a light open boat or canoe 11 to 13 feet long, 30 to 36 inches wide and weighing from 25 to 50 pounds."[20] Two people typically paddled these canoes, each using a single-bladed paddle, and since they were facing the direction of travel they could navigate well in winding streams. A hunter could carry the boat across country fairly easily with the help of a yoke.

Although the canoes of Rushton's childhood were paddled like the Indian bark canoes, and were somewhat like them in form, they had a very different heritage—one going, perhaps, as far back as that of the more famous guideboat. They were probably lapstrake boats built on a keel and related to the lapstrake skiffs brought to the St. Lawrence Valley by British settlers. A larger version of this boat became known as the St. Lawrence River skiff by the second half of the nineteenth century. It was the guide's boat of the Thousand Islands region and a favorite pulling boat in liveries in the Adirondacks.[21]

Samuel H. Hammond got to know many parts of what is now the Adirondack Park; in addition to his trips on the Saranac Lakes (where he was when he described

Arpad Gerster, The End of the Carry, *1893.* 58.273.1.

guideboats in 1857) he spent part of a summer tramping in what he called the "Chateaugay woods"—a much larger region than modern people would call the Chateaugay area. With Joe Tucker, a local guide, and Tucker's large deerhound Shack as his sole companions, he traveled from Chazy Lake southwest to Chateaugay and Ragged Lakes, then south to the Saranacs and Tupper Lake. The little party traveled mostly cross-country on foot, but whenever they came to a navigable body of water, they paddled it—either to get to the other side, to troll for lake trout, or to look for deer. On the lakes he frequented, Tucker usually had hidden a dugout. On Ragged Lake he made a spruce bark canoe. At the next lake, Indian Lake (one of the many Indian Lakes in the Adirondacks), he did not find the right materials to build a bark canoe, so he and Hammond built a raft which wet their feet and blew across the lake but which served their sporting purpose. Near the Indian Carry between Upper Saranac Lake and the Raquette River watershed, Hammond purchased a canoe from the "half-breed" who lived there—probably a birchbark.

While some people moved to the Adirondacks for cheap land, others had their eyes on the region's vast timber resources. The virgin forests of North America had attracted the British in the seventeenth century as they began to build the world's greatest navy. The timber of the Adirondack region was noted well by men campaigning nearby in the valleys of Lake Champlain and Lake George, along the Mohawk and along the St. Lawrence during the colonial wars. The tallest and finest white pines were reserved by the Crown for masts; lesser pine and other varieties of trees supplied ample lumber for planking and frames. By the time of the American Revolution the best timber had been cleared from the land along the banks of the St. Lawrence and the Hudson, and the loggers were moving inland. By 1845 loggers from Glens Falls had moved up the Hudson to the region around Indian Lake in Hamilton County.[22]

Along the larger rivers like the St. Lawrence, transportation to the mills had been relatively easy. As the trees were felled they were grappled together in huge rafts, sometimes a quarter of a mile long.[23] In the spring, when the water was highest, the crews built shanties on board, roughed out some long oars for steering, and cast off to float with their harvest downriver. Some loggers even took their families along for the ride; in the mid-eighteenth century Anne Grant, then a girl living on the banks of the Hudson just above Albany, described the domestic scene on board one such raft, "the mother calmly spinning, the children sporting about her, and the father fishing at one end. . . ."[24] They were bound for Albany, where their logs would be loaded on ships for the trip to their destination.

The central Adirondacks contained great stands of pine, but the rivers were too small and too rough for rafts. Around 1813 two enterprising brothers named Fox, who were logging the Brant Lake tract, began sending their logs down the Schroon River and then into the Hudson to the mills at Glens Falls by letting them float down individually on the spring floods. The new technique, which became known as the river drive, was soon used throughout the northeast.

Engraving after Thomas Cole, Timber Rafts on Lake Champlain, *1850. 68.29.4.*

The Adirondack river drive was considerably harder on the crews than rafting. No fishing or spinning here, and no women except an occasional camp cook. Most of the loggers slogged on foot through the slush and undergrowth all the way from the banking grounds near where the timber was cut to the mills along the riverbanks. They carried peaveys or pike poles twelve to twenty feet long with which they prodded stranded logs back into the flow. The job of the river crews was crucial to the success of the drive because their charge was to pick logs loose from snags in the middle of the river to avoid jams. Snagged logs would quickly become locked tight from the enormous pressure of the "spring freshet" bearing down upon them. A jam was not only dangerous to dislodge, it would delay the river drive—perhaps only long enough to produce grumblings from the drivers anticipating payday, but perhaps so long that the spring flood would subside and leave logs stranded along the riverbank. The delivery of the logs would be an entire year late.

A few men rode in boats downriver with the logs, carrying or lining the boat past obstacles. Generally the boat crews were three: a bowsman, a sternsman, and the oarsman. The man at the oars was the elite of the drive. He was paid more than the ordinary river drivers because the safety of the crew depended on him. On the Hudson around 1900 the ordinary riverman who worked the shores earned $1.50 per day, the bow and sternsmen could earn up to $2.00, and an oarsman, on the treacherous stretch from the mouth of the Indian to the mouth of the Boreas, was paid $4.00.[25]

Barbara Kephart Bird, wife of a forester working on the Moose River in the 1920s, reported that she had never seen such perfect teamwork as that shown by a crew breaking a log jam that had started in the center of the river. She was watching the last generation of river drivers in the Adirondacks, but her description can serve for the nineteenth century as well.

> The men we were watching climbed into their boat and moved swiftly out into the boiling stream. Rowing like mad, they swung over to the island. The bow man immediately caught hold of a solid log with his pike pole. As the boat swung downstream, the other two made fast with peaveys. Bow man hopped out and held the boat while the other two disembarked, the rower first putting on his extra jacket. The reason for this was soon plain, as his job was to hold the boat in readiness for the two workers. The wind was cold, and sometimes he had a long wait before the center "gave way" and his two companions leaped lightly from tumbling logs into the boat. Then there was expert work at the narrow oars until the boat was brought safely to the next center, or to shore, as the case might be.[26]

The oars of river drive boats were indeed "narrow." Typically they were almost bladeless, reflecting a greater concern with staying out of trouble than with efficient propulsion. It is easier to "catch crabs" (catch on the surface of the water when recovering the oar) with wide blades than with narrow ones. These narrow oars were also strong, with no thin blades to catch and split. The oars were "pinned," that is, the horn was fastened to the loom so the oar couldn't slip out or pop up easily. This had obvious advantages in a working boat in which the rower might want to jump for safety or for his peavey at any time without losing his oar, but it hampered his maneuverability a bit since he would not be able to pull the oars inboard to avoid rocks or logs.

* * *

River drivers rowed against the current with their bows pointing upstream in fast or dangerous water. While being carried downstream stern-first, the oarsman used his oars mostly to maintain his position in the river. He didn't attempt to row upstream; since he was actually going backwards relative to the normal direction of a rower, he could see where he was going without craning his neck and, with skill and luck, avoid rocks and snags. It also kept him from going too fast and risking an upset if he hit a rock.

The types of boats used in Adirondack river drives varied throughout the region. The boats Mrs. Bird watched were "not much to look at, being stout, flat-bottomed boats, painted a drab gray."[27] They had broad transoms; other "jamboats" were square at both ends or double-ended. All boats, regardless, were flat-bottomed for work in shallows, had a great deal of rocker for maneuverability, and were sturdily built, with braces fastened across two or three ribs at each oarlock for strength.[28]

The double-ended river drive boats used in the Adirondacks were direct descendants of the military and commercial bateaux of the eighteenth century and were referred to as bateaux by the rivermen. The design had proven itself in conditions similar to those faced by the river drivers and reached its greatest refinement not in

This classic Penobscot-type bateau, photographed on the Ausable River about 1898, was built for the J & J Rogers Company that owned the museum's Ausable River jamboat; see entry 187. P. 24178.

Ferris J. Meigs, son of the
founder of the Santa Clara
Lumber Company, took this
photograph on the company's
drive on the St. Regis River
around 1890. The jamboats
show significant rake to the
bows, like the Penobscot
bateaux, and are rowed by
two oarsmen each. They must
have been stable for the logger
to have hauled the four-foot
pulp logs into the boat. P.
21903.

the Adirondacks, but in Maine, on the Penobscot River in the mid-nineteenth century. The classic Penobscot bateau has an extreme rake to the stem and stern which rolls back waves and allows the crew to leap dry-shod ashore or onto a jam. The sides are flared, a result of building a boat with high, raking ends from straight planks. The boat has a relatively short bottom, which contributes to speed and maneuverability. In the words of John Gardner, it is "a daring watercraft, a combination of extremes that functioned brilliantly under the conditions for which the boat was developed."[29]

Transom-sterned jamboats, like those used on the Moose River in Mrs. Bird's time, were variations on the flatiron skiff, "one of the most common and widespread small utility boats ever built," according to John Gardner.[30] Skiffs provide a steady working platform with great initial stability—that quality that makes one feel as if he can walk around anywhere in the boat without tipping it over. Secondary stability is the quality of remaining upright once heeled; boats like flatiron skiffs have little of this. When they tip past a certain point, over they go.

Adirondack jamboats, like many working small craft, were mostly "built by eye" by craftsmen associated with the logging business, rather than by boatbuilders using plans in boatbuilding shops. Well-documented boats are rare, as is also the case with many workboats. River drive boats were cheap, rugged, and expendable.

Lumbermen on rivers with long stretches of slack water, such as the Raquette River, found that quiet water could be just as difficult to traverse as wild water. At Long Lake, for example, the Raquette broadens out to as much as a mile in width for fourteen miles and there is scarcely a perceptible current. There the river drivers built a raft upon which was mounted a capstan. They then rowed a boom made of logs strung end to end around the main mass of logs and attached the loop to the capstan with a long cable. The raft was rowed or poled out ahead of the logs, an anchor set, and the men trudged round and round the capstan until they drew the logs to them. Then the process began all over again. Often the long hours of tramping lasted through the night when the lake was still and free from the strong winds of early spring; a wind could break the boom and scatter the logs across the face of the lake. On windy nights the men huddled around a fire on shore, ready to row out to work as soon as the wind died down. After steamboats became common in the region they relieved the capstan crews.

Lumbermen were able to use Adirondack waterways to advantage in logging the region, but other entrepreneurs often were not so successful. Miners found rich iron ore in the region beginning in the late eighteenth century, but many enthusiastic developers came to grief and ruin because they failed to look realistically at the inadequate water transportation.

Deposits of iron ore on the edges of the Adirondacks were successfully exploited starting in the late eighteenth century. By 1810 there were eleven forges on the shores of Lake Champlain, and the industry improved when the Champlain canal opened in 1823, providing iron manufacturers with inexpensive access to markets along the Hudson and Mohawk Rivers. The iron mines of the Lake Champlain region flourished through the nineteenth century.[31]

Iron mining ventures in the interior, just a few miles from the ports of Lake Champlain, did not fare so well. The story of the Adirondack Iron Works is typical. A rich

Some lumber companies built floating kitchens for their cooks to facilitate feeding the crews their four daily meals as the river drive moved downstream. This one is probably that of the Sisson and White Company on the Raquette River about 1895. P. 9387.

These kilns at the Narrows between Upper and Lower Chateaugay Lakes produced charcoal to burn in the blast furnaces of the Chateaugay Iron and Ore Company. 1891 photograph by Seneca Ray Stoddard. P. 1729.

bed of iron ore was discovered in 1826 in the town of Newcomb right on the Hudson River, as the developers were fond of emphasizing. What their prospectuses failed to point out was that the stretch of the Hudson they were talking about was practically on the slopes of Mt. Marcy, at 1,804 feet of elevation and forty rugged miles west of Crown Point on Lake Champlain. In 1839 the state surveyor, who ought to have known better, wrote of the situation, "On a partial view of the subject, it might appear that a distance of 40 or 50 miles from water carriage to the great markets, would be an important objection to an establishment which involves in its very nature the transportation of heavy articles. When we further consider, however, that such are the improvements in the construction of railroads and canals, and that scarcely any part of the country is inaccessible by one or the other of these modes, the objection vanishes. . . ."[32]

The owners of the works proposed several schemes to improve transportation to their mine. In 1839 they tried to get legislative support for development of slack water navigation down the Hudson, through what was then a nearly unpeopled wilderness, and through the Hudson Gorge, even now inaccessible by road and known for some of the best whitewater rafting and canoeing in the northeast. A few years later a company was chartered to build what they perhaps thought was a more workable scheme, a system of improvements to existing waterways which would have included a canal from the town of Little Falls on the Erie Canal to Long Lake, whence slack water navigation was possible to Rich Lake and up the Hudson River to the mine—with the trifling addition of another canal from Round Pond to Long Lake. Like many such schemes, this one seems to have been worked out by a hopeful investor in Albany or New York City sitting in his office with one of the rudimentary maps of the day in front of him, not by anyone who had actually walked the land. Nothing came of the various plans for water routes to the Adirondack Iron Works, and the investors pulled out in 1856. The reason, as Benson Lossing put it on a visit to the site two years later, was primarily "geographical and topographical impediments."[33]

The owners of the Adirondack Iron Works did make use of local water transportation. In the 1850s they built a dam across the Hudson below Lake Sanford, north of the present village of Newcomb, to provide slack water transportation to the blast furnace and the village of Adirondac [sic] at the head of the lake, and the settlement of Tahawus at its foot, saving eleven expensive miles of overland transportation. Six heavy boats or barges hauled freight and passengers. The company also built two more pretentious boats, McIntyre and Experiment. Sports like Thomas Addison Richards had found by mid-century that the "Works" provided a "very acceptable headquarters for the tourist" in the High Peaks region, especially since they could admire the view from the Company's boats on Lakes Henderson and Sanford. McIntyre was a sailing vessel forty-seven feet long with a beam of thirteen and a half feet. Richards took a "little voyage" on Lake Sanford in "a noble twelve-oared pleasure-boat belonging to the Company," which may indicate that McIntyre also had oars.[34]

Lack of good water transportation didn't doom all mining enterprises in the region. Iron mining at Lyon Mountain began in 1873, and by the next year there were twenty forges with accompanying charcoal kilns at the outlet of Chateaugay Lake. Both the upper and lower lakes became millponds for the forges. As on Lake Sanford, the Chateaugay Iron and Ore Company used the lakes for local transportation—to move wood and ore in barges towed by steamboats. Even so, the Lyon Mountain mines didn't really become profitable until the completion of the Chateaugay Railroad from Lake Champlain in 1879.[35]

*   *   *

In 1859 Benson Lossing, accompanied by another gentleman and Mrs. Lossing, visited the village of Adirondac at the beginning of a journey down the entire length of the Hudson River. Although ironmaking had ceased only a few years before, the settlement was all but deserted. Robert Hunter had been left in charge of the property, and he and his family had the run of the sixteen houses and cupolaed schoolhouse-church. His cows and chickens wandered at will down the overgrown main street. His neighbors may have left him, but he probably didn't get lonely, at least in the summer, for as the iron industry declined the tourist industry grew. Hunter's was a natural stopping place at one end or the other of a trip through Indian Pass to Keene Valley, or a base camp for an ascent of Mt. Marcy. All over the Adirondacks people who had settled in the region for one reason or another were finding that catering to the tourists presented a lucrative, if seasonal, source of income.

We crossed Champlain to Keeseville with our friends,
Thence in strong country carts, rode up the forks
Of the Ausable stream, intent to reach
The Adirondac lakes. At Martin's beach
We chose our boats; each man a boat and guide,—
Ten men, ten guides, our company all told.

Next morn, we swept with oars the Saranac. . . .

—Ralph Waldo Emerson, 1858[1]

CHAPTER 3

The Way It Looks from the Stern Seat

Seneca Ray Stoddard captured this group of sports embarking from Martin's beach September 21, 1876.
P. 15195.

Visitors to Robert Hunter's home in Adirondac were "trampers." Those looking for a less physically-demanding vacation kept to the central mountains, where the Raquette and Saranac watersheds provided a convenient highway. William F. Martin was Robert Hunter's best-known counterpart in this region. His hotel on Ampersand Bay of Lower Saranac Lake was a landmark from the day it was completed. It stood out initially because it was the only frame building in a scattered settlement of log houses and bark shanties. It was also the first hotel built on purpose to house sportsmen and tourists. The two-story inn commanded "one of the loveliest of quiet Adirondack scenes," in the words of one visitor. "Across the bay, at the right, the shore rises abruptly to a considerable height. At the left, near by, is a dense grove of cedar, balsam, and tamarack. . . . Beyond is the broad lake, with its islands and distant mountains."[2]

The numbers of visitors to the region had been steadily increasing for several years, and Martin had picked an ideal spot to serve them. Lower Saranac Lake was the logical starting point for an expedition into the wilderness, the place where the tourist gave up the "strong country carts" and stagecoaches of overland transportation and set forth on the watery highways which stretched into the interior. Most of them traveled in guideboats rowed by professional boatmen.[3]

In the summers before the Civil War, Martin's was a lively and cosmopolitan place. Gentlemen (and some ladies) from New York and Boston arrived daily, generally having traveled by rail to Whitehall at the head of Lake Champlain, where they boarded a steamboat in mid-morning which deposited them in Port Kent in the evening.[4] The men were attired nattily in india-rubber leggings for trout-fishing or a pair of alligator-leather boots for protection from the unknown creatures of the woods; the ladies wore sturdy flannel dresses which looped up over short crinolines which showed a daring ten or twelve inches of leg.[5]

A particularly noteworthy party arrived one July day in 1858—one member so noteworthy that the townspeople turned out to welcome him. He was the Harvard zoologist and geologist Louis Agassiz; among his nine companions were poets Ralph Waldo Emerson and James Russell Lowell. William James Stillman, the painter, had organized the outing. Stillman had visited the Adirondacks the previous summer under the guidance of Martin's brother, Steve, and had enjoyed the experience so much that he had put together a party of his learned friends from Cambridge and Concord for a shorter sojourn in the woods the next year.

The gentlemen refreshed themselves with one of Mrs. Martin's famous suppers and a night of rest in the cool, balsam-scented air of the mountains. The next morning they assembled on Martin's beach, where they found awaiting them eight local men who were to be entrusted with their safety and comfort for the following month. As was the standard arrangement on such sporting excursions, there was one guide for each gentleman except Agassiz. Stillman himself acted as guide for the eminent scientist, partly to ensure that he had a good time, but primarily, as he admitted, because "I could not have kept in proper subordination so large a company of men collected from all parts of the woods, though with all the care in selection possible under the circumstances, if I had not been ready to do my share of any work I called on them for."[6]

General E. A. McAlpin and his guide Jack Richards about 1890. P. 19986.

Drawn up on the beach were nine guideboats. They must have looked dangerously frail to gentlemen used to the seaworthy Whitehalls and heavy dories of the coast. The boats were elegant, though, curving gracefully from high stem down and

out amidships to a high stern. The guides gently slid the boats half into the water, then, while holding the stem to steady the narrow craft, they invited the gentlemen to step in and walk to the stern, keeping their weight on the flat center of the bottom, and steadying themselves with a hand on each gunwale. The gentleman made himself comfortable in the stern seat, reclining against a light seat back and stretching his legs out almost straight. Then, after stowing his share of the camp duffel and the sport's gear in the center of the boat, the guide put one knee on the bow deck, gave a shove to the beach with his free leg, vaulted gracefully over the deck into the bow seat, and took up the oars. Once in deeper water he turned the boat around and headed out across the waters of Lower Saranac Lake. Emerson was inspired and impressed by the trip across the Saranac Lakes. The weather was clear and the surrounding mountains seemed "grand companions" to him. He was able to concentrate fully on the scenery, as the trip required very little work from him.

When the group reached Bartlett's Carry between Round Lake (now called Middle Saranac) and Upper Saranac Lake, a wagon awaited them to carry over the boats and baggage. When they reached the Indian Carry, Jesse Corey met them with a horse and wagon. Even though the chief distinguishing characteristic of the guideboat was its portability, enterprising settlers at the major carries were quick to provide horsepower to the increasing numbers of tourists.

"Backing" a boat over the carries was also avoided by making use of boats hidden in the woods near frequently-used carries or fishing holes. Many of these, like the canoe used by John Burroughs, were probably sturdy dugouts. H. H. Thompson, camping on Jock's Lake in 1863, used craft that sounded more like flat-bottomed skiffs of some description: "good, large, stout fishing boats . . . kept some distance from shore bottom up on skids and covered with bark" to keep them hidden. Mitchell Sabattis, guiding a sport in 1849 from Long Lake to Blue Mountain Lake, relied on boats—probably guideboats—he knew from friends to be hidden at the carries along the route.[7]

On many carries in the Adirondacks the guides still shouldered the boat, and the sport was expected to carry the duffel. Many sports described the carries with excruciating detail in the books and articles they wrote when they returned. Joel Tyler Headley saw the humor in the situation.

> Nothing can be more comical than to stand and see a party thus passing through the forest. First a yoke is placed across the guide's neck, on which the boat is balanced bottom side up, covering the poor fellow down to the shoulders, and sticking out fore and aft over the biped below in such a way as to make him appear half-human, half-supernatural, or, at least, entirely *un*-natural. But it was no joke to me to carry my part of the freight. Two rifles, one overcoat, one tea-pot, one lantern, one basin and a piece of pork, were my portion. Sometimes I had a change—namely, two oars and a paddle, balanced by a tin pail in place of a rifle. Thus equipped, I would press on for a while, and then stop to see the procession—each poor fellow staggering under the weight he bore, while in the long intervals appeared the two inverted boats, walking through the woods on two human legs in the most surprising manner imaginable. Though tired and fagged out, I could not refrain from frequent outbursts of laughter that made the forest ring.[8]

Emerson calculated that in the course of a full day his guide took thirty thousand strokes and never seemed to tire. The boat that had evolved as an easy-going boat for settlers to row long distances to see their neighbors or to hunt for the market served the tourist industry just as well. The guide sat more or less erect, without putting his back into the rowing and without pushing much with his feet. The guideboat, with its fine lines and light weight, moved easily, and the guide could keep it moving all

Thomas Bangs Thorpe, "Oars and Paddles/Pranks of Paddles and Oars," Harper's Monthly *19, no. 110 (July, 1859): 172–173.*

OARS AND PADDLES.

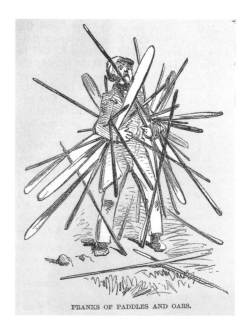

PRANKS OF PADDLES AND OARS.

Seneca Ray Stoddard, The way it looks from the stern seat, *1888.* P. 27677.

day by pacing his strokes to steady, even pulls from the arms only. Stillman and other rowers accustomed to wider craft had to get used to the boat, however, as the guideboat was so narrow that the oars crossed in the middle, and the rower had to row with one hand over the other, or in front of the other, or the two hands rotating around each other, to avoid barking the knuckles of his thumbs.

The sports might also have noted the way in which the guideboat oars were mounted on pins ("tholepins," technically) which fit into the oarlocks. Pinned oars cannot be feathered to reduce wind resistance or pulled shorter in a narrow space, but they can be dropped to shoot or land a fish without fear of losing them. Other guides' boats in the northeast were similarly equipped; the St. Lawrence skiff, soon to be recognized as the standard guide's boat of the Thousand Islands region, had the thole pins mounted on the gunwale of the boat, and the oar had a slot in it which fit over the pin.

Guideboats were well suited to crossing the wide expanses of the Saranac Lakes but less well adapted to the next stage of the journey. After the party of ten boats crossed the Indian Carry, they had to negotiate "Pere Raquette Stream, . . . winding through grassy shallows in and out."[9] If the city men had gained a thorough respect for the tippiness of the boats, the guides might have entrusted them with a long, narrow-bladed paddle for steering. The guides rowed from the bow and the sports sat in the stern, where they were perched on the flat side of an inverted triangle. The slightest movement would cause the rower to "catch a crab" on the recovery of his stroke.

Martin and Stillman had selected for their campsite Follensby Pond, whose outlet enters the Raquette five and a half miles downstream from the Indian Carry. When

The Way It Looks from the Stern Seat 61

Guideboat paddles have long, narrow blades and often a decorative grip. The paddle on the left was made by Caleb Chase of Newcomb. That on the right belonged to William Henry Harrison "Adirondack" Murray. The stone in the grip is a cairngorm, commemorating Murray's Scottish heritage. The ribbon is a replica of a silk scarf tied onto the paddle by a friend of Murray's during a trip with him to the Adirondacks. 90.43, 69.39.

they arrived at their destination, the guides set up camp, cutting young trees for the frames of the lean-tos and a canvas tent the city men had brought along, and peeling spruce bark to "weatherfend" the lean-to roof. The guides then looked after the table, baking potatoes, beans, and "wheat-bread" to accompany the venison and trout. All was washed down with ale and wine—no doubt doubly appreciated because of the trouble required to get it to the sylvan table. The gentlemen gave the campsite the rather prosaic name of Camp Maple; the guides called it the "Philosophers' Camp" in reference to the savants, and their name stuck.

The learned company entertained themselves by swimming, climbing nearby hills, and dissecting and classifying the local flora and fauna. Hunting was not only a way to provide for the table but also an important amusement in that summer forty years before enforced game seasons. If the Philosophers were like many of the other sports visiting the region at the time, they went out after deer merely for the excitement of the chase, sometimes letting the animal go free at the last minute.[10] The swift, silent guides' boats were essential to the two almost universally methods of filling the rustic larder, hounding and jacking.

Hounding was best done with a group of hunters. Some guides rowed their sports into selected coves around a given lake. Other guides, with dogs, set off through the woods to find deer and drive them to the water. The sports waited in their boats for the deer. When a swimming deer was sighted the guides had to bend to the oars to reach the animal before it could gain land again, and then perhaps shoot or club it if the sport missed the mark. Then they had to row back to camp, towing the dead deer.

Jacking, judged an exciting and mysterious experience by many, was also indulged in by the Cambridge luminaries on dark nights. The guide moved the boat silently along the shore where deer fed on the tender aquatic plants, rowing with well-greased oarlocks or paddling with the long steering paddle. When a deer was sighted the jacklight transfixed the animal and the sport shot, backed up by the experienced guide.[11]

The Philosophers of Camp Maple were, as a group, more learned and illustrious than most groups of campers in the nineteenth-century Adirondacks, but they were otherwise typical of the tourists of the day. Generally the travelers were possessed of some leisure and wealth. The vacation had not yet become a part of American life, so it was only those who could afford a protracted absence from home who went to the woods for a month or two. Many were sent to the wilderness for their health. They were men, for the most part; in the years before the Civil War the journey was thought too rough and the destination too remote to appeal to many women. Notable exceptions were Mrs. Lossing and the Honourable Amelia Matilda Murray, a lady-in-waiting to Queen Victoria, who made a "gipsy expedition" from Elizabethtown to Boonville in 1855.

The Philosophers' reasons for going to the woods were typical, as well. Emerson was more articulate and eloquent about the value of nature than most visitors, and indeed, he was in the vanguard of a movement which idealized the Adirondack wilderness as an antidote to industrial civilization. Although Emerson and his colleagues did hunt and fish, their reason for going to the Adirondacks was not

Guide with dogs. P. 1209.

primarily for the hunting. They came for moral and spiritual regeneration, not for utilitarian purposes.

Even while Americans were enchanted with the technology which produced such advantages as inexpensive, high-quality cloth for the masses and instant communication with Europe (Emerson and his friends learned of the laying of the first trans-atlantic telegraph cable while they were in the woods), they were aware of the negative aspects of the new age. Crime and poverty were already apparent among crowded workers in the rapidly-growing cities, and the air and water around the mills and factories were becoming obviously polluted.[12]

In an increasingly industrialized culture an escape to the woods was attractive—and even prescribed by doctors to combat nervous strain, neurasthenia, and dyspepsia. Dyspepsia, chronic indigestion classically accompanied by a sour disposition, was supposedly unknown in the woods. As Stillman reminded Emerson and his fellow Philosophers when they complained about the food at Camp Maple, "'Chronic dyspepsia never came from eating / Food indigestible—'"; it came from the worries and hurries of modern life.

Guiding, boarding, lodging, and outfitting city sports soon represented a significant source of income to many Adirondack residents. Those in the "central valley" who rowed boats or built them were in a particularly good position. The hotelier

This engraving by Theodore R. Davis, "Floating for Deer in the Adirondacks," appeared in Harper's Weekly *in November, 1968.* 66.112.6.

Martin and his brother Stephen were two of the best-known pioneer settlers to take advantage of the business opportunities afforded by the sports. They may have moved to the region for just that purpose. The brothers were raised on a farm near Bangor, New York, one of the villages near the northern edge of the Adirondacks. Apparently farming in the relatively fertile St. Lawrence Valley didn't appeal to them, for as young men they left their home to their parents and sisters and moved up into the mountains. Within a quarter of a century, Martin's was one of the leading hotels in the Adirondacks. Guides from the Saranac region made the inn their headquarters, and guides from the upper Raquette sometimes would wait there for their parties. Knowledgeable travelers engaged a guide by mail before arriving at Martin's; others counted on finding one when they arrived on Lower Saranac.

Adirondack guides soon became well-known to the American public through travel narratives like Headley's, Hammond's, and Emerson's poem.[13] Emerson admired the guides as natural men, unspoiled by the worst aspects of modern life and strengthened by their life in the outdoors. He was also, like many who followed him into the woods, impressed with their ability to live in the wilderness. "Look to yourselves, ye polished gentlemen!" he advised his readers.

No city airs or arts pass current here.
Your rank is all reversed; let men of cloth

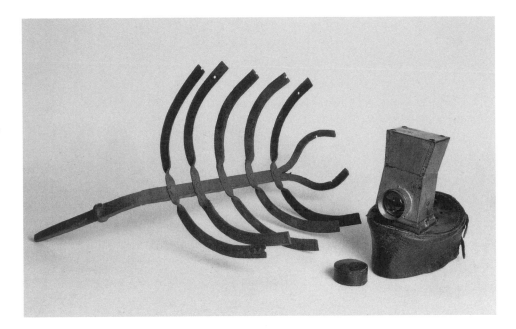

> Bow to the stalwart churls in overalls:
> *They* are the doctors of the wilderness,
> And we the low-prized laymen.[14]

Steve Martin, as we know him from accounts written by his clients, is an example of the classic Adirondack guide. He was Stillman's guide in 1857 and a guide on the Philosophers' trip. A redhead who cut a memorable figure at six foot two, he rapidly gained a reputation for feats of physical strength and endurance which lost nothing in the telling; he could wrestle all comers to the ground, it was said, he once swam five miles after a boat that had drifted away, and he could stalk and kill a deer without a gun.

The most important tool of Steve Martin's trade was a guideboat. Rowing it across lakes, up winding streams, and in pursuit of deer took up the bulk of his time on a trip, and, according to Emerson, he was well-accustomed to it.

> In Adirondac lakes,
> At morn or noon, the guide rows bareheaded:
> Shoes, flannel shirt, and kersey trousers make
> His brief toilette: at night, or in the rain,
> He dons a surcoat which he doffs at morn:
> A paddle in the right hand, or an oar,
> And in the left, a gun, his needful arms . . .
> Sound, ruddy men, frolic and innocent,
> In winter, lumberers; in summer, guides.[15]

As Emerson relates, Martin and his fellow guides worked at that trade only seasonally, and probably intermittently. The sports in search of speckled trout came in the spring, and during the summer deer hunters began to arrive in the woods. For the months of the deepest snow the guides could work elsewhere—in the lumber woods or around their homes and farms.

Guides could pick and choose their clients and the amount of time they would work. Probably most married men spent at least part of the warm months on their farms, leaving the farm labor to their wives and children when it was feasible.[16] When they did work, guiding was lucrative. In the early 1870s the standard rate was $2.50–$3.00 per day. In the lumber woods at the same time a chopper earned less than half as much.[17] Farm labor was even poorer paid; the prevailing wage was $10 per month.[18]

Increasing numbers of sports and tourists in the central Adirondacks meant an increasing demand for the guide's boat, and boatbuilding became another good seasonal occupation. The rapid evolution of the Adirondack boat into a craft perfectly suited to its use is due in part to the fact that many of the builders were guides themselves and knew first-hand the rigors of the carry and the responsibility of taking a heavily-laden boat down Long Lake against a head wind. Other guideboat builders of the middle of the nineteenth century were skilled craftsmen who turned their hands to a variety of trades. The early ones were probably veterans of the bateau shops of Schenectady or at least knew of the type of building practiced there. William McLenathan was a builder early enough to have been credited with being the "father of the Adirondack guide boat" by one of his students at the end of the nineteenth century.[19] A younger contemporary, Caleb Chase, was a skilled gunsmith in addition to being a well-known boatbuilder.

McLenathan was a native of Vermont. At the age of fifty-one he went to work for the young Bill Martin just after Martin moved to Saranac Lake. Martin kept a large number of boats at his hotel for guides who couldn't afford their own boats, or for rental to competent sports.[20] It was "Uncle Mac's" job to build and maintain the fleet.

Caleb Judson Chase lived over the great mountain range in Newcomb. Like many Adirondackers, Chase practiced several trades, but by the time of his death in 1911 it was as a boatbuilder that he had achieved his greatest fame. Chase was born in Ticonderoga in 1830. His father, a Vermonter, died when Chase was an infant, and the boy moved to Newcomb with his brother at the age of twelve, probably to avoid being a burden to his stepfather and his mother's new family. The Chase brothers were moving into a fairly settled part of the woods; in 1842 the neighboring iron works at Tahawus were in full operation. By the time Chase built his first boat at the age of twenty-one, the village of Newcomb was home to 277 souls, including a physician and forty-seven laborers living in two boarding houses.[21] Chase established a home on land he farmed, married Thankful Preston, and started a family. He also established himself as a gunsmith and boatbuilder. His two trades were much in demand and gave him a secure living as the local iron industry died and the tourist industry burgeoned.

Chase's production of guns was probably not prolific; there is no surviving example of his work, and he may have been primarily a repairman.[22] As a boatbuilder, however, he soon became well-known. His early boats were workmanlike square-sterned models built of pine. Like most other guideboat builders, Chase made the paddles and oars for his boats. His guideboat paddles, with their decorative grips, are among the most elegant in the Adirondacks.[23] No record exists of Chase's teacher in the boat-

Caleb Chase about 1898.
P. 11326.

building trade, but like many guideboat builders he established a family name in the trade; his son-in-law William Alden lived next to him and built boats with him until an early death, and his son Edmund J. Chase carried on after his father.[24]

Enthusiastic about the Adirondacks, Emerson and the rest of the Philosophers met in Cambridge the autumn following their trip to Follensby Pond and organized the Adirondack Club. Stillman was delegated to purchase land for a permanent camp, which he did that winter, selecting a tract centering on Ampersand Lake. The group met there in the following year, but in 1860 there was a decline in interest, due partly to the absence of Stillman, who was in Europe. Then the Civil War broke out. As the national crisis deepened, the Cambridge intellectuals lacked enthusiasm for a trip to the woods. Nor did they return as a group after the war ended, and the land eventually reverted to the state for unpaid taxes.[25]

The nation as a whole was disillusioned and spiritually exhausted by the war. But by the end of the decade the appeal of the Adirondack wilderness became even greater to people in search of rest and regeneration.

The Adirondack wilderness, formerly visited by a few adventurous sportsmen . . . has, within a few years, become one of the most popular resorts for tourists. . . . Sporting must continue to afford less and less inducement to visit the wilderness and must be superseded by new objects of interest—the climate, peculiar local institutions, the boating, the rough and salutary exercises and exposure.

—Forest and Stream, 1873[1]

CHAPTER 4

A Popular Resort for Tourists

On Sunday morning, June 15, 1873, a party of eight young women and their four guides rowed onto the still waters of Blue Mountain Lake from the Marion River. They landed on the beach on the lake's eastern edge and stood "spell-bound, for a time," as one of them wrote, "by a scene in which were blended so many natural harmonies. . . . We felt that we were emphatically in the presence of God."[2] The eight women were part of a larger expedition studying the ferns, mosses, and algae of the Adirondacks. The rest of the party arrived within a few days, and the twenty-five women settled down to camp for the rest of the summer, "acquiring renewed vigor for the duties of exploration" when they should return to school.[3] Although unusual in being composed of unchaperoned women, the group was otherwise typical of a new trend in tourism in the Adirondacks. The sportsmen were being joined by "tourists." In contrast to the sports, who came for hunting and fishing and generally traveled by water, the tourists were interested primarily in the scenery, and they often traveled overland to see it.

The botanizing expedition was the summer project of the students in a private ladies' academy in New York City. It was essentially a summer vacation, but the women were also genuinely curious about the region. In the words of Verplanck Colvin, a professional scientist who led his second scientific expedition to the Adirondacks the same summer, "few fully understand what the Adirondack wilderness really is." This desire to know more about the region, particularly that part of it already well described by the writers who traveled the great watery highway of the central Adirondacks, was resulting in a large body of literature. Colvin published government reports, and the lady botanists contributed "The Neglected Plants, Or A Journey Through the Realm of the Cryptogams."

The headmistress of the ladies' academy and president of their "Linaean [*sic*] Society for the Diffusion of Botanical Knowledge" was Amanda Brinsmaid Benedict, sister-in-law of Farrand Benedict, the surveyor who worked on Emmons's 1837 survey.

Seneca Ray Stoddard, West from Blue Mountain Lake House, *1879.*

This is the beach upon which, six years before, the botanizing party had rhapsodized about the beauty and solitude of Blue Mountain Lake. They might have been surprised at the houses and docks, but they would have recognized the guideboats. Two of them are of the square-sterned variety, going out of fashion at the time of the photograph. The Gilbert and Sullivan operetta H.M.S. Pinafore *had premiered the year before this photo was taken, and probably accounts for the name of* Buttercup *on the middle boat.* P. 9597.

Mrs. Benedict and her husband Joel had been spending summers in the Adirondacks for twenty-one years, camping out on Raquette and Long Lakes. As they grew older, they made a spacious corner room at Root's Hotel on Schroon Lake their summer home. Mrs. Benedict's love for the region and its flora no doubt inspired her students to mount an Adirondack expedition.

The ladies all took classical names for the trip, and they divided themselves into a headquarters crew and four corps which were to explore different quarters of the region. Miss Steele, Director of the Expedition, became Themis, and the Misses Spier, Macauley, Callahan, and Poillon became corps commanders Euphrosyne, Aglaia, Circe, and Daphne. The main contingent headed for Root's Hotel in Schroon Lake. While Mrs. Benedict and seven of the ladies settled in at the sign of the moose antlers, Alia and the guide McFredo were dispatched to Newcomb and Long Lake to engage guides to meet the other three corps when they reached the edges of the central valley and take them to Blue Mountain Lake.

Euphrosyne and Aglaia took their corps to the mouth of the Saranac River on Lake Champlain, traveling the well-known and well-used route to Lower Saranac Lake, just as Emerson and Stillman had fifteen years before. The other two corps were practically pioneers, going in by routes that were rough in 1873 but which were soon published as "gateways" to the Adirondacks.

Eight of the women traveled by train from Albany up the Mohawk valley, following the same route west as the bateaumen one hundred years before. At Amsterdam, four women under the command of Daphne left the others and got off to take what they had heard was "the most difficult route into the mountains: northwards up the Jessup River valley from Lake Pleasant."[4] While the Lake Pleasant area was well known to anglers (the first sporting lodge in the Adirondacks was established on

Piseco Lake in 1842), few ventured into the central mountains from there. For the fern-finders, the trip involved a five-day tramp over the Cedar River Mountains. The women and their guides, Sturgis and Holmes, survived a violent thunderstorm and a landslide near Snowy Mountain and went hungry before they reached the south inlet of Raquette Lake—and the Long Lake guides with their boats.

The ladies found out the hard way how little baggage they could take on their backs when traveling overland. Even though the guides reduced their luggage to the minimum, allowing only two suits of clothes, a heavy woolen blanket, a towel, and a piece of soap for each, rejecting mirrors, parasols, perfumes, silk dresses, "and other things too numerous to mention," the women took turns giving their ten-pound packs to the guides to carry. Those long-suffering men already toted seventy-five pounds of gear, plus rifles. Tramping left little time for collection and classification of ferns. Clymene, for one, looked forward to the relative comfort of travel by water. "When we get to the Lake Country," she wrote optimistically to Mrs. Benedict en route, "I can make out my report in the boat, while on the move."[5]

Circe and the remaining three ladies stayed on the train, turning north at Utica and disembarking at the High Falls on the Black River, known today as Lyons Falls. There they engaged guides named Higby and Wood to lead them over the rough seventeen-mile tramp to First Lake on the Fulton Chain. This is the reverse of the route Amelia Murray, Victoria's adventurous lady-in-waiting, had taken in 1855, remarking that her experience scrambling out of bogholes and over decayed corduroy "fully explained why ladies are rare birds in that locality."[6]

James Smillie, Evening on Lake Raquette, Adirondacks, *1874.* 66.98.3.

After encounters with bears and wolves, sleepless nights when they were kept awake by the unaccustomed noises of the forest, and, almost incidentally, some lichen study, the overland corps reached the central valley. At the south inlet of Raquette Lake and First Lake, respectively, the women changed guides. The men who had accompanied them through the woods returned to their homes, and the guides from Newcomb and Long Lake took over. The entire party rendezvoused according to schedule on June 15 at Blue Mountain Lake. As the black flies diminished, the ladies began their vacation. Altogether, the party represented nine boats, twelve guides, and twenty-five young ladies. They camped out for the rest of the summer, since there was neither hotel nor house on the lake.

Female tourists were not unheard of in the back woods in the 1870s, although only a generation before, the six daughters of Otis Arnold had been struck dumb by the appearance of Lady Amelia Matilda Murray because they had never seen another woman besides their mother.[7] But a party so large of women traveling on their own, without brothers or husbands, must have been worthy of comment. The fact that increasing numbers of women were joining the ranks of Adirondack tourists was due not only to the changing role of women in American society, but to general prosperity, better accommodations, better knowledge of the region, and improved and expanded transportation networks. One no longer had to be wealthy, or a gentleman willing to rough it for a month, to visit the Adirondacks.

Although the extravagant railroad expansion of the immediate post–Civil War years precipitated a panic and depression in 1873, it was a mild depression for ordinary people. Real income rose over sixty percent from 1869 to 1879.[8] While an Adirondack vacation was not within the reach of factory workers and laborers, it was possible for middle-class businessmen and their families. In the mid-1870s farm laborers in upstate New York typically made $35 per month, not necessarily including board—not enough to afford a vacation in the Adirondacks. A professional man, on the other hand, probably earned twice as much. A bank clerk or accountant or teacher could count on $1,000 per year, enough over basic necessities to pay for a piano, private school for his children, or a yearly holiday in the Adirondacks. A month in the Adirondacks, figuring in guide-hire, board for guide and sport, transportation from Boston to Saranac Lake, and miscellaneous expenses, cost $125.[9]

While people would continue to camp out in the Adirondacks for generations to come, increasing numbers of visitors wanted more civilized accommodations. Martin's, where Emerson had begun his trip into the woods, had been followed by small and not-so-small establishments all along the well-traveled route through the central valley.

The "St. James of the Wilderness" in the 1870s was the hotel of Apollos A. Smith on Lower St. Regis Lake. "Pol" (or "Paul," as he was known) had built a hunting lodge here in 1859, and by the 1870s the establishment had grown to three stories with accommodations for a hundred guests, a large stable, and a post office. In his boathouse on the sandy beach, reported guidebook-writer Charles Faxon, a hundred of the light, graceful and staunch boats in universal use on these waters are "pigeon-holed," with sterns to the water, reminding one of the scene in "Lucrezia Borgia," where that estimable lady displays her facilities in the amateur undertaking business. These boats are all identical in size and build, are numbered from 1 up, and resemble very much the famous Whitehall boats, except that they are lighter. From the boat house to the water's edge a sloping platform of plank enables the rower to slide his boat out of water.

As many as sixty guides waited at the boathouse, ready to take parties hunting, fishing, camping, or on excursions to other hotels.[10]

While the lady botanists of Blue Mountain Lake had an unusual source of information about the Adirondacks in their headmistress and her husband, many people were not so well informed—at least until after the Civil War. Hunters and fishermen knew of the region through a number of sporting narratives, but few books had addressed the general public, ladies in particular. Beginning in the late 1860s, however, information about the region proliferated for every audience. Much of it extolled the virtues of traveling through the region "more or less," as de Costa would have said, by water.

Certainly the women of the Benedict party had all read the enticingly titled *Adventures in the Wilderness*, which had appeared in the spring of 1869. The book had particular appeal for ladies; its author was William Henry Harrison Murray, a respected Boston minister, and it contained specific instructions for women going into the woods.

"Now, in the North Woods," wrote Murray, "owing to their marvellous water-communication, you do all your sporting from your boat. If you wish to go one or ten miles for a 'fish,' your guide paddles you to the spot, and serves you while you

Seneca Ray Stoddard, Guide House at Paul Smith's, *ca. 1880.*

The thought of one hundred guideboats staggers the modern imagination. According to some sources, the guide house slept sixty guides, each with boat, but sixty is still a large number. Regardless, there was certainly a great deal of business for boatbuilders in the neighborhood, but their names have not been recorded. P. 24173.

handle the rod. This takes from recreation every trace of toil. You have all the excitement of sporting, without any attending physical weariness . . . an excursion to this section [is] so easy and delightful to ladies. There is nothing in the trip which the most delicate and fragile need fear."[11]

While Murray's book resembled the sporting narratives of the previous generation in its tales of running wild rapids and encountering Indian ghosts, its advice to travelers made it a guidebook, a fairly new genre for the region. Guidebooks told the new class of tourists where to go, what to wear, what sights to see, and provided them with lists of guides for hire. Aspiring sportsmen and tourists could also learn about the Adirondacks from accounts published in periodicals. In 1873, the year of the Linean Society's expedition, *Forest and Stream*, the best known of these magazines, first appeared. Over the next thirty years editor Charles Hallock and his successors would devote a great deal of space to Adirondack issues and to the development of small craft for sporting and pleasure use. *Forest and Stream* soon had separate regular columns on canoeing and on yachting, as well as features on hunting in the Adirondacks.

*   *   *

While sports described the hunting and fishing of the Adirondacks and promoters published guidebooks, scientists worked to add to the hard facts known about the region. Ebenezer Emmons's ambitious survey of the late 1830s was the first and only major scientific exploration of the region in the ante-bellum years. In 1872 the second major survey began, the Topographical Survey of the Adirondack Wilderness by twenty-five-year-old Verplanck Colvin.

Colvin, born in Albany in 1847, studied law, but he soon abandoned whatever ambitions he may have had to be a lawyer and developed a deep interest in the natural world and in surveying. In 1865 he began visiting the Adirondacks, fishing and hunting like most young male visitors of the time. Four years later he began making scientific measurements, observations, and reports to the New York State legislature, and in 1872 he applied to the state for an appropriation for a survey which would produce an accurate map of the region. For the next twenty-seven years he surveyed and reported and haggled with the state for funds for his expeditions. He never completed his map, but his measurements and the prose in his reports intrigued and informed the public about the great wilderness in the northern part of the state.

Colvin's reports reached more than the legislators to whom they were addressed. His account of locating the highest source of the Hudson in September, 1872, particularly caught the public imagination; the botanizing ladies included Colvin's story in the manuscript report of their expedition.[12] While his tales of climbing previously untrodden peaks and his descriptions of camping deep in the wilderness fit into the growing canon of Adirondack travel literature, Colvin's reports also revealed details of life in the woods often unnoticed by other writers. Certainly his accounts demonstrate how well suited guideboats were as portable boats. His accounts also describe ways in which other watercraft were used by the hunters, trappers, and settlers of the wilderness.[13]

This engraving, from a drawing by Verplanck Colvin, appeared on his map of the Mud Lake district in his 1874 report to the New York State legislature.

In mid-October of 1873 Colvin set out to explore the region around Horseshoe Pond in southern St. Lawrence County. The season was late, but Colvin was never one to give up field work until forced to by deep snow. With two Saranac guides and their guideboats he rowed up the Bog River to the Chain Lakes, four small bodies of water which have since been subsumed by Low's Lake. Here the party was overtaken by a storm that reduced visibility and hampered his mountaintop work, so the practical Colvin announced that they would explore the sources of the Bog River—a task that could be done just as well in foul weather as fair, "though not so comfortably."[14]

The two boats rowed up the winding Bog River to Mud Lake, aptly named in Colvin's time but made deeper and clearer in the twentieth century by a dam at the river's outlet to Hitchins Pond. There they found a party of guides who had come with boats and dogs to hunt deer for the market. In the space of a week the hunters had shot sixty or seventy large deer and sent them out to the settlements by boat. The hunters told Colvin of a wolf trapper who had visited their camp a few days before and who had traveled from the *west*—exciting news to Colvin, who immediately set off to find the trapper and find out what he knew of the terrain.

Leaving the boats at Mud Lake, Colvin and his men bushwhacked west and found a dugout left by the trapper at the lake, and then the trapper. Rather reluctantly, he divulged his knowledge about the region. Colvin was so intrigued that he determined to explore all the way to Number Four and the Stillwater of the Beaver River that season—even though winter was coming on fast. After Colvin returned to Mud Lake and finished some measurements, he discovered he was running low on provisions. Eager to get on with his explorations, he sent one of his guides back to the settlements for food—a round trip of ninety or a hundred miles, which the man accomplished in two days.[15]

One of the measurements Colvin wanted to finish was Cranberry Lake. On October 26 he and his men set out from their Bog River campsite on a bushwhack of about five and a half miles which included four ponds, a climb of 157 feet, then a drop of 415 feet to the lake. Colvin described their equipment as "light marching order," but the guide who carried the boat might have disagreed. They spent two nights on Cranberry Lake, measuring the altitude and talking with hunters and trappers about other lakes and peaks in the region. On the 28th they crossed the lake, "rolling in heavy foam-crested billows" in their overladen boat, and returned to Mud Lake.

Having gotten Cranberry Lake out of the way, Colvin rendezvoused with his trapper on November 1 and walked off cross country for the Beaver River settlements, with two guides toting two boats. The weather was getting steadily worse—his "minimum thermometer" recording temperatures in the mid-twenties at night until it got broken—but Colvin couldn't resist the lure of unmapped territory. He began to run into ice at the upper end of the lake, but, nothing daunted, loaded the gear in the boats and dragged them out onto the "iced margin" of Mud Lake with ropes.

For a while, in the fairly level country southwest of Mud Lake, Colvin's party hauled their boats and provisions on makeshift sledges with horses they had acquired from the nearest St. Lawrence county settlements. When the terrain became unprac-

Verplanck Colvin, Mud Lake, winter march westward in the unexplored region, *1874. From Colvin's 1874 report to the New York State legislature.*

Verplanck Colvin, Oven Lake, accident to the second boat. The guides' baggage and instruments in danger. *From Colvin's 1874 report to the New York State legislature.*

tical for sledges they went back to overland travel, rowing at every opportunity. They had to break through the ice around the edges of the lakes to launch their "thin, shell-like boats," and on November 8 they abandoned the most badly damaged and continued with one.

Oven Lake was partially frozen, but the guides opted to risk a crossing rather than carry the baggage and boat around the lake through the dense, tangled forest, full of downed timber and riparian thickets. The main party watched the progress of the guides as they themselves struggled along the shore. The guides had rowed to the middle of the lake when they struck thick ice and stove a hole in the boat below the waterline. Unable to help, Colvin and the shore party watched as first one guide and then the other fell into the icy water as they tried to shift the baggage to keep it dry and at the same time draw the boat onto the ice. Eventually the men brought the boat ashore. The craft was so badly damaged that they abandoned it, but when they reached the next lake and Colvin itched for a reconnaissance, they went back for it. They continued their march, stumbling with their loads over the trunks of trees, slippery with deep snow. After crossing a divide and lowering the boat down a steep bluff, they launched it on the still-unfrozen Clear Lake.

At Clear Lake, Colvin and his party were outside the trapper's ken and had to rely on their own resources. There was a foot of snow on the ground, but they were in the home stretch; at Clear Lake, Colvin sent the Saranac guides off to Salmon Lake in search of another trapper said to be wintering there. On November 11 they returned with the trapper, who led them, still carrying their damaged boat, to the waters of the

Beaver River. They finally abandoned the leaky boat they had brought all the way from Saranac Lake and used the trapper's boat to get to within twelve miles of Number Four. There they turned around and headed *back* into the wilderness, carrying and rowing boats as far as Smith's Lake, now known as Lake Lila. At Raquette Lake they found a team and sleigh which took them to Long Lake, whence they sleighed out to North Hudson and back to Saranac Lake for baggage and records they had left there from the first part of their explorations. Their trip from Mud Lake to the Beaver River, on foot and carrying a boat, had taken them on a bushwhack of at least fifteen miles in twelve days. In his 1991 guide to canoe routes, Paul Jamieson describes a trip that follows much of Colvin's trail, even done during the canoeing season, as an unforgettable adventure for qualified persons, and "for the inexperienced, a nightmare."[16]

*   *   *

As Colvin bushwhacked with his guideboats through the downed timber of the back country, less ambitious travelers explored the region in increasing comfort. Improvements in transportation, both to the Adirondack periphery and within the wilderness itself, made a vacation in the North Woods attractive to increasing numbers of people. After 1871 tourists could take the Adirondack Railroad all the way to North Creek. "Adirondack" Murray advocated approaching the Saranac region via steamboat up Lake Champlain; this route was followed by the Philosophers and the Linean Society. By 1879 the approach had improved even more. "The opening of the new railroad on the west side of Lake Champlain is of great interest to sportsmen," wrote a correspondent to *Forest and Stream* in 1879. "At present you can leave New York at six p.m. and reach Plattsburgh at six a.m. and Martin's at five p.m."[17] Once within the wilderness, Murray's "marvellous water-communication" became even more wonderful when steamboats began serving the traveling public. They appeared first on the larger lakes on the periphery of the mountains, but by the end of the decade of the 1870s the toot of the steam whistle was heard echoing off the mountains of the central Adirondacks.

Lake George had steamboat traffic early, as a natural outgrowth of the lively maritime trade on Lake Champlain. The first commercially successful steamer was the 102-foot *Mountaineer,* built in 1824 at Caldwell by John Baird, a local hotelier, and Jahaziel Sherman, builder and master of several Lake Champlain steamboats. In 1837 the newly-incorporated Lake George Steam Boat Association laid the keel of the *William Caldwell,* with which they initiated through service with a land connection at Ticonderoga to Lake Champlain. Tourists especially liked the route because three and a half hours were allowed at the northern landing to visit the ruins of the fort Ethan Allen had taken for the Republic "in the name of the great Jehovah and the Continental Congress" in 1775.[18] The Schroon Lake contingent of the Linean Society expedition stopped here to collect mosses and explore the rooms and passageways of the old fort on their way to Root's Schroon Lake hotel from Lake George.

Andrew K. Morehouse, an energetic businessman in the southern Adirondacks,

put a fifty-five-foot vessel on Piseco Lake in 1840. The settlement at the lake was only two years old at the time but already boasted a hotel, school, church, blacksmith shop, and fifteen families. Although the boat was used primarily for excursion service, it also hauled freight for the inhabitants of the two towns on the lake and probably towed log booms as well.[19]

When the Schroon Lake corps of the Linean Society reached Root's, they found that the sixty-eight-foot, double-deck *Effingham,* launched on the lake the summer of their visit, offered twice-daily excursions on Schroon Lake. *Effingham* was built by the Brooklyn firm of C & R Poillon and had a seventy-five-horsepower engine to drive her single screw.[20]

By the end of the 1870s steamboats had penetrated to the interior lakes. The first in the central valley was probably *Utowana,* commissioned by William West Durant and built at Blue Mountain Lake in 1878. Early that summer she undertook her maiden voyage, carrying employees of a local hotel on an outing. Probably most of them had never been on a powered boat before.[21]

The Saranac Lakes were not far behind; on Independence Day, 1878, hotelier William F. Martin launched *Water Lily* on Lower Saranac Lake. John Philip Sousa's band was aboard to make the occasion suitably festive. *Water Lily* was part of a trans-portation network Martin set up to handle the traffic between his hotel and Bartlett's

Hotel at the carry between Middle (then called Round) and Upper Saranac Lakes. *Water Lily* was met twice daily at the carry between the lower and middle lakes by "large, canopied rowboats." *Mattie*, launched by 1878, crossed Upper Saranac Lake and then connected with carriages and guideboats for Paul Smiths.[22]

Water Lily was average in size for early Adirondack steamers. She was thirty-six feet long, with a beam of nine feet, and carried forty passengers. A crew of three, the captain, engineer, and one purser, ran her. A smaller boat, the ill-fated *Buttercup* (see below), put on Long Lake in 1882, was only eighteen feet long. *Utowana* and *Killoquah*, both built in the late 1870s for the Eckford Chain and Raquette Lake, were between fifty and sixty feet long.[23] *Jennie*, which served Chateaugay Lake from the early 1870s, was a forty-foot lapstrake boat with a capacity of twenty. Her predecessor *Nellie Tupper* was similar in size.[24]

Most tourists and sportsmen welcomed the arrival of steamboats in the central Adirondacks because they made travel more comfortable and cheaper. Passengers on the powered vessels were generally seated on wooden benches under a canopy, with roll-down storm curtains for added protection from the weather. In contrast, guideboat passengers were exposed. They might stay mostly dry by bundling up in mackintoshes and india-rubber blankets, or even carrying an umbrella, but when they reached their destination and the guide ran the boat up on the sand or the sloping dock, any bilgewater inevitably ran down over their feet. And they were cramped; the

The steamboat Water Lily *on Lower Saranac Lake about 1880.* P. 45065.

passenger sat with his legs almost straight in front of him and had few options to change his position. George Washington Sears, a widely-read outdoor writer of the 1880s, complained about being a guideboat passenger even though he was only five feet three inches and normally paddled a twelve-foot canoe. "Yes, the Long Lakers are fast—but cranky and uncomfortable to ride in," he wrote.[25]

Steamboats were also attractive to some "outers" because they provided an independent means of travel. People like Sears, who liked to propel themselves, could take a steamer for a rest now and then, stowing their own boat on the roof. As Arpad Gerster remarked,

> On various tours through the woods much annoyance was suffered through the impatience of the guides, who were always in a "stew" to reach the next hotel on the route, where "grub" was awaiting them. Even in the eighties the Adirondack guide began to change his character. From a woodsman, he was turning into a mere machine for transportation, losing his woodcraft, his leisurely and knowing ways, and his aplomb.[26]

While many hoteliers and tourists embraced enthusiastically the expansion of steamboat traffic in the Adirondacks, some objected to the boats on aesthetic grounds. Many of the narrow, shallow, twisting waterways of the Adirondacks had to be modified for steamboat traffic by blasting, dredging, or constructing dams to raise the water level. *Water Lily* traveled one such "improved" route. The channel between Middle and Lower Saranac Lakes drops around a small island; this drop is now negotiated by the state locks. In 1878 Martin dammed one side of the channel to produce a larger flow for the other side. In the same year, William West Durant raised the water level in the Eckford Chain and the Marion River to facilitate travel by his steamers *Utowana* and *Killoquah*.

George Washington Sears was a vociferous critic of the damming of Adirondack rivers because of the destruction of the natural beauty of the region. Recently-dammed lakes were particularly noisome. Traveling the Fulton Chain in 1881, he stopped to "take in the desolate scene" of Sixth Lake. "The water at and above the dam was clogged with rotting vegetation, slimy tree-tops, and decayed, half-sunken logs," he wrote. "The shoreline of trees stood dead and dying, while the smell of decaying vegetable matter was sickening. . . . None care to stop here longer than is necessary."[27]

The New York State Forest Commission objected to flooding on aesthetic grounds but also, one imagines, because of the destruction of merchantable timber. "The scenery along the Utowana is marred by the effects of this dam," its 1891 report stated about Durant's dam at the foot of Utowana, "whose back-water has in many places overflowed the banks and killed the trees along the shore, while the narrow, winding outlets which were once overhung with foliage have been changed by it into marshes filled by dead, unsightly trees. The shores of the Marion River, below the Carry, present a still worse appearance."[28]

In 1877 a correspondent of *Forest and Stream* objected to plans for *Mattie* because of the progress they represented. "Take notice, O, mighty [Ta]hawus! Look down, O, imperial Whiteface!" he wrote. "Speak in tones of thunder to the rash of intruders, and forbid thy royal domains to suffer as if thy streams were only to turn the mill wheels of manufactures and thy solitudes only made to coin dollars for some traders

Some of the early Adirondack steamboats were driven by stern- or sidewheels, like Colvin, pictured here by Seneca Ray Stoddard about 1878 on Lake George. By the 1880s, however, the small steamers of the central mountains were almost universally driven by propellers, which are more efficient and were readily available. Shoal-draft boats were not essential since many waterways had been deepened by dams. P. 30371.

The steamer Killoquah *with five guideboats on her roof about 1890. Just visible on the starboard side of the roof are two small rowboats of the type usually carried by Adirondack steamboats, probably for aid in emergencies. Photograph by Edward Bierstadt.* P. 7275.

with nature. For when thy realms are traversed by wings of steam thy glory has departed."[29]

Like the Luddites, English weavers who destroyed textile machinery in the early nineteenth century because it threatened their livelihood, some Adirondack guides objected to steamboats on economic grounds. By the late seventies, there was lucrative employment for local men providing transportation or excursions on many of the large lakes. Steamboats represented serious competition. The owners of *Water Lily* received several anonymous letters threatening to sink the boat shortly after she was launched. The boat survived, but one dark night the dam between Middle and Lower Saranac Lakes was destroyed by dynamite.[30]

At least two other steamboats actually did sink under suspicious circumstances in the early 1880s. *Mattie*, the first engine-propelled boat on Lake Placid, was burned at her moorings in 1882. Guides were generally held responsible.[31] *Buttercup*, part of a trans-Adirondack transportation scheme concocted by the central Adirondack real estate developer William West Durant, was launched on Long Lake in 1882. She ran for three years, but one night in 1885 the lines holding her to the dock at the Sagamore Hotel were cut, she was towed to the middle of the lake, a hole chopped in her hull below the waterline, and she sank. That same night, to ensure discontinuation of steamboat traffic, the perpetrators also dynamited the dam Durant had built at the upper end of Raquette Falls to raise the level of the river.[32]

Nobody was ever charged with the scuttling of the *Buttercup*, but in 1959 two amateur scuba divers had no trouble learning the exact location of the boat from an older resident of the town who remembered the guides' talk of his youth. With help from the community, they raised the vessel, and in 1993 she was put on exhibit in the town.

The preference of many people for steamboat travel over guideboat trips was purely economic. By the 1890s, when guides were still commanding $2.50–$3.00 a day, the day trip from Hollands' on Blue Mountain Lake to the Forked Lake Carry could be made by steamboat for $1.75.[33]

Who built the new boats that were revolutionizing travel in the Adirondacks? Some, perhaps most, were built by work crews who came to the region just for the project. The first steamboat on Piseco Lake was built by Benjamin Watson of West Troy in Albany County, who built her on site. He was paid half in provisions and half in land.[34] But local builders got at least some of the business. *Jennie* and *Nellie Tupper* on Chateaugay Lake were built by hotelier and boatbuilder Millard Bellows. The guideboat builder Dwight Grant built *Hunter*, the first steamboat on the Fulton Chain. Fred Rice, who built *Water Lily* with William Allen Martin, moved from the fringes of the mountains to become a resident boatbuilder; he came to the region from Willsboro on Lake Champlain where he had built large craft, and stayed in Saranac Lake to build guideboats.

*   *   *

The post-war increase in Adirondack tourism meant a boom in business for area builders of small craft as well. Faxon's description of Paul Smith's boathouse filled with a hundred guideboats staggers the modern imagination. It must have been fairly impressive even in the days when most travel in the region was by boat. Most other hotels were much smaller, but even so the numbers of guideboats on the water—and boatbuilders in the villages—was substantial and increasing. In the 1870s there were at least sixteen men building guideboats spread across the region from the Saranac Lake area to Boonville. A generation before there were probably only half that.[35]

Henry Dwight Grant was one Adirondacker who took up boatbuilding in this period of increased demand. Grant was born in 1833 on his father's farm near Boonville on the southwestern edge of the Adirondacks. As a boy he hunted, fished, and learned to handle a boat in the woods and waters near his home. By the age of twenty-one he was known as an able woodsman and worked seasonally as a paid guide. The first boats Grant used were heavy dugouts or flat-bottomed skiffs that were generally left on the shore by other users of the woods. Around 1860 he saw the first narrow, light, transomed "Saranac boats" row over the waters of the Brown's Tract. No doubt he, like other Brown's Tract guides, bought one as soon as he could. Perhaps he went to Saranac Lake or Long Lake for it, or perhaps a northern guide, delivering a client to the Fulton Chain at the end of the season, sold him his boat.

After service in the Civil War, Grant returned to Boonville, married, settled there, and began guiding for the Forge House on First Lake when he wasn't working at carpentry. After building a private camp on Fourth Lake for Lewis Lawrence of Utica, Grant took the secure position of caretaker. The Lawrences were resident only in the summer, however, and although there was plenty of work keeping up the structures and grounds, Grant found himself with time on his hands in the winters. Perhaps he also needed to augment his income; in any case, he turned to guideboat building in 1879.

Anxious to have one of his boats photographed even though there was snow on the ground, H. D. Grant hauled it outside the shop one winter day in the 1880s. Grant is "rowing," his workman Lester Fox is in the stern, and Theodore Seeber sits amidships. P. 34109.

Grant had to look far afield to learn his new trade. In the winter of 1879, and then again the following winter, he rented space in a local sash mill and asked Henry Stanton to come from Long Lake to teach him boatbuilding. One can imagine Stanton's arrival in Boonville, perhaps on snowshoes with the patterns for his guideboat in a packbasket on his back.

Grant eventually became one of the most productive and promotion-minded of the Adirondack guideboat builders. He printed an occasional circular, and once he entered a boat in the State Fair—no doubt with a view to advertising. He was unusual in these activities; most guideboat builders relied on word of mouth.

*   *   *

Guideboat builders were not the only craftsmen producing boats for the burgeoning recreational market, and North Country builders of canoes and skiffs were more businesslike in their marketing than their colleagues in the mountains, who were only part-time builders. The best-known of these men, both in his own day and in the late twentieth century, was John Henry Rushton. Rushton built his first boat in 1873, the same summer the young women of the Linean Society went botanizing. Despite having grown up in the Adirondack foothills, Rushton chose for his model not the guideboat in which those ladies spent so many charmed hours, but a small lapstrake boat similar to the skiffs in use on the nearby St. Lawrence River. Rushton had intended the boat for his own use, but a friend saw it while it was still in the Canton barn where Rushton was working and asked if he could buy it. Rushton agreed, and he launched a career as well as a boat in the summer of 1873.[36] Rushton and Grant both built their careers on the nation's increasing interest in outdoor recreation and the Great North Woods. But while Grant remained a traditional, small-town craftsman, building only part-time, Rushton soon adopted truly modern business practices.

J. H. Rushton was born near Russell, in St. Lawrence County, October 9, 1843. In his mid-twenties, he moved to Morley, five miles from Canton, to board with a hunting guide named Tom Leonard. When Leonard wasn't in the woods he built boats and did general carpentry. When Rushton wanted to get away to the woods himself, he borrowed patterns or molds from Leonard for a boat.

Rushton enjoyed building boats, and he also enjoyed the boatbuilding business. "I *love* my business next to my wife and the wild woods," he wrote to a friend.[37] Early in his career he developed practices of constant experimentation, attention to quality, and innovative marketing which eventually made him the best-known canoe-builder in America. He advertised (first locally and then nationally), took exhibits to fairs and expositions, worked closely with his customers, and became a master at the sophisticated practice of getting free advertising by interesting the editors of the sporting press in his work. His first paid advertisement appeared in the classified column of the *St. Lawrence Plaindealer* in 1875. In the next year he took two boats to the Centennial Exposition in Philadelphia, and in the following year he issued his first catalog. By the end of the decade unsolicited endorsements of his work were appearing in the foremost sporting periodicals of the day.

Rushton's first catalog was a small circular which appeared in 1877, when mail-order marketing was in its infancy. Most Americans of the time still conducted retail business on a face-to-face basis. Goods were produced locally or regionally. Purchase through mail-order was regarded as a somewhat risky undertaking.[38] Rushton introduced himself to potential customers not with a handshake but in print. Instead of recommendations from mutual friends, Rushton printed a testimonial from seven leading figures of Canton, including a lawyer, the county clerk, and the county treasurer—men whose word he hoped his readers would trust. "We the undersigned citizens of Canton," they wrote, "being well acquainted with Mr. J. H. Rushton, manufacturer of Rushton's Sporting Boats, are pleased to say to sportsmen in want of light boats for hunting, fishing or pleasure rowing, that in favoring him with their orders they can depend upon their being filled promptly and according to agreement in every respect. His boats are all he represents them to be."[39]

Rushton's catalog grew rapidly as other builders went into business and tried to capture a part of the rapidly-growing leisure market. Catalogs became almost a form of literature. They contained a great deal of copy minutely describing the product and presenting numerous testimonials and accounts of trips taken. The most elaborate example of the boating genre, George T. Balch's *Illustrated Catalogue and Oarsman's Manual for 1871*, ran to nearly five hundred pages and included designs for boathouses and reports of important races in addition to information on the paper boats of Waters and Balch.[40] Aspiring skippers pored over these catalogs each winter, reading the paragraphs of description and advice, comparing measurements, materials, and prices.

The number of boatbuilders producing pleasure boats and advertising nationally

Cover of Rushton's 1881 catalog. AML.

grew in the late 1870s. In New York's North Country alone, Rushton had competition from Herbert M. Sprague of Parishville, a versatile craftsman who also built violins. Sprague had been born in 1856, and in later years claimed to have built his first boat in 1869.[41] Further afield there were A. Bain and Company in Clayton on the St. Lawrence River, and to the south, the Watertown Boat and Canoe Company. James Everson was building Whitehalls and canoes on Long Island, and in the midwest there was the St. Paul and Racine Boat Works, a host of builders in the Peterborough area northeast of Toronto, George Ruggles in Rochester, and W. P. Stephens in the New York City area.[42]

Rushton distinguished himself from these other boatbuilders by an emphasis on light weight, and in this he reveals his Adirondack heritage. He strove to do with his small open canoes what the guideboat builders were doing with the guideboat—provide the lightest boat possible for travel in a region full of portages. He succeeded so well that his masterful designs have been adopted and adapted to new materials for over a hundred years.

You like the feather weight and the backwoods. So do I if I could leave my business for any time, but *as a matter of business and to make the builder known abroad the* decked *sailing canoes are the ones I have to look after.*

—J. H. Rushton, 1884[1]

CHAPTER 5

The Feather Weight and the Backwoods

George Washington Sears sat for his portrait in the late 1870s or early 1880s at the height of his fame as an outdoor writer. P. 13330.

In the winter of 1879–1880, J. H. Rushton received an intriguing order for a boat. The order itself was no less remarkable than the prospective client; it specified a canoe to weigh no more than twenty pounds, and the paddler was George Washington Sears, a writer whose pieces on hunting and fishing had appeared over the name "Nessmuk" in *The Spirit of the Times*, *The Atlantic*, and other periodicals of the 1860s.[2] Sears was a cobbler by trade, with a home, a wife, and three children in Wellsboro, Pennsylvania, but he preferred a life on the move to working on shoes. In his younger days he had gone to sea, hunted in the lumber woods of Michigan supplying meat to the logging camps, and wandered around the Amazon basin working out schemes to improve rubber production. When nearly sixty, he embarked on his first trip through the Adirondacks.

Like many people living in the rapidly industrializing society of the 1870s and 1880s, Sears felt overworked and unwell and felt that a sojourn in the North Woods would be a tonic. Unlike most visitors to the Adirondacks, he planned to "go through alone," without the services of a guide. He couldn't afford a guide on his shoemaker's income, and he was confident that he had enough knowledge of woodcraft to take care of himself. The one thing he did need was a light, inexpensive boat.

As light as it was, a sixty- to eighty-pound Adirondack guideboat was too heavy for Nessmuk. In 1880 he was fifty-nine years old and in failing health, suffering from asthma and probably tuberculosis. He was also a small man, standing five foot three and weighing 105 pounds. A guideboat was also too expensive for a shoemaker. Even a fairly small boat, such as Grant's fourteen and a half footer, sold for $60 in the early 1880s.

Nessmuk attributed the popularity of the guideboat to the guide's desire for speed. "Show [a guide] a Rushton model," he wrote, "light, strong, weatherly and weighing forty-five pounds, and he will say she is slow; he wants a boat that he can 'get somewhere with.'"[3] Nessmuk did admit that the guideboat was "the fastest model of an inland working boat I have seen," on the straightaway, but he felt that a small canoe

89

This photo was taken thirty years after Nessmuk first started looking for a small canoe, but illustrates the use of a hunting canoe in the area in which Rushton grew up. P. 48636.

would have the "bulge" on the guideboat when the way was crooked. He once challenged two guides to a race on a meandering stretch on the Fulton Chain. All three had a modest nip to toast the race. Then Nessmuk took off extra clothing, spit on his hands, and settled down to work. He kept up with the guideboats until the course straightened out somewhat and the way grew less distinct; then the guides literally lost him—Nessmuk ran aground on a deadfall trying to cut across one of the flooded meanders and by the time he was free the guides were nowhere in sight.[4]

Nessmuk also investigated other types of small craft, but none was what he wanted. He tried a tiny dugout, a birchbark, and a kayak; all were too heavy or too cranky. He also dismissed what most people of the time thought of when "canoe" was mentioned, the decked sailing canoe. These vessels, plank-on-frame, sailing versions of Inuit kayaks, were all the rage in the 1880s. They were too heavy for Nessmuk, however, and owed a great deal of their charm to their sails, which were often useless on winding mountain waterways. They were also expensive; Rushton's Rob Roy model sold for $80 in 1880.[5]

After considerable study of boatbuilders who built small craft, Nessmuk sent his order to Rushton. The Canton boatbuilder advertised a thirteen-foot, thirty-five-pound "hunting canoe," the smallest available at the time, and the price was only $27. He also declared he was willing to work with customers to build what they wanted, which in Nessmuk's case was an even smaller boat.

Rushton and Nessmuk shared a love for the wild woods as well as being similar in size. Rushton's interest in lightweight boats was probably a result of his stature as well

John Henry Rushton about 1884. P. 36123.

as his Adirondack upbringing. It should come as no surprise that he and Nessmuk came up with the smallest canoes of the time; Rushton stood five feet tall and weighed "111½ when feeling well."[6]

Rushton exceeded Nessmuk's expectations. The *Wood Drake*, or *Nessmuk*, was ten feet long, twenty-six inches wide, and weighed only seventeen pounds. "She's all my fancy painted her," he wrote in *Forest and Stream*, "She's lovely, she is light. She waltzes on the waves by day and rests with me at night. . . . Propelled by a light double paddle, with a one-fool power in the middle, [she] gets over the water like a scared loon."[7] He cruised her 550 miles through the Adirondacks that summer and returned in 1881 and 1883 for more solo cruising. His letters to *Forest and Stream* that described his adventures, and his 1884 volume *Woodcraft*, which told the novice how to enjoy a similar trip, opened a new world to aspiring "outers." "Going through alone," taking responsibility for oneself in the woods, and going at one's own pace, began to grow in popularity.

*   *   *

With a light boat and a light load, Nessmuk hoped "at no distant day to meet independent canoeists, with canoes weighing twenty pounds or less, at every turn in the wilderness."[8] A generation before, his insistence on independence might have seemed preposterous. In 1880 the time for the message was ripe. "Outers" no longer needed native guides to keep them from getting lost, since maps and general knowledge of the region had improved so much. Those who wanted a break from sleeping under the stars had their choice of hotels and boarding houses almost anywhere in the woods, and stores at the hotels and villages along the major waterways provided quick replenishment of supplies. The wilderness was becoming civilized. "Roughing it" became more and more a matter of choice, rather than necessity.

Verplanck Colvin, who had so much to do with opening the wilderness to travel, noted the change in 1879.

> Viewed from the standpoint of my own explorations, the rapidity with which certain changes take place in the opening up to travel of the wild corners of the wilderness has about it something almost startling. . . . I find following in the footsteps of my explorations the blazed line and the trail; then the ubiquitous tourist, determined to see all that has been recorded as worth seeing. Where first comes one—the next year there are ten—the year after full a hundred. The woods are thronged; bark and log huts prove insufficient; hotels spring up as though by magic, and the air resounds with laughter, song and jollity.[9]

Nessmuk took full advantage of these hotels magically appearing in the woods. On Raquette Lake, where Colvin had found only two bachelor hunters after his cross-country trek in 1873, Nessmuk had his choice of accommodations. Ed Bennett's Under the Hemlocks was his favorite hotel in 1880; within the next six years Bennett would be joined by Blanchard's Wigwams, Isaac Kenwill's Raquette Lake House, and Chauncey Hathorn's Forest Cottages.

The boom in hotel-building was partly due to an increase in the numbers of people who felt that the woods and waters could be enjoyed just as well on day-trips from comfortable hotels as on a two-week camping trip. The former plan allowed for nights between sheets on mattresses instead of blankets on balsam boughs. Confirmed outers argued that trout and venison tasted best eaten off a chip of bark in the woods,

Seneca Ray Stoddard,
Bennett House *(Under the Hemlocks), ca. 1879.*
P. 14957.

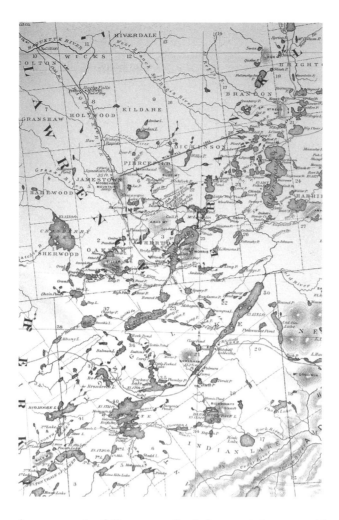

William Watson Ely, section of Map of the New York Wilderness, *1867.*

Ely's map was one of the earliest regional tourist maps. In this section, hotels, guides' houses, and the few roads are shown in the Saranac Lake–Long Lake region. AML.

but many city folk were perfectly happy sitting at a table, because the fresh game was eaten with an appetite sharpened by fresh air. They also enjoyed the novelty of finding white linen and china in the midst of the wilderness.

Nessmuk typically took only a little tea, butter, pork, and sugar in his boat, since he could purchase provisions along the way. Greater numbers of travelers in the region made paddling or rowing a pastime, not a means of transportation. If Nessmuk didn't care to paddle, because he was "fagged" or the big lakes were too rough for his little canoe, he could climb aboard a steamboat, tying his canoe upside down on the roof. He once "drafted" a guideboat going through the Fulton Chain by creeping under its "counter" and taking "the draw of its wake."[10]

Tourists of the 1880s also had the benefit of better maps and more detailed guidebooks. Before the Civil War, travelers relied primarily on the local knowledge of residents—they hired guides. Several sportsmen's travel narratives of the late 1850s were illustrated by maps of parts of the region. Although Colvin's map was never published, by Nessmuk's day there were several maps aimed specifically at the tourist. The most important, William Watson Ely's *Map of the New York Wilderness*, appeared in 1867. It concentrated on the central valley and the high peaks, and marked locations of hotels, guides' houses, and routes. Ely's map was copied and reproduced in

many guidebooks over the next dozen years, adding information on carries, steam-boat fares, and sources of supply. Guidebooks added specifics on the routes, such as sights not to miss and tips for pleasant travel.[11]

Even the knowledge of woodcraft, "the rod, rifle, canoe, camp, and in short the entire list of forest lore and backwoods knowledge" was no longer the exclusive province of the guide.[12] The 1880s was a fruitful decade in the production of how-to books on camping. Some of the earliest were written for boys: W. Hamilton Gibson's *Camp Life in the Woods, and the Tricks of Trapping and Trap Making* appeared in 1881, and Daniel Beard's *The American Boy's Handy Book* in 1882.[13]

It was Nessmuk who wrote the first widely read camping manual written for adults. *Woodcraft* appeared in 1884, and was, in the words of *Forest and Stream*, its publisher, "just the thing that thousands of novices are looking for, and gives them just the advice and practical information they want."[14] It was short, written in plain language, and contained much of the author's contagious enthusiasm for the out-doors. While presuming an ability to read a compass, Nessmuk otherwise started from scratch in advice on what to cook, how to build a camp and a campfire, what to take and, most importantly, what not to take. "Go light, the lighter the better, so that you have the simplest material for health, comfort and enjoyment," he empha-sized.[15] An essential part of Nessmuk's scheme was a light boat. According to Ness-muk, the prospective paddler needed to look no farther than the clinker-built cedar canoes of J. H. Rushton.

What Nessmuk ordered in 1880 was a boat Rushton called a "hunting canoe." "Rushton's Portable Boats are fast becoming a necessity to Gentlemen Sportsmen everywhere, where it is desirable to have a *light* boat," wrote the builder in the cata-log Nessmuk studied. They had a large amount of sheer, which Rushton felt not only gave them "a trim and jaunty appearance," but enabled them to ride safely in much heavier sea than they otherwise would. The open canoes were "*very fast.*"[16]

For carrying his hunting canoes, Rushton sold a frame-style yoke, not the carved yoke used with guideboats. AML.

Rushton's "peculiar and splendid ideas as to hull building"[17] resulted in strong, durable boats which were also light in weight. Rushton's planking and ribs were unusually thin. He recovered strength for the hull by placing the ribs close together. His early ribs were thin, flat strips of red elm; by the early 1880s he began using half-round ribs. These were made by splitting a dowel and were stronger for their weight than conventional ribs. He also boasted that he shaped every plank to fit, rather than forcing it into place, which meant that his boats had less tendency to go out of shape. "It is wonderful how few pounds of cedar, rightly modeled and properly put together, it takes to float a man," he wrote to Nessmuk in 1883.[18]

Rushton's hunting canoes had an Adirondack pedigree possibly as old as that of the guideboat itself. Rushton himself described the type of boat he had used in his boyhood in the 1850s in the northern Adirondacks as "a light open boat or canoe 11 to 13 feet long, 30 to 36 inches wide and weighing from 25 to 50 pounds" which carried two people.[19] The boats were probably lapstrake and built up off a keel, descendants of the small lapstrake boats built and used by the British settlers in the St. Lawrence valley to the north.[20] In the years just after the American Revolution, Loyalists had settled in Upper Canada in great numbers, bringing with them not only their love of the monarchy but their small boats. By about 1784 a narrow, double-

Lapstrake Construction

Small lapstrake boats like canoes or pleasure rowboats were built in the Rushton shop* over a set of five forms. These were one-inch-thick boards that represented the cross sectional shape of the hull at the center and at two points either side of it. These forms were set up on a strongback, upside down, and the stems and keel of the boat attached to them. Then the planking was put on, starting with the garboard; each new plank was clinch nailed to the one below it on the boat. When the boat was planked, it was removed from the forms and turned right side up. The ribs were steamed, bent into place, and clinch-nailed to the planking.

*J. Henry Rushton's construction sequence is described by his son Harry in Appendix A of Atwood Manley, *Rushton and His Times.*

ended lapstrake "skiff" had become a common mode of transportation. Over the next hundred years this boat was modified slightly to meet local conditions. Its best-known, and largest, form became the St. Lawrence skiff.[21]

By the late nineteenth century boatbuilders and users in northern New York and the St. Lawrence valley were using the term "skiff" to describe these round-bottomed boats, and the term stuck. Some contemporaries referred to the Adirondack guide-boat as an "Adirondack skiff." This usage of the term "skiff" may confuse modern readers, who are familiar with the classic definition of "skiff" as a boat with a flat, cross-planked bottom, sharp at one end and with a transom at the other.

Rushton had never previously built a boat as light as the one Nessmuk wanted, but he welcomed Nessmuk's order as a way of testing his boatbuilding theories—and of getting some publicity. "I prefer a larger *canoe*," he wrote to Nessmuk in 1882, "*but this shows what can be done by this system of construction. I know it cannot be attained by any other. If it cannot then a 40 or 50 or 100# boat built on the same system must*

Around the turn of the century, Barney Burns, a Cranberry Lake guide, sits in the stern of his small hunting canoe while a client fishes from the bow. P. 11597.

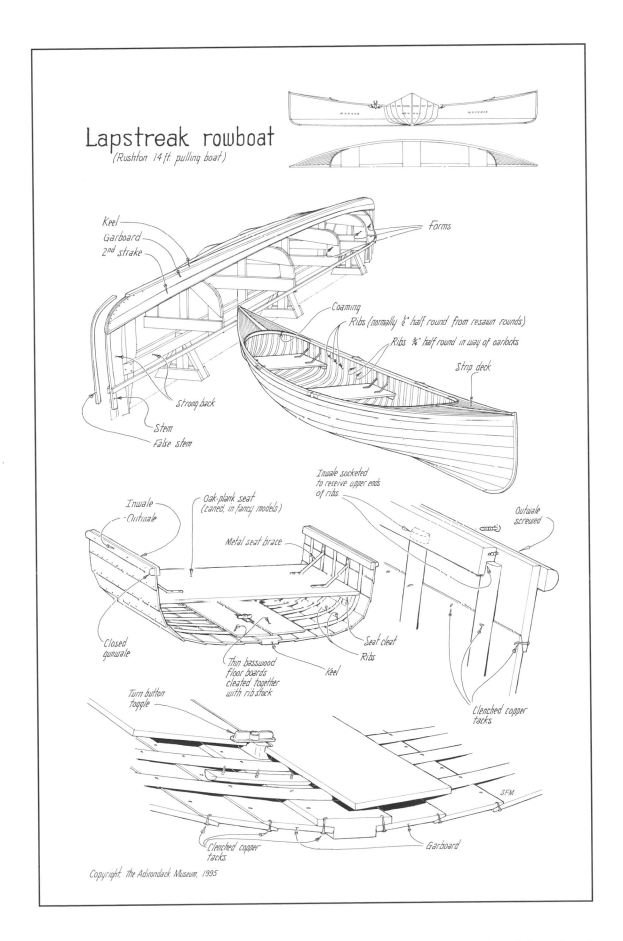

Lapstreak rowboat
(Rushton 14 ft. pulling boat)

Keel
Garboard
2nd strake

Forms

Coaming
Ribs (normally ½" half round from resawn rounds)

Ribs ¾" half round in way of oarlocks

Strip deck

Strong back

Stem
False stem

Inwale socketed
to receive upper ends
of ribs

Inwale
Outwale

Oak-plank seat
(caned, in fancy models)

Metal seat brace

Outwale
screwed

Closed
gunwale

Thin basswood
floor boards
cleated together
with rib stock

Keel

Seat cleat
Ribs

Clenched copper
tacks

Turn button
toggle

S.F.M.

Clenched copper
tacks

Garboard

be *stronger* than one of *equal weight* built in some other manner. That is my position—*you* pay your money and take your choice. . . . By so doing *advertise* me as a builder and *that* is so much *cash* to me."[22]

Nessmuk paddled *Wood Drake* 550 miles through the Adirondacks that summer, from First Lake on the Fulton Chain to Blue Mountain Lake and Forked Lake and back, exciting comment all along the way. Fellow tourists worried that he was endangering his life in such a small craft; guides viewed the boat as an interesting curiosity. The boat was curious not only in its size, but in its paddle; instead of the single-bladed paddles Rushton had used in such a boat in his boyhood, Nessmuk used a long, double-bladed paddle of the type used by Inuit in their kayaks—and by the "modern canoeists" in their decked sailing canoes.

The weather was fine that summer of 1880 and Nessmuk felt well; as soon as he returned to Wellsboro, he began planning another Adirondack trip. That there was a ready market for the accounts of his trips may have helped determine him to go; in his last 1880 letter to *Forest and Stream* he promised to "give some hints for parties who wish to go, in light boats or canoes, through the wilderness without guides."[23]

For his 1881 cruise Nessmuk ordered another Rushton boat somewhat larger than his first. The result was the ten and a half foot, sixteen pound *Susan Nipper*. This boat, he felt, "for a light, comfortable cruising canoe, under paddle, . . . cannot be improved."[24] Nevertheless, Nessmuk paddled her only 206 miles that summer. Plagued by a persistent cough and rainy weather, he returned home early.

Nessmuk stayed in Wellsboro in 1882. His health was failing, but he kept his spirits up by dreaming of a trip the following year, a trip which turned out to be his final Adirondack cruise. For it, he ordered his smallest canoe to date, *Sairy Gamp*, the only one of his boats which has survived. She was only nine feet long and weighed ten and a half pounds. She was optimistically named for the tippling nurse in Dickens's *Martin Chuzzlewit* who "took no water." When *Sairy Gamp* was finished, Rushton wrote Nessmuk, "Now you must *stop* with *this* one, don't try any smaller one. If you get sick of this as a *Canoe*, use it for a soup dish."[25]

Rushton couldn't resist a test run in *Sairy Gamp* when she was finished in early November, 1882. After weighing her, he "took her to the river, put on rubbers, laid a strip of ¼ in. cedar in the bottom and got into her. . . . She closed together an inch or more on top and I did not know but she would collapse. After *feeling* of her, shaking her a little, I paddled off. Steady enough, *four inches out* of water amidship—only *one* danger, 'frailty.' Still, *every piece* is *selected* with *care* and she *may shake* a good deal without *breaking*."[26]

The cruise of the *Sairy Gamp* took place in July and August of 1883. Nessmuk had Rushton ship him the boat in Boonville, from whence he traveled to Paul Smiths and back, a round trip of 266 miles. He sat on a cushion in the bottom, most of the time using his "traveling paddle," a six foot, one inch double-blade. His "pudding stick," a tiny seventeen inch paddle with a single blade three inches across helped him through narrow spots. To cross the carries he put the cushion on his head and wore the boat upside down like a hat. She weighed just ten and a half pounds. Although

Rushton built the boat without thwarts, he braced *Sairy Gamp* for the 1883 cruise with a thwart at each end at Nessmuk's suggestion.

Rushton enjoyed the challenge of building a ten and one-half pound canoe, but he also saw its potential for business. In 1882 he wrote to Nessmuk, "*this shows what can be done by this system of construction. I know it cannot be attained by any other. If it cannot, then a 40 or 50 or 100# boat built on the same system must be stronger than one of equal weight built in some other manner.*"[27] While construction of *Sairy Gamp* was good for business, Rushton did not spend undue time on her. Probably figuring that she would be used only for one summer and would never become a stock model, he planked the boat without his usual care. The bevels along the edges of the planks show beyond the lap in places, and the planking lines do not run up into the stems in fair curves as in a high-quality craft. *Sairy Gamp* cost $20, F.O.B. Canton.

In *Forest and Stream* Nessmuk painted a delightful picture of the life of an independent outer with a light boat. On warm, still days he would create a fragrant cushion in the bottom of his canoe with ferns, lie down in it, and drift "just where it please winds and waves to send me."[28] Fishing in *Sairy Gamp* he regarded as "the culmination of piscatorial sport. With a one-pound trout on the hook it was not necessary to yield more than a yard or two of line at the start, and then play the fish to a standstill by the easy movement of the canoe, reeling up to about ten feet of line, leading the fish about as one pleased, and let him tow the canoe until he turned on his side utterly exhausted, and refusing to raise a pectoral in defense of his life. Then gaff him by sticking a thumb in his open mouth and taking him in."[29] Nessmuk found his tiny canoes remarkably seaworthy, but in rough weather he tied the double paddle into the boat with six feet of strong trolling line and planned to hang onto it in case of an upset.

There wasn't much room for duffel, but, as Nessmuk pointed out, outers were prone to "handicap their pleasures in the matter of overweight." Nessmuk advocated carrying no more duffel than absolutely necessary—a spare shirt and pair of socks were all the extra clothing he took on the cruise of the *Sairy Gamp*. The remainder of the "manifest" was packed in a small oilcloth knapsack: a nine-ounce fishing rod, a hatchet and two knives, a blanket roll, a small tent, two nesting cooking pots made of tin, and a few days' supply of tea, butter, bacon, and sugar.[30]

Rushton himself never became entirely convinced of the utility of boats as small as Nessmuk's. Still, the tiny canoes proved popular. *Sairy Gamp* was finished in November of 1882. Nessmuk had announced his order earlier in the sporting press, and Rushton built the boat right away in case someone inquired after it. Someone did: the central Adirondack developer William West Durant. "He is near six ft. and 170# (guess)," wrote Rushton. "I had hard work to keep him from ordering a duplicate, as it was he ordered a 'Nessmuk.'"[31] In 1886 Rushton wrote Nessmuk, "the trouble is, every d—— fool who weighs less than 300 thinks *he* can use such a canoe too. I get letters asking if the Bucktail will carry two good-sized men and camp duffel and be steady enough to stand up in and shoot out of. I told one fellow that I thought he'd shoot *out* of it mighty quick if he tried it."[32]

Sairy Gamp was optimistically named after the tippling nurse in Charles Dickens's Martin Chuzzlewit *who "took no water." "I once said . . . I was trying to find out how light a canoe it took to drown a man," Nessmuk wrote after his 1883 cruise. "I never shall know. The* Sairy Gamp *has only ducked me once in a six weeks' cruise, and that by my own carelessness." She is nine feet long with a beam of twenty-six inches and now belongs to the National Museum of American History, Smithsonian Institution.*

The "Nessmuk" canoe Rushton sold to Durant was Rushton's stock model on the dimensions of the original *Susan Nipper*.[33] Rushton had been quick to turn this famous custom design into a model anyone could buy, naming it so that potential customers could easily associate it with the renowned woodsman. The Nessmuk models were so popular they were carried in the Rushton catalogs until the shop closed during the First World War. There were eventually seven variations of the Nessmuk-type canoe, in lengths from ten to eleven and a half feet, with conventional lapstrake or smooth skins.

Light hunting canoes like the Nessmuk models were too light and capricious to become widely popular in the nineteenth century. They were primarily built by North Country builders for use in the Adirondacks. One of Rushton's competitors was H. M. Sprague of Parishville. Sprague was a carpenter of diverse talents who also built violins, ax helves, and clothes horses. His shop backed on the West Branch of the St. Regis River, and he ran a livery there stocked with his skiffs and canoes. In his advertising literature Sprague claimed to have gone into business four years before Rushton, in 1869 — but at that time he was only thirteen years old. He first appears in the historical record in 1876, when he advertised "Cedar Boats of any desired length and size" in *Forest and Stream*.[34] By the late 1880s he was offering decked and open canoes as well as lapstrake skiffs for pleasure rowing or hunting — the same types of boats which made up the bulk of Rushton's business. Even his catalog bore a remarkable resemblance to that of his more famous competitor, right down to the wording of some of the testimonials and the engraving on the cover.

Sprague had his own ideas about boatbuilding techniques, however. He sometimes riveted his boats together, rather than clinch-nailing as Rushton did. He also developed improvements, one of which he patented. The technique he thought others might copy was a "new style of lap-strake," in which a thin strip of rubber, "especially prepared," was laid in varnish between the planks to make the boat indubitably watertight.[35] His other idea was to nail scarfs joining planks endwise through a thin strip of tin, presumably to reduce the danger of splitting.

*   *   *

The independent outers posed no threat to the guide's livelihood—yet. While the number of people who guided themselves increased, so did the number of people in the woods in general. Most of these travelers employed a guide, for short trips from their hotel if not for a month-long hunting trip. While there was still work for the old-style independent guide like Emerson's Steve Martin or Murray's John Plumley, the men who rowed, made camp, cooked, and found trout became the rare aristocrats of the trade. Picnicking, occasional trips to a nearby trout hole, and pleasant journeys to the next hotel formed the bulk of the work for men like those who reacted so violently to the introduction of steamboats.

There was usually a corps of guides at a hotel of any size, probably not employed by the hotel, but allowed to solicit the guests. They spent the season in a separate guide's camp, which was sometimes over the boathouse. It was this sort of guide who rowed any one of the hundred guideboats Faxon saw pigeonholed at Paul Smiths.

A more secure position than being a hotel guide was to become a house guide for one of the private camps a few individuals were beginning to erect in the woods. A house guide was assured of steady work during the season, rowing the owner and his guests out for fishing, hunting, or excursions. House guides were also often in charge of the camp boats, and sometimes built them as well. Reuben Cary is one example. Born at Long Lake in 1845, he worked on his father's farm until he was nineteen, when he took his first party out as guide. For the next fifteen years he guided, farmed, married, and started a family, and also began building guideboats. In 1880 he was hired as caretaker by one of his regular clients, an English-born doctor named Benjamin Brandreth, who had recently purchased for a game preserve a large tract of land to the west of Long Lake where the Cary family and their neighbors had been wont to go market hunting. Cary worked as guide,

Guides from Wawbeek Lodge prepare to take clients out for a row in this Stoddard photo from 1889. P. 28220.

caretaker, and boatbuilder at Brandreth Park until three years before his death at the age of ninety.

As tourists and guides increased in number the pressure on the hunting lands became greater. The reputation of the guide as a class also came under question as people repeated stories like one published by Nessmuk in 1880: arriving at the sport's destination, the guide was paid by his client for the return trip to the guide's home, including the cost of carries and board along the way, but he then rowed nonstop and carried his own boat, pocketing the cash.[36] The reaction of the guides was to establish guides' associations to establish prices, enforce observation of game laws, and regulate conduct of the members. The Keene Valley Guides' Association was founded in 1887, the region-wide Adirondack Guides' Association in 1891, and the Brown's Tract Guides' Association, in Dwight Grant's shop, in 1898.[37]

The ever-greater number of people in the woods meant a booming market for guideboats—and not just for purchase by guides. Despite its name (which became current in the 1880s) the guideboat was no longer the exclusive province of the guide. Experienced rowers who so wished could rent guideboats at the hotels for fifty cents per day.

In 1885 the Boonville builder H. Dwight Grant built three boats for a new market, a market which would become increasingly important to him and to other guideboat builders. In that year the names of guides in his shop sales records were joined by those of A. W. Hooper, E. S. Gaylord, and L. H. Lawrence. All three men were regular summer residents of the Fulton Chain.

By 1882 Grant's business was good enough to build his own shop. Grant built the thirty-five-foot *Hunter* there, the first steamboat on the Fulton Chain. His main

Reuben Cary stands on the left with a tool of his trade, a guideboat paddle, at the McAlpin Camp on Brandreth Lake about 1895.
P. 28678.

Hunter *about 1883.*
P. 34105.

product, however, was the "Saranac Lake boat," and he distinguished himself as a steady producer.

Grant's shop was one of the largest guideboat shops in the Adirondacks. Throughout the 1880s he built about a dozen boats each winter; he estimated that it took twenty-one ten-hour days to make a sixteen-foot boat with three caned seats, one caned backrest, one pair of oars, a paddle, and a yoke. Grant's total production in that decade was 115 boats.[38] Even so, in the years when Rushton employed ten to seventeen men year round, Grant employed four to six, primarily in the winter. Of those, only two were the master boatbuilders trusted with hanging the planks; the others cut ribs from patterns, made oars and yokes, and caned seats.[39] The shop all but shut down in the summer when the workmen took jobs guiding, caretaking, or farming.

*   *   *

The winter of 1880 brought Rushton a good deal of interesting correspondence. In addition to the letter from George Washington Sears that resulted in Rushton's development of the Nessmuk model canoes, he received a letter from another prominent canoeist proposing a national canoe meet on Lake George. The canoeists would not be paddling lightweight hunting canoes for the most part. They would be "modern" canoeists paddling the decked sailing canoes Nessmuk had found too expensive and heavy for Adirondack travel. Unlike the guideboats and hunting canoes most people used in the region, which had pedigrees as working boats, these decked canoes were yachts, or boats used primarily for pleasure. Their coming clearly marked a new era in the development of boating in the Adirondacks.

The meet brought together all of the leading canoeists of this country and Canada, furthered an interchange of opinion and increased the range of fraternity and good fellowship among the knights of the paddle.

—Forest and Stream, 1880[1]

CHAPTER 6

The Knights of the Paddle

Seneca Ray Stoddard, Past and Present, *ca. 1890.*

Stoddard summarized the patronizing feeling of most canoeists of the 1880s towards aboriginal craft in this drawing of a "noble red man" gazing longingly at a "modern" canoe. His sentiments were echoed by a correspondent in Forest and Stream *about Indians at the second ACA meet, "If they and their craft were fair samples of the genus and geinus [sic] of the red man, his pale-faced brother has got a long lead on the copper skins, and can discount him in the canoe business badly."* 74.233.35.

Nessmuk's order for *Sairy Gamp* wasn't the only intriguing letter Rushton received in the winter of 1879–1880. He also heard from Nathaniel Holmes Bishop. Bishop, in comfortable circumstances due to a prosperous New Jersey cranberry plantation, had undertaken long-distance expeditions afoot and afloat that had made him well-known to adventurers armchair and otherwise. His first major trek was a thousand-mile hike across Argentina and the Andes to Chile and the Pacific coast. In 1874 he rowed, sailed, and paddled a paper canoe from Troy, New York, to the Gulf of Mexico.[2] When he wasn't traveling he made his home on Lake George, and it was there that he called his fellow canoeists to meet in the summer of 1880 in order to form a national canoe club, and to "take such further action in the interests of the pastime as may be deemed expedient."[3] Rushton made plans to attend, for not only did he support the sport, but his attendance made good business sense. The meeting would be covered by national sporting periodicals, and the most active and innovative of canoeists would attend.

The "Canoe Congress," as the meeting in August of 1880 was billed, attracted a breed of sporting enthusiasts fairly new to Adirondack waters. Few if any brought Adirondack watercraft, either guideboats, the small hunting canoes of Rushton's childhood, or bark canoes. Nor were these "modern canoeists" out for hunting or fishing. They paddled for pleasure, on day-long or month-long cruises to enjoy the waterways and see the scenery. Similar to the Benedict party in their aims, and to Nessmuk in "paddling their own canoes," these sports and their "imported" boats would become an increasingly common sight on Adirondack waters.

In 1880 Lake George was one of America's premier resorts, an ideal site for a regatta of small boats because of its accommodations, accessibility, relatively sheltered waters, and beautiful scenery. Some canoeists took rooms at the Crosbyside Hotel, and others camped on Bishop's land adjacent. Rushton traveled to the meet in comfort by rail, stowing in the baggage compartment a carefully-crated canoe he planned to offer as a prize in a special paddling race. Many of the canoeists attending the

105

congress traveled to Lake George as Rushton did. Others, with more leisure, or a shorter distance to travel, or more utilitarian notions of the purpose of a canoe, paddled to Lake George. The meet was intended for "cruising canoeists," men who, like Nessmuk, liked to explore the continent's waterways under their own power. Nessmuk himself did not go; he was at Moose River, halfway from Boonville to First Lake, fishing from *Susan Nipper* on his first Adirondack trip.

Thirty or forty canoeists attended. Although the organizers of the meet felt it essential that a contingent of Indians in birchbarks attend to "paddle on the Horicon of Cooper," the real focus of the gathering was the racing of "modern" canoes. *The New York Times* correspondent present reported "wooden canoes, canvas canoes, paper canoes, and tin canoes; canoes clincher-built [*sic*] and canoes smooth-built; canoes held together with rivets, and canoes made of successive layers of thin veneers cemented together."[4] Some were decked and paddled with double-bladed paddles, some were decked and sailed, and some were entirely open and paddled with single-bladed paddles.

In establishing a national canoe club, Bishop hoped to provide a "forum for tales of cruising and a comparison of camping equipment and canoe models."[5] Perhaps even more important in his mind was a less tangible purpose: that of fostering among canoeists that "fellow feeling begotten only of thorough organization and a community of interest."[6] Over the four days of the 1880 meeting, twenty-three canoeists met in the rooms of the Crosbyside Hotel and hammered out details of a formal structure for what would soon be known as the American Canoe Association.[7] In addition to by-laws and officers, the group established a five-class system for racing which identified paddling canoes propelled only by paddle (birchbarks and Canadian canoes), sailable paddling canoes with paddling qualities predominant, sailing and paddling canoes with qualities equally divided, paddleable sailing canoes with sailing qualities predominant, and sailing canoes not adapted to cruising where auxiliary power would be needed.[8]

Forest and Stream was the first official organ of the ACA; in 1882 the august journal was joined by *The American Canoeist*, published initially by charter member Arthur Brentano and devoted exclusively to canoeing. Later, *Outing*, *Recreation*, and other journals of outdoor recreation also documented the canoeing scene. Through all these sources, and through the many active local clubs, the ACA became a potent force in popularizing canoeing. Annual encampments, which were held on Lake George or Lake Champlain eight times before the end of the century, publicized the region (at least its periphery) among canoeists and helped introduce "modern" canoes to the Adirondacks.

Bishop did well in fostering "canoebial" *gemütlichkeit*, according to *Forest and Stream's* canoeing correspondent (probably W. P. Stephens, who headed the canoeing column when it was established in 1883). In 1880, "about the camp fire at nights many a rollicking tale of adventure and many an anecdote was passed around while the smoke from campaign stained pipes curled aloft in ringlets." After the following year's gathering on Lorna Island in Lake George, Stephens reported that, of all the

The Canoe Regatta on Lake George.

This engraving of the third ACA meet appeared in Harper's Weekly *on August 26, 1882.* 81.25.1.

features of the meet, "not the least agreeable will be the feature of sociability about the camp fire in the evenings, the swapping of yarns and experiences, the learning of kinks from each other, and a spread of that fraternal spirit essentially characteristic of a body of men engaged in furthering ends at once honest, moral, and strengthening alike to body and mind."[9]

Canoeists were not the only Americans of the time seeking to establish a sense of community through clubs. Nearly half the men in America belonged to fraternal organizations of one sort or another. They were attracted by the sense of community with others of like mind; the clubs filled this need with their ritual and elaborate trappings and costumes. Fraternal organizations and ladies' clubs were generally local, bringing together a group of people with geography in common as well as ethnic or religious background. As the century wore on, regional and national clubs and organizations grew in popularity, providing a group to which people with similar interests could belong regardless of where they lived.[10] Charitable, fraternal, and religious organizations were the most common kind, but educational and study clubs and sporting groups grew rapidly in numbers in the post-war years. The League of American Wheelmen, a bicyclist's group, was founded in 1880, the same year as the American Canoe Association. It had similar aims in fostering fellowship but additionally worked for better roads.

Although the charter members wrote that anyone of good character could join the ACA, most members were middle- or upper-middle-class men. Cruising canoeists were the same social class of men who went on sporting excursions in the Adirondacks. As Bishop wrote in the first year of the Association's existence, "sporting men, so called, will have no part with us. We encourage all that is delightful and pure in the study of nature. We are a band of campers, cruisers and explorers."[11] A correspondent of *Forest and Stream* wrote,

> we have thousands of miles of canoeable water . . . all seeming for years to sing: "come, come, canoe me!" And we have come just as fast as we have learned that "all work and no play makes Jack a dull boy." Even those most pressed by the tireless grind at life's selfish mill of gain have been taught to spare a few weeks at least each year to a wholesome recruiting of their physical systems, and have found in the use of the paddle a cheap and ready means of reaching nature in her primitive state, with whom all love to commune in the solitudes of virgin forests and rocky fastnesses, free from the sordid influences . . . cares and feverish excitement of man's hideous defilements of brick and mortar, misery and squallor.[12]

The most famous person to take up canoeing in its early years was H.R.H. Edward, Prince of Wales, who became commodore of the Royal Canoe Club when it was founded in Britain in 1866. The prince was no doubt the wealthiest, too, by a nautical mile. Most canoeists were of more modest means. One of the attractions of canoeing was that it provided affordable yachting. "Without question the foremost of all manly sports is yachting, encouraging as it does, in the highest degree, self-reliance, decision, quickness of thought and action, endurance and daring, while open to none of those objections on the score of cruelty," wrote W. P. Stephens in an 1881 article entitled "The Poor Man's Yacht." "But yachting even on a small scale is costly. . . . The canoe offers a means of exercise at once safe, pleasant and easily learned at a reasonable cost."[13]

Even though early canoeists did not need to have the resources of the Prince of Wales to go canoeing, they generally had the resources of a gentleman. The "poor man" paddling a "poor man's yacht" was only poor in comparison to the blue-water yachtsmen who competed for the recently-instituted America's Cup. In 1882 Rushton's Princess model cruising canoe cost $120 complete with rig, which might have seemed steep to a carpenter earning $2.25 per day, but cheap to a man considering the expense of berthing and maintaining even an eighteen-foot catboat. After the initial investment was made, canoe cruising appeared even more economical. Stephens estimated the cost of canoe cruising, not including getting to and from the cruising grounds, at two to four dollars per week—this when hire of a guide with guideboat cost $2.50–3.00 per day.

ACA members were "largely professional men, with a sprinkling of business men, and some mechanics," wrote a participant in the 1892 meet. "But they have one common bond—a genuine love of nature. Probably that accounts for the singular courtesy and congeniality—that, and the fact that so many bring their sisters and wives with them." Backgrounds or professions or introductions were not important, she remarked. "The camp sentiment is, that canoeing is common interest enough, and being here is sufficient passport."[14]

The men who attended the first canoe congress were typical of the social class of 1880s canoeists. W. L. Alden, journalist, diplomat, and founder of the first canoe club in America, was elected commodore. Lucien Wulsin, partner in what became the Baldwin Piano and Organ Company, came from Cincinnati as representative of the Cincinnati Canoe Club.[15] Two builders were present, Rushton and William Picard Stephens, from Rahway, New Jersey. Stephens lived to become one of the best-known men in American yachting. Three years after the Lake George meet he became the canoeing editor for *Forest and Stream*, and the next year he became its yachting editor as well. His 1883 book, *Canoe and Small Boat Building: A Complete Manual for Amateurs*, became a classic.

Men with Adirondack interests joined as well. Early association records list, in addition to Rushton and Bishop, five men from Whitehall and seven from Glens Falls, including the lumberman F. F. Pruyn and the photographer Seneca Ray Stoddard. Many summer residents were also doubtless represented; the New York surgeon Arpad Gerster, who had a camp on Raquette Lake, was one.

In the first flush of sociability after the 1880 meet, *Forest and Stream* reported that all who possessed the "spirit and aims of a true canoeist," including ladies, could become members, whether they owned canoes or not. When the charter was finally approved by the membership in November, however, ladies were no longer mentioned, and canoe-less members couldn't vote at association meetings or be eligible for office.[16]

Women remained excluded from full membership in organized canoeing until the middle of the next century. Until 1943 they could become only honorary or associate members without voting rights. Women did participate in the canoeing and socializ-

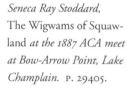

Seneca Ray Stoddard, The Wigwams of Squaw-land *at the 1887 ACA meet at Bow-Arrow Point, Lake Champlain.* P. 29405.

PADDLING MY OWN CANOE

ing of early ACA meets, however. Seven women attended the 1881 meet on Lake George, and at least two, one being Mrs. N. H. Bishop, "paddled their own canoes." All but possibly two were wives or daughters of members. By the late 1890s the association provided special races for women.[17] Mrs. Bishop and the other canoeing ladies were beneficiaries of the trend in which the botanizing ladies were pioneers—the growing participation of women in outdoor sports.

There was a "proper place" for women in the ACA, as in society at large, of course. When they attended an encampment women stayed in a separate "Squaw Camp." Women were only allowed in the regular camping area between the hours of nine and five. By the end of the century, Squaw Camp had its own flag and had become the social center of the meet—much to the disgust of some old-style canoeists.

Some objections to women in canoeing were based on a concern for propriety. Would lady canoeists be tempted to questionable activities with men on unchaperoned outings? One eighteen-year-old woman, asked about the prudence of having spent most of the day and an evening on the water with a young man who was almost a stranger replied, "Oh, the canoe itself is a great protection."[18]

The first canoe congress lasted four days; by 1886 the encampments were two-week affairs. The first week was devoted to cruising, camp sports, and excursions. The second week was taken up with a regatta that included races and a grand review of all boats present.

There was a certain amount of canoe-related silliness along with the races intended to test canoecraft. The dump race at the first meet is one example; by 1886 the hurry-scurry race was popular. In this event contestants were required to run one hundred yards to the beach, dive in and swim twenty yards to their anchored canoes, and then climb in and paddle two hundred yards to the finish line.[19] In jousting, one person standing in the bow of a canoe attempted to knock his opponent out of his boat with a long pole with a padded bag on the end.

In the evenings canoeists enjoyed entertainments and dances as well as yarns around the campfire. Lafayette Seavey, who earned his living in a theatrical property company, created a sensation at the 1891 meet at Willsboro Point on Lake Champlain with a "float" designed to look like the Lake Champlain monster, which he towed behind his canoe. At that same gathering canoeists attended a dance given for the local people who had been hired to serve in the mess tents and set up the tent platforms. The waitresses were "mostly teachers and local farmer's daughters," wrote an ACA member, and "the dances were old fashioned Barn Dances then quite a novelty to us New Yorkers, with the fiddlers sitting on a table."[20]

ACA members developed their own rituals and costumes, most inspired by nautical life. News of events traveled through ACA encampments via flag signals (there was a signal book to decipher them), and officers of the day with nautical titles and gold braid or badges to wear kept order. Pickets selected each day kept the camp area clean and turned away unauthorized people.

The encampments became entertainments in themselves for non-canoeing tourists staying at the local hotels, including wives and daughters of ACA members. Reportedly "several hundred" women and their escorts visited the Lorna Island meet on Lake George in 1881 on Ladies' Day.[21]

Trophies and awards were elements in maintaining the sense of belonging and pride in canoe clubs. The Brooklyn Canoe Club awarded this "Pagan Cruising Trophy" from 1890 through 1913. It was exhibited at the 1934 World's Fair as an outstanding example of the silver engraver's art. 84.79.1.

The canoe club movement, both national and local, grew rapidly. The twenty-three charter members of the ACA were soon joined by many others. Just the next year there were seventy canoes registered with the Association; by 1883 there were 300.[22] One of the aims of the Association was to encourage the formation of local canoe clubs, and in this they succeeded immediately. Only four regional canoe clubs existed at the time of the "First Call" to establish the ACA, but by 1888 there were thirty-one with membership in the ACA and probably many more clubs without ACA status.[23]

The Lake George Canoe Club was typical of canoe clubs of the 1880s. It was founded at the Glens Falls home of photographer Seneca Ray Stoddard on a winter evening in 1882. Dr. Charles Neide, a dentist who had been an officer in the Army of the Potomac and would later serve several terms as secretary of the ACA, was elected "captain" with duties of president, James Knight became "mate" (vice president), and F. F. Pruyn, of the central Adirondack lumbering family, was elected "purser." Like the purser on a ship, he took on the clerical duties of secretary and treasurer. The rank and file addressed each other as "skipper." The club sponsored local meets on Lake George and prided themselves on encouraging independence from "hotels, restaurants, and other inappropriate aids to successful canoeing." With the chauvinism common to men of their station in life, they boasted that "at [a recent] meet the Lake George Canoe Club was credited with being the only party of canoeists present which did its own cooking and catering. . . . Cannot an educated man learn to accomplish what an ignorant Irish girl can do?"[24]

S. R. Stoddard's Cruising Canoe Atlantis *from* Harper's Weekly, *September 10, 1887.*

The photographer Seneca Ray Stoddard was an enthusiastic early canoeist. With a friend, and in three stages, he completed a cruise from New York harbor to the head of the Bay of Fundy in 1885. He paddled and sailed Atlantis, *built by Fletcher Joyner of Glens Falls. Stoddard photographed ACA meets for years, and many of his canoe views ended up in souvenir books purchased by the members. 81.25.2.*

In 1883 Viva, *a Canadian-style open canoe,* Bijou, *and* Maggie, *a decked canoe, all competed in the paddling race. Will Kip, Rushton's foreman, paddles stern in* Maggie. P. 27175.

By the end of the decade canoe clubs had been founded in other towns on the periphery of the mountains. Bishop was a member of the Caldwell Canoe Club at the head of Lake George; it, like the Lake George Canoe Club, was founded in 1882. By 1887 there were canoe clubs in Amsterdam, Watertown, Whitehall, and Canton. Gouverneur had one by 1895, and Port Henry by 1892—just in time to host that year's ACA meet at Willsboro Point. Each club had a totem, flags, and officers with nautical titles. There were no canoe clubs in the central Adirondacks. Despite an abundance of canoeable waters, the region lacked enough upper-middle-class men to support a club.[25]

Although good times around the campfire were important parts of ACA meets, the races were the centerpieces of the encampments, for competitors, spectators, and boatbuilders. Rushton donated a canoe as a prize for a paddling race not only to further the sport but to get some publicity. The prize was won by Thomas Henry Wallace of Gore's Landing on Ontario's Rice Lake, who also won the one-mile paddling race—this one while calmly smoking his pipe.[26] Wallace's racing boat was a long, undecked canoe descended from the Indian dugout, which he paddled with a single-bladed paddle.

By the time he got to Lake George in 1880, Wallace was known in the Peterborough area of Ontario as a champion paddler. Racing open canoes like his had been a hotly contested sport among non-Indian Canadians for over twenty years by the time of the Lake George meet, and the canoes raced by the Canadians were highly refined. When white settlers had moved into the Peterborough area northeast of Toronto in the early nineteenth century, the Indians they found living there used dugouts. The immigrants adopted these dugouts for their own use, hollowing and shaping logs with steel tools to thicknesses and shapes as fine as those possible with conventional

Strip-built Boats

With the development of epoxy glues in the late twentieth century, strip-building has become a familiar technology to builders of small craft. But it is in fact an old and perhaps ancient method and was used by various regional builders in the late nineteenth century, probably as a means of speeding up construction and therefore lowering the cost of their boats. A variation of it was developed by canoe builders in the Peterborough area of Canada for highly refined all-wood canoes.

The basic concept in strip-building is to plank the boats with strips of wood narrow enough (generally an inch or less) to bend edgewise with ease. Whereas the two- or three-inch wide planks of a small lapstrake or carvel-planked boat must be individually cut from wider boards to fit their neighbors, strip planks are straight and uniform from end to end and so can be produced mechanically, in quantity. They are simply sprung to the necessary curvature of their locations in a boat.

Strip builders must cope with the fact that the girth of a boat is not uniform from end to end. If you start strip-planking at the sheer and proceed downward, you will finish the sides and ends of the boat long before you finish the bottom, and the bottom strips will perhaps be required to curve too much even for strips.

Modern builders usually solve this problem by planking each side of the boat in two panels, the planks of one panel fitted to the other along a chosen line. In short boats of low sheer, like the canoes built by Harry Green (entries 16 and 18) and A. Bain and Co. (entry 17), the builder used a greatly tapering garboard and/or tapering strips alternating with the normal planking strips at the turn of the bilge. The Peterborough area builders made planks which, while all alike, were not uniform in width, but were wider in the middle and narrower at the ends.

Another problem inherent in strip-building is the seams: there are many, and the plank edges meet at varying angles. Individual planks are weak and need to be bonded to adjacent ones for overall strength as well as watertightness. The commonest solution is to hollow or "cove" one edge and round the other, as did A. Bain and Co., and Atherton Farr (entry 160). The Peterborough builders used a fine shiplap seam (entry 27 and 30).

If thick enough, strip planks could be nailed to each other through their edges, as was done in rowboats built by the Old Forge Boat Co. and A. Bain and Co.; in lighter boats they would be fastened only to the ribs, which needed in that case to be closely spaced. Today they are usually glued edge to edge, and the function of ribs is performed by sheathings of fiberglass, inside and out, which turns the strip-built hull into a cored laminate with tensile-strength surfaces.

plank-on-frame techniques. Then builders began using dugouts as solid molds over which to build plank-on-frame boats, nailing the planks onto ribs bent over the overturned canoe. The nails went right into the dugout-mold and the new canoe had to be pried off and nails clinched by hand. By the late 1850s construction over a solid mold covered with iron bands which turned the nails, and the use of patterns for planks, had become standard.[27]

While most Peterborough builders used solid molds, they experimented with different methods of planking and framing, motivated both by an interest in quality and by the need to build fast and cheap to supply the burgeoning market. By the time of the first ACA meet, several Canadians built smooth-skinned canoes with wood or metal battens covering the seams on the inside. Daniel Herald of Gore's Landing on Rice Lake built canoes with double skins sandwiching a layer of cotton soaked in white lead. John Stephenson developed a "Rib Boat" in 1879 that had narrow cedar strips all steam-bent into the shape of the cross-section of the boat and driven together with tongue and groove joints. He then developed a "Longitudinal Rib Boat" on the same principle but applying the narrow cedar strips from bow to stern.

It was probably Thomas Gordon of Lakefield who developed the classic cedar strip canoe, the best known of the Peterborough area products. Gordon's method was well adapted to factory production, since all the planks for his boat, narrow strips of cedar about 1¾ inches wide at the center of the boat, are the same shape. The planks are

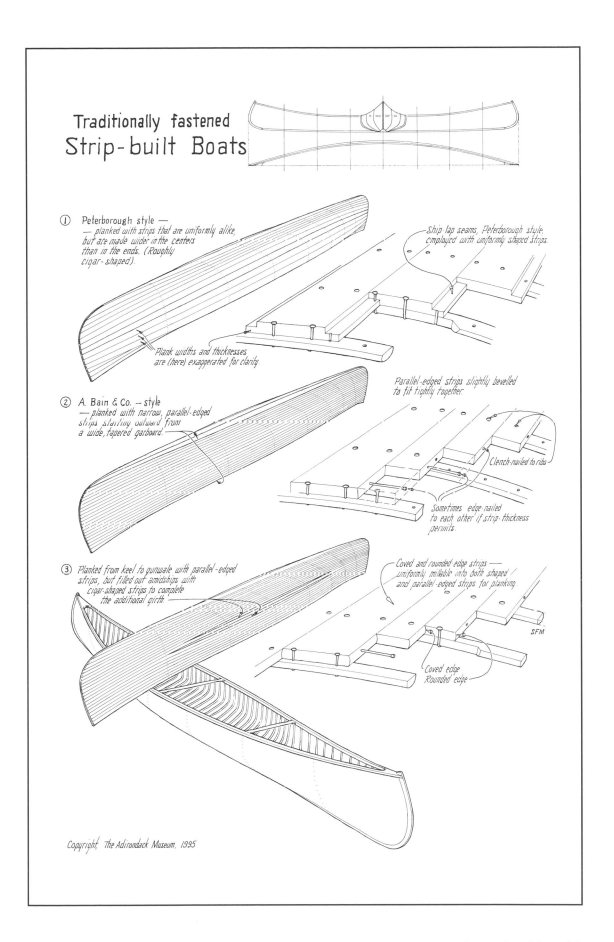

Traditionally fastened
Strip-built Boats

① Peterborough style —
— planked with strips that are uniformly alike,
but are made wider in the centers
than in the ends. (Roughly
cigar-shaped).

Ship-lap seams, Peterborough style,
employed with uniformly shaped strips.

Plank widths and thicknesses
are (here) exaggerated for clarity.

② A. Bain & Co. — style
— planked with narrow, parallel-edged
strips starting outward from
a wide, tapered garboard.

Parallel-edged strips slightly bevelled
to fit tightly together.

Clench-nailed to ribs

Sometimes edge-nailed
to each other if strip-thickness
permits.

③ Planked from keel to gunwale with parallel-edged
strips, but filled out amidships with
cigar-shaped strips to complete
the additional girth.

Coved and rounded-edge strips —
uniformly millable into both shaped
and parallel-edged strips for planking.

SFM

Coved edge
Rounded edge

shiplapped along their long edges, making a watertight joint and eliminating the necessity of the batten.[28]

Peterborough builders developed two distinct hull shapes. Hunting canoes had fairly flat bottoms, and racing canoes had considerable deadrise. The flatter-floored, more stable hunting canoes were particularly recommended for ladies. Florence Watters Snedeker, a pioneering lady canoeist, advised other women to paddle boats "light and swift, yet capable of carrying a good load and of enduring rough usage. Such a craft our Canadian friends have fashioned . . . the famous *Peterborough*. . . . This canoe seems to be the model, both in form and construction, for all the North country . . . especially when a lady paddles with the single blade, kneeling Indian fashion, supported by the round hollow thwart, the grace and movement render the whole the prettiest picture that floats."[29]

The Canadian canoe had advantages not lost on other canoeists. As one aficionado, who wrote in *Forest and Stream* over the pseudonym "Retaw," put it, the Canadian canoe was "certainly the most perfect hunting canoe in existence, and as a paddling canoe it has few, if any superiors."[30] At the first ACA meet, in fact, the "Rice Lake canoe" proved itself "the fastest of all canoes under paddle, as she is also confessedly the fastest under sail." The American canoeists were also surprised to find that a Canadian canoe paddled with a single-bladed paddle beat the double-blades "in the same way as a 'shell' would beat a heavy row-boat." The main objection the Americans at the meet had to the Canadian canoes was that they lacked decks.[31]

*   *   *

Even though the Canadian canoe was well established in its native land in 1880, it was not primarily what N. H. Bishop had in mind when he proposed the first national canoe congress. To him, as to many of the other charter members, a "modern canoe" was a decked sailing boat whose hull form was more like an Inuit kayak than the craft of any of the woodland Indians. Unlike many small-boat types whose origins are obscure, the early history of the decked sailing canoe is well known. It was probably invented, and certainly popularized, by a Scot named John MacGregor. MacGregor, who counted among his ancestors the original Rob Roy of Walter Scott's novels, visited North America in 1859. He paddled dugouts and birchbarks on the Ottawa River, but the kayak he tried out on his way to the Bering Sea particularly intrigued him.

When MacGregor returned to Britain he had a boatbuilder at Lambeth on the Thames build him a small boat with the form of the Inuit kayak but planked in wood instead of covered with sealskin. MacGregor proposed to propel the boat with the traditional Inuit double-bladed paddle, but he added a small lugsail and a jib to the craft, which the natives had not used. The tiny sail was only an auxiliary for use when traveling downwind; he had no centerboard or leeboard and used his paddle as a rudder. *Rob Roy's* length was determined by the maximum allowed on the baggage cars on the German railway, for MacGregor proposed a European cruise using trains to get between watersheds. She was fifteen feet long, had a beam of twenty-eight inches, was nine inches deep, and weighed eighty pounds.[32]

MacGregor set off down the Thames for the Channel on a hot day in July, 1865, with all his duffel for the three-month trip in a little black bag one foot square and six inches deep: a change of clothes, a black Sunday coat, a few extra collars, handkerchiefs and socks, a testament, and a pair of blue spectacles. His object was to try "a new mode of traveling on the Continent, by which new people and things are met with, while healthy exercise is enjoyed, and an interest ever varied with excitement keeps fully alert the energies of the mind."[33]

MacGregor thoroughly enjoyed himself, and when he returned he wrote *A Thousand Miles in the Rob Roy Canoe on Rivers and Lakes of Europe* (1866) to introduce a new pastime to others. His first book, and subsequent books about subsequent journeys (he eventually made five, each with a slightly different *Rob Roy*), were well received. The idea of traveling the countryside in a tiny yacht, with no timetables to adhere to, no appearances to keep up, and with a chance to get off the beaten tourist path was extremely attractive to many men of leisure and means.

In the years between the Civil War and the turn of the century hundreds of canoeists followed in MacGregor's wake, cruising protected waterways on both sides of the Atlantic. Although they made much of being pioneers and explorers, most took some advantage of civilization on their cruises—particularly, as MacGregor had, using railroads in getting to their put-ins. Masts and spars were jointed or short enough that canoeists could stow them and all their gear inside their boats, close up

As he did with the Nessmuk model canoes, Rushton built a stock model canoe based on MacGregor's Rob Roy *which he called his Rob Roy, and, after 1880, the American Traveling Canoe. This illustration is from his 1880 catalog.* AML.

Canoeing in the North
Woods: A Carry.

*The feelings of the Adi-
rondacker this canoeist has
hired to transport his boat
to the next waterway are
obvious in this print from*
Harper's Weekly, *September
22, 1888. A Rushton Princess
model decked cruising canoe
of 1882 weighed about the
same as a guideboat, but its
deck made it more difficult to
carry than a guideboat.*
66.240.2.

cockpit and hatches, and check the whole outfit as baggage to the starting point of
their trip while they rode in a passenger carriage.[34] With their decks making upside-
down portaging difficult, the canoes were too unwieldy to carry easily around rapids
and canal locks, but canoeists were usually able to find a farmer with a cart to help
them.

The waterways of the Northeast were in some ways more civilized in the late nineteenth century than they were one hundred years later. Many canoeists paddled
canals across country, occasionally hitching rides on canal boats and thereby getting
a glimpse of another sort of gypsy life as well as a hot meal. Mill dams forced canoeists
to portage but smoothed out upstream rapids.

Lakes Champlain and George and the canals and rivers that led to them were
prime cruising waters, but few canoeists found their way into the central Adirondacks. A canoeist writing in *Forest and Stream* in 1887 urged his fellows to venture into
the mountains before or after that year's ACA meet at Bow-Arrow Point on Lake
Champlain, but, he admitted, "perhaps it is the swift water, the occasional necessity
of a portage, joined with the fact that the modern canoe is usually decked and built
for sailing and wide expanses of water rather than for rapids and small rivers and lakes,
that the charm of leaving the ordinary routes has not sufficiently presented itself to
the canoeist to induce him to explore the Adirondacks."[35] He might have added that
the Adirondack guideboat, already established, was perfectly suited to the region.

"Modern" canoeists did explore the Adirondacks with decked canoes on occasion. In 1881, accompanied by a friend, Charles Farnham headed for the Hudson in search of white water. He paddled a fourteen-foot Shadow model canoe named *Allegro*. The original *Shadow* had been designed by W. L. Alden; James Everson, a builder at Williamsburgh (now part of New York City) who had made his name building light Whitehall rowing boats, built Farnham's boat.[36] His companion paddled a heavier Nautilus-model canoe. Both were classed by the ACA as "sailing and paddling canoes, with qualities equally divided." In September, not long after an ailing Nessmuk hung up *Susan Nipper* and abandoned his second Adirondack cruise, Farnham and his friend shipped their canoes by rail to Boonville and had them carted to Old Forge. From there they crossed the Adirondacks to Blue Mountain Lake, packed up their canoes once more, and had them carted to North River.

Farnham felt that "to shoot a rapid is to live a new life." He did not try the upper Hudson, however, because he knew it was "so furious in a freshet that only the most reckless lumbermen venture on its rapids." He and his friend put in at the Glen,

Charles Farnham in his Shadow canoe running the Horse Race rapids on the Hudson as pictured in Scribner's Monthly, *April, 1881.* AML.

which they considered the Hudson's "highest navigable waters." "Our canoes were the first that had entered the wilderness," he proudly proclaimed, discounting all but the decked "modern" canoe. The Nautilus capsized in the Spruce Mountain Rift and her discouraged skipper went home by rail. Farnham continued alone, however, and had a glorious time the rest of the way to Albany and fell in love with his canoe. Like Nessmuk and other nineteenth-century canoeist-authors, Farnham personified his "adorable companion." On the "smoking, steaming palace" of a Hudson river steamboat he took home from Albany to New York, he praised not only the canoe's beauty and seaworthiness but "her intrepid spirit, ready for any adventure, and her stanch friendship tried in flood and field, by night and by day."[37]

In 1883 three canoeists belonging to the recently organized Amsterdam Canoe Club made a week-long expedition down the Sacandaga River from Northville to the Hudson at Luzerne in decked canoes. They carried around "the canoeists' greatest trial," a boom of logs, but decided to shoot the six-mile Horse Race Rapids—rapids now subsumed under the Sacandaga reservoir. In their excitement they reported a crowd of 500 people cheering them on, but since the entire population of the nearby village of Conklingville was only 326 according to the 1880 census, this may be an exaggeration. They then traveled through the Glens Falls Feeder Canal and the Champlain Canal to Fort Edward and Schuylerville by canoe, occasionally hitching a ride on a canal boat. They returned home via the Erie Canal. The men spent only one night in their canoe tents, sleeping and taking their meals for most of the trip in towns along the way.[38]

Part of the fun of cruising in little yachts was sleeping at night in their "cabins." Farnham pulled his craft ashore in the evening, settled it in the sand or propped it up with sticks or stones, and made himself a bed in the cockpit. He had only a tarp for his roof; better-equipped canoeists mounted a special canoe tent on the mast or masts. To sleep, the canoeist snuggled in with his legs under the forward deck and head under the rear deck. "Perhaps one of the most important things tending to a comfortable cruise is the matter of shelter," wrote one canoeist. "Under [a tent] the writer has, on a rainy evening, seated in the canoe with a small alcohol stove between the knees, prepared his 'Leibig' soup, coffee, and toasted crackers, written up his log, read awhile by lantern light and turned in snugly to 'sleep the sleep of the just,' oblivious to the elements."[39]

W. L. Alden spoke for many of his fellow enthusiasts when he proclaimed, "the canoeist who does not sleep in his canoe is guilty of treason, and deserves the lasting scorn of all loyal paddlers."[40] A practical editor at *Forest and Stream* countered that "sleeping in the canoe is to be avoided, if possible; it is very uncomfortable for one thing, and strains the craft and causes her to leak, for another. A much better plan is to carry a small cotton tent and make camp in the usual way."[41] It was Alden himself who named "MacGregor's line," an abrasion on the nose suffered by canoeists who woke up suddenly and forgot where they were.

The ACA originally had been conceived as an organization to further the gentle art of canoe cruising, but about its only tangible accomplishment to this aim, beyond

providing a forum for the discussion of camping techniques and routes, was a "canoe pilotage" scheme, in place by 1885. The "ACA Cruises and References" booklet issued in that year listed men who could provide up-to-date information on routes and conditions. The Adirondack region was well covered: Rushton was listed as a contact for the St. Lawrence River, the Oswegatchie, and the Raquette, an E. W. West of Glens Falls for the Hudson River,

In this untitled drawing by Seneca Ray Stoddard a canoeist has erected his tent while afloat—not the normal procedure, but perhaps easier on the boat than doing it ashore. 74.233.33.

the Champlain Canal, and Lake George, and a J. W. Parker of Keene Valley for the Ausable River and "the Adirondack Lakes."[42] One wonders what the local guides thought about the pilots and their advice.

Though not one of its stated aims, the ACA quickly developed into an organization that furthered the development of racing canoes. In the early years, races at the ACA meets tested all combinations of boat skills in quest of the ultimate all-around canoe, as well as the best all-around canoeist; by the late 1880s racing had become the highlight of the encampment. The emphasis on races accelerated development of boats best suited to going fast. Expensive and tricky to handle, these racing boats were not for everyone. By the end of the century an editor for *Outing* magazine had to write, "The perfection of the racing-machine and the extreme acrobatic skill required in attaining perfection in its handling, has driven busy men for the most part from the sailing courses."[43]

Women had been kept from the sailing courses by the additional censure of public opinion. "It should be well understood that canoe sailing," wrote an editor at *Forest and Stream* in 1886, "unless in some special circumstances, is no sport for a lady."[44]

The agility, strength, and daring necessary to skipper a racing canoe of the late nineteenth century were qualities not widely considered "ladylike" at the time—or even possible in the fashions of the day.

By the time of the 1886 meet, it had become apparent that, since the days of Rob Roy MacGregor, canoe building and sailing in England had evolved differently than they had in the United States. In America, canoe racers had increased sail area and reduced weight in their boats so much in the quest for speed that to keep the boats upright in a fresh breeze they had to get out of the cockpit and sit on the windward deck. In a very fresh breeze they found themselves hooking their toes under the leeward side of the deck and hanging out to windward as far as they could. The English, on the other hand, built heavy, ballasted canoes to counterbalance the force of the wind in the sails. They sailed from a reclining position in the bottom of their boats. For the 1886 meet, the ACA issued a challenge to the Royal Canoe Club of Great Britain to test the merits of the two traditions.

The challenge was answered by two gentlemen, Warington Baden-Powell (brother of the founder of the Boy Scouts) and Walter Stewart. The Americans met Baden-Powell's *Nautilus* and Stewart's *Pearl* with a Rushton canoe and one built by Fletcher Joyner, a former Adirondack guide who had moved to Glens Falls. The Rushton boat was built to the specifications of skipper Robert W. Gibson of the Mohican Canoe Club of Albany. *Vesper,* as she was called, was designed as the ultimate cruising canoe—as fast as possible under sail but paddleable and maneuverable, with watertight hatches for all the duffel one would need for a classic canoe cruise, and a centerboard which folded flat when drawn up so the skipper could sleep comfortably in the cockpit.[45] The Joyner boat, *Pecowsic,* made only a pretense at being a true cruising canoe. She came with five suits of sails which made her adaptable to any kind of wind, but which clearly couldn't be taken on a three-week cruise.

The English were soundly beaten by *Vesper* and *Pecowsic,* establishing the superiority of the American method of building and sailing where speed was the object. *Pecowsic* and *Vesper* themselves illustrated a significant change in canoeing within North America. The former was a racing canoe and the latter a cruising canoe.[46] By

Robert Tyson sailing his canoe Isabel *from inside the cockpit, 1885.* P. 27185.

Seneca Ray Stoddard, The Canoe, the Cup and the Captor. *Robert W. Gibson and* Vesper *at the 1886 ACA meet.* P. 9149.

1892 Rushton (by then himself one of the premier builders of racing canoes in the country) wrote, "Here we find two distinct classes, the *Cruiser* and the *Racer*. A few years ago they were one and the same, today they are not. To-day the Racing Canoe, like the race horse, is good for little else."[47]

Even if Rushton regretted the decline in popularity of the decked cruising canoe, he managed to turn the activities of the serious racers to his advantage. Just as he had capitalized on the fame of the canoes he built for Nessmuk, he listed in his catalog a Vesper model canoe the year following the International Challenge Cup, and his shop produced Vespers until Rushton died. The Vesper joined four other models of cruising-racing canoes, plus thirteen different models of pleasure rowboats, seven open canoes, a Canadian canoe, a sailing cruiser suitable for open water, and a steam launch. In just a decade Rushton had expanded his offerings from pleasure rowboats in five lengths, a Rob Roy canoe, and an open canoe. Other builders were similarly expanding their business in an effort to capitalize on the rapidly increasing pleasure boating market. The public had much to choose from in selecting the best boat for a cruise on Long Island Sound, or a picnic in the Adirondacks.

The Knights of the Paddle   123

Within the past fifteen years . . . a new class of boats has sprung up, and the little "Rob Roy" of Macgregor has given birth to a fleet of small craft, scattered over all the world, of such variety as to suit every taste, and offering to all the pleasures of a yacht at a merely nominal cost.

—W. P. Stephens, 1881[1]

CHAPTER 7

To Suit Every Taste

When the young ladies of the Linaean Society arrived at the nearly deserted shores of Blue Mountain Lake on June 15, 1873, they stood for a few moments in awe of the great stillness of the wilderness.[2] Within a decade, summers on Blue Mountain Lake were much livelier. In 1882, for example, visitors to the lake were treated to a nocturnal "water fete" sponsored by the management of the newly opened Prospect House, the largest hotel in the region. The entire lake was illuminated artificially with bonfires on the points and the little blue and red flames of Bengal lights (festive—if smelly—pots of potassium nitrate, sulfur, and realgar) floating on the surface of the water. Over all shone the magnificent Prospect House, electric lights streaming from its six stories of windows.[3] On the water, the recently launched steamer *Toowahloondah* was decorated stem to stern with even more colored lights and Japanese lanterns, and she towed a string of seventy-five rowboats, also illuminated, around the lake. The ladies would hardly have recognized their "Lake of the Skies."

The changes in tourism in Blue Mountain Lake between the 1870s and the First World War were typical of the changes taking place all over the Adirondacks.[4] Summer visitors were increasing dramatically, and the sportsmen were a diminishing proportion of the whole. Probably many spectators of the Prospect House water fete had come to the Adirondacks as they might have gone to the Mohonk Mountain House in the Catskills or the Balsams in New Hampshire—to see and be seen by fashionable society as much as to enjoy pure mountain air and scenery. They were members of the upper economic strata of American society, profiting from the post–Civil War economic boom.[5]

The ease with which they could get to the heart of the mountains encouraged many upper- and upper-middle-class people to try an Adirondack vacation. As rails were laid into the heart of the woods and steamboat routes expanded, wilderness travel became, for many people, less the end in itself it had been for Headley and Nessmuk and more a preparatory stage to be gotten over as quickly as possible. While the ladies of the Linacan Society had taken almost two weeks to get to Blue Mountain Lake by

Around 1890 J. F. Holley photographed the Prospect House from the beach of Holland's Blue Mountain House. In the middle distance are two steamboats, one of them probably the Toowahloondah, and in the foreground are a number of square-sterned guideboats. P. 677.

walking and rowing, by 1886 visitors could board a northbound train in New York in the evening, dine and sleep while rumbling up the Hudson valley, and arrive in North Creek, the end of the line for Thomas Clark and William West Durant's Adirondack Railroad, in time for an early breakfast. At 7:00 A.M. they boarded a stagecoach for the ride to Blue Mountain Lake, theoretically finding themselves at the Prospect House in time for a late lunch. (Delays en route were common.) Formerly remote parts of the western and central Adirondacks got up-to-date service in 1892 when William Seward Webb finished a line from Herkimer to Malone.

In Blue Mountain Lake by the end of the century, three major hotels on the lake could accommodate a thousand guests among them. Patrons of the Prospect House, "a true picture of [the accommodations] presented at the famous watering places,"[6] could relax in a reading room illuminated with electric light and stocked with papers printed only the day before in New York, practice their aim in the shooting gallery or the bowling alley, send a telegram, take a hot bath, and play tennis or golf.[7] In providing tennis and Turkish baths for his guests, proprietor Frederick Clark Durant was competing with other resorts in the Northeast. By 1902, according to one visitor, the "city man" coming to the Adirondacks "must attend parties and receptions, be well posted in golf and tennis and, incidentally, take an interest in amateur theatricals. Occasionally, he may vary the monotony by taking a short row on the lake."[8]

The city man may have taken his short row on the lake in a guideboat manned by one of the hotel guides, or he may have taken out a sturdy rowboat such as those stocked by the Prospect House livery. These craft were probably variants of the Whitehall, a transom-sterned pulling boat then popular in every harbor on the eastern seaboard.

Boat liveries, at hotels as well as in cities and towns, provided a great market for boatbuilders. With improved freight transfer by railroads, as well as better communications through sporting periodicals and mail order sales, livery owners had their pick of models and builders. Craftsmen in New York's North Country certainly got some of the business. The Prospect House livery had a fleet of eighty-two rowboats built by Fletcher Joyner of Glens Falls.[9]

Some builders operated liveries themselves. Fletcher Joyner, builder of the Prospect House fleet and of the 1886 International Challenge Cup contender *Pecowsic*, had his own livery on the Mohawk, and Rushton himself supplied one in Syracuse staffed by his half-brother. Another half-brother ran the livery at the Childwold Park Hotel north of Tupper Lake in the mid-'90s, which was also probably stocked with Rushton boats.[10] At the same time, Myron Nickerson, onetime Rushton workman, went out on his own building boats, some of which he rented through a livery on the Grass River in Canton, and some of which he carted to Tupper Lake every spring to rent for the season.

Most Adirondack visitors who didn't camp out stayed in hotels, but some of the well-heeled elected to enjoy a more private holiday. Between the nation's centennial and the First World War, over sixty private clubs and several hundred additional private camps on smaller parcels of land were established in the region. According to a 1903 Forest, Fish and Game report, these preserves ranged from the 267-acre Saranac Club at the Bartlett Carry between Upper and Middle Saranac Lakes to the Adirondack League Club, which owned or leased 79,172 acres in Herkimer and Hamilton Counties. In some, groups of people held the land as an association, and in others a single family held the property.[11]

The collective clubs were part of the same phenomenon out of which had come earlier sporting clubs in the 1850s, and which was giving rise almost simultaneously

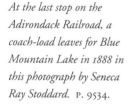

At the last stop on the Adirondack Railroad, a coach-load leaves for Blue Mountain Lake in 1888 in this photograph by Seneca Ray Stoddard. P. 9534.

Edward Bierstadt, brother of the noted western artist Albert, photographed a party leaving the Prospect House livery around 1885. P. 1556.

to the country's first suburban country clubs. Members of clubs could gain exclusive access to larger "pleasuring grounds" than they could afford by themselves, at the same time ensuring the company of social equals. This last motivation was increasingly important as an Adirondack vacation became cheaper and more middle-class people had the leisure time to enjoy one.[12]

As the state Forest, Fish and Game Commission noted in 1903, "the private preserves in the Adirondacks, with a slight exception, have been established within the last sixteen years — most of them within eleven years — and the comparatively sudden exclusion of the public from its old camping-grounds has provoked a bitter hostility on the part of the hunters, fishermen and guides who formerly ranged over this territory."[13] Private preserves kept people off of some of the best-loved traditional waterways of the region, such as Nessmuk's route from the Bog River through Little Tupper, Stony Pond, and Big and Little Slim Ponds into Long Lake.[14] The owners of private preserves were defended by *Forest and Stream* in an 1889 editorial which criticized the "lax and loose morals of that part of the State with respect to game and its protection." The defense was that individuals were forced to post and patrol their own lands because the state would not do so adequately.[15]

The residents' hostility to posting reached its most violent in the murder of Orrando P. Dexter. Dexter had built a "costly cottage" on Dexter Lake, five miles south of St. Regis Falls, around 1900, and insisted on his right to keep people off his land.

He habitually drove himself into town for his mail every morning; on September 9, 1903, someone stepped out from behind a tree and shot him in the back after he passed. The bullet lodged in his horse's rump. "Mr. Dexter had been in continuous contention with many people almost from the day of his coming to Waverly," wrote Franklin County historian Frederick Seaver in 1918. Nobody was ever brought to trial for the crime, "which is not to say," Seaver remarked, "that the identity of the murderer was not strongly suspected in some quarters."[16]

Club members and camp owners built rustic complexes which usually consisted of several buildings. The larger establishments, later called "great camps," often took on the proportions of small villages, with a main lodge, guest cottages, servants' quarters, service buildings, and boathouses. Owners typically stocked the boathouses with an eclectic mix of traditional and up-to-date small craft. Guideboats, sailing canoes, Peterborough canoes, and stable rowing craft of some description were standard. Sailboats were less common. Frequently, the campers (or their caretakers or guides) developed their own subspecies of boats unique to the camp. These became just as much a part of Adirondack folklore and furnishings as the tales of the largest fish caught in the ponds and the moose head over the main lodge fireplace.

Hunters and anglers had established a few clubs in the Adirondacks before the Civil War, but by and large they did not acquire land. The Piseco Lake Trout Club, established in 1842, was the first to build a clubhouse, which they called Walton Hall. Its seven members met annually on the shores of Piseco Lake for two weeks of trout

After leaving the employ of J. H. Rushton, Myron Nickerson established a livery on the Grass River in Canton. In this photo, he sits in the wood-canvas canoe (far right). He also has guideboats, a Rushton-style pleasure rowboat, and a small skiff for rent. P. 21483.

The Adirondack League
Club boathouse on Little
Moose Lake. P. 34140.

This rustic boathouse photographed in 1899 housed
small craft, including a lapstrake pleasure rowboat, seen
here in the water, and a
guideboat, on the ramp dock.
P. 15702.

fishing. The golden age of club founding began in the second half of the 1870s and peaked in the 1890s. The later clubs reflected the trend in Adirondack tourism of their time. While they had as a primary aim the preservation of fish and game on their lands (and often forests as well), they all emphasized establishment of a preserve for the rest and recreation of members.

The Adirondack League Club is one of the largest and best-documented of late nineteenth-century private clubs.[17] It was founded in 1890 for "the preservation and conservation of the Adirondack forests and the proper protection of game and fish . . . , the establishment and promotion of an improved system of forestry, and the maintenance of an ample preserve for the benefit of its members for the purposes of hunting, fishing, rest and recreation." The original club lands consisted of 91,000 acres, on which were several major lakes and "endless possibilities of exploration and discovery" on navigable waterways. Each member received two acres of land for a private camp, and the club built lodges and boathouses for the use of all. In the 1890s wooden tennis courts were built at the club's lodge on Little Moose Lake, and in 1914 the club opened a six-hole golf course.

In spite of the temptations of tennis court and golf course, summer life for ALC members remained strongly tied to the water. Although they were seldom carried (the club left boats at ponds and rivers across the preserve for any who needed them), camp-owning members on Little Moose Lake rowed their own guideboats to meals in the main lodge daily, or on visits to other camps, many of which had no road

Most of the guideboats stored in the boathouse at Little Moose Lake on the Adirondack League Club preserve were built by H. Dwight Grant or the Parsons family.
P. 34107.

access. The club rented guideboats for a dollar a day from the sixty-slip boathouse at Little Moose until 1955. Like many of the private camps and associations, the Adirondack League Club preserved not only game, fish, and forests, but the guideboat itself.

Most guideboats at the ALC were not used as they had been traditionally. They were seldom carried, and they were usually only rowed for day trips around the lakes of the preserve. Nevertheless, Grant, who built many of them, did not compromise in their construction. The club boats are just as lightweight as Grant's working boats in scantlings, but they are sometimes equipped with additions too heavy for a carry boat but which served some decorative or functional purpose in a yacht—detachable floor grates to protect the thin planking from sharp heels, for example.

Grant and his colleagues did finish their boats in untraditional ways, however, as the working boats became pleasure boats. Working guideboats were almost always painted. Paint, in unobtrusive colors like green and black, not only helped camouflage a hunting boat, but it was easier to maintain than varnish. The customers of the 1880s and 1890s, however, appreciated the guideboat for its aesthetic appeal as much as for its sporting potential and often ordered their boats varnished. Builders even occasionally used non-traditional woods. Dwight Grant and Caleb Chase each built a guideboat-yacht entirely of Spanish cedar (varnished), and John Buyce of Speculator built his guideboats of cypress.[18]

Few, if any, Adirondack builders sent their boats out of the region. They built for a local market of hotel keepers and guides, and for summer people who bought the boats for use on their Adirondack vacations. National builders, with one exception, did not take up the guideboat as they did some other regional small craft like the St. Lawrence skiff. The exception was J. H. Rushton. His Saranac Laker model first appeared in his 1888 catalog and was available for twenty years. Saranac Lakers were probably seldom—if ever—purchased by guides. Rushton claimed only that "this boat, used both as a pleasure and hunting boat, we may say forms a connecting link between the two."[19] They are heavier than guideboats built for guides, with decorative deck beams and decks and thick ribs and planking that were scorned by builders striving for a boat that could be carried a mile or two through the woods. Their shape is also fuller in the ends for greater stability.

Although the most famous regional boat of the Adirondacks did not appeal to a wider audience, the small hunting canoe did. Nessmuk's writings probably did a great deal to popularize twelve- and fourteen-foot canoes. The Skaneateles Boat and Canoe Company offered an "Adirondacks [sic] Hunting Canoe" fourteen feet long with a thirty-inch beam in 1910. The very name "Adirondack" apparently held some cachet among small-boat enthusiasts as well. In the 1890s the Boston builder Charles Lawton built a sixteen-foot Whitehall-type boat which he called an Adirondack Canoe, and H. V. Partelow of Boston offered pulling boats called "Adirondacks" in smooth skin, lapstrake, and square stern.[20]

The establishment of private preserves was a boon to the business of local boatbuilders. H. Dwight Grant, his sons, and then the Parsonses, father and sons (who had learned boatbuilding in the Grant shop), did well by the establishment of the

Adirondack League Club. Not only was there a great market for boats among members, but first Dwight and then his son Lewis, became superintendents of the entire club. At least a third of his total output of 358 guideboats, and probably a third of those of the Parsons shop, were purchased by club members or guides. The Newcomb builders Caleb Chase and his son Edmund became the main boatbuilders for the members of the Tahawus Club, established near Newcomb in 1876, as well as building at least four boats for Camp Santanoni, built on Newcomb Lake by Albany banker R. C. Pruyn in 1888.

In 1882 Grant varied his guideboat production with construction of a sailboat. What this boat looked like and where he got the patterns or plans for it is not recorded, but it, too, was probably built for a summer resident. Members of the Adirondack League Club, like many other Adirondack summer residents of their class, were familiar with the yachting scene on the coast. Undeterred by the uncertain winds of the mountains, some of these die-hard sailors brought competitive sailing to the Adirondacks.

Many early Adirondack sailing enthusiasts raced the decked canoes made famous at American Canoe Association meets. League Club members raced canoes by Rushton and the Rochester builder George Ruggles, mostly on the club's Bisby Lake. Rushton had a promoter at the club, since his New York City agent, Henry C. Squires, was an early member. Two of the ALC Rushtons were Vesper models. The Pruyn family also had a Vesper at Camp Santanoni which, like the ALC boats, was not cruised cross-country but used as a small sailboat on a single body of water.[21]

Summer residents of the St. Regis Lakes took sailing races more seriously. When

Eleven of the original twelve Idems remain on St. Regis and Spitfire Lakes nearly one hundred years after they were launched. The twelfth is at the Adirondack Museum (entry 181). Photograph courtesy of Barbara Parnass.

the family of New York banker Anson Phelps Stokes moved up for their first summer on Upper St. Regis Lake in 1876, they built "what was said to be the first sailboat ever seen in this neighborhood—a catamaran made by fastening together two rowboats by a platform and placing a centerboard in the platform." Presumably the rowboats were Adirondack guideboats.[22] The colony of "campers" grew steadily, consisting mostly of wealthy New Yorkers, and they grew progressively more serious about their sailing.

"A cranky flat-bottomed sharpie" won the first "cup race" held by the club in 1885. The St. Regis Yacht Club was formally established in 1897, the year that the young naval architect Clinton Crane visited his uncle Augustus Durkee on the lake. Crane was on his way home from Montreal after an unsuccessful challenge for the Seawanhaka Corinthian Yacht Club Cup on Lake St. Louis and had his yacht *Momo* with him. *Momo* redeemed herself from the disappointing performance in Canada and beat all the boats on the lake. By this time handicapping had become a contentious issue among yacht club members, and they were so impressed with Crane that they commissioned from him a one-design class for the club that would do well in the mountains' capricious winds and in which yacht club members could compete equally.

The class was named "Idem," appropriately, to indicate that they were all alike. The first seven were built in 1900 by the Spalding St. Lawrence Boat Company in

Ogdensburg on the St. Lawrence River at a cost of $750 apiece. The sloops pleased the sailors so much that they eventually bought an even dozen. As the twentieth century advanced, the club established other classes for sailboat racing, but the thirty-two-foot Idems remain queens of the fleet.[23]

The Idems of the St. Regis Lakes and smaller boats like the Barnegat Bay sneak-boxes, adopted as a one-design class by the ALC in 1912, were the rare yachts of a few sailing enthusiasts in the Adirondacks. Most people were much less concerned with exciting sailing than with a stable platform from which to fish, hunt, gather water lilies, or enjoy the scenery. "What kind of boat is the best?" asked the guidebook writer E. R. Wallace for the benefit of his readers in 1894.

> The first and main point to be considered is *weight*, for it must be light enough to be carried for miles, if necessary, by a single person. *Steadiness* is an important point, too, for how many have "missed that deer because the boat was so tottlish," to say nothing of the sufferings from tired cramped limbs and aching back occasioned by sitting for hours in a cranky boat. Capacity for luggage; dryness, both for comfort and the safety of provisions; strength, to enable it to stand the severe hardships it is subject to among the snags, rocks and rapids; and last but not least, very fine lines to enable one to make rapid and especially silent progress through the water in search of "venison for breakfast."[24]

The very characteristics which suited the guideboat so well to the needs of the settlers and professional guides of the mountains became liabilities to many tourists,

Edward Bierstadt, A Cozy Nook in West Bay, Blue Mountain Lake. P. 6777.

The Lake View House,
Bolton, had a livery stocked
with Whitehalls or similar
boats in 1889. Photograph
by Seneca Ray Stoddard.
P. 29957.

even those in search of venison to eat with their pancakes. Its fine lines, originally developed for speed, made the boat too tippy for novices when lightly laden. It was also comparatively expensive, an important consideration for hotel owners who wanted a fleet of boats for customers. Rushton sold his sixteen foot Saranac Laker for $100 in 1903; his fifteen foot three inch double-ended livery boat cost $60.

The upsurge of interest in small recreational boats that resulted in the great variety of canoes paddled by ACA members also produced a cosmopolitan small-boat scene on lakes in the Adirondack interior. Canoes of all varieties were joined by rowboats and sailboats of many descriptions. Builders in the region flourished, adapting designs from elsewhere as well as using guideboat construction techniques to build new regional boat types. This boatbuilding activity in New York's North Country was part of a national trend. The end of the nineteenth century was a period "of immense technical progress in every area, and it was the culmination of refined and perfected boatbuilding techniques extending back over a period of centuries," John Gardner has written. "There was a proliferation of small craft types for sail and oar perfected to the ultimate for speed and convenience. . . . Boatbuilding was to some extent an ethnic melting pot, and this all came to a head, blossomed, so to speak, toward the end of the nineteenth century before the advent of the gasoline engine."[25]

The rowboats participating in the Prospect House water fete were probably transom-sterned craft of Whitehall shape built by Fletcher Joyner, soon to be Rushton's rival and builder of *Pecowsic*. The veritable armada included eighty-two "broad boats of the Champlain type" in addition to a substantial number of guideboats. Joyner's 1883 catalog calls them "open cedar rowboats," suitable for family, hotel, or livery use. "Champlain boat" is not a recognized type, but was used to mean a broad, stable boat as compared to a guideboat.[26]

The Whitehall had emerged as a distinct type in the 1830s for use as a ferry boat and tender in the harbors of New York and Boston. It achieved fame for its speed when used by boardinghouse keepers, who sent Whitehalls to meet incoming ships to solicit tenants.[27] By the 1880s Whitehall-style boats had become popular in yachting circles in addition to being used in every large harbor in the country. These Whitehall-looking craft were soon stock products of all good rowboat builders and in wide use as pleasure boats. Whitehalls were stable, roomy, and could be sailed. They handled well in the choppy water sometimes found on large lakes.

The distinctive Whitehall form, with its plumb stem, rounded bilges, and broad wineglass transom, influenced many regional pulling boats. But many boats superficially similar to Whitehalls lacked the Whitehalls' carvel planking, closed gunwale, and peculiar framing.[28]

True Whitehalls may have been common in parts of the Adirondacks. They were common on Lake George (Stoddard reported a fleet of them there in 1873), and Arpad Gerster, a seasonal resident on Raquette Lake who preferred light canoes, noted in 1898 that friends visited from Blue Mountain Lake "in a big tub of a Whitehall boat."[29]

A Lake George rowboat forms part of the picturesque scene of Concordia Bay, Lake George, sold by the Detroit Publishing Company in 1904. P. 11432.

Builders on Lake George adopted the Whitehall style for a boat well-suited to their waters. By the 1890s at least two prolific builders on the lake, Wildman Hall Sexton of Hague, and F. R. Smith and Sons of Bolton Landing, were producing a pulling boat which has become known as the Lake George rowboat.[30] This distinctive craft has a slightly tumblehome stem and caned seats hanging from knees rather than plank seats on "risings"; the framing and stern planking are different from a true Whitehall.[31] The most distinctive difference between the two is the shape of the transom. A true Whitehall has a much broader transom, forming a more exaggerated "wineglass" shape than the transom of a Lake George rowboat.

The Lake George rowboat became a feature of summer life on "the Queen of American lakes." Local fishing guides used them, as did hotels and camps, large and small. The Smiths sold over two hundred to the Sagamore Hotel and over eighty to Mohican Lodge between 1890 and 1910. The workmen at the Smith shop turned them out at the rate of one every twenty-one man-days—about the same rate at which their contemporary Dwight Grant built guideboats.[32] On a still evening, a favorite occupation of the young patrons of the large resort hotels was to engage a small steamer to tow a string of Lake George rowboats around the lake, the musical passengers providing accompaniment by singing or playing the ukelele.[33]

The Whitehalls were only a part of the cosmopolitan boating scene on Lake George in the late 1870s. From 1878 to 1887 it was the site of a major intercollegiate rowing race for fours, second in importance only to the Harvard-Yale race.[34] Most of the competition sculls and shells in America at the time were made of paper, built primarily by the firm of Elisha Waters and Son, down the river in Troy.[35] Paper boats were popular until the 1890s because of their light weight but fell into disuse by the turn of the century because, despite a proprietary waterproofing finish, they tended to get soggy after much use.

While many pleasure rowers preferred a transom-sterned Whitehall-style boat, others chose a fairly narrow, double-ended lapstrake rowboat. The most popular was the skiff used on the St. Lawrence River which, like the guideboat, originated as a workboat for residents of the Thousand Islands region. Although invention of the skiff is attributed to Clayton boatbuilder Xavier Colon about 1868, it seems to have evolved gradually from the same lightly-built lapstrake skiffs built by British settlers in the St. Lawrence valley as the Adirondack hunting canoe.[36] By the time large numbers of tourists began coming to the Thousand Islands region for rest and recreation (as they came to the Adirondacks at the same time), the skiff was well established as the native craft.

Classic St. Lawrence skiffs are usually between eighteen and twenty-two feet long with beams from thirty-nine to forty-two inches. They are lapstrake boats built on a keel, rather than the flat bottom board of a guideboat. Their stem profile is distinctive: the stems tip slightly outward from the vertical. They are commonly not symmetrical fore and aft, but are wider forward of the center than aft. They are rowed from a single thole pin mounted on the gunwale over which is passed an oar with a leather-lined hole. Skiffs meant for fishing were fitted with pole hooks, butt boards,

Two women prepare to take their St. Lawrence skiff out for a row from Assembly Point on Lake George around 1900. P 35103

and fishboxes. There are often one or two caned armchairs mounted stern and center for comfortable trolling. They typically have a rub rail just below the sheer plank, metal seat hangers, and attached floorboards which cover the bottom of the boat well up the inside towards the seats.

In this golden age of inland small craft, the St. Lawrence skiff seems to have been a particular favorite because it was stable and easy-going. *Rudder* magazine claimed in 1905 that St. Lawrence skiffs could be found in every boathouse in the United States. If true, it may have been partly due to *Rudder* itself, whose founding editor Thomas Fleming Day had formerly been a salesman for the Saint Lawrence River Skiff, Canoe and Steam Launch Company.[37] Certainly private camp owners as well as livery proprietors in the Adirondacks stocked their boathouses with skiffs. General Richard U. Sherman, a founding member of the Bisby Club, a forerunner of the Adirondack League Club, had a twenty-foot skiff with sail and centerboard on Bisby Lake by 1886. *Sylph* was, in the words of an enthusiastic journalist, "the most graceful craft on this side of the wilderness."[38] William West Durant equipped Camp Pine Knot with a St. Lawrence skiff by Colon's successor, A. Bain and Company, before 1893. Rocky Point Inn, like the Prospect House, catered to both sports and tourists; by 1900 this hotel near Eagle Bay had "a fine fleet of St. Lawrence and Adirondack boats" for the use of guests.[39] Commercial skiff builders (there were a dozen by the 1880s) were particular in pointing out in their catalogs the suitability of their skiffs for livery use.[40]

"Ralph's," on Upper Cha-
teaugay Lake, was "one of the
most prominent of
the wilderness hostelries,"
according to E. R. Wallace's
Guide. *It was easy to get to
via the Chateaugay Railroad,
and, as this 1896 Stoddard
photograph shows, well-
stocked with a livery of Bellows boats.* P. 28017.

Palatial resort hotels like those found in the Adirondacks were common in the Thousand Islands, where the skiff evolved. In Alexandria Bay, for example, visitors could choose among a number of lodging-places, including the Thousand Island House, with capacity for 700 guests, and the Crossman House, which could house 300. Like Blue Mountain Lake's Prospect House, these hotels catered to sports as well as to tourists.

The Thousand Islands region provided some of the nation's best muskellunge fishing, as well as abundant waterfowl shooting. The skiff was beautifully suited to such sporting. It was roomy enough to carry a sport or two, guide, bushel baskets full of decoys, and a retriever. It was steady to shoot out of and stable for the guide to help his sport land a large fish. It was also fast and seaworthy, so that the guide could get his client on the Forty-Acre Shoal before all the other anglers, and get him home safely even if heavy seas should blow up. Perhaps most important to the guide, who often rowed twenty miles or more in a day's work, it pulled easily and could be sailed when winds were favorable.

Like the Whitehall, the St. Lawrence skiff was copied and "improved" by North Country builders. On the Chateaugay Lakes, which lie between the high country of the Adirondacks and the alluvial lowlands of the St. Lawrence River, a family of hotel keepers built boats very similar to St. Lawrence skiffs. They became so identified with them and the Chateaugay Lakes that these boats, like the Lake George rowboats, became known by a distinct name: "Bellows boat."

Jonathan Bellows, an emigrant from New Hampshire, opened his Lake House on Lower Chateaugay Lake around 1840. A few outdoor enthusiasts found their way to his establishment (the artist A. F. Tait painted his earliest Adirondack scenes there), but business boomed only after the Ogdensburg and Lake Champlain Railroad passed close by in 1852. By 1880 Jonathan's grandson Millard was in charge. Millard taught himself boatbuilding in the course of keeping up the livery fleet, and by 1890 he was working full time to supply the hotel and the camp owners around the lake. His cousin, Cassius ("Cash") Bellows, soon joined him, and the two eventually turned out over 150 skiffs as well as several steam and gasoline launches.

Compared with St. Lawrence skiffs, Bellows boats were smaller on average (usually fouteen to seventeen feet long with beams of thirty-six to fifty-one inches). The smaller size is probably due to the fact that they were not sailed, and that the Chateaugay Lakes, while large as Adirondack lakes go, are not as large and dangerous as the broad reaches of the St. Lawrence River. Bellows boats have plumb stems, in contrast to the outward-tipping stems of St. Lawrence skiffs, and much flatter bottoms. They are rowed with the distinctive single-tholepin arrangement of the St. Lawrence boats.[41]

J. H. Rushton's version of this double-ended lapstrake skiff was the mainstay of his boatshop until the turn of the century. In early catalogs Rushton claimed his version was an "improved" version of the skiff. Rushton pleasure rowboats and skiffs may at least have shared a common ancestor, since the Rushton boats were grown-up versions of the light sporting boats with which he had begun his career. Rushton's boats were smaller and more lightly built than most St. Lawrence skiffs, however, and had flatter bottoms and plumb stems instead of the significant deadrise and outward-tipping stems of the skiff.[42]

In 1877 Rushton built his "pleasure rowboats" in five lengths from eleven to fifteen feet. By the year of the World's Columbian Exposition he offered a dozen different models (identified by number in 1893; in 1895 they were distinguished by names of states), each of which could be ordered in one of five different grades, with a square stern, or as a sailing skiff with a centerboard. Rushton was building an impressive (though theoretical) eighty-four different pleasure rowboats. The skiffs ranged in size from twenty-one to twelve feet long and forty-two to thirty-two inches in beam.

The sport in this Rushton Pleasure Rowboat no. 113 is rowing with Lyman's patented bow-facing oars.
AML.

A. Jackson's boat shop in
Brushton, ca. 1900.
P. 61673.

Rushton had competition for his lapstrake skiffs from at least four other builders
in nearby North Country villages. Although there must have been a healthy regional
market for little skiffs, only two builders, Rushton and H. M. Sprague, advertised
nationally.

Sprague was Rushton's chief rival in his immediate area. Sprague claimed to have
gone into business prior to Rushton and hinted in his advertising (and it may only
have been advertising) that Rushton owed much to Sprague's designs. Sprague had a
shop in Parishville, on the West Branch of the St. Regis River, where he employed
"skilled workmen . . . at low prices." (He presumably hoped to attract business by
promising to pass on to his customers his savings in labor costs.) In addition to sailing canoes, a type of duckboat known as a sneakbox, and violins, he turned out a line
of pleasure boats for sportsmen, and row and sailboats for families.[43]

In the hamlet of Brasher Falls on the St. Regis River, the L. D. Rogers Company
built skiffs before 1919 that are almost copies of Rushton's, and Alfred Jackson hung
out his shingle further east, in Brushton on the Little Salmon River.[44]

While some of these Adirondack builders adopted the construction techniques of
boats that had evolved elsewhere, others used the methods with which they were familiar in building what Rushton called "Pleasure Rowboats." The result was several
different models of rowing boats and canoes built with the sawn frames, flat bottom
board, and feather-lapped planking of the Adirondack guideboat.

People who wanted to carry more passengers or more freight than was possible in
a standard guideboat built or bought an extra-long guideboat. Guideboats longer
than eighteen feet became known as church boats, freight boats, or family boats.

They are guideboats in every detail except that they have no yoke cleats or yokes. Even with the techniques of guideboat construction a boat that long is too heavy for one man to carry comfortably. Dwight Grant built his first church boat in 1887. Out of the 358 guideboats built by Dwight Grant and his sons, twenty-two were church boats.[45]

Adirondack craftsmen also built shorter-than-average guideboats as the guideboat's original functions became less important to users. The standard boat of the working guide ranged in length from fifteen to sixteen feet. Builders and guides had learned empirically that this was the length at which the boat reached its maximum hull speed. As Willard Hanmer, a Saranac Lake builder, stated in 1961,

> Sixteen was a standard length and that seemed to be the ideal boat for racing or carrying a load or anything else. Speed you never would gain over sixteen feet, and you would drop off sharply on anything under sixteen feet. For instance, the twelve, thirteen and fourteen foot models I build today are nice, light boats to get back where the trout are supposed to be, but you can't make the speed in them.[46]

Hanmer was only one of a number of builders who built boats less than fourteen feet in length; the Grants, whose production is well documented, built sixty-three boats shorter than thirteen-and-one-half feet, which they called "Raiders."

Guideboat builders also turned out double-ended pleasure rowboats built in guideboat fashion. By strict definition these boats are almost guideboats: they have the sawn frames, elliptical bottom boards, and smooth skin of the classic guideboat,

On the way to church from Camp Pot Luck on Spitfire Lake, 1893. P. 312.

but they are heavier all around because of heavier scantlings. Because they are so heavy, they have no carrying yokes. These guideboat-built rowboats were stabler and sturdier than traditional guideboats. The Old Forge Boat Company in Old Forge built some around the turn of the century that may have been attempts at capturing the St. Lawrence skiff market. They are shaped much like St. Lawrence skiffs and have the decorative deck beams and finish of the skiff (a varnished sheer strake with a rub rail below it, and then a painted hull). The Old Forge Boat Company (1896–1910) was the corporate name of Theodore Seeber, who worked for Dwight Grant in Boonville and then set up shop in Old Forge with Ben and Ira Parsons, other Grant workers.[47] An unknown builder in the northeastern Adirondacks supplied the Ausable Club with similar boats, which became known as "Westport guideboats."

John F. Buyce carried the tradition of guideboat-built rowing boats into the twentieth century. The standard product of his shop was lapstrake rather than smooth-skinned but with sawn frames and an elliptical bottom board. His boats became known as "Buyce boats." Buyce opened his first shop in Speculator, in the southern mountains, in 1890, at the age of twenty. He was a true jack-of-all-trades. At one time in his career, which lasted until his death in 1947, he hung a sign over his door which advertised "Odds and Unusual Things that You Can't Get Done at the Other Place." The shop was nominally a blacksmith's shop, which gradually became a garage as times changed, where Buyce repaired automobiles and motor boats. He also dealt in agricultural implements, saddlery, and hardware and did considerable woodworking.

The tools of John F. Buyce's various trades, as well as a boat on the jig, surround him and a friend in 1920. P. 11439.

Boatbuilders experimented with many different construction materials as well as different types of small craft in the second half of the nineteenth century. Paper, tin, steel, and canvas were all tried; builders also experimented with boats that folded up or came apart. Dot, ca. 1880, is a model of a canvas sailing canoe: waterproofed fabric stretched over an open wooden frame of ribs and stringers. 61.20.

Over the course of nearly sixty years he turned out andirons and weathervanes, fireplace utensils, carriages, cutters, and boats.

Around the turn of the nineteenth century, as canoes became more popular with people guiding themselves, Adirondack guideboat builders began to receive orders for canoes. Not surprisingly, many of them produced guideboat-built canoes with the sawn frames, flat bottom board, and flush-lap construction they were used to. At least five Adirondack builders produced these boats: H. K. Martin, Myron Nickerson, A. H. Billings, George and Bliss, and Willard Hanmer.[48]

Adirondack boatbuilders turned out many glamorous craft in the decades around the turn of the century; however, Lake George rowboats, Old Forge Boat Company rowboats, and other highly finished yachts do not represent the region's entire production. Punts and flats have been a part of the American maritime scene since colonial times, and they were well used in the Adirondacks as well. These humble craft were built not only by boatbuilders, but by carpenters, caretakers, and handymen.

The punt or scow is the simplest of all small workboats. In its most basic form it is a rectangular floating box with both ends slightly lifted for easier going. It has straight sides, a flat bottom amidships, and is flat across the top; it has no sheer curve.[49] The bottom is generally cross-planked. Punts have great initial stability and are good work platforms, whether for painting a steamboat or flycasting for brook trout. Their disadvantage is that they row hard.

Scores of Adirondack working punts have no doubt disappeared without a trace. Just hints remain in the historical record of how they were used. They were left at remote ponds for fishing, at streamside for ferries, for muskrat trapping or beaver hunting, or for transporting construction materials to remote camps, dams, and homes. Since visitors have always documented their Adirondack lives better than natives have, however, the story of punt-yachts is better known. Punts with guideboat-style oarlocks were used for fishing on the ponds of the North Woods Club, the favorite Adirondack haunt of artist Winslow Homer. Punts for fishing became such a part of club life at the nearby Tahawus Club that they have been built well into the end of the twentieth century. The Bisby Club, a progenitor of the Adirondack League Club, used punts for fishing and as ferries beginning in the 1870s. Some of the Club's ferry punts had no oars at all, just ropes rigged to pull the boats across the Moose River.[50]

A slightly more refined craft is the flat, or flatiron skiff, also known as a sharpie rowboat. This boat also has a cross-planked bottom but is sharp at one end to make going through a chop easier. It has great initial stability but must be used in sheltered or semi-sheltered waters since it can be thrown right over by heavy seas.[51]

The best-known Adirondack example is a boat that was called the "Bisby scow," in its incarnation as a fishing boat on the waters of the Bisby Club and its successor the Adirondack League Club. General R. U. Sherman, an early member, was so proud of the design that he sent a description and specifications to *The American Angler* in 1888, where the editors published them as "A Good Club Boat for Large Waters." "A boat of this form and material will weigh 120 to 130 lbs., and will carry safely 1,200 to 1,500 lbs. weight," they wrote. "It will be steady on the water, easily propelled, and one may stand in it to cast the fly without fear of being overturned, or may pass from bow to stern or stern to bow without endangering his life or that of his fellow-passengers."[52]

*   *   *

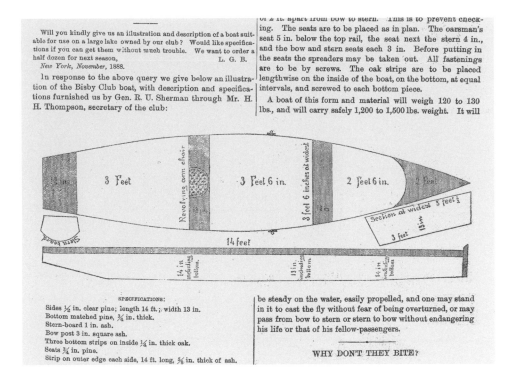

Will you kindly give us an illustration and description of a boat suitable for use on a large lake owned by our club? Would like specifications if you can get them without much trouble. We want to order a half dozen for next season, L. G. B.
New York, November, 1888.

In response to the above query we give below an illustration of the Bisby Club boat, with description and specifications furnished us by Gen. R. U. Sherman through Mr. H. H. Thompson, secretary of the club:

of 2 ft. apart from bow to stern. This is to prevent checking. The seats are to be placed as in plan. The oarsman's seat 5 in. below the top rail, the seat next the stern 4 in., and the bow and stern seats each 3 in. Before putting in the seats the spreaders may be taken out. All fastenings are to be by screws. The oak strips are to be placed lengthwise on the inside of the boat, on the bottom, at equal intervals, and screwed to each bottom piece.

A boat of this form and material will weigh 120 to 130 lbs., and will carry safely 1,200 to 1,500 lbs. weight. It will

SPECIFICATIONS:

Sides ⅜ in. clear pine; length 14 ft.; width 13 in.
Bottom matched pine, ¾ in. thick.
Stern-board 1 in. ash.
Bow post 3 in. square ash.
Three bottom strips on inside ¼ in. thick oak.
Seats ¾ in. pine.
Strip on outer edge each side, 14 ft. long, ⅝ in. thick of ash.

be steady on the water, easily propelled, and one may stand in it to cast the fly without fear of being overturned, or may pass from bow to stern or stern to bow without endangering his life or that of his fellow-passengers.

WHY DON'T THEY BITE?

In the spring of 1893 a wave of bankruptcies destroyed major firms across the country, and stock prices fell to all-time lows. In the resulting panic 600 banks and 15,000 businesses failed. The depression that followed lasted until 1897. It was the deepest the nation had known because never before had the fortunes of industry, labor, and farmers been so interdependent.[53]

Most Adirondack and North Country boatbuilders did not suffer the reverses of urban workers. Instead, the boatbuilding industry—if one can call it that—continued to flourish.[54] Boatbuilders in the region still operated more at the level of craftsmen than industrial workers. Like Dwight Grant they had other sources of income. Nor were they dependent on the national market; their products were sold by word of mouth to local or regional patrons.

J. H. Rushton was an exception. Since the late 1870s he had worked hard to develop a wide market, and in the mid-'90s he sent boats to Michigan, Louisiana, and possibly even Samoa.[55] In addition to national marketing, he met increasing competition in the small craft field by offering something for everyone. "Surely, in all the number [of boats in this catalog] you can find something to meet your wants, to please your taste," he wrote in his 1888 catalog.[56] In 1893 he issued a special edition of his catalog as he prepared to go to the World's Columbian Exposition in Chicago, the best showcase of the decade for reaching a large audience. The catalog listed a total of fifty-two different models which, when the different optional grades were counted, totaled 135 different boats he would build (not including nineteen different "outfits" for the sailing canoes). There were pleasure boats (twelve models), dinghies, an Adirondack guideboat, four different types of open paddling canoes, fourteen models of decked sailing canoes, a large cruising sailboat ("large" in comparison to the decked sailing canoes), and a Barnegat Bay Sneak Boat. In the open paddling canoe category, he began offering not only his original small hunting canoes but Canadian models. These he built not with the strip-building techniques of the Peterborough builders but with the flush-lap construction of the guideboat builders.

Rushton installed electric lights in his shop and replaced the original water turbine with a gasoline engine in the early 1890s; the debt incurred on these improvements was increased by the costs of sending an exhibit to the Exposition. He was thus in a poor position to deal with the depression. His profits depended on a national market, and that market was ailing. Rushton closed his shop for a few years in the middle of the decade because he couldn't keep his workmen employed, and during the hiatus several of the men struck out on their own. Myron Nickerson and Isaac Hurst set up shop in Canton, taking with them some elements of Rushton's style.[57]

Rushton's shop notebooks from the period after he reopened have survived, and they give a good picture of his efforts to cope with the effects of a national depression. They record Rushton's detailed cost accounting, a practice unusual for the time in small business.[58] In two little shop notebooks he labeled "Knowledge," Rushton recorded cost-finding rules he had worked out himself—computing the cost of cedar planking by multiplying the length in feet by beam in inches of the proposed boat, and then adding ten percent to arrive at the cost in cents, for example. He also records a breakdown of the cost of several of his most popular models, by grade. The cost of every part of Boat #109, a standard lapstrake pleasure rowboat, is listed, from bang irons and ringbolts ($1 and 20 cents respectively) to time to "fit out," or attach that hardware, and crate. The bottom line of each such cost list is "share running expenses," or a proportion of shop heat, lights, power, machinery, superintendence, and advertising. The higher-grade boats bore a greater proportion of the overhead than did the lower-grade boats.[59]

Rushton's "Books of Knowledge" also contain offsets for the molds, keel measurements, and the spilings for several of his most popular models: nearly all the information one needs, in fact, to record the boat's shape. With the offsets one can build the mold over which the boat is built. The spilings are tables of figures from which the planks for the boats can be produced. They were for Rushton's record only, not for actual construction, since the boats were routinely built from wooden patterns. But Rushton knew that patterns change and become inaccurate over time, and he wanted to make sure that he could ensure a standardized product. The spilings make it possible to produce accurate plank patterns efficiently whenever needed.[60]

Rushton also produced quantities of parts at a time; "Knowledge" records production of 1,600 ribs in three standard sizes, for example. While not exactly an advanced system of interchangeable parts, this and much of the other information recorded in the notebooks are evidence of attempts to make his shop more systematic and efficient. Even though he was present all the time (getting there in the mornings before the workmen to select the stock for that day's work), he seems to have

A bird's-eye view of Rushton's exhibit at the World's Columbian Exposition, 1893. He took a dinghy, a Vesper, a racing sailing canoe, a Vaux model small hunting canoe, a Saranac Laker, two Canadian model canoes, a pleasure rowboat, a Cruiser model sailboat, and a square-stern livery boat. In cases were hardware and models. AML.

wanted to modernize the shop: to make production of his boats as little dependent on individuals and whim as possible.

The "Books of Knowledge" do not record how effective Rushton's cost-accounting and mass-production were in keeping his business afloat. Certainly the greatest credit can go to his introduction of a new boat in 1901: the canvas-covered Indian Girl canoe. Rushton felt the new technology of canoe construction was inferior to that of the all-cedar boats on which he had made his reputation, but there was no doubt that the boats appealed to a wider audience. Canoeing had faded from the public imagination since the 1880s as the decked canoes became more specialized and expensive. Also towards the end of the century bicycles became cheaper. People wanting outdoor recreation were increasingly more likely to choose wheels than water. The wood-canvas craft brought canoeing back to prominence in outdoor recreation and enabled more people than ever before to "paddle their own canoes."

With the advent of the canvas-covered canoe, built somewhat after the lines of the Indian birch bark, but with flatter floor, and in everyway [sic] a stronger, stauncher craft than that of the red man, the interest in canoeing increased rapidly, and many who had fancied that a canoe was an invention of the evil one discovered the error of their ways.

—Yachting, 1907[1]

CHAPTER 8

Rag Boats in the Wilderness

Early in July, 1906, Mr. and Mrs. C. H. Mattison of Syracuse swaddled their canoe in burlap and put it on a freight car bound for Eagle Bay. A few days later they and their fox terrier boarded the train themselves, taking the Adirondack Division of the New York Central Railroad to Clearwater, and then the Raquette Lake Railway to Fourth Lake. They arrived in the woods late in the morning. After lunch, they unwrapped their canoe and paddled off on a 150-mile trip through the woods and waters to Tupper Lake. They were true disciples of Nessmuk, traveling in a canoe, without a guide, and sleeping in a tent rather than a lean-to or hotel. They paddled an open canoe as the old shoemaker had, but it was a fairly new craft for Adirondack waters, not the more traditional lapstrake cedar cockleshell Nessmuk recommended. The Mattisons' canoe was a product of the Maine woods, a sixteen-foot, sixty-five-pound cedar boat covered with waterproofed canvas.[2]

The Mattisons' wood-canvas canoe was a direct descendant of the Algonquin birchbark. Birchbarks were used in great numbers in the Maine woods by professional hunting and fishing guides—the contemporary counterparts of Adirondack guides who were using guideboats at the same time for the same purposes. The inventor of the wood-canvas canoe was supposedly a Penobscot Indian guide. Dillon Wallace, a contributor to *Outing* magazine, who took wood-canvas canoes on several Labrador adventures, wrote that in patching his birchbark with a scrap of heavy canvas in the 1850s, the Penobscot had the bright idea of completely replacing the bark with canvas.[3]

The popular story of the origins of the wood-canvas canoe does not take into account, however, that such craft are built in a completely different manner from the birchbark canoe. As with the guideboat, the technology was probably perfected over a period of time by several different builders familiar with non-native boatbuilding. In any case, by the late 1870s the wood-canvas canoe had reached its modern method of construction. Unlike its Indian ancestor, built largely by eye on the ground, the wood-canvas canoe is built over a solid mold.[4]

Wood-Canvas Canoes*

A wood-canvas canoe is built over a solid mold that represents the shape of the inside of the canoe, upside down. Crossing the mold like ribs, at the locations of the ribs, are strong metal bands. The mold has a recess along the bottom of each side for the inwales and is notched at the ends to receive the pre-bent stems. Building a mold is tantamount to building a complete wooden boat, but once built it makes repeated building of a single canoe design rapid and efficient.

After the inwales and stems are in place on the mold, the flat cedar ribs are steamed and bent tightly over the form at the metal bands and fastened at each end to the inwales, which they run by.

The planking seams need not be water-tight, so the thin planks (³/16" or so) will be merely butted edge to edge. They are straight and uniform in width (perhaps 3½") and can be applied without much fitting, except in one section of tapered or "gored" planking on either side. Slightly beveled butt joints are swiftly cut with a sharp knife and hidden on top of ribs.

The planks are laid over the ribs starting at the centerline and tacked, usually with special brass canoe-tacks that have rounded heads, through the ribs, three or four tacks at each rib. The points of the very sharp tacks are turned back and clinched by the metal bands.

Owing to the usual tumblehome sides and stems of canoes, the planking cannot be completed on the mold. The shell is removed, decks fastened in, thwarts installed to stiffen the structure, and the planking finished at the ends and sheer. The planking is re-clinched as needed, the outside smoothed, and then a single piece of canvas is stretched on, so as to envelope the whole boat. It is tacked all around, at the tops of the ribs, into the inwales. At the ends, it is slit on the center line and tacked, one side at a time, the second overlapping the first, with smaller tacks, up the leading edge of the stem.

The canvas is "filled" by rubbing into it a waterproofing compound that dries to a hard, but not brittle, surface. The contents of canvas fillers were shop secrets; Rushton's recipe was "5 lbs Silacks [shellac], 1½ qt. Turpentine, 1 qt. oil, 1 pt Japan [a drier], 2 lbs. white lead."[†] When this has cured, the surface is sanded and painted and the outwales attached.

*For complete information see Stelmok and Thurlow, *The Wood and Canvas Canoe.*

[†]Rushton notebook no. 3, St. Lawrence Historical Association, Canton, N.Y., 64.

Mrs. George Whitfield Butts was photographed by her husband on their Adirondack canoe trip in 1907. P. 47636.

Wood-Canvas Canoes

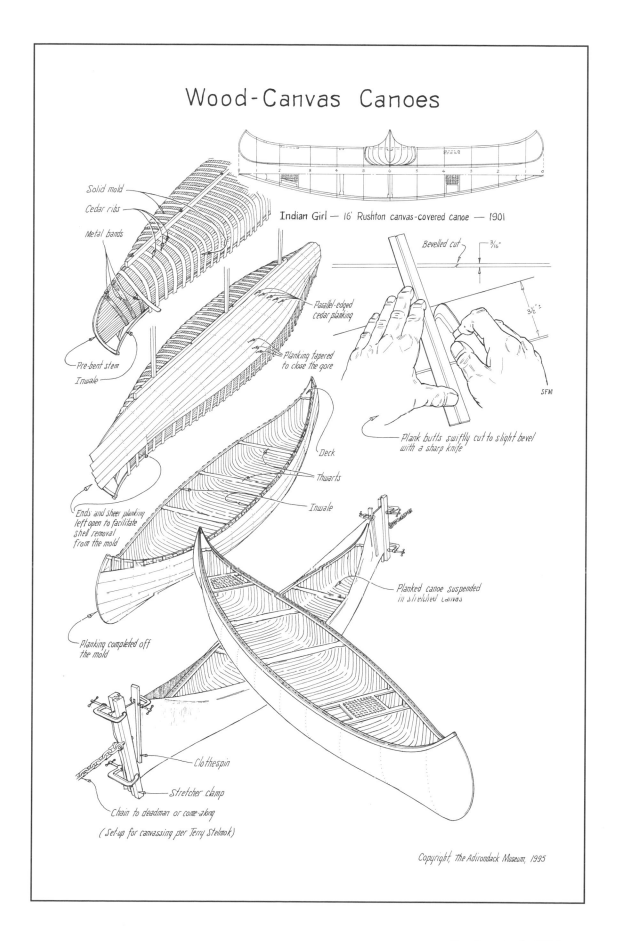

Indian Girl — 16' Rushton canvas-covered canoe — 1901

Solid mold

Cedar ribs

Metal bands

Pre-bent stem

Inwale

Parallel-edged cedar planking

Planking tapered to close the gore

Bevelled cut

3/16"

3½" ±

Plank butts swiftly cut to slight bevel with a sharp knife

SFM

Ends and sheer planking left open to facilitate shell removal from the mold

Deck

Thwarts

Inwale

Planking completed off the mold

Planked canoe suspended in stretched canvas

Clothespin

Stretcher clamp

Chain to deadman or come-along

(Set-up for canvassing per Terry Stelmok)

The wood-canvas canoe does incorporate native elements of building and hull shape. Thin planking braced with thicker ribs and a hull sheathed with a strong, independent flexible covering for resilience and responsiveness were inherited from the birchbark. The form of the early canoes, as well, was copied from Penobscot Indian models. These boats were easy to paddle because they were slender and shallow and had low-profile sheerlines.

Early wood-canvas builders departed from native tradition not only in the hull covering but in method of construction. Canvas replaced bark, tacks and screws replaced spruce root, and uniform materials overall resulted in a stronger boat.[5] The solid mold used by wood-canvas canoe builders enabled them to build boats over and over again to the same model. The canvas covering meant that the planks did not have to be fitted water-tight. This eliminated a good deal of fine joinery, saving labor and therefore cost.

The result was a durable, cheap canoe—less vulnerable to damage from a tyro and more affordable than traditional all-wood craft.[6] In 1907, the year C. H. Mattison published an account of his Adirondack canoe cruise in *Field and Stream*, J. H. Rushton sold his fifteen-foot wood-canvas Indian Girl, grade A, for $41. The same boat in traditional all-cedar construction was $65. His popular Canadian-inspired all-wood Arkansaw [*sic*] Traveler, in a comparable grade, was $56. (At the same time an Adirondack guideboat built by Lewis Grant cost $130.72.)[7]

By the 1880s the wood-canvas canoe was widely used by the hunting and fishing guides in the Maine woods. It did not take long for enterprising sports and guides to export the boat to urban waters. Canoe clubs along the Charles and Connecticut Rivers in Massachusetts, formerly bastions of decked canoe sport, accepted them readily. Many of these recreational paddlers were uncomfortable with the business-like, somewhat tippy, designs which had been perfected for the guides, so builders developed more stable boats. These boats had wide, flat bottoms for good stability and were fitted with keels so they could be paddled in a straight line easily. They often had picturesque high ends and fancy details like long decks with coamings, two caned seats (a guide's model has only one), and decorative paint jobs. Around the turn of the nineteenth century recreational canoeing spread to an even wider market, and canoe liveries along the Charles became major businesses.[8]

Fred Lee photographed a couple paddling a wood-canvas canoe with a low sheer profile on Fourth Lake in 1905.
P. 14504.

J. R. Robertson of Auburndale, Massachusetts, was one of the earliest designers of wood-canvas canoes for the recreational market. Earlier in his career Robertson had worked for Rushton; in a catalog published before 1886 Robertson noted that he had formerly lived in Canton and claimed that he had designed "Adirondack Boats and Canoes (Known as Rushton's Portables)."[9] After leaving Rushton, he built all-wood Rushton models for a short period, but he soon took up the wood-canvas model. Robertson's wood-canvas canoe was designed specifically for the Charles River market. In the 1890s several of the established Maine builders followed suit in producing boats for pleasure paddlers.

High ends proved quite popular among recreational canoeists, even though wood-canvas canoes of the well-established builders had less extreme sheerlines. Old Town's Otca model, introduced in 1906, became Everyman's idea of a canoe in the first half of the twentieth century. High ends did make it easier to turn the canoe over to sleep under it, but most canoe campers of the wood-canvas era used tents or lean-tos instead. The reason for the high profile is probably less practical than romantic: the public's notion of an Indian canoe, absorbed from sources like Currier and Ives's popular prints from A. F. Tait paintings, was one with high ends. Canoeists of the twentieth century were more removed from the age when Indians were a real threat than the American Canoe Association members who scorned the canoe of the "savage." They could now afford to emulate and romanticize the native canoes.

Builders and paddlers remained attached to the Indian heritage of the wood-canvas canoe—or what they thought was its Indian heritage. Rushton named one of his later wood-canvas models the "Navahoe," despite the fact that the real Navajo are desert

This selection of paddles from the Adirondack Museum collection includes, from left, a paddle sold by J. H. Rushton with Indian motifs added by the owner, a paddle made by a young medical student on vacation in the Adirondacks about 1900, and paddles made by James McCormick about 1914 for use on the Fulton Chain, and by George Everett, a summer resident of Lake Ozonia, in the 1930s. 72.27, 83.73.1, 80.63.15, 90.34.1.

dwellers and have no tradition of canoeing whatsoever. Old Town offered factory paint jobs in ersatz Indian motifs, and individual canoeists decorated their canoes and paddles with what they thought were Indian designs. This romantic attachment of canoeists to the "noble savage" was part of a national sentiment which resulted in phenomena like Ernest Thompson Seton's Woodcraft Indians, a camping organization for boys.[10]

Recreational paddlers appreciated the wood-canvas canoe not only for its low price, stability, and romantic aura, but for its durability. Since the canvas and the wooden hull it covers are independent of each other, the boat is flexible and resilient. The Mattisons traveled through the Adirondacks in 1907 with two companions who learned of the flexibility of their canoe first-hand. While the Mattisons pulled their boat ashore at the rapids below Buttermilk Falls, near the head of Long Lake, their friends tried to run the white water and shortly wrapped their canoe around a rock.

They were able to pry it loose, but three ribs and some of the planking were broken. The canvas remained intact, however, and they were able to complete the trip to Tupper Lake without a leak. Edward Breck, whose "practical manual on wilderness life" appeared in 1908, suggested that canoeists on long trips take along a one-pound can of white lead, a small can of shellac, and a thin piece of oiled silk for making repairs to the canvas. Small copper tacks could be used to put on a large patch which would "not improve the appearance of our craft," Breck admitted, "but we are in the forest and not figuring in a canoe parade in a suburban park."[11]

It wasn't until the beginning of the twentieth century that wood-canvas canoes really caught on in the Adirondacks. Much of the credit for popularizing the craft must go to a canoe-building company established in Old Town, Maine.

George Gray was an entrepreneur whose family owned several businesses in Old Town. He had no special expertise in canoe building, but he brought capital, connections, and a keen understanding of marketing and distribution to the business of small-craft construction. Gray started his canoe company by buying the business of Henry Wickett, an established builder in Old Town. The company grew rapidly with additional investment from George's brother Herbert, and Gray purchased a four-story factory in town to meet demand. In 1902 he hired J. R. Robertson away from his business on the Charles River to be superintendent of the Robertson–Old Town Canoe Company. Robertson probably did not remain with the company; in 1904 its name was changed to the name which would become synonymous to many with the wood-canvas canoe: the Old Town Canoe Company.[12]

A couple canoes in a Rushton Indian Girl on the Grass River near Canton about 1920. p. 36223.

Probably in direct response to the challenge from Old Town, Rushton designed two canvas-covered cedar canoes in 1901. One of them, the Indian Girl, quickly became the mainstay of the shop. Just five years later Rushton built 750 Indian Girls, a production record.[13] Rushton had trouble accepting the new craft, however. "I am a staunch believer in the Cedar Canoe without the canvas cover, and no less so now than heretofore," he wrote in his 1903 catalog, "but I cater to the wishes of many, and among the number are those who prefer the canvas covering. To the several builders of this class of work in the 'Pine Tree State' belongs most of what credit there is in the production up to nearly the present time. I say this most willingly, although I cannot concede their claims to the superiority of the canvas covered vs. all wood canoes."[14] No other North Country builder tried to make a business of wood-canvas canoe production.[15]

Although Rushton designed the Indian Girl, he did not interest himself as much in its production as he did in all-wood canoes. Contractors hired the help and supervised the work in his Canton boatshop: the first was an experienced builder Rushton brought from Maine named Melvin Roundy, who was succeeded after 1908 by Frank Fox.[16] Wrote one contemporary of the shop during this period, "I think they were paid by the boat—and how they jumped. Of course the all wood boats were patiently and lovingly made by skilled workers. I mean with the skill of a violin maker, differing from the slap-dash skill of the rag boat makers."[17]

*   *   *

The craft may have changed, but the reasons outers went to the Adirondacks after the turn of the century had not. As a canoeist writing in *Recreation* in 1905 pointed

In the first two decades of the twentieth century canoeing held a place in the popular imagination. The covers of sheet music reflected the canoe's possibilities for independence and romance; pictured here are only a few of the museum's thirty-two examples. AML.

out, "The free life of the open, the sweet influence of the woods and waters, the utter absence of worldly cares and responsibilities is a grand good tonic."[18] The region's appeal was not that it was a trackless wilderness, however. Amenities of civilization were even more available to canoe cruisers of the early twentieth century than they had been for Nessmuk. "The Adirondack Mountains afford a splendid field for beginners," wrote one adviser to canoeists in 1913, "because of the semi-settled conditions of some parts, the wilderness of others, and the ease with which habitation can be reached."[19]

The waterways of Headley's "central valley" remained the most popular canoe route for cruisers in wood-canvas canoes. After the New York Central Railroad put through a spur all the way to Old Forge in 1896, canoeists could board a sleeper in New York City at 7:15 Friday night and be in Old Forge at 6:30 Saturday morning in time for a hearty breakfast and an early start on the Fulton Chain.[20] If they grew tired of black flies or paddling or any other aspect of the great outdoors they could abandon ship at Raquette Lake and go home on the train. If they were having a great time and wanted a side trip, they could paddle the Eckford Chain and climb Blue Mountain for its glorious view. Those completing the standard trip continued down the Raquette River through Forked Lake, Long Lake, a dozen miles of the Raquette River, and then made the carry into the Saranac Lakes. At Saranac Lake village they could wrap up their canoe again and take the train for home.

Canoeists with their own boats, like the Mattisons, could send their boats by train to their put-in. Others could rent canoes once they got to the mountains. In Old Forge in the 'teens and 'twenties, Rivett's Boat Livery and an "old native" rented fifteen-

George Whitfield Butts, A
Carry Between 2 Lakes,
Adirondacks, *1907.*
P. 47654.

foot canoes for five dollars a week. A packbasket and a carrying yoke could be added for fifty cents.[21]

By the late 1920s canoes with complete camping outfits could be rented at several of the other gateways to the Adirondacks as well. Scott B. Smith of Warrensburg advertised in the 1929 Delaware and Hudson Railway's promotional guide, "A Summer Paradise," a "complete cruising outfit" intended for two weeks' camping and cruising on Lakes Champlain and George. The canoe was of the "'Adirondack Guide' type; [with] broad lines to give steadiness and carrying capacity." The builder of Smith's canoes is not recorded, and "Adirondack Guide" model canoes show up in no known catalogs. Whether it was the builder or Smith himself who named the model, he probably felt that "Adirondack" had cachet among canoeists. Smith's rental outfit also included "paddles, tent, beds, kitchen utensils, trappings," all for thirty dollars.[22]

Rental firms did not supply groceries, and savvy canoeists did not overburden their canoes with food, for they could stop at villages along the way to replenish supplies. Two ladies traveling with their husbands had ice cream served to them in their canoes on a hot day on the Fulton Chain in 1921, and they refreshed themselves with bottles of ginger ale while toting packbaskets over the carries.[23]

Local residents continued to provide carry service for canoeists, just as they had for the guideboat travelers of the previous generations. Generally a man or boy with a wagon and team waited for canoeists at major carries like Buttermilk Falls or Raquette Falls. There was an electric signal box at the Raquette Falls carry in 1907 for summoning the team; by 1912 it had been replaced by a telephone. The carriers at Buttermilk Falls modernized, too, and eventually used a car. The carry service wasn't cheap; it cost four dollars to cover the mile and a half from the top of Buttermilk Falls to the end of the rapids below it. If the canoeist were anxious to get to civilization, another four dollars would take him the remaining four miles into Long Lake village.

Canoeists had their choice of accommodations. Some, like the Mattisons, took a tent. Others slept in boarding houses or hotels, as Nessmuk had done some of the time. In 1919 the state constructed the first of its log lean-tos on hiking trails to Mt. Marcy, and in subsequent years canoeists, too, found lean-tos along the major waterways. The state's Recreation Circulars, which also started appearing in 1919, identified these major routes and the locations of the lean-tos on them.[24]

The wise canoeist dressed for the woods and took no excess. For her two-week trip, Mrs. Mattison carried only a bathing suit and a skirt and sweater in addition to her paddling clothes. She attracted some comment and admiration for her everyday wear, which was a blue flannel shirt, knickerbockers, and leather leggings. A man they met whose female companions wore white shirtwaists and skirts with low shoes and drop-stitch stockings ("which must have a been a cinch for the punkies and mosquitoes") vowed to persuade the ladies in his party to dress more practically.[25]

Like the botanizing Benedict party, the Mattisons were sightseers, not hunters or anglers. They did take firearms, however, and Mrs. Mattison potted a muskrat with

This paddler did not go so far as to wear knickerbockers and leather leggings, but she did sport a practical corduroy skirt and warm cardigan for her canoeing trip in 1911. Photograph by Grace Cogswell. P. 25292.

This group of campers used an established lean-to on their trip in the Saranac Lake region around 1900. Photograph by F. W. Rice. P. 59776.

a pistol on the last day of their trip. They found rest and relaxation in the woods as had others before them, but the experience seemed new—particularly for a woman. "It will probably be a great surprise to many canoeists to learn that a nervous and frail little woman, weighing less than one hundred and twelve pounds, could sleep with only one blanket and poncho between her and the ground," wrote Mattison with a gently patronizing attitude typical of the time, "but that is what my wife did, and she invariably enjoyed a night of refreshing sleep."[26] The Mattisons not only enjoyed the woods and waters but also civilized scenes. Mattison noted in his article the summer homes of steel magnate Andrew Carnegie and Governor Timothy Woodruff on Raquette Lake, and the cabin site of dime-novelist Ned Buntline on Eagle Lake. They paused in their paddling for side trips by foot, climbing Black Bear Mountain overlooking the Fulton Chain, and making a special detour through the Eckford Chain to climb Blue Mountain.

Like Nessmuk, C. H. Mattison complained about other uses of the waterways that detracted from their beauty as canoe routes. He particularly disapproved of the standing dead timber around Sixth Lake, caused by artificially impounded water, and harangued his readers to vote down a bill before the New York State Legislature in the 1907 session that he felt would threaten Buttermilk and Raquette Falls by permitting power dams. "As nearly all such bills are carried . . . when submitted to the vote of the people, it behooves all lovers of the woods to wake up and do their utmost to defeat it," he wrote.[27]

The spirit of independence—and an interest in economy—was strong in these early twentieth-century canoe cruisers. "Opinions differ as to whether guides are a necessity," wrote Borden H. Mills, echoing Arpad Gerster a generation before. Mills, whose articles on Adirondack canoeing appeared in such journals as *Country Life in America, Recreation,* and *Adirondac,* wrote, "My advice is, if you want to fish or hunt and go for that alone, by all means take a guide, otherwise don't. The expense is considerable, and while one certainly has an easier time of it, the presence of an opinionated guide in camp has its drawbacks."[28]

Unguided trips in the Adirondacks were easier than ever, not only because of the semi-civilized nature of the Adirondack woods, but because of the topographical maps of the United States Geographical Survey and the written guides and manuals available to the aspiring outer. Nessmuk's *Woodcraft* remained in print and had been joined on the shelf by a number of other publications on outing in general and canoeing in particular. These new canoeing handbooks almost universally recommended the cedar-canvas canoe, although some, particularly those written by Canadians, advocated the all-wood Peterborough models. Edward Breck had J. H. Rushton read his chapter on canoe selection and management just before Rushton died in 1906. Rushton disagreed with him on one point, the toughness of the all-wood canoe. He had "a high opinion of their strength and general usefulness, even in swift waters, an opinion which I do not share, so far as the waters of the north woods . . . are concerned," wrote Breck.[29]

Brochures from the New York Central Railroad, 1915–1928.
AML.

Advice about canoeing was also carried in the proliferating outdoor and sporting periodicals of the early twentieth century. These reached people who already knew about the joys of outdoor recreation, and journals of more general interest promoted canoeing for new audiences. Articles about canoeing appeared regularly from the turn of the century through the First World War in *Recreation, Outing, Woman's Home Companion, Good Housekeeping*, and the *Four Track News*, "An Illustrated Magazine of Travel and Education Published Monthly by the Passenger Department of the New York Central and Hudson River Railroad." They frequently singled out the Adirondacks as prime cruising grounds. The authors were usually writing in the first person about a trip they had taken and gave more or less specific information about what to take and where to go.

Women's magazines advocated canoeing as particularly suited for female outers. Charlotte Cheesbro Hough, wife of Emerson Hough, writer and conservationist, described the canoe in terms which appealed particularly to women in her article, "Canoeing Seems Made for Girls," which appeared in the *Ladies' Home Journal* in 1915. "Everything about the canoe is light, compact, graceful, delicate, dainty, serviceable," she wrote. She liked the sport because it compelled women to "get into the game" and acquire an honest tan. She urged lady canoeists to paddle in style by sporting a blazer or jaunty hat: "Indeed, this is the most pictorial of all sports, as any wise woman will not be slow to realize."[30]

The railroads that served the Adirondacks saw an opportunity to promote themselves as they promoted canoeing. The Adirondack Division of the New York Central Railroad, which began service in 1892, offered stops along the popular Fulton Chain and near Tupper Lake, Saranac Lake, Lake Placid, and the St. Regis Lakes. In addition to the *Four Track News*, the New York Central published vacation guides from the early 1890s through the 1930s, most of which had people in boats on the covers. The early guides were illustrated with pictures of guideboats; by the 1920s the small craft were wood-canvas canoes. The Delaware and Hudson also issued vacation guides to "A Summer Paradise" from the late 1890s through the early 1940s, with advertisements and advice focusing on the canoeing possibilities of Lake George and Lake Champlain.

In spite of the large numbers of people now guiding themselves, the guiding profession continued to expand until 1930—an indication of how much the tourist business as a whole was growing. Sportsmen or tourists, whose primary aim in coming to the region in the early 1900s was to have an Adirondack holiday rather than to find a good canoe trip, probably chose the security of a guided excursion. "Parties have 'done' the Adirondacks with map, book and compass, without the aid of a regular guide," admitted the venerable guidebook-writer Seneca Ray Stoddard, "but the way is full of hardships for such that may be avoided by those accustomed to the contrary."[31] A guide's charge was $3.00 per day, on the same terms as a generation earlier: the guide provided the boat, shelter, camp kit, and evening entertainment. Guided parties commonly stayed in hotels or boarding houses along the way, and the client was responsible for the guide's room as well as his own. He also paid the guide's expenses on the return trip even if, as was usual, it was a one-way excursion. So, while canoeists who guided themselves might spend only $16 to $30 on a two-week holiday in the North Woods, those who hired a guide had to spend $42 for the guide's pay alone. The cost of hotel accommodations, meals, carries, and the guide's return costs were added to that. Borden Mills, who owned his own canoe, spent only $16 on a two-week vacation for two in 1909.[32]

Most guides seem to have preferred a guideboat for their work. "Guides and lumbermen never say a good word" for the canoe, preferring the guideboat for speed, wrote the editor of the New York Central's 1914 guide. He went on to editorialize, "but there is nothing congenial about a guide-boat, and, besides, one works when one rows. The man who rows also is always going away from somewhere, and never seems

It took a lot of concentration for a small girl to paddle a big canoe at the Moss Lake Camp, 1935. P. 43117.

to be getting anywhere else, until the nose of his boat, which is at his back, of course, bumps the shore."[33]

Some guides did use canoes. Many fishing guides on the Oswegatchie used canoes in the 'teens and 'twenties. One of the best known, Wilfred Morrison, paddled not a wood-canvas canoe, however, but a cedar-strip Peterborough.[34] The route up the Oswegatchie from Inlet to High Falls is winding and crosses rapids; a canoe that could be poled was more useful than a guideboat.

In the long run, though, the availability of a cheap, easily paddled boat with which the general public was widely familiar contributed to the decline of guiding as a profession beginning in the late 1920s. Herbert Keith, a guide who came to the Oswegatchie in 1907, had little good to say about the new generation of self-guiding outdoors enthusiasts. He felt that they lacked woods skills and true appreciation of the wilderness. Guiding in his region lasted longer than in the Adirondacks as a whole because of the area's remoteness.[35]

As the number of guides began to decline, so did the demand for guideboats. Lewis Grant, who went to work in his father's shop in Boonville in 1895, built only nineteen guideboats from 1916 through 1934, none of which was for a guide. All but two went to camps on Adirondack League Club lands. Since his guideboats cost almost three times the most expensive wood-canvas canoe from Old Town, most people wanting simple backwoods transportation passed him by.[36]

*   *   *

Many city dwellers who saw an Adirondack canoe trip as a "grand good tonic" for themselves sought a similar draught for their children by sending them to camp for the summer. The theory was that spending a summer in the balsamic air, without the distractions of family or, until the 1920s, the opposite sex, children could grow in health and character away from the "dust, dirt and dangers" of the city streets.[37] Eighteen camps were established nationwide in the 1890s, 106 between 1900 and 1910, and by 1929 over a million campers attended 7,000 summer camps, ninety percent of which were in the Northeast.[38] The first summer camp for children in the Adirondacks (and one of the first in the country) was Camp Dudley on Lake Champlain, established in 1884. By 1925 there were fifty-four children's camps in the Adirondacks, including thirty-four in the central mountains, seven on Lake Champlain, and thirteen on Lake George.[39]

In the first three decades of the twentieth century Adirondack children's camps aimed to teach woodsmanship, cooperation, and character-building, as well as giving campers plenty of healthy outdoor exercise. Boating accomplished all these aims. Many camps were equipped with a variety of watercraft, from small sailboats to rowing shells, but St. Lawrence skiffs and canoes—particularly sponson canoes—were common because of their stability. Sponsons are long, narrow air chambers attached to the outside of the canoe along each side for practically its entire length, and make the boat virtually untippable. Around 1906 the Adirondack Camp for Boys on Lake George brochure stated "a fleet of St. Lawrence skiffs and a number of canoes are pro-

A war canoe team at the
Moss Lake Camp for Girls
around 1935. P. 44293.

vided, and there will be one boat to every three boys. The St. Lawrence skiff is well-
known as an especially safe boat, and at the same time it is light and easily rowed. The
canoes are those made by the Old Town Company of Maine."[40]

Young Adirondack campers fished, paddled around in front of their camps, and
went on longer trips in camp canoes. Managing the camp "war canoes" taught teamwork. These extra-long canoes had initially become popular as club canoes in Canada
in the late 1890s among men who liked canoe racing but could not afford to own their
own boats. The most common size by the 1920s was twenty-five feet, but some camps
had thirty-four-foot canoes. Crews of six to ten paddled the shorter war canoes, while
the longer ones held twelve to twenty. Generally the paddlers were arranged in pairs,
with a single paddler in the stern to call cadence, much like the cox in the rowing
shell. Sometimes the strongest, most capable paddler was put in the bow for the rest
of the crew to watch. Some camps had special camp paddling songs to help keep the
crew in sync. A war canoe plowing through the lake was an impressive sight, especially when the paddlers ended their exertions by simultaneously saluting with their
paddles, blades up and grips on the seat. The Old Town Company claimed in its 1910
catalog that one of their thirty-four-foot war canoes manned by eighteen young men
had beaten every launch it encountered in short sprints on a lake in New Hampshire.[41]

War canoe races were part of the water festival some camps held on parents' weekend or at the end of the season. These festivals were a chance for campers to show off
their skills as well as advertisements for the camps. The annual Water Carnival at the

Harry Rushton posed for his photograph in his shop with an Indian Girl canoe around 1910. P. 36221.

Adirondack Camp for Boys on Lake George in 1904 included rowing and paddling races, diving, swimming, and canoe jousting. The camp boasted that "the sports attract a large gathering of people, coming in launches small and large, and in decorated steam yachts, presenting a beautiful sight."[42]

Children's camps launched an impressive number of wood-canvas canoes on Adirondack waters. The best-equipped camps could put all the campers on the water at the same time. Like the Adirondack Camp for Boys, Camp Pok-O-Moonshine near Willsboro boasted enough boats to allow one to every two or three boys. This was nearly forty canoes for Pok-O-Moonshine.

*   *   *

J. H. Rushton, the only North Country builder of wood-canvas canoes, had difficulty competing with Old Town and the other national builders. The chief drawback of Rushton canoes was probably cost, which was high because of Rushton's remoteness from major markets, insistence on quality, and comparatively low volume. Rushton's fifteen-foot Indian Girl, best grade, cost $41 in 1907. A comparable boat from Old Town, the Charles River model, cost $36.[43] Rushton himself did not live to see his business eclipsed. In 1906, in the midst of what looked like full recovery from the lean years of the 1890s, Rushton died of Bright's disease at the age of sixty-two.

Rushton's eldest son Harry took over the business and incorporated it. He showed his father's flair for advertising by issuing a catalog devoted solely to the Indian Girl. In 1909 and 1910 he published a little magazine called *Indian Girl Paddler*, which purported to be a general canoeing magazine, but was clearly meant to promote J. H. Rushton, Inc.'s, most popular product. Articles on organizing a canoe club, canoe maintenance, and how to make a good impression while out "girling" were interspersed with testimonials about the quality and performance of the Indian Girls.

The *Indian Girl Paddler* for January, 1910, carried a photograph of a three-horsepower Thrall motor, and the announcement that J. H. Rushton, Inc. stood ready to install it in an Indian Girl canoe. The motor cost $60, $11 more than the cost of a Grade A boat. Harry, with his father's attention to the latest trends in canoeing, was trying to keep his company competitive. The motorized canoe ultimately did not keep the company alive. The shop doors closed for the last time in the winter of 1916–1917. But Harry was right about the gasoline engine: by 1910 it was fairly trouble-free and inexpensive, and traditional boat types, large and small, were being fitted with motors around the country. Boats—and boating—were changing irrevocably.

The Doris *was formerly a steamboat, but this year the old boilers and the clumsy machinery have been removed and a 45-h.p. Fay and Bowen motor installed, thus marking another triumph for the internal combustion motor.*

—MotorBoat, 1910[1]

CHAPTER 9

The Triumph of Internal Combustion

The excursion launch Doris *was a popular subject for postcard photographers. In the two right-hand postcards she is shown with her pre-1910 steam engine.* AM *collections.*

Doris was already a distinctive fixture on Lake Placid when the *MotorBoat* writer saw her in 1910. She had been built in Paradox Bay twelve years before for hotelier H. C. Stevens. At seventy-seven feet long, she was one of the largest steamboats in the central Adirondacks, and was licensed for 154 passengers. Her skipper, who from 1903 until 1951 was Stevens's son Arthur, surveyed the lake from a distinctive octagonal wheelhouse with a conical roof topped by a turned finial. In addition to carrying passengers she delivered the mail to lakeshore residents two times a day. For a decade, she also carried fire pumps to protect lakeshore camps; in 1900 the recently-established Shore Owner's Association had purchased a pump for the vessel which ran off the steam boiler.[2]

Summer residents of camps on Lake Placid that were inaccessible by road used *Doris* for transportation, but most of her passengers did not take her to get anywhere in particular. For these people, boat travel was an end in itself. "REMEMBER! You haven't seen Lake Placid until you have taken one of these gorgeous boat tours," declared the brochure of the George & Bliss livery, which purchased the boat from Stevens in 1919 and ran her until 1951. "Nothing can be more invigorating and restful than a boat trip on Lake Placid," they claimed, rather paradoxically.[3]

Many people, like the Mattisons, still built their Adirondack holiday around a cruise through the region's waterways in a guideboat or canoe. But beginning around the turn of the century, others, who formerly stayed several weeks or the summer at a hotel or club lodge, eating and sharing piazzas and boathouses with many other people, looked for a place where they could rest and recreate in small family groups. Some booked one of the cottages that hotel-owners were building in response to the trend. Others purchased their own piece of the Adirondack wilderness and built a private camp.[4] While they might take a boat like *Doris* to get to their camp or hotel from the nearest railhead, boats were, for them, primarily recreational vehicles, not means of transportation.

The excursion launch Miss Saranac, *operated by the Thomas Boat Lines, offered a tour from Saranac Lake village through all three Saranac Lakes, viewing the "Grandest Lake and Mountain Scenery in the Adirondacks." Broadside for Thomas Boat Lines, n.d., ca. 1918.* AML. P. 58977.

The boathouses of private camps were filled with a rich variety of craft. Modest camps on the Fulton Chain might have a canoe or a flat-bottomed rowboat for the children and a guideboat for the adult anglers in a small frame structure with a sloping ramp dock to the water. More extravagant boathouses on Upper St. Regis Lake or Upper Saranac Lake might be filled with guideboats, skiffs, and canoes, and perhaps an annex for a large sailboat. They were smaller versions of the hotel and club boathouses they were replacing, with one notable addition. In the first two decades of the twentieth century, Adirondack camp owners were increasingly likely to purchase an inboard motorboat for their fleet.

Motorized boats found an eager audience in a growing population of people who wanted to get out on the water and had the time and the disposable income to spend on boats but not always the athletic abilities or interests to row or paddle themselves. The popularity of boating as a recreation that had begun with the cruising canoeists of the 1870s accelerated as power boats became reliable and cheap. The attraction of power boats is also probably due to a general American fascination with the internal combustion engine—the same fascination that had conditioned the American people for a rapid acceptance of the car.[5]

Privately-owned power boats had cruised Adirondack waterways since the wealthy began buying small steam launches in the 1870s and 1880s. In 1891 one could purchase a twenty-two-foot steam launch from H. V. Partelow in Boston for $500.[6] Charles Wright Durant, uncle of William West Durant, brought the forty-two-foot *Stella* to his camp on Raquette Lake the year after she was built in 1881.[7] But steam yachts were ill suited to amateur operation. They had a limited capacity and were expensive,

Developer of the Adirondack and St. Lawrence Railroad, William Seward Webb, had a naphtha launch, two skiffs, and what looks like a long, open racing canoe at his Camp Nehasane on Lake Lila around 1900. Photograph by T. E. Marr. P. 23742.

complicated, and dirty to run. Time was needed to get up steam before embarking, and the engineer had to be licensed.

In 1883 a Swedish immigrant named Frank W. Ofeldt introduced an engine that promised to make power boats more practical for the amateur. His machine was essentially a steam engine in which the expansive gas was vaporized naphtha, a petroleum product, instead of steam. The naphtha engine was easier to run and cleaner than a steam engine, but most important, it was about one fifth the weight per horsepower of a steam engine. This meant that the engine could be placed in the stern near the propeller, freeing the midships area for passengers, and that the engine itself, and the hull in which it was placed, could be more lightly built. Also, a naphtha launch could be fired up and underway in about five minutes, no matter how cold the weather.[8] Prices for naphtha launches were comparable to those for small steam launches. In 1898 a twenty-one-foot naphtha launch cost between $750 and $850, depending on finish.[9]

Naphtha launches enjoyed a large but brief popularity. In 1903 reportedly 3,000 were in operation around the world. The first power boat on Upper St. Regis Lake was a naphtha launch, and there were naphtha boats also on the Eckford Chain, Raquette Lake, the Saranacs, Forked Lake, and Long Lake. There were at least eleven on Lake George, including two over thirty feet long.

Electricity seemed another alternative to steam, and by the early 1890s electric launches were commercially available. A fleet of more than fifty of them cruised a million people around the waterways of the World's Columbian Exposition in 1893. They did not become widely popular, however, because of the weight of the batteries, limited cruising range, and because of a higher cost even than naphtha launches. In 1896 a twenty-one-foot electric launch from the Gas Engine and Power Company cost between $1,175 and $1,225, depending on finish.[10]

Within two decades naphtha and electric launches were largely supplanted by boats powered by gasoline engines. "Explosive engines," as they were initially called, were first perfected for inboard use, and then, by the 1920s, were reliable enough to be widely popular in the form of outboard motors. Like the wood-canvas canoe, the internal combustion engine helped make pleasure boating available and attractive to a greater number of people. "One must be poor indeed who cannot avail himself of

This camp on Gull Lake on the Webb preserve had a typical small boathouse with ramp dock. The denizen of the Gull Lake Camp, a hermit named Muir, had his old square-sterned guideboat tied at his dock when this photo was taken by T. E. Marr around 1900. P. 23764.

Seneca Ray Stoddard photographed the steam yacht Stella *(later* Osprey, *entry 167) on Raquette Lake around 1885.* P. 27812.

the privileges and pleasures afforded by the motor boat of to-day," wrote an editor of *Yachting* magazine in 1907.

> A boat may be knocked together and fitted with power at a cost of from $35 upward.
> . . . The motor boat has not only made water exploration both feasible and fashionable
> but it has rendered the title of "cap'n" no longer an empty one. . . . The motor boat in
> its various ramifications is essentially a boat for the many.[11]

The Thrall engine Harry Rushton advertised as ideal for his Indian Girl canoes was typical of the small inboard marine gasoline engines common by the first decade of the twentieth century. The technology for building these engines was by then so simple and so well known that any well-equipped machine shop could produce them—and many did. The engines of the pioneers were copied if available; if not, skilled machinists could find articles and books that gave plans for simple engines. The most common small engine of the day was a single-cylinder, two-cycle engine which developed about two horsepower in the smallest model.[12]

Engineers and builders made rapid progress in increasing the reliability and speed, and decreasing the weight, of marine engines. These lighter, faster engines in turn forced a change in the design of the boats they powered. The displacement hulls of traditional rowing, paddling, and sailing craft became unstable and unpredictable when driven much faster than their natural hull speeds. A displacement boat naturally creates a wave as it moves through the water; when driven too fast it is forced to "run uphill" on its own bow wave and, at best, squats, and at worst, becomes unstable and capsizes. By 1911 boat designers had developed the planing hull—a new shape that would not only stabilize the boat but help it realize previously undreamed-of

Planing and Displacement

When driven at a fast enough speed, the pressure of the water it is trying to force out of its way begins to lift the boat up on top of the water. It tends to *plane* over the water, rather than *displace* the water and slice through it. To encourage this tendency, and to give stability, the planing hull evolved—relatively short, flat, and broad, in contrast to the traditional long and narrow displacement hull.

DRAWING #1 Waves move at a speed related to the square root of their lengths (i.e., the distance between crests). A 100-foot wave moves at 13.4 knots, a 25-foot wave at 6.7 knots. A boat of *full displacement* shape is most easily driven when the waves she is making are less than her own length.

DRAWING #2 When an increase in speed extends the waves to the full length of such a boat, it becomes impractical to make her go faster. Resistance increases out of proportion to power and she may become unstable.

DRAWING #3 A boat can be shaped to generate waves longer than her own length by making her shallow-bodied with straight and almost level bottom lines at the stern. Such a boat can exceed displacement speed with moderate power and is called *semi-displacement*.

DRAWING #4 As the boat is driven still faster, the pressure of water forced out of her way begins to lift her higher in the water, and the waves become shallower as well as longer. The boat is then called *semi-planing*.

DRAWING #5 At a still higher speed, the pressure is so great that the boat runs almost entirely on top of the water. The waves become so long and shallow that they are no longer significant, and the boat is called *full-planing*.

DRAWING #6 At very high speeds, the boat can be supported on top of the water with smaller areas of bottom. The *stepped hydroplane* at speed runs on only its steps and is an example of the *full-planing* type.

Text and Drawings by Philip C. Bolger

Old meets new in this photograph of John Goldev's naphtha launch taken around 1906; in the foreground is a small gasoline launch.
P. 17221.

speeds. Instead of the long, narrow, deep hulls of fast displacement boats which cut through the water, the new hydroplanes were relatively short, with broad, flat bottoms that rose up and planed over the water.

Inexpensive and reliable marine engines made the pleasure-boat industry flourish all over the country, in spite of the fact that the shipbuilding industry as a whole was in decline. Through the first decade of the twentieth century power boats increased

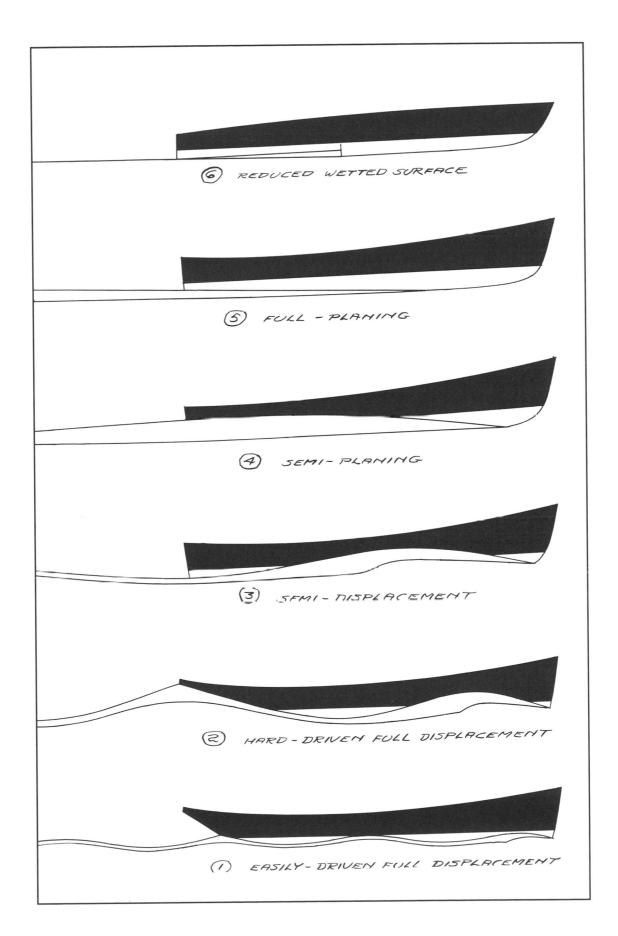

⑥ REDUCED WETTED SURFACE

⑤ FULL - PLANING

④ SEMI - PLANING

③ SEMI - DISPLACEMENT

② HARD - DRIVEN FULL DISPLACEMENT

① EASILY - DRIVEN FULL DISPLACEMENT

A party on the Fulton Chain gets cozy with the motor of their launch in this scrapbook photo labeled "All ready to start to Old Forge, July 1909, in the Gull." P. 22746.

rapidly as a proportion of new boats built. In 1898, according to a poll taken by *The Rudder*, gasoline-powered boats were twenty-eight percent of the boats built in the country. By 1903 that figure had grown to fifty-two percent and an increasing proportion of those boats were pleasure craft.[13]

By 1910 Lake George had become "a cradle of motor boating" with a fleet of 600 vessels. A correspondent for *MotorBoat* wrote,

> Boats of many different models and makes are now to be found on these waters. It is interesting to note that most of the new motorboats are of the moderately speedy type. A popular type is the semi-fishing boat, not very fast and suitable for trolling. The fishing grounds of the lake are almost daily the scenes of angling parties, aboard boats whose motors are throttled down to trolling speed. Many of the larger motorboats on the lake are used to convey the party, with lunches, tackle and the like, to the spots where fish are biting; but a small motorboat, or sometimes a rowboat, is usually taken in tow, and from this craft the fishermen cast their lines.[14]

In the same year there were 150 motorboats on Lake Placid, and on Lake Flower in the village of Saranac Lake, four small motorboats "and about half a dozen electric guide boats."[15] The favorite type of boat on Placid was "a runabout with a canopy top," no doubt used for the same purposes as the "semi-fishing" boats on Lake George.

Just as canoe enthusiasts had banded together in canoe clubs to regulate racing and promote their sport, motorboat enthusiasts formed clubs to encourage motorboat recreation and to regulate the rapidly growing sport of motorboat racing. The Lake George Regatta Association was founded in 1887, only seven years after the American Canoe Association on the same lake. Not only the really fast boats were featured; by the turn of the century the Association was sponsoring launch races for boats other than racing machines.[16] Within two decades, it was joined by two other boat clubs. Their chief activities were the regulation of racing, to which end they sponsored a joint championship cup, and formulating handicapping rules to allow different models to compete evenly in races.[17] As it had been since the early days of the American Canoe Association, Lake George was right up to date; the parent organization for motorboat racing, the American Power Boat Association, was founded in 1903.

Adirondack motorboat clubs typically had broad interests beyond racing. The Shore Owners Association of Lake Placid, founded in 1893, was particularly concerned with marking hidden rocks and removing "floating logs, one of the most serious menaces to pleasure boating." The Saranac Boat and Waterways Club was founded in 1913, its object being "to encourage boating on the Saranac Lakes, rivers

This single-cylinder, two-horsepower inboard motor was built by the Waterman Marine Motor Company around 1912. It was then one of the lightest inboards made and was intended for use in canoes and light rowboats. 90.62.

The whole gamut of Lake George watercraft around 1910 is seen in this photo of a Hague regatta: steamboats, gasoline launches, canoes, and rowing craft. P. 35933.

and tributaries; to promote and stimulate aquatic sports and contests; to keep (as far as possible) channels free from obstructions and properly buoyed; to protect the property and camps of its members from injury and theft; and to exercise a general care and supervision of the whole Saranac littoral."[18] Such clubs performed a much-needed service in marking channels and hazards, a service which was not taken up by New York State until the mid-1960s.

The regattas sponsored by motorboat clubs had similar features to those of the canoe club meets of the previous generation. The races were the centerpiece events, but there were also teas, swimming races, decorated launch cruises, races for non-powered craft, novelty events such as jousting, and, beginning in the 1920s, races for outboard boats. Racers and spectators continued the festivities into the evenings at banquets and balls. "The annual event of the Lake George Regatta Association crowns each season on the 'Queen of American Lakes,'" reported *Yachting* about a typical event.[19] Spectators rode special excursion trains from Albany and Plattsburgh to watch the fun.

Motorboat club members frequently debated means of restricting the all-out development of boats that were good only for speed—just as had the American Canoe Association. It was essentially a democratic movement; the people who could win unrestricted races tended to be only a few very wealthy individuals who could afford a new model with the latest in technology every year. In 1907 *Yachting* magazine remarked rather ambiguously in reporting on that year's regatta, "if all were to be believed Lake George this summer will be the speed center of the country. It no doubt, however, will be found that the racers to come will not depart structurally from the trend to be observed throughout the country towards a boat that is not only swift but wholesome, a cruiser as well as a craft that wins races."[20]

Races sponsored by the Iroquois Association, which replaced the Glens Falls Club in 1912, attempted to encourage the development of these "wholesome" boats. Their "bang and go back" races could be entered by any make or model. The craft raced around a course and then when a blast sounded they were to turn around and retrace their course. The first boat to cross the line was the winner, but any boat which exceeded its outgoing time by more than one and one-half percent coming back was disqualified.

Despite a wide interest in races for "wholesome" boats, no regatta was complete without some events for really fast machines. Most major lakes had a national-class competitor, either an up-to-date speedboat or an outdated boat that had been turned out to pasture.

Lake George was the first Adirondack lake to become home to a national-class speedboat. In 1899 the Philadelphian E. Burgess Warren, part owner of the Sagamore Hotel, brought his magnificent eighty-foot-long *Ellide* to his summer home on Lake George. *Ellide* was an elegant steam yacht with such amenities as a china closet and ice chest, but her truly noteworthy quality was the ability to run at forty miles per hour. She was powered by a patented quadruple-expansion 910-horsepower steam engine, modified versions of which were used in U. S. Navy torpedo boats. *Ellide* was reputedly the fastest steam yacht in the world until 1902, and she was a feature of regattas and carnivals on the lake for years.[21]

A few years after *Ellide* appeared on Lake George, another unusually long speedboat, powered by gasoline rather than steam, made her first run on Raquette Lake. *Skeeter* was only half the length of *Ellide*, and she went a little more than half as fast, but she still must have been impressive to people used to travel by guideboat or excursion steamer. *Skeeter* had been built in 1905 for the second running of the Gold Cup, the American Power Boat Association's annual championship, and was purchased in 1906 for his Adirondack camp by publisher Robert Collier. With a length of forty-five feet, going her top speed of twenty-six miles per hour, she was difficult to turn. Collier seriously damaged the boat when he failed to calculate correctly his course in the path of the oncoming steamboat *Adirondack* and was broadsided.[22]

In the 'teens, Lake George was home to *Show Me III*, *Canny Scot*, and *Araby III*, thirty-mile-per-hour boats built in Watervliet, not far away.[23] By the early 1930s *Skeeter* had been joined by other Gold Cup class boats on other Adirondack lakes. Edmund Guggenheim of Saranac Lake bought *El Lagartito*, a raceboat built on Long Island for Lake George resident George Reis, and renamed her *Miss Saranac*. Lake George's Melvin Crook owned *Betty V*, which looked like "nothing so much as a peanut mounted on an ironing board," according to the *Washington Post*.[24]

Speedboat races, such as those run by the Lake George clubs or the Saranac Boat and Waterways Association, were popular spectator events. The public seemed to en-

Skeeter, *with her port bow*
damaged from the collision,
is tied to the steamer Lillian
at the Raquette Lake dock,
about 1910. P. 7294.

joy the spectacle of speed and technology. In the Depression years, watching a boat that cost thousands of dollars skim over the water was, for many, an appealing escape from financial worries. There was no more exciting and crowd-pleasing race than that for the Gold Cup.

The Gold Cup was run on Lake George in 1914, 1934, 1935, and 1936. The shores of the "queen of American lakes" were dotted with summer estates built by people with enough wealth to buy and maintain power boats. A. L. Judson, Commodore of the American Power Boat Association from 1916 until 1923, summered there, as did the owners of *Hawk-Eye. Hawk-Eye* was designed by one of the best-known names in power-boat design, John L. Hacker. He claimed fifty-seven miles per hour for her in 1915.[25]

The rules of the Cup provide that the defending champion names the site of his defense. The winner in 1913 was Casimir Mankowski, a reputed Polish count who summered on Lake George.[26] Mankowski's boat was *Ankle Deep*, designed by Clinton Crane, whose first design for the Adirondacks had been the Idem class sailboats for the St. Regis Lakes. Mankowski hit a log and didn't finish his defending race. In 1934 George Reis brought the cup races back to Lake George for the following three years.

The years of Reis's domination of the Gold Cup races came in the era of the "gentleman's runabout." The American Power Boat Association had established the Gold Cup race to encourage the development of high-performance motorboats. The competition had accomplished its aim, just as the races sponsored by the American Canoe Association had encouraged, albeit not on purpose, the development of high-performance sailing canoes. Power-boat racing had never been a sport for Everyman, but in the late 'teens it grew further and further out of the reach of even ordinarily wealthy people. The boats themselves were not only expensive, and champions had to build a new one each year, but they became machines for speed only, with less and less utility as a boat.

*   *   *

For a decade after Mankowski's defeat the sport was dominated by Garfield Arthur Wood, who had made a fortune from having invented the hydraulic lift system for dump trucks. In the late 'teens Wood bought an interest in the Christopher Columbus Smith Boat and Engine Company, which would later make their "Chris-Craft" name practically synonymous with "runabout." The Wood-Smith combination was nearly unbeatable. In 1920, their first *Miss America*, a twenty-six-foot long, seven-foot-wide sled-like hull, powered by two World War I surplus Liberty aircraft engines, won the British International Harmsworth trophy. Later in the summer Wood drove *Miss America* 77.85 miles per hour, a new world water speed record.[27]

Only two boats ran in the 1921 Gold Cup. In reaction to this declining interest, and to Wood's domination of the sport, the APBA restricted the Gold Cup race to more "wholesome" boats: boats without the stepped hulls characteristic of hydroplanes, with normal marine engines instead of aircraft engines, and with a second cockpit for a passenger. The restrictions had the desired effect—a few practical runabouts actually did enter the 1922 race. They did not seriously threaten the raceboats, but for the next decade and a half wealthy amateurs ("gentlemen" in the nineteenth-century sense) could again afford to compete for the Gold Cup.[28]

Perhaps the era's quintessential gentleman amateur speedboat racer was George Reis, an heir to Pennsylvania steel money, who spent his winters acting on the stage of the Pasadena Playhouse and his summers racing boats on Lake George. Reis's family began summering at the Sagamore Hotel on Lake George in 1901, when he was twelve. They built a boathouse on the mainland which was filled with a succession of craft, and young George spent his summers tinkering with them. By the age of twenty-two, he was racing *Krazy Kat*, a launch capable of thirty-one miles per hour. A few years later he was a spectator at the 1914 Gold Cup races. Reis's abilities and interest caught the eye of other racers on the lake. In 1916 he drove in his first Gold Cup race in Detroit at the wheel of Commodore Judson's *Hawk-Eye*. The following year he drove the Bolton Landing-built *Hawk-Eye II* in the Cup races, with Bolton resident James Kneeshaw as riding mechanic.

In 1925 Reis bought a used boat in Buffalo named *Miss Mary*, which had been designed in 1921 by John L. Hacker to meet the new Gold Cup restrictions. Reis renamed the boat and gave her a new engine. As they crossed the finish line on her first time trial Reis's riding mechanic Anderson "Dick" Bowers took one look at his stopwatch and joyfully tossed it overboard. *El Lagarto* had hit fifty-two miles per hour, eight miles per hour more than her previous owner had been able to achieve.[29]

Reis raced *El Lagarto* on the national circuit for the next nine years. Before he retired in 1937, he had won all the major laurels for speedboats of the restricted class in America: three President's Cup victories, one National Sweepstakes victory, and three consecutive Gold Cup victories. In 1935 *El Lagarto* was clocked at just over seventy-two miles per hour in a one-mile trial, the fastest straightaway speed ever attained by a boat of the restricted class.

Civic boosters loved the Gold Cup races. The citizens of Bolton Landing made Reis their honorary mayor for bringing the community to the attention of a national audience in a time of national depression. In 1934 the Lake George Gold Cup Regatta Committee urged "all who will benefit directly or indirectly from increased summer business, or who from sheer civic pride in Lake George would like to have it known nationally as the ideal mountain-lake resort to give generously to the Lake George Gold Cup Regatta Fund." They predicted "a strengthening of real estate values, increased business for hotels . . . more business for the transportation lines, the gasoline and oil companies, the public utilities, . . . the laying of a solid foundation for the future development of the lake," and general prosperity.[30] The public loved *El Lagarto*, too, probably because of the spectacle of the "old warhorse" that refused to be put out to pasture and continually beat the best that money could buy.

El Lagarto's crew was a mixture of amateurs and professionals, "summer people" and natives. The restricted era of the Gold Cup marked the last years that the race was dominated by true amateurs as drivers and owners, and that also must have been part of its appeal to the general public. In the cockpit beside Reis usually rode Dick Bowers. A summer resident of Pilot Knob on the east side of Lake George, Bowers had been a naval mechanic in the First World War. Although the press referred to Bowers as a mechanic, he was more accurately called the riding mechanic. His job was to watch the gauges for the driver and make what adjustments he could while they were running. Reis and Bowers made many decisions on what would be done to *El Lagarto*, but the majority of the work was done by professional shop mechanics and boatbuilders, experienced men who added their store of racing knowledge to that of Reis and Bowers.

*   *   *

Reis kept one professional mechanic on his payroll. Bolton Landing native Ferris "Smoke" Gates had originally been hired as caretaker for the Reis boathouse, but his real love was *El Lagarto*. His brother Robert was an employee of F. R. Smith and Sons, who were located next to the Reis boathouse, and he was often called in to help as well. The Gates brothers frequently traveled with Reis and the boat, as there was constant tinkering and checking and repair work to be done on a racing circuit. Bob Gates, because he was the smaller of the two, was often asked to crawl into the engine compartment between heats to work on the engine. Sometimes it was so hot that it would burn all the hair off his arms. The Gates brothers attended the Gold Cup in Detroit when *El Lagarto* won her first victory. The rules stated that the first-place winner must have her engine torn down for inspection. Smoke and Bob did so, and then worked around the clock to put the engine back together and reinstall it to have it ready for a race in Montreal three days later. The boat ran in the race with only a brief preliminary check-out—and won.[31]

The boatbuilders at F. R. Smith and Sons, the shop that had made its name building Lake George rowboats in the 1880s and 1890s, made most of the modifications to the hull of *El Lagarto*. The most significant was a set of five one-half-inch steps built onto the bottom of the hull. Reis and Bowers had seen the way in which steps helped Victor Kliesrath's *Hotsy Totsy* plane over the water in the 1930 Gold Cup race, and when they went back to Bolton Landing they put their heads together with the Gates brothers and designed a new bottom for *El Lagarto*. It was installed next door at Smith's.[32]

Reis himself was saluted by the editors of the 1934 Gold Cup souvenir program as "one of motorboat racing's true Corinthians. The game boasts no better sportsman, no one who gets so much pure fun out of speedboat competition and the preparation therefor," they wrote.[33] The Corinthian ideal was one adopted by sailing-yacht racers in the early years of the twentieth century to distinguish themselves from the professional crews that had raced for high stakes in the second half of the nineteenth century.

George Reis and *El Lagarto* retired from competition in 1937. In that year, the American Power Boat Association removed most of the remaining restrictions on the Gold Cup class. Participation in the race had been dropping steadily for over a

George Reis and Anderson Bowers in El Lagarto *about 1935.* P. 50030.

decade; commentators like *MotorBoat* attributed the decline in interest to the squelching of innovation and pointed to the twenty-five-year-old *El Lagarto* as evidence.

Gasoline-powered boats, just like steamboats a generation earlier, were not greeted with universal enthusiasm in the Adirondacks. Competitors preparing for races, especially when they ran without mufflers, were particularly annoying to many. Motorboats were banned entirely from some privately-controlled lakes. Not long after its founding, the Adirondack League Club banned motors on Little Moose Lake and Bisby Lake. Shoreowners and campers not so fortunate to have complete control of water traffic voiced their objections to the noise and wash of fast motorboats in the press and through local ordinances or the agreements of shore owners' associations.[34]

*   *   *

However much notice they received in the press because of their noise, speed, or style, racing-calibre motorboats did not become a feature of daily life on most Adirondack lakes until the 1950s. Slower and somewhat quieter craft did become a part of the Adirondack picture, however, even for people who did not own a motorboat themselves. Although some excursion and freight steamers continued in service—in some cases into the 1920s—gradually most service boats were either modernized, as was *Doris*, or simply replaced by modern gasoline-powered inboard vessels.

Before good roads and more common use of the automobile made going and coming from camp a casual thing, many lakeshore residents relied on boats for services like mail and groceries. As with the excursion launches like *Doris*, these service boats were increasingly gasoline-powered, rather than steam-powered, as the twentieth century wore on. A writer in the *New York State Conservationist* remembered in 1960,

> Before World War II, the hum of a motorboat was often a solitary, yet welcome sound. To thousands of cottage vacationers and campers of the 1920's and 1930's the purr of the early morning milk boat was a gentle alarm clock and reason enough for arising to scan the swirling mist-drifts on the mirror surface of lake or river.[35]

Boats regularly delivered groceries and mail on some lakes, and all over the region they performed a host of other occasional services, such as delivery of construction materials for lakeside camps and provision of fire protection. *Doris* served the camps of Lake Placid in the latter capacity, and *Mary Jane*, a twenty-five-foot open utility boat, patrolled for forest fires on Raquette Lake in the mid-1920s.

Grocery boats saved people the trouble of going into town frequently for vegetables, milk, and staples. In Long Lake, patrons' orders were filled by the various stores in town and the boxes were taken to the marina providing the service for delivery to camps. Patrons could have orders from Jennings's Liquor Store delivered, as well as their mail, and the all-purpose boat occasionally doubled as tugboat or hearse. Sightseers went along for the ride to see the spectacular view of the Seward Range.[36] Big Moose Lake also had a grocery boat which ran around the lake twice daily during the tourist season. It delivered groceries and took orders for the next day on the morning trip and delivered milk on the afternoon run. It was owned and operated by the village grocery store.

On the Fulton Chain, the Marks and Wilcox grocery outfitted a launch as a floating grocery store, complete with cashier. Their "pickle boat" ran from 1905 through 1939, visiting hotel docks every other day. Private individuals came to the nearest hotel or children's camp dock to pick up their supplies. The boat's 300 feet of shelf space was stocked with lamp wicks, batteries, canned soups, pork chops, and produce. A barrel of pickles stood on the stern deck.[37] There was even occasionally enough business among summer campers on the Fulton Chain for specialty boats. Lenhart's bakery in Old Forge delivered fresh bread and doughnuts by boat for several years, and one year an entrepreneur cruised an ice-cream boat up and down the Chain.[38]

Mailboats served lakeshore residents on many lakes, including the Saranacs, Cranberry, Raquette, Long, and the Fulton Chain. The residents of the Fulton Chain got rural mail delivery just after the turn of the century—earlier than many parts of the region, owing to the influence of Benjamin Harrison, who had a summer home on Second Lake. In 1901 Maurice Callahan of the Fulton Navigation Company won the contract for mail delivery from Old Forge to Inlet. He held the contract until 1929, when W. Donald Burnap, a local resort proprietor, took over. For most of his career, which lasted until 1975, Burnap cruised a route of twenty-two miles seven days a week, from June 1 to October 1, serving as many as 208 patrons.

The Fulton Chain mailboat was staffed by two people, the skipper and the clerk. The cabin was fitted out like a post office, with a pigeonhole for each camp. Before leaving town, the clerk would sort the route's mail, then put the mail into individual bags under way. Each home, camp, and hotel had two mailbags, each labeled with its name—one usually onboard the boat and one at the residence. As the boat

The steam-powered "pickle boat" Mohawk *was drumming up support for the Southern Adirondack Mission on this August 17, 1917, run; on other trips its cabin carried movie posters for the Old Forge theater.* P. 14608.

approached, the skipper sounded the horn to summon someone to the dock. If
nobody appeared the boat continued on. If there was someone on the dock, the skipper drew his port side alongside the dock and the clerk leaned out an open door to
hand the incoming mailbag to the waiting camper with his left hand and take the outgoing mailbag with his right. After 1929 the clerk's door had a waist-high chain across
it to prevent a recurrence of a fatal accident which happened when a clerk fell out of
the door and was crushed between the boat and the dock. Most transfers were made
on the fly—the boat stopped only if there was a large package or if it could not coast
past the dock. The clerk was busy all the time sorting and hand-cancelling the outgoing mail so that it would be ready for the train when they returned to Old Forge.[39]

Even hunting and fishing guides joined the mailmen and grocery-store proprietors
in making use of power boats. In 1910 *MotorBoat* magazine reported that on Lake
Placid,

> Everyone recognizes the necessity of the motorboat and its superiority, but it is inter-
> esting to watch the genuine enthusiasm of the old guides and backwoodsmen whenever
> they see a neatly modeled speed boat cutting through the water. So popular is the gaso-
> lene [*sic*] engine becoming that a number of St. Lawrence skiffs and guide boats have
> been equipped with motors, the 1½-hp. Ferro proving very suitable for this purpose.[40]

All over the country regional boat types were being adapted for power. In Maine
and Massachusetts, dories were turned into inboards. St. Lawrence skiffs were certainly suitable for installation of a motor; up on the river "skiff-putts" became quite
popular around this time. In the Adirondacks, twenty-foot church boats, the extra-
long guideboats, were the ones most often motorized. The motor was mounted in
the middle of the boat, at the widest part of the bottom board, and a long propeller

shaft was run through a stuffing box and was supported outside by a little strut. A rudder operated by tiller ropes was mounted on the stern. According to Charles Keough, the boats "scooted right along, but it took a ten-acre lot to turn them around."[41]

About the same time, fishermen in Wanakena built *The Beast*, a flat-bottomed boat with a tunnel-stern protecting a propeller driven by a single-cylinder Truscott engine. Some guides of the area used it to get up the Oswegatchie, but one of them, Herbert Keith, bemoaned it as a "forerunner of the most destructive device ever invented by man to ruin fishing on the upper Oswegatchie and other rivers" because it brought greater numbers of fishermen upstream, many of whom were not interested in the value of wilderness beyond the fishing.[42]

*   *   *

History does not record whether the builders of *The Beast* were professionals or amateur "backyard" builders. There were plenty of both in the region. As power boats increased in popularity and reliability and decreased in price, many small shops started building the new craft. Firms like that of former guideboat builders Tom George and Herman Bliss, and Jack Rivett, a newcomer to the trade, carried on the Adirondack heritage of boatbuilding in the first two decades of the twentieth century. In addition to the professionals, enthusiastic skippers with "elbow grease and gumption" could build their own boats.

When the editor at *Yachting* spoke of a $35 inboard motorboat that made everyone a "cap'n" he was assuming the "cap'n" was also the boatbuilder. Plans and kits were available from a number of sources. Someone wanting a small launch for her Adirondack camp could, for example, order a knocked-down sixteen-foot "combination" (a boat that could be powered by an engine, oars, or sails) for $34.90 from the Brooks Boat Company of Bay City, Michigan, one of the larger mail-order motorboat companies. This was the price for the hull only, however. The Brooks two-horsepower, single-cylinder engine cost $50. Brooks also sold plans only.[43]

Brooks was also one of the many small firms around the country that sold modestly-priced launches ready to put in the water. There were several such builders in upstate New York alone who sold their craft to Adirondack customers. On Fourth Lake in the 'teens and early 'twenties at least four private camp owners had Oneida Lake Fishing Boats built by Lindley of Canastota. These were sixteen-foot craft powered by three-horsepower motors built by Cady, another Canastota firm. They cost $150, complete.[44]

J. H. Rushton, ever ready to read the market, got into the power boat business in 1882. In that year he built a small steam launch, his first power boat. In 1892 he advertised steam, naphtha, and electric boats in his catalog. About 1902 he ventured into the field of internal combustion with a seventeen-foot-long, thirty-three-inch-wide hull with a fantail stern powered by a two-cylinder, two-cycle engine built by the Tuttle Engine Company of Canastota. Rushton built as he knew best—the boat was basically an all-wood canoe, with steam-bent ribs of the same scantlings as those used in his larger rowboats. The engine was started by a crank on its forward end; the skipper then had to climb over it to sit down and steer. The boat was apparently not a success. Probably only two were built, and in 1903 Rushton emphatically announced in his catalog, "I BUILD NO POWER BOATS OF ANY KIND."

There were other, more successful, powerboat builders on the edge of the Adirondacks. The Lozier Motor Company built high-quality yachts in Plattsburgh for three years around the turn of the century. They sold a set of four to a group of families who built camps on Eagle and Blue Mountain Lakes in 1905. Their chief designer, Frederick Milo Miller, was a Malone man, but they brought their capital and managerial expertise from (and soon returned to) the Midwest.[45]

One of power boating's most famous designers, John L. Hacker, set up shop in Watervliet, near Albany, in the mid-'teens and built fast runabouts powered by Van Blerck engines. Hacker soon returned to his home in the midwest, but the firm changed its name to The Albany Boat Corporation and stayed in business until the Great Depression. *Canny Scot* was built by Hacker's company in Watervliet as the first of a one-design class for Lake George. She could run at twenty-seven miles per hour (a speedboat for 1915), but also made a comfortable runabout. She had a one-man top, storm curtains, cushions, lazy backs, disappearing windshield, and electric lights, and could be throttled low enough for trolling. *MotorBoat* magazine predicted that the class would "do much to increase enthusiasm and promote speed-boat racing on this beautiful lake."[46]

A little further afield was another firm with an energetic dealership program that managed to sell many launches in the Adirondacks. The Fay and Bowen Company, which manufactured the new engine for *Doris*, was located in the Finger Lakes region. There were two Fay and Bowen dealers on Lake Placid alone—the George and Bliss establishment and that of G. M. Richardson. Richardson advertised "Modern Adirondack Power Boats": Fay and Bowen and Niagara hulls, powered by Fay and Bowen engines. "The perfect power plant, as quiet as an electric auto," claimed a 1915 *Adirondack Daily Enterprise* advertisement about the engines.[47] On Lake George by the 1920s there were three Fay and Bowen dealerships. The largest one in the entire country was that of Walter Harris at the southern end of the lake, a fact due perhaps in part to Harris's organization of regattas especially for the brand-name boats. Harris held separate races for each Fay and Bowen model over a course between the Sagamore Hotel and Dome Island.[48]

Within the Adirondack region itself were several powerboat builders, who built not only yachts but commercial vessels as well. They were probably more successful, in fact, with their tour boats and mail boats than they were in competing with larger builders of boats for the pleasure market. Most seem to have done their own design work.

Jack Rivett of Old Forge is one example of an Adirondack boatbuilder who taught himself and designed his own boats. According to W. Donald Burnap, one of his customers, he started building boats in the early 1920s by "taking the measurements he needed" from a commercially-built boat belonging to the Burnap family on Fourth

J. H. Rushton and two workmen test his launch on the Grass River behind the shop, watched by a man driving real horsepower along the bank. P. 36180.

Lake and lengthening and widening these figures. The resulting vessel was forty feet long instead of twenty-five, and six or seven feet wide instead of five. In the winter of 1928–1929 Rivett built a boat for one of the Burnap sons to use in delivering the mail; it was a further modification, a foot and a half wider. "It made quite a little work-up around the bow, drawing it into the bow," Burnap remembered, "but it worked out pretty good. Rivett did the designing as well as building it."[49]

Rivett turned to boatbuilding in 1910 as part of his excursion business. He had purchased a little four-passenger launch with a five-horsepower inboard motor in 1905, from the St. Lawrence County landowner and lumberman A. A. Low, to run passengers between Old Forge and Inlet. Business was so good that he built the thirty-five-foot *Geraldine* from his own design, possibly inspired by St. Lawrence River excursion boats. Rivett eventually built at least five other commercial launches.[50]

Doris's second owners, Tom George and Herman Bliss, were versatile Adirondack boatbuilders. They purchased the boatshop of Albert Billings, a guideboat builder for whom they had both worked, after Billings's death in 1904. There they built all-wood canoes with sawn frames as well as guideboats.[51] Later they took up the internal combustion engine by expanding the shop's boatbuilding facilities to include construction of motorboats. Their close copies of the then popular Chris-Craft boats were known

Jack Rivett in the launch he acquired from A. A. Low.
P. 36113.

around the area as "George and Bliss Specials." Mechanics in the machine shop repaired engines and turned their skills to automobiles in the garage when needed.[52]

Freeman Baker, whose shop stood on Lake Flower in the village of Saranac Lake, ran another all-around livery and boatshop. Baker built and ran at least one large excursion launch, the thirty-five-foot *Bluebird*, as well as inboard raceboats for the locally-popular 151-cubic-inch class. In 1936 he patented an arm-powered sternwheel catamaran, which he offered in child, adult, and tandem models.[53]

The Lake George Boat Company, which built production runabouts beginning in 1935, attracted some national attention. An article in *MotorBoat* in 1936 recorded their ideas for expansion: "Heretofore the company has been making boats only for the summer colony at New York State's most famous lake, but the local enthusiasm for the boat prompted the idea of expanding the sales territory." Their thirty-foot-long runabout complete with cabin was designed for this new market. The company was the winter work of Clarence Livingston, a trained naval architect and livery owner on Harris Bay.[54]

Other Adirondack builders used plans or kits instead of designing their own boats. Brooks offered several plans for raceboats, as well as a fantail-stern launch "adapted to a number of commercial purposes" such as workboat or passenger boat. The cost for the knocked-down boat, which could be built in lengths from thirty to forty-five feet, was $220.65.[55] Melvin A. Brush, another Fulton Chain builder, built at least two boats from plans "from a boat company." His two *U-Go-I-Go*'s were excursion launches and carried forty and fifty-five people or more, respectively.[56]

It is impossible to measure accurately how successful builders like George and Bliss, Baker, and Brush were in selling their boats in the Adirondacks. It is safe to say, however, that they sold few, if any, powerboats outside the immediate area. Even for the Adirondack market they competed with other, larger firms. By the 1920s, it was clear that the center of powerboat manufacture was in the Midwest, particularly in Michigan, close to the center of automobile production.[57]

The great variety of local and regional builders and the launches they built began to disappear in the mid-twenties in the face of competition from much larger, national firms. In Michigan, Christopher Columbus Smith, who had earned the nickname in racing circles of "the Wizard of Algonac" for over a decade of good showings on the national and international circuits, produced his first line of standardized runabouts in 1924. Within five years Chris Smith and Sons controlled one-sixth of the American market. Other builders and designers of raceboats, Gar Wood, John Hacker, and Horace Dodge, built most of the rest of the country's runabouts.

National firms like Chris-Craft were successful not only because of low prices resulting from economies of scale, but because of their wide marketing network. Liveries and dealerships introduced the boats to the public and made purchase convenient. By the 1930s national brands were available throughout the Adirondacks. George and Bliss rented Chris-Crafts, "fine motor boats accommodating 8 to 25 people." They also ran a marina, selling and servicing Chris-Crafts as well as Fay and Bowens.[58]

*   *   *

Not only did the number of builders of inboard launches diminish as boatbuilding for the recreational market became big business, but the rich variety of smaller craft diminished as well with the development of marine motors. In the 1880s there was something to suit every taste, whether it was wilderness cruising or exciting sailing or safe fishing or family picnicking, and these boats varied from region to region. By the time of the Second World War there was a much more uniform boating scene. As John Gardner has observed, "you could stick a gasoline engine in any old tub. Such craft didn't have to be hydrodynamically perfect any more."[59] The perfection of the outboard motor in the 1920s accelerated the trend.

There have been days when one could not commune with Mother Nature without an amount of laborious travel that did much to dull the keen edge of enjoyment. The outboard engine has been one of the great factors in the increasing love of open spaces and the possibility of reaching these places from the marts of trade without labor to which office-bound muscles are not suited. . . . The modern outboard is probably the best example of multum in parvo *that science has perfected.*

—Rudder, 1922[1]

CHAPTER 10

Kickers and the Keen Edge of Enjoyment

In late August of 1924, the Davies family of Ridgewood, New Jersey, loaded up their Buick touring car with all their camping gear and headed for their annual fortnight's camping holiday on the north shore of Blue Mountain Lake. Mr. Davies remarked that they looked like "gypsies going to war." The Buick had no trunk, so everything was either stuffed inside or packed into a wooden box and clamped onto one of the running boards. On the other running board was carefully strapped Mr. Davies's newest piece of equipment: a twin-cylinder, two-horsepower Johnson outboard motor.

Mr. and Mrs. Davies and their nine-year-old son Richard took two days to get to Blue Mountain Lake. They spent the first night with relatives in Schenectady. The road was hard-surfaced as far as Indian Lake, but from then on it was a single-track dirt road. When they finally arrived, they checked in with Chester Stanton, who ran a livery at Merwin's Blue Mountain House, and rented one of Stanton's small "fishing dories." Mr. Davies had read carefully the directions for the Johnson, but he had not had a chance to actually start it. "I can still see him very clearly trying to get that motor started," wrote his son in 1994,

> Turning this valve and twisting that pet-cock and always (or not always) getting one or two puffs and having it go dead. . . . It kept getting later and later, but it finally got going and kept going and off we went. It resulted in our first experience at setting up camp in the dark.[2]

Outboards were rare on Blue Mountain Lake in 1924, and the Davies family attracted attention whenever they ventured out with theirs. These trips away from camp became more frequent once they had the outboard than they had been the previous year. The Davieses became regulars for the morning mail and for the *New York*

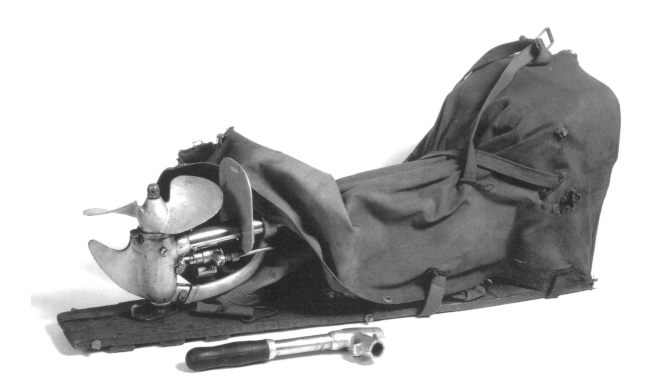

Times, and their fishing excursions increased in frequency and scope. They trolled for lake trout in Blue Mountain Lake and motored over to Utowana Lake, six miles away, for bass, stopping in season to pick raspberries near the head of the Marion River.

*   *   *

Engineers and boatbuilders had tinkered with detachable rowboat motors since the 1890s. The first widely successful developer of the outboard motor was Ole Evinrude. Evinrude, a self-taught engineer and mechanic in Milwaukee, introduced his two-cycle, single-cylinder outboard motor in 1909. Evinrude's success was due not only to the engineering of his "kicker," but to the marketing and advertising skills of his wife and business partner. Bess Evinrude captured the public's imagination with her advertisement for their first outboard, urging "Don't Row! Throw the Oars Away!"[3]

The original Evinrude developed one and one-half horsepower and weighed sixty-two pounds. It did well on the market in part because it was reliable and fairly easy-starting. By the early 1920s the outboard motor industry had progressed tremendously; the best motors were not only easily started but dependable enough to be really successful with the pleasure-boating public. They were light, too, as manufacturers began using aluminum instead of bronze and iron. Indiana's Johnson Brothers introduced their two-cylinder Light Twin outboard in 1922, which weighed only thirty-five pounds.

The outboards of the 'twenties also brought true motorboat speed within range of the average boater. Most kickers of the 'teens were primarily substitutes for rowing: single-cylinder motors that developed about two horsepower and would propel the displacement hull of a standard rowboat at the same speed as an energetic rower, albeit with much less effort. By the mid-1920s the small "detachable rowboat motors" had been joined in liveries and dealerships by big, twin-cylinder engines designed for speed. Johnson became even better known when they introduced their six-horsepower Big Twin on July 4, 1925, and set a new world's outboard speed record of almost fifteen miles per hour.[4]

When outboard motors were basically substitutes for rowing, traditional displacement hulls performed well with them. But boatbuilders working on boats for fast outboard motors ran into the same problems with their hulls as had the builders of fast inboard boats. They responded the same way: by building planing hulls for the more powerful power plants. The Johnson Brothers's 1925 record-breaking motor did so well in part because it was mounted on *Baby Buzz*, a broad-transomed "mono-plane" with a flat bottom aft. By 1926 several builders were producing Baby Buzz models. As with previous national trends in boating, the Baby Buzz fad ran through the Adirondacks. In 1928 the Saranac Lake Boat and Waterways Club had a Baby Buzz class outboard race in its twentieth annual regatta. High speeds did not deter the flappers; Hallie Sheldon, with her Baby Buzz *Baby Joan*, was only one of the women who entered the outboard races at the 1928 Saranac Lake regatta.[5]

Adirondack boatbuilders built some boats designed specifically for outboards, with varying degrees of success. Fred Rice of Saranac Lake, guideboat builder and son of a guideboat builder, built *Gull* for his own use in 1926. She was made just like a

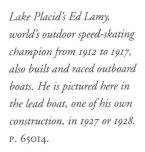

Lake Placid's Ed Lamy, world's outdoor speed-skating champion from 1912 to 1917, also built and raced outboard boats. He is pictured here in the lead boat, one of his own construction, in 1927 or 1928.
P. 65014.

traditional guideboat with the exception of heavier scantlings all around and, as Rice described it, extra length added in the middle to carry a bigger load. He also constructed a wide, heavy transom to carry a four-horsepower outboard motor.[6]

Rice's *Gull* was unique. Willard Hanmer of Saranac Lake, who started building guideboats with his father in the 1920s and continued until his own death in 1962, designed, built, and sold at least several outboard boats. Some were simple flat-bottomed, broad-transomed skiffs. Others had the flat bottoms and broad transoms of standard planing outboards but were built entirely with guideboat construction techniques: they had flat bottom boards, sawn ribs, and smooth-skinned planking of the same scantlings as his guideboats.

Like Hanmer's outboard skiffs, some traditional Adirondack boat types were already well suited to use with an outboard. Flat-bottomed Bisby scows were the first outboards of the Adirondack League Club—on the lake where motorboats were allowed.[7] F. R. Smith and Sons, on Lake George, sold many of their wineglass-transomed Lake George rowboats for use with outboards, although they were a little "touchy" when motorized.[8]

Adirondack boat owners and builders also made modifications—sometimes drastic ones—to existing boats when they wanted to follow Bess Evinrude's advice. There wasn't much buoyancy in the extremely fine end of the average guideboat to support a heavy motor, but some "putt-putters" clamped outboard brackets to their guideboats and mounted a little motor to one side of the stern. The brackets were popular among canoeists, and both canoes and guideboats went fairly well as long as the boat was ballasted forward. Sawing off the pointed stern of a guideboat and adding a transom was another, more drastic, modification to accommodate a motor. This provided a flat surface at the stern for mounting. It also placed the motor on a wider cross-section of boat.[9]

Aspiring outboarders could also build their own boats, as could people who wanted an inboard launch. Journals such as *Popular Mechanics* published kits and plans. The appearance and performance of some of these home-built outboards of the 1920s at the Adirondack League Club can be guessed from their names: *Baby Whale*, *Floating Kidney*, *Tomato Can*.[10]

Ultimately, however, Adirondack builders could not compete in the outboard market with better-capitalized factories that advertised nationally. Most outboard boats used in the Adirondacks were built by firms like Penn Yan and Thompson in upstate New York and some of the Maine builders like the Old Town Canoe Company.

$$*\qquad*\qquad*$$

The real "triumph of internal combustion" as far as Adirondack transportation went, of course, was not marine engines like the Fay and Bowen that powered Lake Placid's *Doris* or the Johnson that drove the Davies's rental boat, but the automobile. The car transformed life and leisure for both residents and visitors in the Adirondacks just as it did in the rest of the country.

Cars were so inexpensive that they were available even to Adirondack residents,

A steamboat pushes the Raquette Lake car ferry between Raquette Lake village and North Point, whence automobilists drove the Old Carthage Road (now the North Point Road) to Long Lake village. P. 45524.

many of whose incomes were marginal. As roads in the region were improved, cars transformed their lives. Like rural folk throughout the nation, Adirondackers rapidly became less isolated because their cars made it possible to drive periodically to villages for shopping, socializing, and schooling. In consequence, smaller communities withered.[11] Places like Deerland, Wevertown, and Faust lost post offices and stores.

Cars also began to change patterns of Adirondack tourism after the First World War. Cars gave tourists freedom to travel when they liked, where they liked. The low cost of automobile ownership made recreational travel cheaper and more accessible—just as had the railroads and steamboats for previous generations. After World War I, the automobile supplanted the train as the principal mode of mass pleasure travel in the country, and in the Adirondacks.[12]

People who either didn't want to vacation in a hotel full of other people or couldn't afford to, took to the roads "gypsying," stopping to camp wherever they wished. Soon commercial and state campgrounds offered amenities like fire rings and safe, running water; in 1920 the New York State Conservation Department opened its first campground on Forest Preserve land in the Adirondacks. By the late twenties automobile tourists had their pick of more and better accommodations as cabin courts sprang up, offering many of the comforts of home along with the privacy and freedom of camping.[13]

Low-cost automobiles created an even bigger revolution in Adirondack tourism than did trains and steamboats, since the new automobile "outers" did not use their

Camp Comfort in Piseco was a typical campground for the "auto-gypsies" of the 1920s.
P. 13780.

cars just to get to the Adirondacks. Many of them used their cars, not boats, as their recreational vehicles once they got here. Comparing the costs of cars and boats perhaps reveals why. In 1908 Henry Ford introduced the Model T as a car for the masses. By 1923 a Ford roadster could be purchased for $260. Contemporary canoes were fairly economical ways of getting out on the water; the Old Town Canoe Company sold its popular eighteen-foot Charles River model canoe for $46. A boater wanting more speed and less effort could outfit herself with a "Standard Outboard" boat from the Penn Yan Boat Company. Powered by Johnson's popular Light Twin outboard, the entire rig would cost $288—more than the cost of a car. At the top of the recreational boat price scale was an inboard launch. A camp owner wanting one for cruising around Lake Placid would have to spend $1,450 for Fay and Bowen's twenty-four-foot Junior Runabout.

The automobile not only increased the numbers of short-term tourists in the Adirondacks but also made it possible for the long-term summer population to grow. With the new mobility afforded by the automobile, people were not restricted to the main waterways and could easily reach more isolated lakes. The Adirondack region is peppered with examples of small- and medium-sized lakes that sprouted rings of camps. Big Wolf Lake in Franklin County, which was developed as a summer colony by lumberman Ferris Meigs starting in 1916, is an example of a group of camps organized into a private association during this period. In the northern Adirondacks, the Northern New York Land Trust sold logged-off lands around Lake Ozonia starting in 1921 to eager buyers from towns in the nearby St. Lawrence valley. The population of summer campers on the lake doubled between 1921 and 1930. The new people were primarily from nearby towns like Hopkinton, Potsdam, and Canton—easily reached by automobile for weekends away.[14]

*   *   *

Although getting around in the Adirondacks became easier for vacationers as use of the automobile increased, it was several decades before they routinely brought their boats with them. Until the mid-1930s wide sheets of steel were not available and car tops were constructed with an insert of waterproofed fabric. The fabric tops would not support a boat, nor were roof racks widely available. Likewise, it wasn't until the late 'twenties that passenger cars were powerful enough to pull trailers. Trailering a boat was not even an option for most until then; nor does it seem that even afterwards many people wanted to tow their boats. The State of New York did not start constructing boat ramps onto publicly-accessible waters in the Adirondacks until 1960.

Even when people could cartop their boats, many found the boats of the day too heavy to lift very high. The Penn Yan Boat Company in New York's Finger Lakes region introduced their popular Car Top model outboard boat in 1936 to address this

Mr. Fisher looks proud of the rig he has engineered to carry his wood-canvas canoe on top of his Ford Model A coupe to the Adirondacks about 1930.
P. 50564.

problem. The "Car Topper" was carefully designed to fit most cars and be handled by most people; the gunwales were at a standard width to fit on a car roof, and the sixty-pound weight was supposedly just right for a couple to load. "*Actual tests* show that the light end of a 60 pound boat (*about 25 pounds*) is the *absolute maximum* that a woman can be expected to handle," Penn Yan claimed in its brochure.[15]

Standard canoes were somewhat more portable, but even so, Penn Yan felt it profitable to introduce an "Auto Canoe" in the 1920s that was short enough to be strapped to the running board of a car. It was ten feet long, thirty-four and a half inches wide, and weighed only thirty-eight pounds, light enough to "be handled like a market basket."[16]

Vacationers and residents alike used outboard motorboats in the same ways in which they used inboard launches. Both recreation and work became increasingly motorized by the cheap, reliable outboards. Why *not* throw the oars away?

When her husband brought home the Johnson outboard motor he proposed to use on their camping trips to Blue Mountain Lake, Mrs. Davies disapproved. She worried that the noise of the machine would "defile the wilderness." She soon came around, however, perhaps remembering, as *Rudder* put it, the "amount of laborious travel" it had taken to get to Callahan's store for groceries or to Utowana Lake for bass fishing. She was typical of many vacationers.

By 1938, when this picture was taken, the guideboat was becoming a rare boat. Most people preferred wood-canvas canoes or outboard boats for their small craft.

P. 47529.

is designed to provide a handle for easy carrying.

In Summer Homes

NOWHERE is the popularity of the Evinrude more in evidence than at the summering places. Run wherever you like—distances are nothing. You go fast and your ride is always cool and refreshing because the motor does all the work.

With an Evinrude you can go where you like—across the lake to dance or dine, over to the island for a picnic or beach party, or to town to bring guests or supplies. The whole family will enjoy the Evinrude; mother or even the youngsters can "run 'er."

The Adirondack Forest Preserve provided many opportunities for families to camp for a few weeks or the summer. An outboard motor made it easy to haul gear back and forth from town to camp or around the lake. In 1916 the state authorized private construction of wooden tent platforms on Forest Preserve land. The Saranac Lakes were especially popular with platform tent campers, who sometimes built several platforms and erected clusters of tents, or even installed gas stoves, lights, and ice-boxes. Others camped on the Fulton Chain, or on state land on lakes like Indian Lake or Long Lake. Even if they came by car they might not be able to carry all their gear; if they came by train they certainly had to find a local resident or business that would store their equipment for them between seasons. Until cartopping and trailering became possible, their boats were part of the equipment to be stored unless, like the Davies family, they rented a boat once they got to the mountains.[17]

With the lightweight outboards of the 1920s, cruising by outboard canoe became possible. As in the days of the decked sailing canoes, probably not many people traveled through the central Adirondack region with a motor because they would have to double the carries in order to get boat, motor, and gear to the other side. A 1958 outboard cruising guide did recommend Lake Champlain and Lake George to outboard cruisers, however.[18]

James Fynmore, Speed Boat
Racing *[on Indian Lake]*.
P. 15993.

An outboard motor saves a
good deal of work for these
two men, possibly guides,
with their impressive take of
whitetail deer. The boat is a
modified St. Lawrence skiff.
P. 61811.

Starting in the mid-1920s, outboard racing became increasingly popular. Local regattas featured outboard races, and spectators of the Gold Cup races on Lake George in the 1920s were treated to outboard races between heats.

Just as Adirondackers had taken up the inboard engine in the early years of the twentieth century, they appropriated the cheaper and more versatile outboards for caretaking chores, hunting, and guiding. But even as the price of outboards came down, so did the disposable income of most Americans, whether potential Adirondack vacationers or Adirondack residents. Human-powered craft remained the most common type on the waters of the north woods until after the Great Depression. In the 1950s, as the nation recovered from the Depression and the Second World War, pleasure-boat traffic picked up again. As when canoe builders began to exploit wood-canvas construction methods around 1900, new technologies fueled a boom in recreational boating.

Nothing is more central to the American boatbuilding tradition than a readiness to try new things and to accept worthy innovations when they appear. —John Gardner, 1984[1]

The rapid growth of boating on reservoirs and lakes may result in an overuse problem within a few years . . . and the boating experience may degenerate to that of driving a car at rush hour. —Echelberger and Moeller, 1973[2]

CHAPTER II

Hot-Rudders, Trailer-Sailors, and the Wooden Boat Revival

The Long Haul on the Canoe Trip. *Boonville photographer James Fynmore took this photo of a party from an Adirondack boy's camp crossing a carry with an aluminum canoe for an exhibit at the 1964 World's Fair.* P. 15932.

Over the Memorial Day weekend in 1944, as the Allied Forces in Europe massed for the invasion of Normandy, William J. Hoffman took a short fishing vacation in the Adirondacks. Hoffman was chief tool engineer for the Grumman Aircraft Engineering Corporation on Long Island, a company that was busy building airplanes for the Navy. From Inlet he and his friend Len Harwood flew into Limekiln Lake. There the fast, modern phase of their trip ended. Harwood had an aged, thirteen-foot wood-canvas Old Town canoe which they used on Limekiln Lake. After a few days they decided to try their luck on Squaw Lake, so they shouldered the boat. The Old Town had been advertised as a fifty-pounder when new, but Hoffman felt sure it must have weighed twice that by the time he reached Squaw Lake. The boat may have soaked up water, and probably had a few extra coats of paint over the years, and perhaps the black flies were particularly bad that year on a particularly muddy carry. In any case, Hoffman decided on the spot that what the country needed was a lighter canoe.

Although he was not familiar with canoe construction, Hoffman was very familiar with the technology his company was using to build aluminum airplanes. Sitting by the campfire on Squaw Lake, he studied the shape of the canoe and decided that it would be comparatively simple to draw two halves out of aluminum and then rivet them at the keel. When he returned to the factory Hoffman worked up a thirteen-foot prototype aluminum canoe which weighed thirty-eight pounds—little more than half the actual weight of the new Old Town thirteen-footer he purchased for a model.

With the help of Russell Bontecou, an Alcoa employee, Hoffman worked further on the design of his aluminum canoe, ultimately modifying it beyond any similarity to the Old Town model except length. The manufacturing process was the first major

207

hurdle; an aluminum canoe could not be formed to the same shape in the ends as a wooden canoe, so the metal boat had a blunter bow and stern. Hoffman and Bontecou reduced the sheer and increased the freeboard to come up with a safer-looking design they felt would be popular with a general public.

Hoffman's supervisors were intrigued with his work. Leroy Grumman no doubt was beginning to wonder how he could keep production up at his factory once the military contracts stopped coming in, and an improved canoe seemed as if it might help do the trick. As soon as peace was declared, Grumman gave Hoffman a 20,000-square-foot area in the Bethpage plant to produce canoes. By the end of 1945 the factory had ninety-five orders; by the end of the next year 10,000 orders were on the books. By 1947 Grumman was the nation's largest canoe manufacturer.[3] Within a few years Grumman moved canoe production from Long Island to a larger facility in Marathon, New York.

At about the same time as Grumman was developing aluminum into the country's most popular material for canoes, other entrepreneurs were adapting fiberglass, another new technology, to small craft production. Fiberglass had become commercially available in 1948, right after World War II, but boatbuilders took a few years to realize the great advantages of the material for watercraft in both production and

Homer Dodge, called "the dean of American canoeing" in the 1960s and 1970s, competed in the Hudson River Whitewater Derby well into his eighties. Born in Ogdensburg in 1887, he had a lifelong love of the St. Lawrence River. In 1956, just before construction of the St. Lawrence Seaway began, Dodge ran the Long Sault Rapids in an open Grumman, the only person on record to have conquered the rapids in an open boat. In this photo, taken by W. Grishkot for the Whitewater Derby Supplement of the Warrensburg–Lake George News (May 2, 1974), he runs the 17th annual race.

maintenance: fiberglass was virtually care-free and could be mass-produced by unskilled labor in about one quarter of the man-hours needed for a wooden boat. By the mid-1950s the fiberglass boat industry had taken off.[4] Fiberglass was more successful as a boatbuilding material for outboard boats and sailboats than for canoes. Although sturdy and cheap, and having the potential for light weight, production fiberglass boats weighed twenty to twenty-five percent more than their aluminum counterparts.

Post-war prosperity fueled the recreation industry all over the country. Canoe manufacturers began courting not only the traditional audience of those with experience in the out-of-doors, but also a more general public not familiar with small craft. Stability and sturdiness were, to many, more important in a canoe than the fine lines, traditional appearance, and handling characteristics which took experience to appreciate. Price was also a consideration; factory-built aluminum and fiberglass boats were even cheaper than the products of the big wood-canvas building shops. In 1947 a seventeen-foot Old Town Otca model wood-canvas canoe weighed eighty-five pounds and cost $199 in the highest grade. A contemporary Grumman of the same length weighed sixty-seven pounds (fifty-three in the lightweight version) and cost $157.

The people who came to the Adirondacks to recreate in the post-war boom were freed by the automobile from depending on the waterways for transportation. The region's lakes and rivers became playgrounds instead of highways. Boats increased in numbers but decreased in variety as mass production, synthetic materials, and the influence of the gasoline engine on boat design took effect.

Guideboats practically vanished from public sight. When the guideboat scholar Kenneth Durant began his research in the late 1950s he had trouble finding boats to study, and those he did find were mostly in the boathouses of private preserves like the Adirondack League Club. Aluminum and fiberglass had completed the popularization of canoes begun by wood and canvas at the turn of the century.

*   *   *

The New York State Conservation Commission both responded to the increasing numbers of canoeists and encouraged them. Starting in 1919 the Commission began a series of recreation circulars describing various aspects of state-owned lands for recreationists. One of the first, *Adirondack Canoe Routes*, described the central valley route famous since the days of Joel Tyler Headley, the 125-mile trip from Old Forge to Saranac Lake.[5] The Commmission also built lean-tos on popular canoe routes, just as it was building lean-tos on well-used automobile and hiking routes. In 1925 there were twelve open camps listed in *Adirondack Canoe Routes*. By 1939 the number had doubled. The state also developed campsites without lean-tos for the growing numbers of canoeists. In 1954 1,480 canoeists camped at Alger Island on Fourth Lake and 986 at the Forked Lake campsite. Just ten years later the numbers had increased to 5,501 at Alger Island and 3,347 at Forked Lake.[6]

By the early 1970s Grumman was building 20,000 canoes each year. They were as ubiquitous in the Adirondacks as guideboats had been a century before. Cross-

country cruisers carried them around Buttermilk Falls and Raquette Falls and across the Indian Carry on their way from Old Forge to Saranac Lake; liveries rented them for day-long fishing trips; and children's camps and housekeeping cottages had fleets for their guests. The resonant "boink" of spruce paddle hitting aluminum had joined the burble of inboard engines, the roar of outboards, and the call of the loon as the sounds of the Adirondack waterways.

In 1975 the state's recreation circulars were joined by a major guidebook devoted to the canoe waters of the northern half of the Adirondacks. Paul Jamieson's *Adirondack Canoe Waters: North Flow*, a response to the great numbers of cruising canoeists in the region, was a model for books of the sort.[7] It went far beyond the recreation circulars in giving information on the rich natural and human history of the region in addition to tips on where to put in and where to camp. The year after Jamieson's book appeared, the number of state lean-tos on Adirondack canoe routes had jumped from the twenty-four available before the Second World War to nearly fifty.

Increased popularity of canoe cruising was not the only result of the post-war boom in recreational boating. Several races for non-powered craft began in the 1950s and 1960s as well. The Hudson River Whitewater Derby was first held in May, 1957, with runs from North River to Riparius as well as shorter slalom courses. This race, with its course strewn with rocks, was a competition for craft of modern, durable canoe materials like aluminum and fiberglass, not for wooden boats.

Rubber was another modern boatbuilding material which made its appearence in the Adirondacks in the post-war period. Whitewater aficionadoes across the country were adopting army surplus rubber rafts for river running, and an adventurous group from the North Woods Club began rafting the Hudson from Newcomb to North Creek in the 1950s. It wasn't until the spring of 1979, however, that commerical companies began taking paying passengers down the river. For a few years they enjoyed only a short, two-week season, but soon the town of Indian Lake was cooperating with a release of water from its dam on the Indian River, allowing a longer rafting period. Commercial rafting followed on the Sacandaga, the Moose, and the Black Rivers, and by 1995 an average of 47,000 people annually were being guided down Adirondack rivers on rubber rafts.

Even though traditional wooden boats were fast disappearing from general use, a small group of competitors revived guideboat racing. They were led by Howard

Robert F. Kennedy running the rapids of the Hudson River Gorge on Whitewater Derby weekend, 1967. The kayak is in the collections of the Adirondack Museum, entry 13.

Seaman, a Long Lake native who returned to his home town after service in World War II. When he wasn't running his contracting business, he coached younger rowers and competed in both guideboat races and war canoe races. Seaman had little time for working out, but he felt that he kept in shape in his daily work; many of his fellow racers rose at dawn to practice before going to their regular jobs. By the 1960s several central Adirondack towns sponsored war canoe and guideboat races. The best-known competition became the Willard Hanmer Guideboat Race, begun on Hanmer's death in 1962 and rowed on Lake Flower and the Saranac River each Fourth of July weekend. By the late 'seventies and early 'eighties racers could also compete in a six-mile whitewater course on the East Branch of the Ausable River, a forty-four-mile race from Long Lake to Tupper Lake, and a three-day, ninety-mile competition through the central valley from Old Forge to Saranac Lake.

Post-war prosperity and synthetic materials increased the number of power boats as well as canoes in the Adirondacks. The fleets of small inboards and outboards that motored out of boathouses were joined by transient boaters. "Since 1946, the number of power boats in use on New York State waters has more than doubled," wrote a consultant for the New York State Division of Motorboats in 1960.

> The boom in boating is due largely to the application of modern, mass production methods and technological advances to the boating industry. . . . While the use of such materials as aluminum and fiberglass have brought new ease of manufacture and hull maintenance, perhaps the greatest revolution has occurred in the development of power plants, especially the outboard motor. . . . Topping even these advances is the growth

Posters announcing various boating events and competitions. AML

Howard Seaman and his son John race down Long Lake in 1971. Photograph by Peter Lemon. p. 255).

of lightweight, easy-to-handle trailers, giving rise to an armada of "trailer-sailors" who, in the span of a few hours, can hitch their boats behind the family car, journey to a nearby lake or stream, launch, take a spin and return with ease.[8]

As early as 1930, upwards of 10,000 people annually picnicked and camped on the Lake George islands, many of whom got there by motorboat. By 1962 the number had reached 31,757, and the state had built "cruiser docks" at Log Bay, on Long Island, and on other islands with rough shorelines.[9]

The docks on the Lake George islands were part of an effort on the part of the state to catch up with the rapid increase in the number of trailer-sailors. "Frankly, the recent expansion of our inland mosquito fleet of trailer-borne outboards and car-tops has taken most of us by surprise," wrote Roy Irving, a state educator, in the 1958 *Conservationist*.[10] State campsites such as Rollins Pond and Lewey Lake provided limited access for power boats to public waters in the late 1950s, and in 1960 the state began building boat launch ramps in the Adirondacks. Individuals and private groups like the Saranac Lake Boat and Waterways Association had been marking channels and hazards since the 1920s, but it wasn't until the mid-1960s that the state began to take over the job of setting out adequate, standardized buoys. The Conservation Department's goal was not only safe boating but encouragement of people to try new, unfamiliar waters and to reduce the concentration of boaters in a few popular areas.

Construction of boat launches and the marking of hazards were part of a general awareness in the Conservation Department of not only the popularity of power boating but the dangers posed by the increasing fleet. In 1959 the legislature created a Division of Motor Boats to address what Charles Cusick, writing in *The New York State Conservationist*, had called "The Problem With Boats."

> With the increase in the number of cottages and camps and the even greater increase in popularity and availability of boats and motors, we now find 250 boats on a lake where once there were only 50. . . . Not only does every camper own and operate a boat for one purpose or another, but we also find great numbers of boats being brought to our lakes and launched from trailers. . . . The whole thing adds up to a scene of confusion, resentment and a growing conflict of interest which must be brought to an end if the equitable enjoyment of our lakes as places for healthy recreation is to be preserved.[11]

James Fynmore, Water Skiing in the Adirondacks, *1964.* P. 15916.

Cusick cited fishermen angry because their privacy was violated and the fishing ruined, dangers to "little tikes" and other swimmers, campers whose temper and di-

James Fynmore, Boy's
Camp, *1964.* P. 15934.

gestion were ruined by the noise, and property owners objecting to shoreline erosion from wakes. Cusick particularly blamed water-skiing, writing that it was only after that sport became popular that people began to demand some regulation of boating. Boating accidents also made headlines, especially after the Division of Motor Boats began requiring accident reports in 1960.

A legislative committee studied the situation in 1957 and found that substandard watercraft and ignorance of basic boat handling and safety were chiefly responsible for the accident rates. In 1960 the Conservation Department began registering pleasure boats. It also set up a Public Information Section and developed a Young Boatman's Safety Course. Laws such as those requiring a Safety Course certificate by anyone under fourteen operating a boat and one requiring two people in any boat pulling a water skier were passed, and speed limits established for restricted or populated waterways. The numbers of power boats on the water continued to increase, but the accident rate began to fall.

The government also responded to the conflict between power boaters and skippers of quieter craft. The State Land Use Master Plan of 1972 established a category of wilderness area in which no motorboats were allowed. The first of these, set aside as an antidote to the tremendously popular Fish Creek-Rollins Pond campsite, was the St. Regis Canoe Area. In addition, no power boats were allowed on river segments classified as scenic or in wilderness areas.[12]

Willard Hanmer cuts ribs on his bandsaw, 1961. Photograph by James Fynmore. P. 10370.

*　　*　　*

As power boats of fiberglass and aluminum became more numerous, the numbers of builders of wooden boats diminished almost to the vanishing point. The situation was the same in the Adirondacks as it was all over the country. Rushton's business had gone under during the First World War. One of Rushton's workmen, Everett "Cyclone" Brown, had taken the molds for the Indian Girl to his farm on the DeKalb Road when the boatshop closed, and he built Indian Girl canoes into the 1930s. In 1926 J. H. Rushton's half-brother Judd had sold the shop itself to a farmer who tore it down and built a dairy barn with the lumber. The patterns were burned for kindling. Lewis Grant lived until 1960. He built his last guideboat in 1934, although he built flat-bottomed outboard boats into the 1950s and continued to do repair work on his boats and those of his father.

Willard Hanmer of Saranac Lake was one of the few Adirondack boatbuilders who hung on into the 1960s and the only one who continued to build guideboats. He kept his shop going not only by building skiffs and outboard boats in addition to guideboats, but by mechanizing every possible phase of boat production. "Machinery was something special to Willard Hanmer," wrote John Gardner. "If it was possible to mechanize an operation that was formerly done by hand, he worked out a procedure and a jig to do it with machinery. His shop was full of jigs, some of them ingenious but far from automatic."[13]

One of Hanmer's better systems was the one he used in getting out ribs. When he and his father, Theodore, had cut and sanded the ribs by hand, it took them a day and a half to produce the framing for a guideboat; by cutting the ribs with a band-saw, finishing them with a power shaper fitted with a forty-five-degree cutter, then sanding them on a drum grooved to produce just the round he wanted, Willard could do them alone in half a day. Hanmer modified his guideboat design somewhat to accommodate his use of power tools. For example, he did not "back out," or hollow the inside of his planks to fit the curve of the ribs.

* * *

Although the building of boats died out in the Adirondacks, repair, servicing, and running them for various purposes continued to supply Adirondackers with cash. As people increasingly brought their own boats into the region, the livery business declined, but marinas equipped with gas pumps, mechanics, and facilities for seasonal hauling and storage found ready customers. There remained some camps inaccessible by road (on Upper St. Regis Lake, for example, and on parts of Raquette and Long Lakes) which still needed service by water. When an addition to a camp was built, the local contractor loaded his gasoline-powered excavating equipment onto a barge

J. S. Apperson, Delivering Garbage to French Point (Lake George), *1953.*
P. 48788.

John Gardner made a careful study of the museum's Grant guideboat Virginia (entry 101) between 1959 and 1963. The results were published in Outdoor Maine in 1960 and as an appendix to Kenneth and Helen Durant's The Adirondack Guide-Boat in 1980. Photograph by Helen Durant, MS 80-3, AML.

and towed it down the lake, and caretakers hauled garbage by boat from private camps and public campsites.[14]

Willard Hanmer died in 1962, and with him, it must have seemed, died the Adirondack boatbuilding industry. Nobody watching would have been surprised, for the building of small wooden boats nationwide was moribund. By the end of the decade there were no wooden boats in the New York Boat Show, perhaps the country's premier showcase for recreational watercraft.[15] But as people all over the country planted petunias in their old wooden skiffs and took to the water in new

Kenneth Durant rows his Warren Cole guideboat before giving it to the Adirondack Museum (entry 69). Photograph by Helen Durant, MS 80-3, AML.

aluminum and fiberglass outboards, there was a quickening of interest in traditional types of small craft. As it had been during the great flowering of boat construction and use in the late nineteenth century, the Adirondack region was a center in the new era of small-craft construction and study.

Since the 1930s, Howard I. Chapelle, a naval architect and self-trained historian, had been documenting and writing about America's rich heritage of small craft. His stated objective was to open the eyes of the recreational boating public to America's boating past so that yachtsmen might find boats better suited to their home waters and tastes than the mass-produced craft used by almost everyone across the country. Chapelle's two major popular works, *Boatbuilding* (1941) and *American Small Sailing Craft* (1951) documented traditional boats as well as boatbuilding.[16]

In the 1950s Chapelle was joined by others writing about and documenting traditional small craft. John Gardner, who had completed a master's degree in education at Columbia in the depths of the Depression and then went to work in the boatyards of Massachusetts, began writing articles about small craft for the *Maine Coast Fisherman* in 1951. A few of his earliest essays were about the Whitehall boat. These were read by a recently-retired journalist, Kenneth Durant, the son of Prospect House proprietor Frederick Clark Durant. Kenneth Durant had spent his summers at the family's Camp Cedars on Forked Lake and had grown up rowing guideboats. In the late 1950s Durant realized that the guideboat was a vanishing breed, and he began research into the history of the craft. Durant's query to Gardner about Whitehall origins for the guideboat was the beginning of a long and fruitful relationship.

In 1957 the Adirondack Museum opened in Blue Mountain Lake. It was conceived by its founder, mining company executive Harold K. Hochschild, as a regional museum exploring all aspects of man's relationship to the Adirondacks, so boating was naturally an important part of the story. From the museum's inception, Durant worked closely with the first director, Robert Bruce Inverarity, and in 1958 the museum mounted an exhibit of guideboats. For the next fourteen years Durant continued to study the Adirondack guideboat, helping the museum acquire many fine examples of the craft as well as tools, patterns, accessories, and a great deal of archival material. Durant died before he had finished his research to his satisfaction, but his wife, the internationally-known cinematographer Helen van Dongen Durant, carried on the work. The result was the publication in 1980 of *The Adirondack Guide-Boat*, one of the country's finest and most complete studies of a regional boat type.[17]

Durant was part of a new movement. Interest in wooden boats continued to grow, in the Adirondacks and in the rest of the world. What later became known as "the wooden boat revival," a reaction against mass-production and machinery-made goods, grew out of the 1960s. Chapelle, Gardner, and Durant helped give the revival its scholarly underpinnings. Magazines (particularly *WoodenBoat*, founded in Maine in 1974) publicized the movement. Schools in traditional boatbuilding both fueled it and helped resurrect forgotten skills and boat types; Mystic Seaport Museum hired John Gardner and began offering wooden boatbuilding classes in 1969, and in 1972 an ex-Outward Bound instructor named Lance Lee started an apprentice program at the Maine Maritime Museum.

In 1975 the Adirondack Museum held a conference to assess the state of the guideboat building business and to give builders an opportunity to exchange ideas and experiences. John Gardner gave an introductory address, and ten builders attended who were interested in construction of Adirondack boats. Only seven of those were trying to make a living in the boat business, and most had other sources of income. None had been very prolific.

Nine of the builders attending the 1975 Adirondack Museum conference used traditional construction in their boats. The tenth, Dick Shew of South Bristol, Maine, advocated the use of ribs made by laminating thin strips of spruce with epoxy. He was seconded by John Gardner, who advocated the use of glued strip planking as well, in order to reduce the cost of the boat and make it more competitive in the small-craft market, but most of the builders present preferred traditional methods.

In subsequent years the Adirondack region participated fully in the wooden boat revival. Carl Hathaway, who had taken over Hanmer's shop in 1962, began giving courses in guideboat construction that were sponsored by nearby North Country Community College. Some guideboat builders adopted modern technology for parts of their boats, producing guideboats with laminated ribs, strip planking, or fiberglass hulls. As this book is written, there are fifteen shops in or near the Adirondacks building small craft suitable for use in the region. Ten of them use primarily traditional materials and designs. Four build boats primarily of wood but of a new design or with the extensive use of modern technology like epoxy laminations for ribs. Their output

Olmstedville builder Peter Hornbeck with one of his pack canoes on a pack frame, 1993. Courtesy Peter Hornbeck.

ranges from a few boats over twenty years to forty to sixty in a decade. Not surprisingly, those who use some modern technology have fared best.

The fifteenth builder, Peter Hornbeck of Olmstedville, is the most modern in construction and the most successful in sales. He has built over a thousand boats since going into business in 1973. His boats are of modern materials but traditional North Country design. He builds guideboats and has even made a mold for a Rushton Princess model decked sailing canoe, but his most popular models are versions of Rushton's *Wee Lassie* and *Sairy Gamp*. He can supply hardware for mounting these small canoes on an aluminum frame backpack, in a modern version of the carrying yoke used by nineteenth century Adirondack guides.

Hornbeck's boats are fiberglass and Kevlar, the latter just one of several synthetic materials boat manufacturers have popularized since the early 'seventies. In 1977 the outdoor equipment manufacturing giant Coleman introduced a canoe made of high-density polyethylene that had the primary virtue of being inexpensive. It quickly became the "Model T of the industry," despite flexibility which made the bottom "oil-can," or ripple, as it went through the water. Other materials were higher priced but performed better. The Old Town Canoe Company, the most successful makers of wood-canvas canoes, was only one company that began making canoes of Acrylonitrile Butadiene Styrene (ABS), a hard rubber product which sheaths a layer of foam. It was rigid and performed well in whitewater as well as flatwater, but it was expensive—$200–$250 more than fiberglass or aluminum canoes in the mid-'seventies. Kevlar 49, a Du Pont product supplied in cloth form, was even more expensive but produced a better performing boat. Kevlar was durable and could be formed to finer lines than ABS, which is vacuum-molded. It was also light in weight; a seventeen-foot polyethylene boat might weigh eighty pounds, and ABS and aluminum seventy to seventy-five, but a Kevlar boat of the same length would weigh only fifty-five to sixty pounds.[18]

Although people in the Adirondacks still use the waterways for recreation in great numbers, there are many more attractions competing for their attention than there were a century ago. In the late twentieth century they must consciously choose to take a boat to get through the region; everyone comes and goes at least part of the way by road. It is perfectly possible to take an Adirondack vacation and have little or no contact with the water. One may shop in outlet stores, play mini-golf, dine in gourmet restaurants, ride water slides at amusement parks and generally participate in any number of activities found in any other resort area in the country.

In the preface to his *Adirondack Canoe Waters: North Flow*, Paul Jamieson commented on the decline in the importance of Adirondack waters for small boating and their decline in importance as travel corridors as the automobile changed American life. "But the network of waters is still there," he continued. "The past can be recovered. Many Adirondack rivers are authentically wild. . . . In re-exploring this network, I have often felt like the city dweller who began new life in the sticks: I have seen the past and it works."[19]

Although the great variety of small craft of the late nineteenth century is gone, its heritage continues. The boating past does work for many who live in or visit the Adirondacks. It worked for Christine Jerome, a writer who in 1990 bought a Lost Pond canoe, Peter Hornbeck's version of *Sairy Gamp*, and retraced most of Nessmuk's 266-mile, 1883 trip. The experience gave her an appreciation for Adirondack history which turned the necklace of lakes along her route into a necklace of stories, and also a love of canoeing, which "takes us to places where silence calms the spirit and where perspective returns."[20]

The past also works for those who enjoy flying down Long Lake in front of a 115-horsepower outboard motor, silver glitter embedded in a purple gel-coat replacing the mahogany aesthetic of *El Lagarto*, traveling at *El Lagarto* speeds, blue sky and white clouds wheeling overhead, deep green forest flashing past on either side.

The past works for antique-boat enthusiasts, who rescue cedar relics from under porches and up in haylofts, clean out the remains of generations of squirrels, and spend years in loving restoration, then paddle their glowing canoes at every regatta and show they can find.

The past works for those who enjoy the instant camaraderie of the mile-plus carry around Raquette Falls on a summer Sunday, when the north-bound stream of paddlers commiserates with the south-bound stream about the length of the carry and shyly but proudly tells of a beaver they saw just downstream. "The forest makes friends of all," wrote Alfred Billings Street in 1860.[21]

And the past works for those who travel in the spirit of Verplanck Colvin and his guides and carry their canoes the third of a mile into Colvin's Smith's Lake, now Lake Lila, to float at twilight on the glass-calm lake suspended between sky and sky, listening to the haunting cry of a loon.

Notes

INTRODUCTION
This Venice of America

1. Samuel Eliot Morison, *The European Discovery of America: The Northern Voyages* (New York: Oxford University Press, 1971), 389–390, 410–415.

2. Lewis Evans, "Analysis" in Lawrence Henry Gipson, *Lewis Evans* (Philadelphia: Historical Society of Pennsylvania, 1939), 11.

3. Thomas Pownall, *A Topographical Description of the Dominions of the United States of America*, ed. Lois Mulkearn (Pittsburgh: University of Pittsburgh Press, 1949), 51.

4. James Fenimore Cooper, *The Last of the Mohicans* (New York: Bantam, 1981), 208, 213.

5. Joel Tyler Headley, *The Adirondack; or, Life in the Woods*, introduction by Philip G. Terrie (New York: Baker and Scribner, 1849; reprint, Harrison, N.Y.: Harbor Hill Books, 1982), x–xi.

6. Harold K. Hochschild, *Lumberjacks and Rivermen in the Central Adirondacks, 1850–1950* (Blue Mtn. Lake, N.Y.: The Adirondack Museum, 1962), 40.

7. Benson J. Lossing, *The Hudson, From the Wilderness to the Sea* (New York: Virtue and Yorston, 1866), 21. Ted Aber and Stella King, *History of Hamilton County* (Lake Pleasant, N.Y.: Great Wilderness Books, 1965), 750.

8. On the establishment, function, and accomplishments of the New York Natural History Survey in the Adirondacks, see Philip G. Terrie, *Forever Wild: A Cultural History of Wilderness in the Adirondacks* (Syracuse: Syracuse University Press, 1994), 27–43. On the naming of the region and Mount Marcy, see Russell M. L. Carson, *Peaks and People of the Adirondacks* (Glens Falls, N.Y.: Adirondack Mountain Club, 1986), 8–10, 55–58.

9. Ebenezer Emmons, "Fifth Annual Report of Ebenezer Emmons, M. D. of the Survey of the Second Geological District," *New York State Assembly Document 150* (Feb. 17, 1841), 114–115.

10. Emmons, 119.

11. Emmons, 120.

12. Emmons, 128.

13. In "Nature" (1836), Emerson had written, "In the wilderness, I find something more dear and connate than in streets and villages," advancing the familiar romantic distinction between nature and civilization. Ralph Waldo Emerson, *The Complete Works of Ralph Waldo Emerson* (Centenary Edition, Boston: Houghton, Mifflin, 1903–04), I: 10.

14. See Hans Huth, *Nature and the American: Three Centuries of Changing Attitudes* (Berkeley: University of California Press, 1957), 102–128.

15. See Philip G. Terrie, "Urban Man Confronts the Wilderness: The Nineteenth-Century Sportsman in the Adirondacks," *Journal of Sport History* 5, no. 3 (Winter 1978): 7–20.

16. On the publishing history of Headley's *The Adirondack*, see my Introduction to the Harbor Hill edition. The last edition to appear in Headley's lifetime was published by Charles Scribner's Sons in 1882. On the rituals, values, and aesthetics of the romantic travelers, see Terrie, *Forever Wild*, 44–67.

17. Headley, *The Adirondack*, 167–68.

18. Alfred Lee Donaldson, *A History of the Adirondacks* (New York: Century, 1921), 1: 292–304.

19. Ralph Waldo Emerson, "The Adirondacs: A Journal Dedicated to My Fellow Travellers in August, 1858," *May-Day and Other Poems* (Boston: Ticknor and Fields, 1867), 41–62. For a full account of Emerson's encounter with the wilderness, see Paul F. Jamieson, "Emerson in the Adirondacks," *New York History* 39 (July 1958): 215–237.

20. William H. H. Murray, *Adventures in the Wilderness; or, Camp-Life in the Adirondacks* (Blue Mtn. Lake, N.Y.: The Adirondack Museum; Syracuse: Syracuse University Press, 1970).

21. Warder H. Cadbury, *Introduction to Adventures in the Wilderness*, 11–75.

22. Paul Russell Cutright, *Theodore Roosevelt: The Making of a*

Conservationist (Urbana: University of Illinois Press, 1985), 34–37.

23. David Strauss, "Toward a Consumer Culture: 'Adirondack Murray' and the Wilderness Vacation," *American Quarterly* 39 (Summer 1987): 270–286. Ann Douglas, *The Feminization of American Culture* (New York: Avon Books, 1977). T. J. Jackson Lears, *No Place of Grace: Antimodernism and the Transformation of American Culture, 1880–1920* (New York: Pantheon, 1981).

24. *First Annual Report of the Commissioners of State Parks of the State of New York. Transmitted to the Legislature May 15, 1873* (Albany: Weed, Parsons & Co., 1874), 21. The members of the Commission were former governor Horatio Seymour, William A. Wheeler, Franklin B. Hough, Patrick H. Agan, William B. Taylor, George Raynor, and Verplanck Colvin. Colvin is generally thought to have been the primary author of the report.

25. See Lears, *No Place of Grace*, 47–58.

26. See Peter J. Schmitt, *Back to Nature: The Arcadian Myth in Urban America* (New York: Oxford University Press, 1969), and Ralph H. Lutts, *The Nature Fakers: Wildlife, Science, and Sentiment* (Golden, Colo.: Fulcrum Publishing, 1990).

27. Harold K. Hochschild, *An Adirondack Resort in the Nineteenth Century* (Blue Mtn. Lake, N.Y.: The Adirondack Museum, 1962), 25–42.

28. Donaldson, *History*, 2: 159–162. Philip G. Terrie, "Behind the Blue Line," *Adirondack Life* 23 (January–February 1992): 46–51, 60–62.

29. See John F. Sears, *Sacred Places: American Tourist Attractions in the Nineteenth Century* (New York: Oxford University Press, 1989).

30. Edwin R. Wallace, *Descriptive Guide to the Adirondacks* (Syracuse: Watson Gill, 1895), 41.

31. On the conservation story, see Terrie, *Forever Wild*, 92–108. The ostensible threat to the watershed as the main stimulus to conservation is arguable. Some historians have seen the watershed argument as a cover for wealthy land owners and club members who wanted the state to protect the Forest Preserve and gradually eliminate logging from the region—all this to make their private inholdings more valuable. See Roger C. Thompson, "The Doctrine of Wilderness: A Study of the Policy and Politics of the Adirondack Preserve-Park" (Ph. D. diss., State University College of Forestry, Syracuse University, 1962); Brenda Parnes, "Trespass: A History of Land Use Policy in the Adirondack Forest Region of Northern New York State, 1789–1905" (Ph. D. diss., New York University, 1989); and Louise A. Halper, "'A Rich Man's Paradise': Constitutional Preservation of New York State's Adirondack Forest Preserve, A Centenary Consideration," *Ecology Law Quarterly* 19 (1992): 193–267. Of these only Halper rises above predictable paranoia about the machinations of the rich. On how much damage was actually done (or not done) to Adirondack Forests, see Barbara McMartin, *The Great Forest of the Adirondacks* (Utica: North Country Books, 1994).

32. Terrie, *Forever Wild*, 130–35.

33. Matthew Russell, "DEC Backs Sierra Club in Fight for River Access," *Adirondack Daily Enterprise*, Aug. 15, 1991; Elizabeth Edwardsen, "Battle Stewing over River Access," *Glens Falls Post Star*, 2 September 1991; Mary Hill, "Mountain Club Joins Waterway Fray," *Lake Placid News*, Sept. 16, 1991.

34. "Law Gives Canoers Greater Access to Streams," *Glens Falls Post Star*, March 4, 1991.

35. "Judge's Ruling Tips Waterway Issue in Favor of Canoeists," *Adirondack Daily Enterprise*, Sept. 23, 1993.

36. David Bauder, "Ruling Opens Rivers to Canoes," *Glens Falls Post Star*, Aug. 19, 1994.

CHAPTER I

Of Bark and Bateaux

1. Samuel de Champlain, *The Works of Samuel de Champlain*, ed. H. P. Biggar (Toronto: Champlain Society, 1922; reprint, University of Toronto, 1971), 2: 79–80.

2. Biggar, *Champlain* 2: 79.

3. These dimensions are from the canoes Champlain saw on the St. Lawrence near Tadoussac in 1603 and I assume they were similar to boats he used on the 1609 trip to Lake Champlain. Biggar, *Champlain*, 1: 104. See also Edwin Adney and Howard I. Chapelle, *The Bark Canoes and Skin Boats of North America* (Washington, D.C.: Smithsonian Institution, 1964), 7.

4. William Sturtevant and Bruce Trigger, eds., *Handbook of North American Indians* (Washington, D.C.: Smithsonian Institution, 1978), 15: 793.

5. Sturtevant and Trigger, *Handbook*, 303. Lafitau's evidence from Caughnawaga in 1712 and Kalm's from the Champlain valley in 1749 confirm that the standard boat of the Iroquois was elm.

6. See William N. Fenton and Ernest Stanley Dodge, "An Elm Bark Canoe in the Peabody Museum of Salem," *The American Neptune* 9, no. 3 (July 1949): 192, and Adney and Chapelle, *Bark Canoes and Skin Boats*, 212–219.

7. Adney and Chapelle, *Bark Canoes and Skin Boats*, 7.

8. Emmons, *New York State Assembly Document 150*, 115.

9. John MacMullen, "The Adirondacks in 1843," *St. Lawrence Plaindealer*, Aug. 24, 1881. Typescript in Kenneth Durant Collection, Adirondack Museum Library; cited hereafter as AML. See also Kenneth Durant to Holman J. Swinney, April 22, 1966, AML for background on MacMullen.

10. MacMullen, "The Adirondacks in 1843," 10.

11. Morton Cross Fitch, "History of Ragged Lake in Franklin County, New York" (Providence, R.I., 1934), 52. One of 25 mimeographed copies, AML.

12. Samuel H. Hammond, *Hills, Lakes, and Forest Streams, or, A Tramp in the Chateaugay Woods* (New York: J. C. Derby, 1854), 28–29.

13. Sewell Newhouse, *The Trapper's Guide; A Manual of Instructions for Capturing all Kinds of Fur-Bearing Animals, and Curing Their Skins; with Observations on the Fur-Trade, Hints on Life in the Woods, and Narratives of Trapping and Hunting Excursions*, ed. Oneida Community, 3rd ed. (New York: Oakley,

Mason & Co., 1869), 128. The charismatic and controversial leader of the Community, John Humphrey Noyes, held the copyright to Newhouse's book.

14. Adney and Chapelle, *Bark Canoes and Skin Boats*, 213.

15. Bruce Raemsch, "Preliminary Archeological Survey for the Adirondack Museum, 1973," MS 73–9, AML.

16. See entry 9.

17. *Indian Girl Canoes: J. H. Rushton, Inc., Canton, N.Y.* (n.d.; after 1906, probably 1909), 3; MS 81–17, AML.

18. Arthur H. Masten, *The Story of Adirondac*, ed. William K. Verner (Blue Mtn. Lake, N.Y.: The Adirondack Museum; Syracuse: Syracuse University Press, 1968), 38.

19. John Burroughs, *The Writings of John Burroughs: Wake Robin* (Cambridge: The Riverside Press, 1923), 1: 85–90.

20. Verplanck Colvin, *Report on a Topographical Survey of the Adirondack Wilderness of the State of New York* (Albany: Argus Co., 1873), 22.

21. John Gardner, *The Dory Book* (Mystic, Conn.: Mystic Seaport Museum, 1987), 18. Gardner discusses in great detail the origins of the form and its subsequent impact on colonial history.

22. Bateaux were certainly not the only boats of European design used on the peripheries of the Adirondacks during the colonial period. They are the only ones treated here because of their significance as ancestors to the later boats used in the mountains, which are the subject of this book.

23. See Russell Bellico, *Sails and Steam in the Mountains* (Fleischmanns, N.Y.: Purple Mountain Press, 1992), 64–66 for an account of the expedition.

24. See Gardner, *Dory Book*, 18–24 for a thorough discussion of the origins of the bateau.

25. John Gardner, "Small Boats Important in Building Young Nation," *National Fisherman* (Aug. 1976): 4C.

26. John Gardner did the analysis and drawings of the remains and reported them in a series of articles for the *National Fisherman/Maine Coast Fisherman* (combined); the above comments are from "Relics of Ghost Fleet are Small Craft Bonanza" (October 1966): 8A–9A.

27. Gardner, *Dory Book*, 24.

28. Philip Lord, Jr., "'1 New Threehanded Batteau': The Mohawk River survey of Philip Schuyler and The Western Inland Lock Navigation Company, August 21–September 4, 1792" (Schenectady, N.Y.: Schenectady Urban Cultural Park, 1992).

29. Pownall, *A Topographical Description*, 51.

CHAPTER 2

The Lake Their Only Path

1. John Todd, *Long Lake* (Pittsfield, Mass.: E. P. Little, 1845), 7.

2. Headley, *The Adirondack*, vii.

3. Headley, *The Adirondack*, v-viii. The description of the country was actually that of Headley's cousin, Farrand Northrup Benedict, a mathematician and professor of civil engineering at the University of Vermont who worked with Ebenezer Emmons on the 1837 survey of the region.

4. Sturtevant and Trigger, *Handbook* 15: 150.

5. Aber and King, *Hamilton County*, 427 and 749.

6. Aber and King, *Hamilton County*, 754.

7. The descriptions of the outsiders are the only ones extant; there are no descriptions of their boats from the people who developed them. The earliest documented guideboat-prototype probably dates from 1848.

8. Jeptha R. Simms, *Trappers of New York, or a Biography of Nicholas Stoner and Nathaniel Foster, Together With Anecdotes of Other Celebrated Hunters, and Some Account of Sir William Johnson, and His Style of Living*, 2nd ed. (Albany: Joel Munsell, 1851), 201.

9. Samuel H. Hammond, *Wild Northern Scenes; or, Sporting Adventures With the Rifle and the Rod* (New York: Derby and Jackson, 1857), 201.

10. Thomas Bangs Thorpe, "A Visit to the 'John Brown's Tract,'" *Harper's New Monthly Magazine* 19, no. 110 (July 1859): 172.

11. Kenneth and Helen Durant, *The Adirondack Guide-Boat* (Blue Mtn. Lake, N.Y.: The Adirondack Museum and Camden, Maine: International Marine Publishing Company, 1980), 133.

12. See Gardner, *Dory Book*, 3–17, for a full discussion of this type of construction.

13. John Gardner outlined the influence of the gig on the guideboat in his lecture at the Annual Meeting of the Small Craft Curator's Conference, Adirondack Museum, Sept. 26, 1987.

14. Farrand N. Benedict, *New York State Senate Document No. 73, 69th Session* (Albany 1846), 10.

15. Ebenezer Emmons, "New York State, Report of Geological Survey, 1839," *New York State Assembly Document 275* (Feb. 27, 1839).

16. Headley, *The Adirondack*, 316.

17. Todd, *Long Lake*, 7–9.

18. Headley, *The Adirondack*, 232.

19. This boat-rocking can drive some rowers to distraction; later, when the guideboat became the main vehicle in which professional guides took clients out hunting, the famous hotelier Paul Smith warned a fidgety sport not to hire a guide who wore the same size clothes he did.

20. J. H. Rushton, "Single vs. Double Blades," *American Canoeist* (July 1882): 93.

21. Early history of the St. Lawrence skiff was explored by Philip Gillesse in an untitled paper delivered at the Museum Small Craft Association Annual Meeting, Clayton, N.Y., Sept., 1987; also in Philip Gillesse to author, March 20, 1990, curatorial research files, Adirondack Museum.

22. Aber and King, *Hamilton County*, 915.

23. William Freeman Fox, *History of the Lumber Industry in the State of New York* (1901; reprint Harrison, N.Y.: Harbor Hill Books, 1976), 27; a quarter of a mile was the size of one observed in 1808 on Lake Champlain.

24. Mrs. Anne Grant, *Memoirs of an American Lady, With Sketches of Manners and Scenes in America, as They Existed Previous to the Revolution* (Albany: Joel Munsell, 1876), 323.

25. Hochschild, *Lumberjacks and Rivermen*, 31.

26. Barbara Kephart Bird, *Calked Shoes: Life in Adirondack Lumber Camps* (Prospect, N.Y.: Prospect Books, 1952), 122–123.

27. Bird, *Calked Shoes*, 122.

28. The museum has five examples of river drive boats; see entries 186–189.

29. Gardner, *Dory Book*, 135.

30. John Gardner, *Building Classic Small Craft* (Camden, Maine: International Marine Press, 1984), 2: 43–44.

31. Richard A. Allen, "Adirondack Mining and Mineral Industries—An Overview," For more see MS 80-11, 5–6, AML.

32. Emmons, "Geological Survey," 295. The navigation scheme was actually worked out by Farrand Northrup Benedict, mathematics and civil engineering professor at the University of Vermont, who worked with Emmons on the survey.

33. Lossing, *The Hudson*, 24. Bruce Seeley, "Adirondack Iron and Steel Company: 'New Furnace', 1849–1854," Historic American Engineering Record, NY–123, 1978, 155; MS 78–14, AML.

34. Thomas Addison Richards, "The Adirondack Woods and Waters," *Harper's New Monthly Magazine* 19, no. 112 (Sept. 1859): 461–462. Masten, *The Story of Adirondac*, 133–135.

35. Allen, "Adirondack Mining," entry for Lyon Mountain (Chateaugay District), n.p., MS 80–11, AML.

CHAPTER 3

The Way It Looks from the Stern Seat

1. Ralph Waldo Emerson, "The Adirondacs: A Journal," in *Poems* (Boston: Houghton Mifflin and Co./Cambridge, Mass.: The Riverside Press, 1892), 159.

2. Seneca Ray Stoddard, *The Adirondacks Illustrated*, 18th ed. (Glens Falls, N.Y.: S. R. Stoddard, 1888), 98.

3. Alfred A. Donaldson covers the history of Martin's in *A History of the Adirondacks* 1, Chapter 24. According to Kenneth Durant, the term "guideboat" did not start appearing until the mid-1870s.

4. This was the route taken by Benson Lossing and his wife in 1859 and reported by him to be the most popular route among travelers; Lossing, *The Hudson*, 4.

5. Joel Tyler Headley wore leggings around 1848; Headley, *The Adirondack*, 17. Murray mentions alligator boots in *Adventures in the Wilderness*, 26. Helena Lossing wore the bloomer costume in 1859; Lossing, *The Hudson*, 27.

6. William J. Stillman, "The Philosophers' Camp: Emerson, Agassiz, Lowell, and Others in the Adirondacks," *Century Magazine* 46, no. 4 (Aug. 1893).

7. H. H. Thompson, "Camping on Jock's Lake in 1863," *American Angler* 5 (July 5, 1884): 1–4, and "Letter from a Sporting Naturalist," *Spirit of the Times* 19 (Sept. 8, Oct. 27, Nov. 3, 17, 24, and Dec. 8, 1849).

8. Headley, *The Adirondack*, 172–173.

9. Emerson, "The Adirondacs," 160.

10. See Hammond, *Hills, Lakes and Forest Streams*, 32–33; and Headley, *The Adirondack*, 382–383, for other examples.

11. See Philip G. Terrie, *Wildlife and Wilderness: A History of Adirondack Mammals* (Fleischmanns, N.Y.: Purple Mountain Press, 1993), for a thorough discussion of deer hunting and game laws in the Adirondacks.

12. For a complete discussion of Emerson's philosophy of wilderness in relation to the Adirondacks, and the development of a wilderness aesthetic, see Philip G. Terrie, "The Intellectuals," *Adirondack Life* 15, no. 2 (March–April 1984): 34–40, and *Forever Wild: Environmental Aesthetics and the Adirondack Forest Preserve* (Philadelphia: Temple University Press, 1985), 59–69, by the same author. In his "Urban Man Confronts the Wilderness," Terrie discusses the equipment and activities of the sports and notes that they wanted to get close to the wilderness, but not *too* close.

13. Richard Patrick Roth, "The Adirondack Guide (1820–1919): Hewing Out an American Occupation" (Ph.D. diss., Syracuse University, 1990), examines the Adirondack guide primarily from a romantic perspective. For comparison see Nathan S. Lourey, "A Historical Perspective on the Northern Maine Guide," *Maine Historical Society Quarterly* 26, no. 1 (1986): 2–21.

14. Emerson, "The Adirondacs," 162.

15. Ibid.

16. In the early period, many guides were found on their farms, according to early travel accounts. The diaries of Julia Baker Kellogg, who lived near Minerva in the 1850s and 1860s and Lucelia Clark, who farmed near Cranberry Lake in the 1880s and 1890s, record being left on the farm when the menfolk went out guiding. Mrs. H. M. Clark Diary, 1897–1922, Cranberry Lake, N.Y., MS 87–18, AML. The term "guide" is not distinguished as an occupation by census-takers in the Adirondacks until 1880.

17. $25–30 per month plus board. Harold K. Hochschild, *Township 34: A History with Digressions on an Adirondack Township in Hamilton County in the State of New York* (New York: privately printed, 1952), 94. Guides provided some of the board, in a sense, in that they were to see to it that game and fish were on the menu. The sport provided staple groceries like pork, tea, and cornmeal. Guides' wages are from E. R. Wallace, *Descriptive Guide to the Adirondacks and Handbook of Travel* (New York: The American News Company, 1873), 260.

18. See D. M. Ellis, *Landlords and Farmers in the Hudson and Mohawk Region, 1790–1850* (New York: Octagon Books, 1967), 213.

19. "Juvenal," "One of the Veterans," *Forest and Stream* 61, no. 16 (Oct. 17, 1903): 295. The man who learned from McLenathan was N. S. Graves, who later built boats at Blue Mountain Lake.

20. Donaldson, *History*, 1: 305.

21. U.S. Census for 1850, Newcomb, Essex County, New York.

22. Holman J. Swinney to Kenneth Durant, April 22, 1966. Kenneth Durant MS 70/10–32, AML, mentions that Chase was probably like many other small gunsmiths in rural locations who built guns but had no stamps with which to strike their names on the barrel.

23. Biographical information from *Biographical Review of Leading*

citizens of Essex and Clinton Counties (Biographical Review Publishing Co., 1896); *Field and Stream* (Sept. 1901); and Newcomb census 1850–1870.

24. See entries 75, 76, 77 for examples of Chase's work.

25. Donaldson, *History*, 1: 188, documents the end of the Adirondack Club.

CHAPTER 4
A Popular Resort for Tourists

1. William Watson Ely, "Ampersand Mountain," *Forest and Stream* 1, no. 6 (Sept. 18, 1873): 84.

2. Amanda Brinsmaid Benedict, "The Neglected Plants. Or, A Journey Through the Realm of the Cryptogams," 1873, f. 163, MS 88–9, AML. Hereafter referred to as "Benedict MS." The above citation is the way in which the only public copy, a photocopy that is in the Adirondack Museum Library, is cataloged. The manuscript was probably a collective work by a group of students who are not all known; Amanda Brinsmaid Benedict was their teacher. The original was not numbered consistently or consecutively; folio references are for the separate sheets as numbered by the museum.

3. Benedict MS, f. 164.

4. Benedict MS, f. 77.

5. Benedict MS, f. 151.

6. Amelia Matilda Murray, *Letters from the United States, Cuba and Canada* (London: John W. Parker and Son, 1856), 2: 283.

7. Murray, *Letters*, 282, reports it so; David Beetle, *Up Old Forge Way, a Central Adirondack Story* (Utica, N.Y.: Utica Observer Dispatch, 1948), 21, claims this was untrue and that Mrs. Arnold took her daughters shopping in Boonville periodically for their education.

8. Robert Wiebe, *The Search for Order, 1877–1920* (New York: Hill and Wang, 1967), 2.

9. The figure of $125 is from William H. H. Murray, *Adventures in the Wilderness*, 25. Laborer's wage is from the New York State manuscript census for Oneida County, 1875. Sally McMurry, Pennsylvania State University, to author, Feb. 22, 1994, notes the wage rate for Oneida County and the fact that board was often not included. John A. Garraty, *The New Commonwealth, 1877–1890* (New York: Harper and Row, 1968), 130, and Paul S. Boyer, ed. *The Enduring Vision: A History of the American People* (Lexington, Mass.: D. C. Heath and Co., 1990), 680, discuss middle-class incomes during this period.

10. Edward S. Sears, *Faxon's Illustrated Hand-Book of Summer Travel to the Lakes, Springs and Mountains of New England and New York* (Boston: Charles A. Faxon, 1875), 174.

11. Murray, *Adventures in the Wilderness*, 18–19. The delicate and fragile may have had no worries, but the modest might have; for the recommended "ladies' outfit," Murray specified the revolutionary "bloomer costume" described on page 59 as "short walking-dress, with Turkish drawers fastened with a band tightly at the ankle."

12. Clymene's knowledge of literature was better than her understanding of geography; she had an idea that the region near Snowy Mountain included Colvin's "minute, unpretending tear of the clouds." Benedict MS., f. 146.

13. Philip G. Terrie in "Verplanck Colvin, Adirondack Surveyor: Response to Wilderness," *Environmental Review* (Fall 1983): 275–290, discusses Colvin's significant differences from other nature writers of the time, his interest in the minute workings of nature as well as the grand, sublime vistas.

14. Verplanck Colvin, *Report on a Topographical Survey of the Adirondack Wilderness of New York for the Year 1873* (Albany: Weed and Parsons, 1874), 53.

15. Colvin's guide must have been going all the way to Long Lake.

16. Paul Jamieson and Donald Morris, *Adirondack Canoe Waters, North Flow* (Lake George, N.Y.: Adirondack Mountain Club, 1991), 31.

17. "D. L.," "Adirondack Notes," *Forest and Stream* 6, no. 5 (March 9, 1876): 67.

18. Bellico, *Sails and Steam*, 293–294.

19. Aber and King, *Hamilton County*, 301.

20. Carl M. Lathrop, "Effingham and the Summer People," *The Iron Man Album* 37, no. 4 (March–April 1983): 1–3. The botanists may have had a particular interest in the boat; the party included one young lady named Poillon. C & R Poillon were in business as shipwrights at least from 1842 until the turn of the century, according to the New York City directories.

21. Harold K. Hochschild, *Adirondack Steamboats on Raquette and Blue Mountain Lakes* (Blue Mtn. Lake, N.Y.: The Adirondack Museum, 1962), 1.

22. Stoddard, *The Adirondacks Illustrated*, 104. The Adirondack Museum has at least two guideboats that were once fitted with canopies. The boats Stoddard refers to may have been guideboat-built or of a more conventional build.

23. This is based on deduction from photographs, assuming a length of 15–18 feet for the guideboats on the steamboats.

24. Henry Ruschmeyer, "Chateaugay Lake: A Case Study of Adirondack Resorts, 1840–1917" (honors paper, Department of History, Union College, 1966), 84, MS 70–10, AML.

25. Dan Brenan, ed., *Canoeing the Adirondacks with Nessmuk: The Adirondack Letters of George Washington Sears* with revisions by Robert L. Lyon and Hallie E. Bond (Blue Mtn. Lake, N.Y.: The Adirondack Museum; Syracuse: Syracuse University Press, 1992), 109. The story of "Nessmuk" in the Adirondacks is told below in Chapter 5.

26. Arpad G. Gerster, *Recollections of a New York Surgeon* (New York: Paul Hoeber, 1917), 276.

27. Brenan, *Canoeing the Adirondacks*, 101. The Fulton Chain dams at this time were actually built to impound water for power and canal systems downstream, rather than navigation, but the aesthetic effect was the same.

28. Forest Commission Report 1891, quoted by Harold K. Hochschild in *Adirondack Steamboats*, 3 and 5.

29. "Icharod," "A Steamboat on Upper Saranac," *Forest and Stream* 8, no. 2 (Feb. 15, 1877), 19. Low-lying lands along navigable waterways were flooded not only for steamboat traffic

but also to impound water to ensure a supply for river drives and mills downstream. Henry David Thoreau was ambiguous about the meaning of the steam-whistle of the railroad he heard at Walden Pond; see Leo Marx, *The Machine in the Garden, Technology and the Pastoral Ideal in America* (New York: Oxford University Press, 1964), 250–251.

30. Donaldson, *History*, 1: 308.

31. Donaldson, *History*, 1: 383. Donaldson assumes this was a different *Mattie* than the one Stoddard records as being on Upper Saranac in 1878, but steamboats were often sold to new owners and moved to different lakes.

32. Hochschild, *Adirondack Steamboats*, and Frances B. Seaman, "The Buttercup Mystery of Long Lake" (Long Lake: privately printed, 1991), 3–4.

33. The Blue Mountain Lake–Forked Lake trip would perhaps not be a full day's trip for a guide trying to "make time," but it was a reasonable excursion. It was not unusual for guides to make it from Martin's to Palmers on Long Lake in a day, a longer trip.

34. Aber and King, *Hamilton County*, 301.

35. See appendix of boatbuilders. It is difficult to know exactly who was building boats. The term "boatbuilder" does not appear in the census until 1870, but in that decade and before, men now known as boatbuilders do not appear in the census as such.

36. The story of J. H. Rushton is well and completely told in Atwood Manley, *Rushton and His Times in American Canoeing* (Blue Mtn. Lake, N.Y.: The Adirondack Museum; Syracuse: Syracuse University Press, 1968). Manley repeats local tradition that Rushton's first boat was a canoe, 10. For a tribute to Manley from his friend and assistant on the book, see Paul Jamieson, "Atwood, Rushton and the Chickaree," *Adirondack Pilgrimage* (Glens Falls, N.Y.: Adirondack Mountain Club, 1986), 174–180.

37. J. H. Rushton to George Washington Sears, April 25, 1884, MS 78–2, AML.

38. Tom Tyson, "The Nature and Function of Cost-Keeping in a Late Nineteenth Century Small Business," (unpublished paper, AML, 1990).

39. J. H. Rushton, *Rushton's Portable Sporting Boats and Canoes* (Canton, N.Y.: Plaindealer Steam Presses, 1877), 9.

40. George T. Balch, *Illustrated Catalogue and Oarsman's Manual* (Troy, N.Y.: Waters and Balch, 1871). There apparently was never another issue. The museum owns two Waters paper boats: see entries 152 and 164.

41. Since he was only thirteen years old in 1869, Sprague probably did not start building boats until the mid-1870s at the earliest.

42. Stephens later became a designer of ocean-going yachts and, for many years, was yachting and canoeing editor of *Forest and Stream*.

CHAPTER 5
The Feather Weight and the Backwoods

1. J. H. Rushton to George Washington Sears, Sept. 14, 1884, MS 78–2, AML.

2. For more on Nessmuk's adventures and his relationship with Rushton, see Brenan, *Canoeing the Adirondacks*.

3. Brenan, *Canoeing the Adirondacks*, 59.

4. Ibid., 107.

5. *Rushton's Portable Sporting Boats and Canoes For Hunting, Fishing, Trapping or Pleasure Rowing*, 1880, 13. Sears claimed that a Shadow or Stella Maris would cost considerably more than $100 in his *Woodcraft* (1920; reprint, New York: Dover Publications, 1963), 88. The development of the decked sailing canoe is covered below, in Chapter 6.

6. Rushton to Sears, May 2, 1880, MS 78–2, AML.

7. Brenan, *Canoeing the Adirondacks*, 33.

8. Ibid., 138.

9. Verplanck Colvin, *Seventh Report on the Progress of the Topographical Survey of The Adirondack Region of New York to the Year 1879* (Albany: Weed and Parsons, 1880), 7–8.

10. Brenan, *Canoeing the Adirondacks*, 107. Nessmuk is using poetic license here. "Counter" in the nautical sense is an overhanging stern. Most guideboat sterns are just the opposite.

11. Paul G. Bourcier, *History in the Mapping: Four Centuries of Adirondack Cartography* (Blue Mtn. Lake, N.Y.: The Adirondack Museum, 1986), 33–39.

12. "Nessmuk," letter to the editor in *Forest and Stream* 14 (July 8, 1880): 451.

13. These books were perhaps stronger on outdoor crafts and general encouragement to enjoy the woods than they were on practical woodcraft. Building and sailing boats were important parts of their message, however. The boys' books were part of a concern that as America industrialized, its future leaders were being raised without enough exercise and fresh air which supposedly helped build character and manliness. Building and handling small craft was often part of this movement, which, by the end of the century, had resulted in the birth of innumerable children's camps, as well as the foundation of the Boy Scouts of America.

14. Advertisement in a list of books published by *Forest and Stream* in the back of "Seneca," *Hints and Points for Sportsmen* (New York: Forest and Stream Publishing Co., 1891).

15. Sears, *Woodcraft*, 4.

16. *Rushton's Portable Sporting Boats and Canoes*, 1880, 3–9.

17. A. H. Siegfried in the Louisville *Commercial*, Aug. 12, 1876, quoted in Manley, *Rushton and His Times*, 18.

18. Sears, *Woodcraft*, 91. Nessmuk is quoting a letter Rushton wrote to him Nov. 18, 1883.

19. J. H. Rushton, "Single vs. Double Blades," *American Canoeist* (July 1882): 93.

20. Philip Gillesse to Hallie Bond, March 20, 1990, Adirondack Museum curatorial research files.

21. See entries 133, 134, 135.

22. Rushton to Sears, Nov. 8, 1882, MS 78–2, AML.

23. Brenan, *Canoeing the Adirondacks*, 90.

24. Ibid., 96.

25. Rushton to Sears, Nov. 1, 1882, MS 78–2, AML. Sears had two other boats made by Rushton which he used in Florida: *Bucktail*, named for Nessmuk's Civil War regiment and 10½ feet long, 22 pounds, and the *Rushton/Fairbanks*, the smallest of all at 8½ feet and 9 lbs., 15 oz.

26. Rushton to Sears, Nov. 8, 1882, MS 78–2, AML.

27. Ibid.

28. Brenan, *Canoeing the Adirondacks*, 80.

29. Ibid., 140.

30. Ibid., 172.

31. Rushton to Sears, Nov. 11, 1882, MS 78–2, AML.

32. Rushton to Sears, March 7, 1886, MS 78–2, AML.

33. The boat itself, named by Durant *Wee Lassie*, is in the collections of the Adirondack Museum, entry 15.

34. Sprague's advertisement for cedar boats appeared in *Forest and Stream* 5 (Jan. 27, 1876): 396.

35. Copy of article in *Sail and Paddle* (March 1887): 59 in Kenneth and Helen Durant Collection, Folder 16–16–5, MS 80–3, AML.

36. Brenan, *Canoeing the Adirondacks*, 68.

37. See also Nathan S. Lourey, "A Historical Perspective on the Northern Maine Guide," *Maine Historical Quarterly* 26, no. 1 (1986): 2–21.

38. The total is taken from the Grant tally boards, thin planks of pine on which Grant kept a running record of his production. The data from Appendix A in Kenneth and Helen Durant, *The Adirondack Guide-Boat*, 167–199.

39. Kenneth and Helen Durant, *The Adirondack Guide-Boat*, 47 and 49.

CHAPTER 6
The Knights of the Paddle

1. "The Canoe Congress," *Forest and Stream* 15 (Aug. 12, 1880): 36.

2. He actually started his voyage from Quebec City in a heavy 18-foot cedar canoe with a New Jersey waterman as crew, but in Troy fell in love with the paper boats of Elisha Waters, bought one, dismissed the waterman, and continued alone. The Adirondack Museum has two Waters boats; see catalog, and Bishop's book, *The Voyage of the Paper Canoe* (Boston: Lee and Shepard Publishers, 1878).

3. "A Canoe Congress," *Forest and Stream* 13 (Jan. 1, 1880): 953–954.

4. "The Canoe Convention," *New York Times*, Aug. 17, 1880. The correspondent was probably W. L. Alden, who was on the editorial staff and who had just been elected Commodore of the American Canoe Association.

5. Nathaniel H. Bishop, "First Call," text of which is quoted in Ronald Hoffman, "The History of the American Canoe Association, 1880–1960" (Ph.D. diss., Springfield College, 1967), 18.

6. "A Canoe Congress," 953–954.

7. The association was initially named the National Canoe Club, but within a few months the name was changed to the American Canoe Association in deference to the Canadians, who were encouraged to join.

8. "The Canoe Congress," *Forest and Stream* 15 (Aug. 26, 1880): 76.

9. Nathaniel H. Bishop, "The American Canoe Association," *Forest and Stream* 16 (April 21, 1881): 237.

10. Donna Braden, *Leisure and Entertainment in America* (Dearborn, Mich.: Henry Ford Museum and Greenfield Village, 1988), 37–42, gives a quick overview of the subject.

11. Nathaniel H. Bishop, "The American Canoe Association," *Forest and Stream* 16 (April 21, 1881): 237.

12. "Rushton Canoes," *Forest and Stream* 16 (March 17, 1881): 137.

13. William Picard Stephens, "The Poor Man's Yacht," *Forest and Stream* 16 (July 7, 1881): 460.

14. Florence Watters Snedeker, *A Family Canoe Trip* (New York: Harpers Black and White Series, 1892), 86 and 97. The composition hadn't changed from a decade earlier, when *Forest and Stream* observed that all ages and classes were represented, although business and professional men from 25 to 50 years of age predominated. *Forest and Stream* 22 (Dec. 11, 1884): 136.

15. Wulsin paddled a Rushton Rob Roy to the headwaters of the Mississippi in 1879. The Adirondack Museum has his journals and photographs from that trip, as well as a later Wulsin canoe, a Rushton Princess model (see entry 52).

16. "X," "The American Canoe Association," *Forest and Stream* 15 (Sept. 16, 1880): 136.

17. R. B. Burchard, "Back to the Grindstone: the Canoe Camp," *Outing* 29 (Nov. 1896): 142, lists a ladies' paddling race and a ladies' race for one crew and passenger.

18. "The Safety of a Canoe," *Forest and Stream* 25 (July 23, 1885): 518.

19. J. B. McMurrich, "ACA Official Business," *American Canoeist* 5, no. 5 (May 1886): 83.

20. D. B. Goodsell, "A Canoeing Reminiscence" (paper in the American Canoe Association Collection, B4, New York State Historical Association, Cooperstown, New York, n.d.).

21. *New York Times*, Aug. 13, 1881.

22. Ronald Hoffman, "The History of the American Canoe Association, 1880–1960" (Ph.D. diss., Springfield College, 1967), 53–56.

23. Benjamin A. G. Fuller, "Canoeing in America: 100 Years of Sport," 4, curatorial research files, AM.

24. "Lorna," "The Lake George Canoe Club," *Forest and Stream* 22 (March 3, 1884): 137.

25. "Canoe Clubs," *American Canoeist* 6, no. 3 (March 1887): 64, lists contemporary canoe clubs.

26. "The Canoe Congress," *Forest and Stream* 15 (Aug. 12, 1880): 36.

27. The complete history of the Peterborough builders is not

easily accessible in one spot. See John Marsh, "The Heritage of Peterborough Canoes" in Bruce W. Hodgins and Margaret Hobbs, eds., *Nastawgan: The Canadian North by Canoe and Snowshoe* (Toronto: Betelgeuse Books, 1985): 210–222, and Dr. G. D. W. Cameron, "Birth of the 'Peterborough' Canoe: Four Builders Start a Revolution," *Wooden Canoe* 9 (Winter 1982): 4–9.

28. Cameron, 8.

29. Snedeker, *A Family Canoe Trip*, 134–135. Despite her advocacy of the Canadian canoe, Mrs. Snedeker cruised from New York to the 1892 meet on Lake Champlain with her husband and young son in a decked sailing canoe.

30. "Retaw," "The Canadian Canoe," *Forest and Stream* 29 (Dec. 29, 1887): 456.

31. "The Canoe Convention," *New York Times*, Aug. 17, 1880.

32. A complete description of *Rob Roy* is in John MacGregor, *A Thousand Miles in the Rob Roy Canoe on Rivers and Lakes of Europe* (Boston: Roberts Brothers, 1867), 5. *Rob Roy* was built by a craftsman named Searle, who was already established as a builder of light rowing craft for recreation and racing.

33. MacGregor, *A Thousand Miles in the Rob Roy*, 5.

34. The museum's Vesper (entry 54) has a complete set of cockpit covers.

35. R. K. Wing, "Cruises about Lake Champlain," *Forest and Stream* 28 (July 7, 1887): 522.

36. The museum has an Everson Whitehall; see entry 127.

37. Charles Farnham, "Running the Rapids of the Upper Hudson," *Scribner's Monthly* (April 1881): 857–870.

38. "Seven Days of It," *American Canoeist* 2, no. 9 (Oct. 1883): 138–139.

39. "Tent for Small Boats," *Forest and Stream* 16, no. 1 (April 14, 1881): 217. "Liebig" soup was named for its inventor, a German who developed the first widely-available soup concentrate.

40. W. L. Alden, *The Canoe and the Flying Proa, Or, Cheap Cruising and Safe Sailing* (New York: Harper and Brothers, 1878), 30.

41. "CMD", "Canoe Cruising. Number Three," *Forest and Stream* 2, no. 23 (July 16, 1874): 364.

42. "A Scheme for Canoe Pilotage," *Forest and Stream* 25 (March 5, 1885): 116.

43. Burchard, "Back to the Grindstone: The Canoe Camp," 142.

44. "A Bid for an 'Accident,'" *Forest and Stream* 26 (May 6, 1886): 295.

45. See catalog entries 54 and 55 for information on the museum's Vespers.

46. There were actually two races between *Vesper* and *Pecowsic*, the prearranged International Challenge Cup and another race arranged at the meet. *Vesper* won one and *Pecowsic* won one, confusing the public and giving Rushton and Joyner plenty of advertising copy for years to come. See Manley, *Rushton and His Times*, Chapter 10.

47. *J. H. Rushton*, 1892 catalog, 4.

48. "Lake George Meet," *Forest and Stream* 17, no. 3 (Aug. 18, 1881): 44.

CHAPTER 7

To Suit Every Taste

1. William Picard Stephens, "The Poor Man's Yacht," *Forest and Stream* 16 (July 7, 1881): 460. The same essay appeared as the introduction to Stephens's catalog in the same year. Stephens is talking primarily about the different models of cruising and sailing canoes, but his comments could equally apply to the great variety of all sorts of recreational small craft of the time.

2. Benedict MS, f. 163.

3. Harold K. Hochschild quotes the *New York Telegram* for Aug. 16, 1882, when he describes the event in *An Adirondack Resort*, 53.

4. Blue Mountain Lake is not entirely typical perhaps, since it had become the most fashionable mountain resort in the northeast by the mid-1880s. Hochschild, *An Adirondack Resort*, 43.

5. For a discussion of the growth and distribution of hotels and private camps see William B. Conroy, "The Changing Recreational Geography of the Adirondack Mountain Area" (Doctor of Social Science diss., Syracuse University, 1963). Jeffrey Limerick, Nancy Ferguson, and Richard Oliver's *America's Grand Resort Hotels* (New York: Pantheon, 1979) is primarily an architectural history of existing structures, but it also examines the growth of grand resorts as a phenomenon in American history.

6. Edwin R. Wallace, *Descriptive Guide to the Adirondacks* (Syracuse, N.Y.: Forest Publishing House, 1899), 407. The summer population was further swelled by guides, chambermaids, and waiters.

7. Stoddard, *The Adirondacks Illustrated*, 190B.

8. Thomas G. King, "Adirondack Guides," *Recreation* 2 (May, 1895): 386.

9. F. Joyner, *Practical Pleasure Boat and Canoe Builder*, 1883, photocopy of an incomplete copy of catalog in AML, 17.

10. Manley, *Rushton and His Times*, 131, and "Childwold Park," MS 61–187 B3, AML. The latter livery was run by Judd W. Rushton, who, after J. H. Rushton's death, briefly ran the boat shop in Canton. In the mid-1890s Judd had his own sash and door factory in Canton, where he also made paddles.

11. "Private Preserves Within the Limits of the Proposed Adirondack State Park," *Forest and Stream* 43 (Dec. 22, 1894): 563, and "Private Preserves," *New York State Forest, Fish and Game Commission, Eighth and Ninth Reports* (Albany: J. B. Lyon Co., 1902–1903), 36–44, which counted 419 camps in the region, including ones on large and small holdings. Also "Private Camps in the Adirondacks in 1896" table in Conroy, "Changing Recreational Geography," 121.

12. Schmitt, *Back to Nature*, 11–12, discusses the growth of hunting and country clubs. Braden, *Leisure and Entertainment*, 305–308, describes the exodus of the wealthy from their for-

mer recreational haunts because of increasing numbers of middle-class tourists.

13. "Private Preserves," *Fish and Game Commission, Eighth and Ninth Reports*, 36.

14. "The number of beautiful lakes and ponds in this wonderful region no man knows, and Little Tupper is among the finest," wrote Nessmuk on his 1883 cruise. Whitney Park, enclosing this region, was closed in the late 1890s, and remains so into the late twentieth century. Nessmuk's letter of Aug. 12, 1883, printed in Brenan, *Canoeing the Adirondacks*, 159.

15. "Adirondack Preserves," *Forest and Stream* 32, no. 11 (April 4, 1889): 209. The feeling that private individuals are better stewards of the land than the state remains a defense for private ownership into the late twentieth century.

16. Frederick J. Seaver, *Historical Sketches of Franklin County* (Albany, N.Y.: J. B. Lyon Company, 1918), 553–555.

17. Edward Comstock, Jr., ed., *The Adirondack League Club, 1890–1990* (Old Forge, N.Y.: The Adirondack League Club, 1990). Chapter 1, "'Our Forest Home': Camp and Lodge Life," by Roger Yepsen, and Chapter 4, "Tests of Integrity: Boats of a Hundred Years," by Mason Smith.

18. See entry 76 for the Chase boat.

19. J. H. Rushton, *Illustrated Catalogue: Pleasure Boats and Canoes*, 1895, 17.

20. John Gardner, "Lines of Lawton's ADK," from an article in *Outdoor Maine* (March 1960): 11. Photostat in Kenneth and Helen Durant Collection, MS 80–2, Folder F-2, AML; *The Partelow Standard Boats, Canoes and Steam Launches*, 1891 catalog, 5–7.

21. See entry 55.

22. Anson Phelps Stokes is quoted in his daughter Mildred Phelps Stokes Hooker's *Camp Chronicles* (Blue Mtn. Lake, N.Y.: The Adirondack Museum, 1964), 1.

23. *St. Regis Yacht Club Fiftieth Anniversary, 1897–1947* (Upper St. Regis, N.Y.: St. Regis Yacht Club, 1947), 20–27. See also Clinton Crane, *Yachting Memories* (New York: D. Van Nostrand Co. Inc., 1952), 19–20.

24. Edwin R. Wallace, *Guide to the Adirondacks*, 486. Wallace went on to "emphatically" endorse the boats of J. H. Rushton.

25. "John Gardner in his Own Words," in Peter H. Spectre, *Different Waterfronts: Stories from the Wooden Boat Revival* (Gardiner, Maine: Harpswell Press, 1989), 42.

26. F. Joyner, *Practical Pleasure Boat and Canoe Builder*, 1883, 17, prints a letter from F. C. Durant reporting satisfaction with his order of 82 boats. Stoddard, *The Adirondacks Illustrated*, 201B, states that the Prospect House has "a fleet of light lake boats, larger and steadier than the ordinary traveling boat of the Adirondacks." The St. Lawrence River Skiff, Canoe and Steam Launch Company offered the Champlain model, a "square stern high grade row-boat . . . built more especially for first-class hotels and boat liveries" which had a Whitehall look. St. Lawrence River Skiff, Canoe and Steam Launch Company, *Illustrated Catalogue, 1893* (1893; reprint, Clayton, N.Y.: Thousand Islands Shipyard Museum, 1983), 26.

27. Gardner, *Building Classic Small Craft*, 1: 194–197. Gardner

28. Gardner, *Building Classic Small Craft*, 1: 212. On page 213 Gardner writes, "There are so many small boats, similar in some respects and different in others, which have been called Whitehalls, that in discussing them complete confusion reigns unless there is some established and recognized norm to which they can be related and compared. While it is common and convenient to use the term, Whitehall, to describe a boat, it is often inaccurate and misleading to do so, for many variations of the type have appeared at different times and in different places." Howard I. Chapelle also wrote about Whitehalls, *American Small Sailing Craft* (New York: W. W. Norton, 1951), 198. See entry 127 for a detailed description of the Everson-built Whitehall *Grey Bonnet*.

29. Stoddard, *The Adirondacks Illustrated*, 59, says there was "a large fleet of skiffs, mostly of the kind called 'Whitehall'" on the lake, but we have only Stoddard's word that these were true Whitehalls. They may have been variations of the type which became so common. Arpad G. Gerster, Journal, Aug. 8, 1898, MS 71–6, AML.

30. Dorothy Backus Offensend, *The Sexton Boatbuilders of Hague* (Pawlet, Vt.: privately printed, 1982), 79.

31. Compare entries 131 and 132 to 127 for a more complete discussion of the differences.

32. That is, three men working together took seven days to finish one. Interview with Bob Gates, Bolton Landing, Nov. 15, 1989. Grant evidence from Kenneth and Helen Durant, *The Adirondack Guide-Boat*, 49.

33. Frank Schneider, "The Lake George Rowboat," *Adirondack Life* (July 23, 1964): 14.

34. Cornell or Penn usually won; Wesleyan, Bowdoin, Columbia, and Princeton also competed.

35. Gretchen A. Meyers, "Paper Rowing Shell Building in the United States, 1867–1900" (master's thesis, Springfield College, 1981), quotes from an 1890 *Outing* article. Waters began work in 1867.

36. Untitled paper by Philip Gillesse delivered at the Museum Small Craft Association Annual Meeting, Thousand Islands Shipyard Museum (Clayton, N.Y., Oct. 1989).

37. Howard A. Lennon, "The St. Lawrence Skiff," *Bulletin of the Jefferson County Historical Society* 7, no. 1 (Jan. 1966): 9. Howard I. Chapelle, *American Small Sailing Craft*, 178, says they were well known to eastern sportsmen by the 1870s and 1880s.

38. Thomas C. O'Donnell, *Birth of a River* (Boonville: Black River Books, 1952), 57, quotes the reporter without attribution.

39. Rocky Point Inn brochure, ca. 1900, AML.

40. Harold Herrick, "A Stable Boat is a Blessing," *Ducks Unlimited* 17, no. 6 (Nov.–Dec. 1983): 64, counts "at least a dozen" commercial builders with other skiffs built by guides.

41. John H. Conover, "The Bellows Rowboat," *Adirondack Life* 24, no. 6 (Sept.–Oct. 1993): 20–24; and Henry Ruschmeyer, "Chateaugay Lake: A Case Study of Adirondack Resorts,

41. 1840–1917" (master's thesis, Union College, 1966). Ralph Bellows interview by Kenneth Durant 1958, Kenneth and Helen Durant Collection, MS 80–2, folder 50–11/1, AML.

42. See catalog entries for St. Lawrence skiffs: 133, 134, and 135 and for Rushton's Pleasure Rowboats: 136, 137, 139, 140, and 141.

43. *Sprague's Improved Cedar Boats and Canoes for Exploring, Hunting or Pleasure Rowing*, catalog, ca. 1888. Curatorial research files, AM. See entries 18 and 145.

44. See entry 143.

45. See entry 116.

46. Willard J. Hanmer interview by Robert Bruce Inverarity, transcript, March 12, 1961, 64–65, curatorial research files, AM.

47. Marylee Armour, *Heartwood: The Adirondack Homestead Life of W. Donald Burnap* (Baldwinsville, N.Y.: privately printed, 1988), 210, and Mason Smith, "Tests of Integrity," *The Adirondack League Club*, 181. Ben Parsons built strip-built (¾"-wide strips) rowboats with steam-bent frames as well.

48. See entries 23, 24, 25, 26.

49. Gardner, *Building Classic Small Craft*, 1: 11.

50. Mason Smith, 170–171.

51. Gardner, *Building Classic Small Craft*, 2: 43.

52. "A Good Club Boat for Large Waters," *American Angler* 14 (Nov. 24, 1888): 327.

53. A brief overview of the depression of 1893 in James West Davidson et al., *Nation of Nations: A Narrative History of the American Republic*, 2nd ed. (New York: McGraw–Hill, 1994), 788–791.

54. Available information reveals no drop in the number of boatbuilders active during this period. In fact, there were more than ever before. The information summarized in the Boat Builder's List has to be taken primarily as an indicator, however, rather than an accurate count because of the dearth of biographical information about builders, especially from the middle of the nineteenth century.

55. J. H. Rushton, "Books of Knowledge," vol. 1, 126–131, MS, 80–13, AML, is a table of freight rates including Virginia, Michigan, and Samoa which may, of course, have been recorded in response to inquiries rather than actual orders. The customer in Apia, Samoa, may have decided to get a locally-built boat rather than pay the $50 shipping charge—half the price of the expensive Vesper. The Michigan boats are better documented. At least nineteen went to the Huron Mountain Club, a sporting preserve founded in 1889 in the northern part of the state.

56. *Rushton's Portable Sporting Boats*, 1888, 2.

57. See entries 23 and 95.

58. Tom Tyson, "The Nature and Function of Cost-Keeping in a Late Nineteenth-Century Small Business," (unpublished paper, AML, 1988). Rushton's "Knowledge" is in two volumes. They and a companion volume at the St. Lawrence County Historical Association in Canton, New York, are the only records of the shop that have survived, prompting speculation as to whether Rushton always kept such detailed cost-accounting records, or whether they were a response to the depression. Tyson assumes the latter.

59. Hallie E. Bond, "J. Henry Rushton's 'Books of Knowledge,'" *The Apprentice*, no. 12 (Autumn 1990): 12–15.

60. The spilings have been tested in modern times. Mason Smith, a restorer then living at Lake Ozonia not far from Rushton's hometown, used the spilings to make a plank for a pleasure rowboat built in the 1890s. He cut it out without reference to the boat, using only the written record, and it fit perfectly. Interestingly, the experiment tried on a boat built after Rushton's death didn't work.

CHAPTER 8

Rag Boats in the Wilderness

1. E. T. Keyser, "The Joys of Canoeing," *Yachting* (April 1907): 237.

2. Old Town Canoe Company, *Old Town Canoes, 1910* (1910; reprint, Madison, Wis.: Wooden Canoe Heritage Association, 1981): 14; C. H. Mattison, "Canoeing in the Adirondacks: A Practical Account of a Two Weeks Vacation Spent in the Woods on a Hundred and Fifty Mile Cruise," *Field and Stream* 12 (June 1907): 107–118.

3. Dillon Wallace, "The Canoe Yesterday and Today," *Hunting and Fishing* (March 1929).

4. Jerry Stelmok and Rollin Thurlow, *The Wood and Canvas Canoe: A Complete Guide to its History, Construction, and Maintenance* (Gardiner, Maine: Harpswell Press, 1987), 22–24, suggests that the early Maine builders improved on each other's methods, all the while feeling the technology was well-known. Most builders were guides, not boatbuilders, to begin with. The idea of building the canoe upside down over a solid mold seems to have been developed by the Maine builders independent of the Peterborough builders, who had been building all-wood canoes that way since the 1850s.

5. Credit should be given to *more* fastenings, as well; where birchbark canoe planks and ribs are merely held in by the tension of the different parts of the hull, the same elements on a wood-canvas canoe are tacked and screwed in place.

6. Stelmok and Thurlow, *The Wood and Canvas Canoe*, 23.

7. *Rushton's Rowboats and Canoes*, 1907 catalog, 48, 39, 27. Lewis Grant Collection, MS 70–7, AML. This is actually the price for a 16-foot Grant guideboat bought in 1917. Figures are not available for prices closer to the 1907 date.

8. Stelmok and Thurlow, *The Wood and Canvas Canoe*, 28.

9. *Adirondack Portable Sporting Boats and Canoes for Hunting, Fishing, Trapping, Pleasure Rowing and Sailing*, Holmes and Robertson, Manufacturers, catalog, n.d., probably between 1883 and 1886.

10. Schmitt, *Back to Nature*, 106–114, discusses the Woodcraft Indians in the context of "backwoods brotherhoods."

11. Edward Breck, *The Way of the Woods: A Manual for Sportsmen in Northeastern United States and Canada* (New York: G. P. Putnam's Sons, 1908), 96.

12. Stelmok and Thurlow, *The Wood and Canvas Canoe*, 31–33.

13. Manley, *Rushton and His Times*, 142.

14. J. H. Rushton, 1903 catalog. Reprinted in William Crowley, ed., *Rushton's Rowboats and Canoes: The 1903 Catalog in Perspective* (Blue Mtn. Lake, N.Y.: The Adirondack Museum and the Wooden Canoe Heritage Association, Ltd., 1992), 43.

15. After the Rushton shop closed in the winter of 1916–1917, Everett Brown, one of his workers, took the Indian Girl molds and produced the canoes for a while but does not seem to have made a success of it.

16. Rushton Notebooks 2: 53, St. Lawrence County Historical Association, Canton, New York.

17. Ibid., 50. Quote from Selden T. "Pont" Williams, ca. 1965.

18. "Canoeing in the Adirondacks," *Recreation* 23 (August 1905): 186.

19. Kenneth R. Smith, "Through the Adirondacks by Canoe," *Forest and Stream* 80 (May 31, 1913): 686.

20. That's what the men did as described in R. H. Nash's "Overland Canoe Trip," *Forest and Stream* 79, no. 14 (Oct. 5, 1912): 434–435, 443–446. They had to pay an extra fare for the two miles of the Fulton Chain Railway trip from Thendara to Old Forge. The Fulton Chain Railway ran until 1932; after that passengers for Old Forge got off in Thendara. Michael Kudish, *Where Did the Tracks Go: Following Railroad Grades in the Adirondacks* (Saranac Lake, N.Y.: The Chauncy Press, 1985), is the reference guide to rail service in the region.

21. The name of the "old native" of 1913 is not recorded; other writers mention a Mr. Marks in addition to Rivet. Kenneth R. Smith, "Through the Adirondacks by Canoe," 686; Harriette Syms, "Our Adirondack Canoe Trip," *Conservationist*, no. 4 (Sept., 1921): 135–139; Arthur Kelleye, "An Auto and Canoe Trip to the 'Dacks,'" *Fur-Fish Game* 42, no. 6 (June 1926): 1 and 6.

22. *A Summer Paradise*, Delaware and Hudson Railway 1929 brochure, 137.

23. Syms, "Our Adirondack Canoe Trip," 136.

24. See Paul Jamieson, "Camping on State Lands Through the Years," *Conservationist* 19, no. 4 (Feb.–March 1965): 3–7, for an overview of changing state camping facilities.

25. Mattison, "Canoeing in the Adirondacks," 107–118.

26. Ibid., 117.

27. Ibid., 118.

28. Borden H. Mills, "Canoe Cruising in the Adirondacks," *Recreation* 2 (June 1908): 262–263, 294–295. Mills wrote the canoeing advice for the Delaware and Hudson guides, as well as publishing in *Four Track News*, and, as late as 1961, in *Adirondac*, the journal of the Adirondack Mountain Club.

29. Breck, *The Way of the Woods*, 104.

30. Mrs. Emerson Hough, "Canoes Seem Made for Girls," *Ladies Home Journal* (July 1915).

31. Stoddard's guidebooks 1904–1914 had the same advice.

32. Borden H. Mills, "By Paddle and Portage," *Country Life in America* 16 (June 1909): 156, 158, 160.

33. *The Adirondack Mountains*, New York Central Lines 1914 advertising brochure, 24–25, AML.

34. Herbert Keith's *Man of the Woods* (Blue Mtn. Lake, N.Y.: The Adirondack Museum; Syracuse: Syracuse University Press, 1972) is one of the few books on the subject of Adirondack guiding written from the inside, by a guide.

35. Keith, *Man of the Woods*. It is Paul Jamieson, in his introduction, who analyzes the continuation of the guiding profession on the Oswegatchie. George Marshall analyzed the decline of the profession of mountain guides in "Adirondack Guides of the High Peak Area," in *The Adirondack High Peaks and the Forty-Sixers*, ed. Grace Hudowalski (Albany: The Adirondack Mountain Club, 1970), 129–130.

36. In 1917, the year Grant sold a 16-foot guideboat to W. G. Gallowhur for $130.72, an AA grade Old Town Charles River model, with closed mahogany gunwales, cost $45. *Old Town Canoes*, 1917 catalog, 11.

37. Brant Lake Camp For Boys brochure, n.d., AML. Of course, even after the 1920s many single-sex camps continued in operation.

38. Schmitt, *Back To Nature*, Ch. 9, "The Customary Thing."

39. Fay Campbell Kaynor, "The Golden Era of Private Summer Camps," *Vermont History News* (May–June 1990): 46–50. *A Handbook of Summer Camps: An Annual Survey*, 2nd ed. (Boston: Porter Sargent, 1925) lists and describes camps throughout the country.

40. Evidence for the types of boats used at Adirondack children's camps comes from the collection of camp ephemera in the Adirondack Museum Library. Brochure photographs of waterfront activities are common, but, unfortunately, clear statements like the one from the Adirondack Camp for Boys are rare. *Adirondack Camp for Boys* brochure, n.d., AML.

41. *Old Town Canoes*, 1910 catalog, 29.

42. *Adirondack Camp for Boys* brochure, n.d., AML.

43. *Rushton's Rowboats and Canoes*, 1907 catalog, 48; *Old Town Canoe Company*, 1910 catalog, 14.

CHAPTER 9

The Triumph of Internal Combustion

1. Harry Belknap, "On Lake Placid," *MotorBoat* 7, no. 15 (Aug. 10, 1910): 33.

2. They bought their own fireboat when installation of a gasoline engine on *Doris* made the pump obsolete.

3. David H. Ackerman, ed., *Placid Lake: A Centennial History, 1893–1993* (Lake Placid, N.Y.: The Shore Owners Association of Lake Placid, Inc., 1993), 47; "See Beautiful Lake Placid by Motor Boat," undated George and Bliss brochure (ca. 1915), AML.

4. Of 103 private camps existing on the Adirondack League Club in 1990, nearly a quarter had been built before the turn of the century. But in the next three decades, until the stock market crash, over half of the remaining camps were built. The trend was more pronounced on the Adirondack Mountain Reserve. Of seventeen camps on the Ausable Lakes, fourteen were built before 1929, and none before 1900. Lists of camp construction dates from Comstock, ed., *The Adirondack League Club*, 252–262, and Edith Pilcher, *Up the Lake Road:*

The First Hundred Years of the Adirondack Mountain Reserve (Keene Valley, N.Y.: The Adirondack Mountain Reserve, 1987), 166–173. The trend towards construction of private camps was the same in more public parts of the Park as it was in the clubs. On Lake Placid there were forty-three private camps before the turn of the century, but twenty-four of those had been built after the railroad reached the village of Lake Placid in 1893. From 1900 until 1929 seventy-three camps were built. In the southwestern Adirondacks, on Twitchell, Big Moose, Seventh, and Raquette Lakes, sixty-three camps existed in 1984. Of these, only a dozen were built before 1900 and five after 1929; the remaining forty-six were built between the turn of the century and the beginning of the Great Depression. (Data for Lake Placid camps: David H. Ackerman to author, July 8, 1994, curatorial research files, AM; for Big Moose region, Karen D. Lux and Karen Creuziger, "A Survey of Selected Camps on Big Moose, Raquette, Seventh, Sixth and Twitchell Lakes," 1985, MS 83–16, AML.)

5. Mark S. Foster in his essay "The Automobile and the City" discusses this fascination; David L. Lewis and Laurence Goldstein, eds., *The Automobile and American Culture* (Ann Arbor: University of Michigan Press, 1983).

6. H. V. Partelow, Boston, Mass., 1891 catalog, 16.

7. *Stella* was later sold and renamed *Osprey*; she is now in the collections of the Adirondack Museum. See entry 167.

8. For background on the naphtha launch, see Kenneth Durant, *The Naphtha Launch* (Blue Mtn. Lake, N.Y.: The Adirondack Museum, 1976); Richard K. Mitchell, *The Steam Launch* (Camden, Maine: International Marine Publishing Co., 1982), 202–215; and D. W. Fostle, *Speedboat* (Mystic, Conn.: Mystic Seaport Museum Stores, 1988), 21–30.

9. *Gas Engine and Power Company*, 1896 catalog, 16.

10. Fostle, *Speedboat*, 27–29; *Gas Engine and Power Company*, 1896 catalog, 69.

11. "The Poor Man and the Motor Boat," *Yachting* (July 1907): 48. Fostle, *Speedboat*, 79, discusses the availability and popularity of small inboards.

12. John Gardner, "Old Marine Engines," *National Fisherman* (June 1973) 4-B; Benjamin A. G. Fuller, "The Coming of the Explosive Engine, 1885–1910," *The Log of Mystic Seaport* (Autumn 1993): 34–42.

13. Fuller, "The Coming of the Explosive Engine," 40.

14. Herman Broesel, "Lake George, A Cradle of Motor Boating," *MotorBoating* (Aug. 1961): 17; H. A. Schermerhorn, "The Season of 1910 on Lake George," *MotorBoat* 7, no. 14 (July 24, 1910): 20.

15. Harry Belknap, "On Lake Placid," *Motorboat* 7, no. 15 (Aug. 8, 1910): 33. The "electric guideboats" may actually have been church boats with electric motors like the motorized church boats remembered by Charles Keough.

16. Dorothy Backus Offensend, *The Sexton Boatbuilders of Hague, Lake George, New York* (Pawlet, Vt.: privately printed, 1982), III.

17. H. A. Schermerhorn, "The Season of 1910 on Lake George," *MotorBoat* 7, no. 14 (Sept. 25, 1910): 21–23.

18. Program of the Saranac Boat and Waterways Club, 20th Annual Regatta, 1928, AML.

19. *Yachting* (June 1907): 364–365.

20. Ibid.

21. Fostle, *Speedboat* 42–43; Betty Ahearn Buckell, *Lake George Boats* (Lake George: Buckle Press, 1990), 83–84.

22. See entry 170.

23. Albany Boat Corporation catalog, n.d., ca. 1915; copy at Antique Boat Museum, Clayton, N.Y.

24. *Washington Post*, Sept. 24, 1934.

25. Albany Boat Corporation catalog, ca. 1915.

26. Mankowski was known as a member of the Polish aristocracy, but Buckell suggests he was an American. Buckell, *Lake George Boats*, 39.

27. Fostle, *Speedboat*, 123–175; see also J. Lee Barrett, *Speedboat Kings* (Detroit: Arnold Powers, Inc. 1939). The fact that the first Miss America beauty pageant occurred in 1921 is apparently a coincidence, unless the beauty queens were named after the boat. Naming speedboats "Miss ——" is a tradition going back at least to Chris Smith's 1915 Gold Cup winner *Miss Detroit*.

28. The restrictions on the race were modified nearly every year until they were lifted in 1936. See Fostle, *Speedboat*, ch. 12. Lower speeds meant safer races, too, which also made the sport more attractive to amateurs.

29. See entry 176.

30. "A Preview of the Lake George Gold Cup Regatta," from 1934 scrapbook kept by George Reis; private collection.

31. Robert Gates, Bolton Landing, interview with author, July 7, 1989, curatorial research files, AM.

32. The President's Cup program for 1934 stated that *El Lagarto*'s bottom had been redesigned by "one of the best naval architects in the country," but does not say who that was. Bob Gates remembered that it was the work of Reis, Bowers, himself, and his brother. Robert Gates interview.

33. 1934 Gold Cup program, copy in AML. "Corinthian" was a term coined by amateur yacht racers, circa 1900, to distinguish themselves from the professionals who raced for high stakes; see Clinton Crane's *Yachting Memories*, 126.

34. "Campers Protest Racket of Motor Boat Engines Roaring Through Night," *Adirondack Daily Enterprise*, Aug. 29, 1935, and "New Muffler Law Being Enforced," *Lake George Mirror*, Aug. 8, 1931.

35. Warren Stout, "Boats! Boats! Boats!" *The New York State Conservationist* 14, no. 3 (Dec.–Jan. 1959–1960): 6.

36. Virginia Jennings, "Dwindling Demand Makes Mailboat Service Thing of the Past," *Tupper Lake Free Press*, July 19, 1989.

37. Armour, *Heartwood*, 216–217, and David H. Beetle, *Up Old Forge Way/West Canada Creek* (Utica, N.Y.: North Country Books, 1972), 46–47.

38. Armour, *Heartwood*, 218.

39. Armour, *Heartwood*, 167–175.

40. Belknap, "On Lake Placid," 33.

41. Charles Keough, interview with author, Feb. 2, 1994.

42. Keith, *Man of the Woods*, 76–79.

43. Brooks Boat Manufacturing Company, catalog number eleven, 1906, 11, 45, 51, AML. Brooks also offered the finished hull, still without motor, for $100.

44. John H. Chamberlin to author, July 28, 1994; Lindley Boats catalog, n.d., ca. 1910, 6. AML.

45. The Lozier Motor Company is discussed below and in entry 169.

46. "Lake George One-Design Speed Boats," *MotorBoat* 12, no. 14 (July 25, 1915): 27.

47. *Adirondack Daily Enterprise*, Feb. 4, 1915, 32.

48. Jay Higgins, "Haute Boat," *Adirondack Life* 18, no. 4 (July–Aug. 1987): 96–99; John V. D. Hilton, "A Factual History of the Fay and Bowen Engine Company," curatorial research files, n.d., AM.

49. Armour, *Heartwood*, 211–212. Charles Keough remembers that many Adirondack builders designed their own inboards, especially before the 1930s. Keough is a longtime Saranac Lake boat restorer and dealer and onetime mayor of the village. He purchased the shop of Freeman Baker on Lake Flower. Interview with author Feb. 2, 1994, curatorial research files, AM.

50. Frank Rivett, son of Jack Rivett, interview with Edward Comstock, Jr., July 9, 1976, and with John R. Collins, Sr., Jan. 16, 1976, by Edward Comstock, Jr. Accession files for 75.259.1. The Adirondack Museum has in its collection the 1915 Rivette launch *Fulton*; see entry 174.

51. The museum owns a guideboat-built George and Bliss canoe; see entry 25.

52. Ackerman, *Placid Lake*, 54; Keough interview.

53. The Adirondack Museum owns a child's model; see entry 194.

54. "Lake George Boat Company," *MotorBoat* (Oct. 1936): 16.

55. Brooks 1906 catalog, 29.

56. Armour, *Heartwood*, 213–214.

57. John B. Rae, in his essay "Why Michigan?" suggests that it was primarily a fortuitous concentration of technical and entrepreneurial talent that resulted in Michigan's becoming the center of automobile manufacture. Lewis and Goldstein, eds., *The Automobile and American Culture*, 1–9.

58. Meet the Town: Saranac Lake, N.Y., pamphlet, 1932–1933, 31; *Adirondack Daily Enterprise*, advertisement, June 8, 1917.

59. John Gardner in Spectre, *Different Waterfronts*, 42–43.

CHAPTER 10

Kickers and the Keen Edge of Enjoyment

1. *Rudder*, 38, no. 4 (April 1922): 3. *Multum in parvo* is a Latin expression that means "a great deal in a small compass," according to the Compact Oxford English Dictionary. The O.E.D. cites an 1876 reference to a "multum-in-parvo pocket knife" by Thomas Hardy that makes the modern reader think of a Swiss army knife.

2. Richard E. Davies to author, Nov. 27, 1994, 4, curatorial research files, AM.

3. Peter Hunn, *The Old Outboard Book* (Camden, Maine: International Marine Publishing, 1991), and W. J. Webb and Robert W. Carrick, *The Pictorial History of Outboard Motors* (New York: Renaissance Editions, Inc., 1967), cover the development of outboard power.

4. Webb and Carrick, *Pictorial History of Outboard Motors*, 101.

5. Program for the 20th Annual Regatta on Lower Saranac Lake, Saranac Lake Boat and Waterways Club, Inc., Aug. 6 and 7, 1928, AML. The Adirondack Museum's Baby Buzz-type boat was built by the Old Town Canoe Company; see entry 178.

6. This boat is in the collections of the Adirondack Museum: see entry 177.

7. Comstock, ed., *The Adirondack League Club*, 186.

8. Author's interview with Robert Gates, former employee of Smith's, July 22, 1994, curatorial research files, AM.

9. See entries 68 and 72.

10. Comstock, ed., *The Adirondack League Club*, 186.

11. See the essay by Joseph Interrante, "The Road to Autopia," in Lewis and Goldstein, eds., *The Automobile and American Culture*.

12. Braden, *Leisure and Entertainment*, 323–352, discusses the impact of the automobile on American leisure travel.

13. See Warren Belasco, *Americans on the Road: From Autocamp to Motel, 1910–1945* (Cambridge, Mass.: M.I.T. Press, 1979).

14. William G. McLoughlin, "Camps and Hotels at Lake Ozonia, 1872–1968," MS 77–16, AML, highlights the importance of the automobile to the development of the lake.

15. "The Story of the Famous Penn Yan 'Car Top' Boat," undated brochure, ca. 1960; copy in Kenneth and Helen Durant Collection, MS 80–3, Folder 14–3, AML.

16. Penn Yan catalog, ca. 1925, 20–21; copy in AML.

17. The museum's wood-canvas rowboat (entry 157) was used by a camper on Indian Lake; documentation also from interview with Clarence Petty, whose family stored camping gear for visitors at the Indian Carry in the 1920s. Clarence Petty, interview with author, Jan. 21, 1994, curatorial research files, AM.

18. Fessenden Seaver Blanchard, *An Outboard Cruising Guide to New England, Eastern New York State and Adjacent Canadian Waters* (New York: Dodd, Mead, 1958).

CHAPTER 11

Hot-Rudders, Trailer-Sailors, and the Wooden Boat Revival

1. Gardner, *Building Classic Small Craft*, 2: x.

2. Herbert E. Echelberger and George H. Moeller, "Toward a Better Understanding of Recreational Boating in the Adirondack Lakes Region," *Water Resources Bulletin* 9, no. 6 (Dec. 1973): 1266.

3. "Aluminum Canoes," memorandum from William J. Hoffman, Grumman Aircraft Engineering Corporation, to Dudley Field, July 23, 1964, AML; and Dwight Rockwell to David Seidman, January 21, 1989; curatorial research files, AM.

4. Fostle, *Speedboat*, 203–207, discusses the development of fiberglass for small craft.

5. George D. Pratt, Commissioner of the Conservation Commission in this era, was a great promoter of recreational use of the Forest Preserve. Pratt was also an early official in the Boy Scout movement and president of the Adirondack Mountain Club. The state department that began life as the Conservation Commission in 1911 changed its name to the Conservation Department in 1926, and then to the Department of Environmental Conservation in 1970.

6. New York State Conservation Department, *Forty-Fourth Annual Report for the Year 1954* (Albany, N.Y.: Williams Press, Inc., 1955), and New York State Conservation Department, *Fifty-Fourth Annual Report for the Year 1964*, n.p.

7. Paul Jamieson, *Adirondack Canoe Waters: North Flow* (Glens Falls, N.Y.: Adirondack Mountain Club, 1975).

8. Stout, "Boats! Boats! Boats!," 6.

9. State of New York, Conservation Department, *Twentieth Annual Report for the Year 1930* (Albany: J. B. Lyon and Company, 1930), 76; State of New York, Conservation Department, *Fifty-Second Annual Report for the Year 1962*, 57, n.p.

10. Roy Irving, "Boats and Boating on New York's Inland Waters," *The New York State Conservationist* 12, no. 5 (April–May 1958): 10.

11. Charles A. Cusick, "The Problem With Boats," *The New York State Conservationist* 11, no. 4 (Feb.–March 1957): 12.

12. Paul Jamieson and Donald Morris, *Adirondack Canoe Waters: North Flow*, 3rd ed. (Lake George, N.Y.: Adirondack Mountain Club, 1991), 117.

13. John Gardner, "Willard Hanmer and the Adirondack Guide-Boat," *The Small Boat Journal* 11 (March 1980): 28–30.

14. Charles Brumley, "Blue Collar Boats," *Adirondack Life* 20, no. 4 (July, 1989): 18–19, 22.

15. The disappearance of wooden boats from the New York Boat Show is pointed out by Peter Spectre in his chapter on the wooden-boat revival in his collection, *Different Waterfronts: Stories from the Wooden Boat Revival.*

16. Howard I. Chapelle, *Boatbuilding: A Complete Handbook of Wooden Boat Construction* (New York: W. W. Norton & Company, Inc., 1941); and Chapelle, *American Small Sailing Craft.*

17. In the opinion of Benjamin A. G. Fuller; for bibliographic information on regional boat studies see his essay in The Museum Small Craft Association's *Boats: A Manual for their Documentation* (Nashville, Tenn.: American Association for State and Local History, 1993), 388–390.

18. James West Davidson and John Rugge, *The Complete Wilderness Paddler* (New York: Vintage Books, 1975), 40–45, discuss the canoe-building materials of the mid-seventies.

19. Jamieson and Morris, *Adirondack Canoe Waters*, viii.

20. Christine Jerome, *An Adirondack Passage: The Cruise of the Canoe* Sairy Gamp (New York: HarperCollins, 1994), 210.

21. Alfred B. Street, *Woods and Waters: or, The Saranacs and Racket* (New York: M. Doolady, 1860), 31.

Catalog of Boats in the Adirondack Museum Collection

The museum boats are described below in groups according to their general type: canoes, rowing craft, power boats, and a special category including hybrids and oddities. Within the subdivisions in each category (listed below) boats are arranged chronologically from earliest to latest, with those of unknown construction date last.

The builder and designer are assumed by the author to be the same person, unless stated otherwise.

Boat names are in italics (*Allegra*). Model names are in roman type with an initial capital (Nomad).

The date of construction is given as accurately as records allow. In some cases this may be a range of some years, and in some cases catalog records allow a specific period to be stated. Boats for which nothing more specific than forty years can be estimated are not given a date. In this context, "ca." indicates a range of ten years before and after the given date and "about" indicates a closer range of years.

The place of construction given is assumed to be in New York State unless noted otherwise.

Source of all information is assumed to be in the accession folder for the given boat or in the boatbuiler's catalog unless otherwise cited. These accession folders are kept in the registrar's office of the Adirondack Museum and contain secondary material as well as information from donors. The catalogs are in the museum library's vertical file.

Most of the sailing boats had to be jury-rigged to some degree for the photographs because of missing hardware.

The subdivisions of the catalog are as follows:

Canoes

A canoe is a light, narrow, double-ended, round-bilged boat, generally twenty feet in length or less. Technically speaking, it has a length-to-beam ratio of 4.5 to 1 or greater and a bare-hull displacement-to-length ratio of less than thirty.* Canoes are generally paddled. As W. P. Stephens put it in 1885, "the principal point of difference between a canoe and other boats is mode of propulsion, the paddle being held and supported by both hands, while in boats the oar or scull is *supported* on the boat, and its motion is *directed* by the hand."[†] Canoes are also sailed. Sailing canoes are some of the fastest single-hull sailboat types in the world.

The term "hunting canoe" is used in this catalog in the way J. H. Rushton used it, to refer to small, light canoes under fourteen feet in length. Boats of this size today are often referred to as "pack canoes."

*Steve Redmond, "Herreshoff's Double Paddle Canoe," *WoodenBoat* 60 (September–October, 1984): 140.

[†]William Picard Stephens, *Canoe and Boat Building. A Complete Manual for Amateurs*, 8th ed. (New York: Forest and Stream Publishing Company, 1898), 67.

Aboriginal Types

1. Birchbark Canoe

L: 14'7"   B: 38"   wt: 58 lbs

Built by an unknown builder, ca. 1879

If the donors' construction date is correct, this is an unusually early birchbark to have survived; these fragile craft usually do not last long. It was used in the Saranac Lake region.

DONORS: Jeannette and Leonie Dieschbourg   71.137.4

2. Birchbark Canoe

L: 12'6"   B: 31"   wt: 45 lbs

Built by an unknown Canadian Indian between 1896 and 1913

The financier and millionaire J. Pierpont Morgan bought Camp Uncas from William West Durant in 1896. According to tradition, he brought an Indian to the camp from Canada to build this canoe for his use at Uncas. The metal fastenings and general construction make this canoe typical of such craft built for sports around the turn of the century.

DONOR: R. W. Birrell   56.48.5

3. Birchbark Canoe

L: 11'11"   B: 36"   wt: 47 lbs

Built by Penobscot Indians in the Old Town area of Maine [?], ca. 1897

This is a sophisticated example of the Malecite-type birchbark canoes built in the Old Town area, mostly for white sports. The decoratively carved thwarts are mortised into the inwales. The boat is closely gored, giving it a nice, fair shape. The gores are fitted edge-to-edge, rather than being overlapped, as in some more hastily-built birchbarks. The stem profile is modern, influenced by the contemporary wood-canvas canoes then being turned out in much greater numbers in the same area. The diamond-shape of the hull as seen in plan-view, however, is traditional, as is the "winter bark" decoration. Winter bark is birchbark that is peeled during a thaw, and it comes away from the tree with the dark rind which lies between the bark and wood of the trunk adhering to it. The rind turns darker with age and can be scraped off to delineate decorations.*

The father of the donors bought this canoe for use at his Lake George camp.

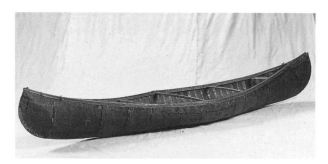

DONORS: Helen and Florence Meyers   57.221.1

*Edwin Tappan Adney and Howard I. Chapelle, *The Bark Canoes and Skin Boats of North America* (Washington, D. C.: Smithsonian Institution, 1964), 14–15.

4. Birchbark Canoe

L: 12'8"   B: 32"   wt: 49 lbs

Built in Quebec, ca. 1915

A manager of the Ticonderoga paper mill acquired this canoe from Indians in eastern Canada and used it for fishing on Lake George. It was paddled with a double-bladed paddle from Abercrombie and Fitch rather than by the single blade of the Indians.

The builder used care in constructing this craft. The pierced decorative flaps below the gunwale are traditional, but unusual in this period, having been abandoned by most builders intent on producing boats quickly for the market. Varnish on the hull is not traditional but may be original, as some birchbarks from the Algonquin tradition were so finished.

Construction details are a mix of traditional and modern. The one-piece stem is carved from a curved root. The birchbark skin is nailed to either side of it; traditionally, the stem was pierced and the bark lashed on. The thwarts are in two pieces. The boat is built with light thwarts lashed to the inwale; when the structure of the boat was finished, heavier thwarts were nailed on over them to strengthen the frame. The "keelson," nailed in the bottom, is common in late birchbarks and was added to keep the ribs in place.

5. BIRCHBARK CANOE

L: 13'   B: 33"   wt: 38 lbs

Built by an unknown builder, ca. 1880(?)

Isaac Simonin purchased this canoe for use at his Camp Ninomis on Second Stony Creek Pond. The thwarts are decoratively carved with "W.W.K.," a later owner of the boat and its donor to the museum. The donor suggested the date for this Algonquin-style canoe built with metal fastenings.

6. BIRCHBARK CANOE

L: 14'3"   B: 33½"   wt: 58 lbs

Built by Matthew Bernard, Golden Lake, Ontario, 1926

Even after Europeans brought their own types of watercraft into eastern Canada, the Algonquin Indians there continued to find ready markets for their birchbark canoes—first fur traders and then tourists and sports. This canoe was built for a dedicated "outdoorist" for $2 per foot by Matt Bernard, one of the best-known builders of birchbarks for the tourist trade of the 1920s. Golden Lake lies about sixty miles due west of Ottawa.

Bernard used techniques and details from contemporary wood-canvas canoe construction as well as from his own Algonquin heritage in this boat. The piece of wood lashed on over the stem is a typical Algonquin detail, but the bolted thwarts and seats, and the style of the thwarts, is typical of wood-canvas canoes.

7. BIRCHBARK CANOE

L: 13'   B: 33"   wt: 47 lbs

Built by Dan Emmett, Corey's, about 1928

Every summer from around 1910 until near his death in the early 1950s "Indian Dan" Emmett camped at Corey's, making birchbark canoes, sweetgrass baskets, and packbaskets to sell to the summer residents. Emmett was a Mohawk from the Caughnawaga Reservation near Montreal. The aboriginal Mohawks were not traditionally birchbark canoe builders. They took up canoe building in the eighteenth century after moving into the St. Lawrence valley.

Dan Emmett built this canoe in a hybrid Algonquin-Abenaki-Ojibway style which had become common by the early twentieth century because of the influence of canoe manufacture for the white market. The new style is characterized by iron fastenings, less turn-up at the ends, less decoration, and often less attention to fairness in the hull than is found in traditional craft.

This canoe was built for Anna and Avery Rockefeller and was used only on Ampersand Lake for paddling—by adults only. Emmett, a friend of the family, maintained the boat, using patches of cotton fabric in addition to more traditional pitch. Nevertheless, it always leaked. It was not used after his death.

DONOR: The family of Anna and Avery Rockefeller   90.53.1

8. BIRCHBARK CANOE

L: 12'11"   B: 35"   wt: 55 lbs

Built by "Indians in Canada" according to the donor

This birchbark is typical of canoes built for the tourist trade by Indians in Quebec and Ontario around the turn of the century. It has carved thwarts but otherwise not much distinctive style.

DONOR: Ed Blankman   77.224.1

9. DUGOUT CANOE

L: 14'1"   B: 20"   wt: unknown

Built at Lake Ozonia, St. Lawrence County, between 1344 and 1504

The builder of this canoe fashioned it by using a combination of edge tools and fire to hollow out a log. It was found on the bottom of a lake, probably sunk on purpose to protect it from rodents and uninvited borrowers.

DONOR: William Cubley   58.350.1

10. DUGOUT CANOE

L: 16'4"   B: 29"   wt: 300 lbs

Built by Charles Fenton, Number Four, ca. 1880

Orin Fenton was an early hotelier and guide in the western Adirondacks, establishing his popular Fenton House at Number Four in 1826. His son Charles took over in 1870 and ran it until 1899. Charles is the probable builder of this remarkable dugout. Rather than being a result of necessity or whimsy, as are most historic Adirondack dugouts, this one seems to have been built as a test of skill with hewing tools by a man well familiar with contemporary boat types. It has a little wineglass transom and a hewn-in stern seat. Its elegantly-shaped hull has a well-defined chine. The final "civilized" touches to this aboriginal boat type are outrigger oarlocks and the word CANOE painted on the transom.

DONOR: George Davis   71.135.1

11. DUGOUT CANOE

L: 13'1"   B: 15"   wt: 142 lbs

Built by Ernest Berry and Paul [?], Raquette Lake, 1953

This narrow, rather crude dugout reportedly "sailed the lake daily" with the aid of outriggers. Ernest Berry once owned Camp Fairview on Osprey Island in Raquette

Lake. The surname of his fellow builder is not recorded. The two men probably built this as an experiment.

DONORS: Mr. and Mrs. Leonard Levine   56.62.1

12. GREENLAND KAYAK

L: 17'   B: 20"   wt: 40 lbs

Built in the Umanak district of Greenland, ca. 1933

"The kayak, in its highest state of evolution and in skillful hands, is perhaps the most seaworthy of all primitive small craft," wrote Howard I. Chapelle in 1964. One hundred years before, "Rob Roy" MacGregor had appreciated the rapid and easy paddling, maneuverability, and light weight of the kayaks of Greenland in choosing that New World form for his new Old World boat.

If the shape of the traditional Arctic kayak influenced nineteenth-century cruising canoes, native construction methods were entirely ignored. The strength of the kayak lies primarily in the deck, while the hull of a wooden canoe is supported by its frames, keel, and stems. A kayak is covered with skin rather than wood. Kayaks, like birchbarks but unlike European-tradition boats, are built without plans or molds.

This boat was acquired by the artist and writer Rockwell Kent (1882–1971) in Greenland in the early 1930s. It is built with sawn lumber and metal fastenings. Traditionally, the wood in kayaks was split by hand and the frame

was lashed together. The Greenland kayak is built with a slight vee-bottom, but this one has flattened out with age.

DONOR: Rockwell Kent   64.177.1

13. WHITEWATER KAYAK

L: 13'2"   B: 26"   wt: 32 lbs

Built by Bart Hauthaway, Weston, Massachusetts, 1965

The Hudson River Whitewater Derby calls for extreme maneuverability in a boat. First used in the 1965 world championships, this model was a very successful slalom design for many years. It is also notable for its construction, since it is one of the earliest all-fiberglass kayaks. Prior to the mid-1960s builders had no good way of joining the hull to the deck and so made cloth decks. Hauthaway solved the problem in the deck of this kayak by fastening it to the hull with pop rivets.

This boat was built for David Binger, who loaned it to Robert F. Kennedy during the Whitewater Derby of 1967. Kennedy and several companions ran one of the roughest parts of the Hudson River gorge from Gooley Landing to North River.

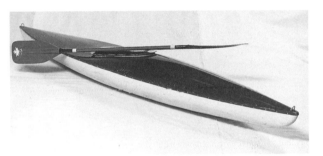

Museum purchase   68.244.1

Open Paddling Canoes

14. HUNTING CANOE

L: 13'   B: 31"   wt: 50 lbs

Built by J. H. Rushton, Canton, ca. 1880

The first boats Rushton built in the early 1870s were similar to this one. He marketed them as "portable hunting boats," to be carried with square yokes and probably paddled by two people with single-bladed paddles. This

example has quite fine entry, and an elaborate stern seat that may once have had the builder's name painted beneath it. It was purchased second-hand in 1888 for use at a camp on the old Hollywood Stillwater on the Raquette River, now the Carry Falls Reservoir.

DONOR: Clifford Judd   65.5.1

15. NESSMUK MODEL CANOE *Wee Lassie*

L: 10'6"   B: 27"   wt: 20 lbs

Built by J. H. Rushton, Canton, 1883

William West Durant purchased a Nessmuk model canoe from J. H. Rushton in 1883 and named her *Wee Lassie*. He paddled her in the central Adirondacks and probably took her to American Canoe Association meets as well, for he lists her as his canoe in the 1892 yearbook. Like most skippers of Rushton's lightweight canoes, he used a double-bladed paddle and sat on a cushion in the bottom, which he protected with a carpet. As originally built, the boat had no thwart.

After Nessmuk's cruise with his first Rushton boat in 1880, Rushton offered a ten-and-a half-foot stock model and named it after the famous woodsman. He carried the Nessmuk line until the end of his life. *Wee Lassie* has become almost a generic term for small canoes in the late twentieth century, and it has been copied in all sorts of modern and traditional materials; see entry 22.

DONOR: Harold K. Hochschild   60.53.1

(See Appendix for lines drawing of *Wee Lassie*.)

16. HUNTING CANOE

L: 13'4"   B: 34"   wt: 30 lbs

Built by Harry Green, Hermon, ca. 1886

Harry Green was a "fine mechanic" and carpenter as well as boatbuilder who worked out of his barn. He designed the Hermon school, as well as building rowboats and canoes. He was a contemporary of J. H. Rushton, but used strip planking, which Rushton never did. Green's strips were rounded on one edge and hollowed on the other and

edge-fastened. This type of planking was also used by A. Bain & Co., the much-better-known builders on the St. Lawrence River. In his heyday, about the time this boat was built, Green built many of the boats used on Cranberry Lake, not far from his home.

Museum purchase   59.16.1

17. HUNTING CANOE

L: 11'11"   B: 28¾"   wt: 40 lbs

Built by A. Bain & Co., Clayton, 1888

The noted New York physician Arpad Gerster used this boat for solo trips through the Adirondacks from bases at his camps on Raquette Lake and Long Lake. He took to the waterways alone to avoid the "annoyance . . . suffered through the impatience of the guides, who were always in a 'stew' to reach the next hotel on the route, where 'grub' was awaiting them." His kit included a tent of raw China silk and a fly made by David Abercrombie, a pair of Jaeger blankets, an air pillow, a two-pound ax, a sheath knife, a rifle, and a cooking kit of aluminum. "In 1888 aluminum was a precious metal; but, undaunted, I ordered a nest of four kettles, the largest one holding two quarts. They cost $12.00, but were worth the price," he reported.* Gerster's canoe also came with a set of floorboards and a yoke into which he carved, in Latin, the legend "It is light because it is well borne, 1887."

The Peterborough canoe builders are the best-known nineteenth-century users of strip planking, but other builders experimented with it, too. A. Bain & Co. differed from the Peterborough builders in that they used planks which were hollowed on one edge and rounded on the other. After the planks were fitted together they were edge-fastened.

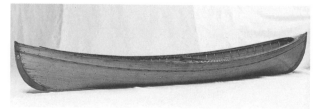

DONOR: J. C. A. Gerster   56.61.3

*Arpad Gerster, *Recollections of a New York Surgeon*, 172.

18. HUNTING CANOE

L: 10'7"   B: 34"   wt: 35 lbs

Built by Herbert M. Sprague, Parishville, ca. 1890

Superficially, this boat looks as if it were built by J. H. Rushton, but the ribs are too big, oddly-sized, and irregularly spaced. The clinch nailing is coarser. Herbert Sprague had a small shop in which he did most of the work with only local men as occasional help. He built guideboats, rowboats, and decked cruising canoes. In his later years he turned to making violins.

From the late 1920s until the mid-'50s this boat was owned and used by William McArthur, guide or caretaker at the St. Regis Fishing and Hunting Club on the upper St. Regis River.

Museum purchase   63.146.1

19. HUNTING CANOE

L: 11'   B: 34"   wt: 32 lbs

Built by Harry Green, Hermon, 1895

Harry Green built this "carry-boat" in 1895 for a Judge Irving Vann, who used it in the Cranberry Lake region. Its last owner reported that he had "spent many happy hours in the craft, and have seen many nice trout taken in over her gunwhales [sic]. And I've carried it as much as ten miles in a day." Like *Wee Lassie*, and a number of other, lesser-known boats, this is an alternative to the guideboat for portable water transportation in the Adirondacks. It

has a carrying yoke. Its wales are spruce, ribs are elm, and the strip-planking is pine.

DONOR: Henry Bragdon   65.18.1

20. HUNTING CANOE

L: 10'2"   B: 26"   wt: 28 lbs

Built by: Merle Austin and Ed [?] Hamner, Long Lake, ca. 1910

Merle Austin was a guideboat builder, but he built this little canoe using hull shape, construction techniques and a model more like those of J. H. Rushton—a rabbeted keel, smooth skin, and clinch-nailed ribs. It has been patched with canvas. Hanmer used the boat for beaver trapping around Long Lake.

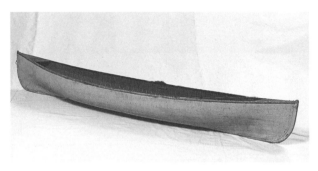

Museum purchase   75.258.1

21. HUNTING CANOE

L: 12'5"   B: 29"   wt: 32 lbs

Built by Lewis Grant, Boonville, before 1940

Grant built this boat for his personal use on little ponds and streams. A versatile builder, he used Rushton-style construction techniques rather than adopting guideboat construction like so many guideboat builders did when called on to build a canoe. Grant's fine craftsmanship is as evident in this boat as in his guideboat *Virginia* (entry 101) and his flat-bottomed rowboat (entry 148).

Grant was aiming for light weight, and one of the ways he achieved this was by placing the ribs farther apart in the ends, where they were less important structurally than in the center of the boat.

Like a guideboat, this canoe has a carrying yoke. Grant probably paddled it with the single-bladed paddle traditionally used on these boats in the Adirondacks.

Museum purchase   73.54.1

22. PACK CANOE

L: 10'6"   B: 27"   wt: 18½ lbs

Built by the Old Town Canoe Company, Old Town, Maine, 1960

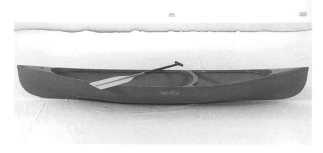

"Here is a fine piece of equipment for those who enjoy fishing or hunting remote mountain ponds or other small bodies of water otherwise inaccessible to the sportsman." Although these words sound like they were written by J. H. Rushton in the 1880s, they actually describe this fiberglass canoe offered by the Old Town Canoe Company eighty years later. The need for certain types of boats does not change.

Nor does the usefulness of a good design change. This boat is meant to be a copy of Rushton's *Wee Lassie* (entry 15). What does change is the technology by which boats are made and, consequently, the precise form. When Bart Hauthaway designed this boat, he tried to copy Rushton's lines as closely as he could, but slight changes in the end profiles were necessary to produce a design that could be made in fiberglass.

The handling of this boat has changed, as well. Hauthaway originally thought he could paddle it kneeling with a single blade, rather than sitting with a double blade, as *Wee Lassie* was paddled. He thought that the double blade was too cumbersome for packing long distances, and the drips which might travel down the shaft too chilling in the hunting season. He found the canoe too tender to kneel in, however, so he added the thwart for back support while sitting and the cushion for comfort but retained the single-bladed paddle.

DONOR: Old Town Canoe Company   71.10.1

23. GUIDEBOAT-BUILT CANOE *Allegra*

L: 14'7"   B: 29½"   wt: 56 lbs

Built by Myron Augustus Nickerson, Canton, ca. 1900

Allegra is the result of one builder's interest in providing a canoe with some of the outstanding characteristics of a guideboat. She has a smooth skin for quiet paddling, and sawn frames (instead of the steam-bent frames more usual in canoes) give great strength for light weight. A sister boat, *Allegro*, is rumored to have run the rapids of the Hudson gorge and survived. The extreme upswept bow and stern, a most unguideboat-like feature, were no doubt added for a romantic look but made the boat difficult to handle in a breeze. *Allegra* also once had a carrying yoke like a guideboat.

DONOR: William Oliver   67.209

24. GUIDEBOAT-BUILT CANOE *Minne Wawa*

L: 15'   B: 30"   wt: 53 lbs

Built by Albert Henry Billings, Lake Placid, 1903

This canoe was one of a pair purchased by neighbors on Lake Placid to give to their daughters, who were chums. Both canoes were built in 1903 by guideboat builder Billings, who was also caretaker at one of the camps where the boats were to reside. They were the only canoes Billings ever built. Like several other guideboat builders, when he was asked to build a canoe, he built it in guideboat fashion.

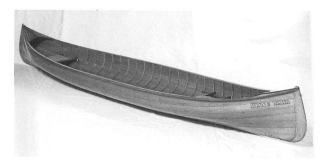

DONOR: Blanche Buttfield Pratt   65.75

25. GUIDEBOAT-BUILT CANOE

L: 14'10"   B: 34"   wt: 53 lbs

Built by George & Bliss, Lake Placid, ca. 1910

Built for recreational paddling, this canoe has strip-planked decks supported by scalloped deck beams. It has never had a carrying yoke. It has a conservative shape, with neither the high stems of the museum's Nickerson canoe (entry 23) nor the tubby shape of the Hanmer canoe (entry 26).

Museum purchase   56.75.2

26. GUIDEBOAT-BUILT CANOE

L: 12'11"   B: 32"   wt: 40 lbs

Built by Willard J. Hanmer, Saranac Lake, between 1920 and 1962

Willard Hanmer was a guideboat builder, and when asked to build canoes or even outboard boats, he often used guideboat construction techniques. This canoe has a guideboat-style carrying yoke. Unlike a guideboat, it has an extremely wide sheer strake and un-guideboat-like floor timbers between the ribs, which are made out of rib stock.

The boat has Hanmer's trademark decks, built with a plywood layer on the bottom and cut-out for a handhold. Its shape is a result of short length (for light weight) combined with width and tumblehome sides (for stability).

DONOR: Dickenson J. Richards   71.194

27. CANADIAN OPEN PADDLING CANOE

L: 15'10"   B: 31"   wt: 50 lbs

Built by Walter Dean, Toronto, Ontario [?], ca. 1885

Canadian builders experimented with many different types of planking in the 1850s, 1860s, and 1870s; this is one variation. The seams between the three extremely wide planks on each side are made watertight by means of metal battens, the edges of which are turned down into the planks on each side staple-wise. Walter Dean, a builder who moved to Toronto from Orillia to build boats in 1883, patented this "Close-Rib Metallic Joint Construction" and became well known for it. When the patent ran out, several other builders began using the technique.

Wide planks were soon abandoned by canoe builders; you can see why by examining the many cracks in this canoe. It was used at the Adirondack League Club near Old Forge.

DONOR: Herbert Hanson   59.6.1

28. PETERBOROUGH CANOE

L: 16'   B: 33"   wt: 84 lbs

Built by the Peterborough Canoe Company Ltd., Peterborough, Ontario, between 1892 and 1923

A Manhattan couple who vacationed in the Adirondacks purchased this boat second-hand from the Interstate Boat House on Dykman Street in the 1950s for use on Loon Lake in Warren County. There are no seats; the paddlers kneel on the bottom, leaning against the thwarts. There is a mast partner which probably took a mast with a lateen

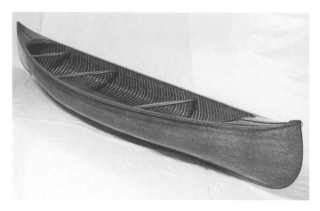

sail. The boat was probably sailed with leeboards, but there is no rudder. Probably the sailor merely tucked a paddle under his arm, using the blade for steering.

The term "Peterborough canoe" has become a generic one referring to all-wood canoes built in the Peterborough area. This boat is a genuine Peterborough, built with the strip-planking which the company made famous. The Peterborough Canoe Company appeared in 1892 and gradually bought up most of the small shops in the region which had pioneered canoe-building technology—like the cedar-strip method. By 1920 Peterborough had become the premier builder of all-wood canoes in Canada; three years later, by merger with Chestnut, the company (later Canadian Watercraft, Ltd.) built virtually all the canoes in Canada.

DONORS: Susan and Larry Zweigbaum   81.51

29. PETERBOROUGH CANOE *Voyager*

L: 16'   B: 34"   wt: 79 lbs

Built by the Peterborough Canoe Company, Ltd., Peterborough, Ontario, 1904

The builders of this canoe called it "The Acme of Perfection in canoe construction" because of its patented tongue-and-groove vertical planking. They claimed that the arches formed by the thin planks were naturally the

strongest type of canoe skin, and the boat was unrivaled for lightness and durability. The planks were steam-bent over forms, kiln-dried, then assembled inside a mold for fastening with lengthwise oak battens. The drying, combined with the tongue-and-groove seams, was supposed to keep shrinkage and therefore leakage to a minimum. This type of construction has much less lengthwise strength, however, than a conventionally-built canoe.

The "cedar rib canoe," as this type of construction was called, was patented in 1879 by John S. Stephenson, one of the earliest innovators in canoe building in the Peterborough area. Shortly thereafter, the Ontario Canoe Company bought the patent. The Peterborough Canoe Company, successor to the O.C.C., built the boats well into the twentieth century.

St. Lawrence County judge Ledyard P. Hale ordered this canoe from the factory and, with his son, paddled it home to Canton in the summer of 1904. Thereafter the Hales criss-crossed the Adirondacks in *Voyager*, paddling her with two single-bladed paddles.

DONOR: The Hale Family   64.137.1

30. CANADIAN TANDEM RACING CANOE

L: 16'   B: 32"   wt: 53 lbs

Built by the William English Canoe Company, Peterborough, Ontario, ca. 1915

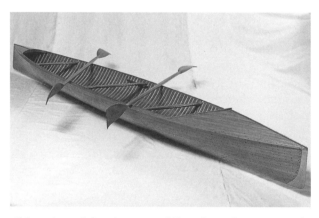

Although used for pleasure paddling from the 1920s until the 1960s, this boat was originally designed as a racing canoe. The vee-bottom made for an unstable boat but did contribute to speed. Racers competed in this type of boat either with single-bladed paddles while kneeling on one knee, or with double-bladed paddles which were used while they sat on box-like seats. A solo paddler could reposition or remove the center thwart. This canoe, best at going fast in a straight line, seems a strange choice for use on the winding Raquette River. It was used there at the Raquette Falls camp owned by Charles W. Bryan, onetime president of the Pullman Car Company.

William English went into business in 1861 and was still building boats around the time of the First World War. He was known for first-class craftsmanship. This boat is planked in Peterborough-style strips. English also built rib-and-batten canoes.

DONOR: Mrs. Charles W. Bryan   66.165

31. CANADIAN OPEN PADDLING CANOE

L: 12'9"   B: 31"   wt: 60 lbs

Built by the Lakefield Canoe Company, Lakefield, Ontario, 1946

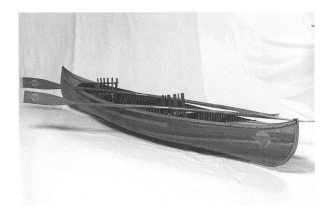

"The ordinary open canoes are coming into greater use each year in the United States," editorialized *Forest and Stream* in 1889. "For pleasure paddling and exercise, and especially for 'girling,' they are unequalled." The owner bought this canoe at the factory in Ontario for $110 in 1946 for just those reasons. It was, he said, "ideal for cruising on quiet water, with a well-provisioned picnic basket. Sometimes when the moon was full, spending the day and not leaving the river until 2 A.M., we loved to drift just before twilight and watch the swallows circle and dip in the water."

This craft is rather short for a tandem paddling canoe, and relatively flat-bottomed, which did gain stability. The seats and seat backs make cruising and picnicking comfortable. The wooden rub strips on the bottom add weight but protect the bottom. They also aid in tracking, or traveling in a straight line, but make the boat harder to turn. This is a substantial boat; the ribs are significantly larger than those in other Peterborough area canoes.

The boatshop which became the Lakefield Canoe Company was founded by Thomas Gordon, one of the pioneers of the Peterborough-style strip-planking seen in this canoe. He also pioneered the use of patterns for planking and the use of a solid mold in building canoes, both of which were widely adopted because they made production of uniform quality much easier and cheaper.

DONOR: Mr. and Mrs. J. H. Denniston   75.208.1

32. OPEN PADDLING CANOE

L: 15'9"   B: 33"   wt: 68 lbs

Built by an unknown builder, probably Canadian

The braces which support the thwarts on the inside of this canoe's sheerstrake are like those commonly used by Canadian builders, as are the wide outwales and the tight upsweep of the bow and stern. Other features make attribution problematic. The ribs are wider than those used by most Canadian builders, and the boat is riveted, instead of clinch-nailed. The fancy deck, strip-built of walnut and mahogany, suggests a special or high-grade order, whoever the builder.

This canoe was paddled on Lake George.

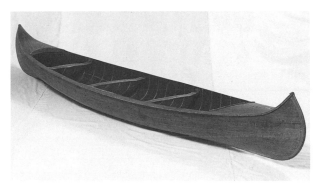

DONORS: Mr. and Mrs. Dudley B. Morrison   72.62.1

33. OPEN PADDLING CANOE

L: 12'11"   B: 33"   wt: 55 lbs

Built by Mahlon C. Freeman, Fulton, ca. 1900

Mahlon Freeman built both small pleasure craft and large boats for the canals and lakes of upstate New York. His small craft, like this canoe, were strip-planked, with the edges of the planks concave and convex and then edge-fastened. The frames were riveted to the planks on ten-inch centers. The carrying yoke is unusual (and not very comfortable-looking) and may be Freeman's own design.

This boat was purchased by Fulton hardware merchant Lewis Parry Smith for use at his camp near Old Forge. The paddle he used with it was a guideboat paddle he acquired in the Adirondacks, rather than the paddle Freeman sold with the boat.

DONOR: Mrs. Willson Parry Smith   90.13.1

34. CANADIAN #3 [?] MODEL OPEN PADDLING CANOE

L: 14'1"   B: 28"   wt: 57 lbs

Built by J. H. Rushton, Canton, 1895

This is an example of one of Rushton's models that he built to meet competition from the Canadian builders. The thwart brackets and the wide outwales are similar to the features of popular Peterborough canoes of the time. The smooth-skinned, guideboat-like planking is totally unlike anything used by the Canadian builders, however, and neither the stem shape nor the sheer profile are Canadian. It was last used on Blue Mountain Lake.

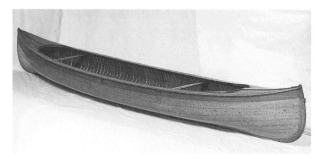

DONOR: Mr. and Mrs. John Collins   66.67.1

35. ARKANSAW TRAVELER MODEL OPEN PADDLING CANOE

L: 15'   B: 28½"   wt: 56 lbs

Designed by Benjamin F. Kip, Canton, 1892
Built by J. H. Rushton, between 1903 and 1906

Rushton's Arkansaw Traveler was one of his later designs, first offered in 1903. It proved popular and was carried in his catalogs through the closing of the boatshop. It was intended for racing—or at least for swift cruising by an experienced paddler. It is narrow and has considerable deadrise, which makes it tippy but fast. The influence of Canadian designs on Rushton showed in the Arkansaw Traveler in the wide outwales and smooth skin, although Rushton achieved the smooth skin with a guideboat lap rather than the strip-building techniques being used by the Peterborough builders. Either single- or double-bladed paddles could be used in this canoe.

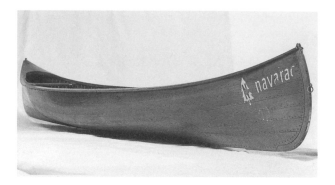

This boat was originally purchased by Adolph Lewisohn, a New York City mining magnate and philanthropist, for Prospect Point, his new camp on Upper Saranac Lake. The camp consisted of forty structures on 4,000 acres, including an enormous rustic boathouse. The boathouse was furnished with the latest in Rushton canoes; Lewisohn eventually bought at least one other, an Indian model which the museum also owns (entry 37). After his death the camp was run as a resort, and then, in 1951, became Camp Navarac, a summer camp for girls. The Rushton canoes became part of the fleet; one wonders if the campers were allowed to use them, or whether paddling them was reserved for counselors and owners.

DONORS: Mr. and Mrs. I. E. Blum   76.61.1

36. #5 ARKANSAW TRAVELER MODEL OPEN PADDLING CANOE

L: 16'   B: 28"   wt: 62 lbs

Designed by Benjamin F. Kip, Canton, 1892
Built by J. H. Rushton, Canton, between 1903 and 1906

The Arkansaw Traveler was one of Rushton's lightest Canadian models. About it he wrote, "this is a canoe that requires some care in handling. . . . It is not built like a racing shell, but at the same time is fast enough to be in a class with them." Harry Rushton recommended "when you take her out for a paddle be sure your hair is parted in the middle."

DONOR: Ralph W. Burger   60.44.1

(See Appendix for lines drawing of Arkansaw Traveler.)

37. INDIAN MODEL OPEN PADDLING CANOE

L: 15′   B: 32″   wt: 47 lbs

Built by J. H. Rushton, Canton, between 1901 and 1912

Around the turn of the century Rushton realized that the largest market for canoes was in wood-canvas models. He remained a staunch believer in the superiority of the all-cedar canoe, however, and his Indian model seems to be a compromise. In form it is like a wood-canvas canoe, but its beveled-lap planking is like the all-wood canoes Rushton loved to build.

Great sheer and wide, flat ribs show the influence of the wood-canvas canoe. Rushton's Indian resembles his canvas-covered Indian Girl model, except for being three inches higher in the ends. It was offered in wood-canvas as well, but ultimately that option did not prove as popular. The lower-profile Indian Girl became the mainstay of the shop after 1902 (entry 35).

DONOR: Mr. and Mrs. I. E. Blum   76.61.2

38. WOOD-CANVAS PADDLING CANOE

L: 16′5″   B: 32″   wt: 68 lbs

Built by E. H. Gerrish, Bangor, Maine, between 1888 and 1902

E. H. Gerrish was the earliest commercial builder of wood-canvas canoes and one of the largest at the time this canoe was built. His canoes reflect their Indian ancestry clearly. Their shapes and the gentle upsweep of the stems are reminiscent of Penobscot and Malecite bark canoes. This canoe is much rounder-bottomed than many other wood-canvas canoes. Canoes built primarily for the recreational market, in contrast to the market of professional guides, tend to be flatter-bottomed for stability.

The stems of this boat have rotted, probably as a result of the boat's having been left upside down on damp ground. Despite the deteriorated exterior, the boat retains the original arc to its bottom.

DONOR: Howard Bullard   77.162.1

39. WOOD-CANVAS PADDLING CANOE

L: 15′1″   B: 31″   wt: 80 lbs

Built by B. N. Morris, Veazie, Maine, ca. 1895

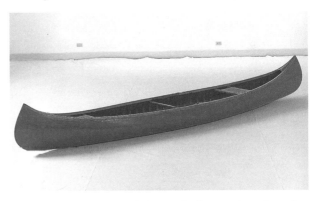

New York surgeon Arpad Gerster had a number of small craft at his camp on Long Lake, but he preferred this boat to any of the guideboats for camping trips and daytime excursions. It has no keel, and its maneuverability was especially useful in the winding Brown's Tract Inlet from Raquette Lake to lower Brown's Tract Pond.

The floor grate protects the interior of the boat but adds weight, suggesting that this canoe was designed more for pleasure paddling than for travel over carries. The moderate upsweep of the stems is reminiscent of Indian canoes after which Maine craft were fashioned.

Dr. Gerster was given this canoe in the late 1890s by William West Durant. The cleat for the guideboat-like carrying yoke was added after the boat got to the Adirondacks. Although the cleat is shaped like a classic guideboat cleat with the forward end longer than the after end, it is fastened flush to the inwale so it does not afford the same secure handgrip as a guideboat yoke. The Morris yoke clamped to the gunwales.

DONOR: John C. A. Gerster   70.205.1

40. WOOD-CANVAS CANOE *Pumpkinseed*

L: 12'   B: 34"   wt: 39 lbs

Built by Charles F. Maurice, Sr., Bisby Lake, about 1908

Building a wood-canvas canoe is not something amateurs generally do to produce a single boat, since constructing the solid mold is such a big project. Nevertheless, Maurice, a member of the Adirondack League Club, built this in the early years of the wood-canvas canoe's great popularity. It is nicely built. In most of the boat Maurice used tapered planks instead of uniform-width ones as in many wood-canvas canoes. Maurice was also a guideboat man; see entry 98 for his early Grant boat, *Ghost*.

DONOR: Charles F. Maurice   72.127.1

41. WOOD-CANVAS ROWING CANOE

L: 18'4"   B: 37½"   wt: 98 lbs

Built by B. N. Morris, Veazie, Maine, about 1908

The canoe evolved for paddling, but canoes also make good rowboats. This boat probably made a relatively fast pulling boat and had the added advantage of quick conversion to a paddling canoe in a narrow passage or if the passenger wanted to help with the propulsion. The fancy outrigger oarlocks add a few inches to the effective beam, and a low stool raises the rower to a comfortable height.

This canoe is also equipped with a mast step, although the sailing rig has not survived.

The Morris rowing outfit included rowlocks, spoon-bladed oars, and detachable rowing-stool, and cost $7.50.

DONOR: Henry N. B. Noss   73.60.1

42. INDIAN GIRL MODEL WOOD-CANVAS PADDLING CANOE

L: 16'10"   B: 34"   wt: 76 lbs

Built by J. H. Rushton, Inc., Canton, between 1911 and 1916

J. H. Rushton never conceded the superiority of all-wood canoes over canvas-covered craft, but when he introduced the Indian Girl in 1902, it quickly became the mainstay of the shop. The Indian Girl was aimed at a public concerned with stability, paddling ease, good looks, and low price; Rushton's previous open canoes had been designed for those interested in speed or lightness. The Indian Girl

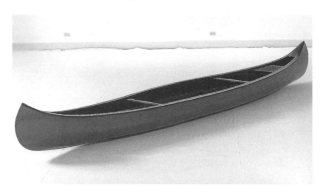

has a keel and little rocker for easy tracking, a flat floor for stability and carrying capacity, greater depth than the Canadian models for safety, and a moderately high bow and stern, "adding the touch of the birch bark canoe to a craft immeasurably strong and more durable." In 1903 an Indian Girl cost $30 and an all-wood Indian model canoe cost $65.

This canoe was produced shortly before the shop closed, and at that time the Indian Girl was offered in five grades and four lengths. This is an "OI" grade, which was "third best." The three-piece open gunwales were cheaper to produce than those on the two higher grades, but they had the important advantage of allowing water and sand to be dumped out easily.

DONOR: Caleb Brokaw, Jr.   83.37.1

43. INDIAN GIRL #4 WOOD-CANVAS CANOE

L: 17'11"   B: 32"   wt: 78 lbs

Built by J. H. Rushton, Inc., between 1906 and 1915

This is a low-grade canoe from the last years of operation of the Rushton shop. It is in poor condition and was collected for its research value.

DONOR: Charles Keough   73.92.1

44. AMERICAN BEAUTY MODEL WOOD-CANVAS PADDLING CANOE

L: 17'1"   B: 32"   wt: 80 lbs

Designed by Harry Rushton, built by J. H. Rushton, Inc., Canton, between 1912 and 1915

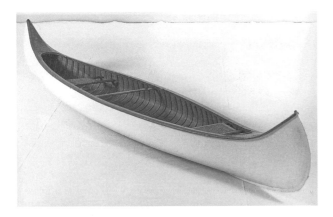

"If you want to get something a trifle better than your neighbor has, a canoe which represents the very best in canvas canoe building—buy an AMERICAN BEAUTY," wrote Harry Rushton the year after his father died and he assumed management of the boat shop. Harry designed the American Beauty by adding high stems for a romantic look to the basic hull shape of the Indian Girl. It had the easy paddling lines of the Indian Girl with a keel that helped in tracking, but the high stems made the boat difficult to handle in a breeze.

The profile appealed to a public whose notion of Indian canoes was stereotyped. The boat was built by special order only, and in only one grade, which included extra-long decks and deluxe materials and fittings. The American Beauty was never a big seller, probably because of its price. In 1912 this boat cost $67.50, while the grade A Indian Girl could be had for only $50.

DONOR: O. M. Edwards   63.182.1

45. WOOD-CANVAS SPONSON CANOE

L: 18'3"   B: 45"   wt: 190 lbs

Built by the E. M. White Co., Veazie, Maine, ca. 1918

While technically a canoe because it is basically double-ended and built like any other of the boats of this important Maine builder, this canoe was probably never paddled. Instead, it was set up for easy operation by one person with oars or with a 2½ horsepower Elto outboard motor. The oars were mounted on outrigger oarlocks to clear the sponsons. The sponsons made the boat more stable for use on a large lake like Lake George.

John S. Apperson, a passionate defender of the "forever wild" amendment of the state constitution, used this boat in his work. Apperson was an engineer by training and brought his engineer's attention to detail to the Adirondacks; he usually knew the areas he campaigned for better than anybody on either side of the controversy. His favorite part of the region was Lake George. He used this boat there, as well as a larger inboard launch he named *Article VII, Section 7* after the "forever wild" clause.

E. M. White was one of the better-known Maine builders. White canoes were produced from 1898 until 1947, when the Old Town Company bought the White name (but not the forms). In 1975 two graduates of Maine's Washington County Vocational and Technical School, Jerry Stelmok and Rollin Thurlow, obtained the White molds and resumed building White canoes.

Somewhere along the line this canoe was fiberglassed, a common, but often short-lived, solution to leaks.

DONOR: William M. White   72.92.1

46. WOOD-CANVAS CANOE

L: 15'5"   B: 33"   wt: 92 lbs

Built by James McCormick, Potsdam, 1920

James McCormick was a Civil War veteran and a North Country jack-of-all-trades. At one time or another he was

an innkeeper, carpenter, lumberman, or carriage maker. Although a contemporary of J. H. Rushton, McCormick did not take up boatbuilding until the wood-canvas era.

This crude canoe is one of a fleet McCormick built for his Iroquois Lodge on Fourth Lake. It was used there until 1942, and then fiberglassed twenty years later.

DONOR: Edwin Barry   80.63.14

47. FOLDING CANOE

L: 11'2"   B: 3'   wt: 42 lbs

Built by the King Canvas Boat Company, Kalamazoo, Michigan, ca. 1890

This is another in the boatbuilder's quest for portability and lightness. It was patented in 1886, and King boats were built into the 1920s. The company boasted in 1922 that the Survey Department of Canada had been using its boats exclusively since 1902. King also claimed that the "time required to set up our boat in any place you desire, is about ten minutes. There are no loose parts to lose or misplace, you cannot go wrong in setting up." As originally sold, this eleven-foot boat formed a 4' x 10" x 8" package weighing seventy pounds, that included a carry-

ing case, jointed double paddle, and air chambers for each end which are now missing.

DONOR: John C. A. Gerster   61.16.2

48. LINKANOE

L: 14'6"   B: 35"   wt: 65 lbs

Built by The Link Manufacturing Co., Gananoque, Ontario between 1945 and 1949

One solution to the problem of portability in small boats is collapsibility. Edwin Link introduced his version of a collapsible boat at a gala "coming out" at the Hotel Lexington in New York on December 12, 1945. The components of the "Linkanoe" were brought in in two satchels, and the boat was assembled in ten minutes. Ten sections of wood-reinforced Mikarta, a plastic commonly used for electrical insulators, were locked together to form the hull, which was then waterproofed by fitting over it a canvas sheath which was hooked over a series of studs beneath the outwale with a continuous shock cord, giving the boat a vaguely Indian look. Thwarts, seats, and two sectional paddles completed the outfit. Early advertising brochures touted the canoe's sturdiness, good handling, and portability. "Check it like luggage, stow it in the closet, or leave it in the trunk of your car," the canoeist was urged. Capacity was also a selling point; a 1945 advertising photo showed Ed Link in his canoe with a moose he had bagged on a hunting trip.

Edwin Link, heir to a piano and organ factory in Binghamton, became enamored of flying as a young man. He started a flight school in the basement of the piano factory at the age of twenty-five, and his first (and ultimately most successful) product was a stationary flight trainer. In the early 1930s he received an order from the British Royal Air Force for several hundred trainers which had to be built in the Empire, so he opened a factory in Gananoque, Ontario. He used a Grumman Widgeon to commute. He also liked to fly into remote Canadian lakes for fishing. His need for a boat he could take with him led to his development of the Linkanoe. The Widgeon had a small cargo compartment and no pontoons upon which a conventional canoe could be carried.

Within a year, Link rowboats, outboard boats, and skiffs joined Link's sectional boat line, and over the next three years about 4,000 sectional boats were manufactured at the Canadian plant (the Binghamton plant had

been dedicated to production of Link Trainers), but they had only limited commercial success. On November 1, 1949, Link Aviation announced a closeout sale to get rid of existing stock and ceased production.

DONOR: Earl Hendee/Phelps Hose Co.　　　87.64

Sailing Canoes

49. DECKED CRUISING CANOE

L: 14'　　B: 30"　　wt: 80 lbs

Built by an unknown builder, ca. 1885

This center-board-less canoe is the closest thing the museum has to MacGregor's *Rob Roy*. It is primarily a paddling canoe; only the substantial keel provided lateral resistance for sailing. The simple pin-and-lateen rig could be doused from the cockpit and then lashed on deck for paddling. The bottom is more vee-bottomed than a boat designed primarily for sailing.

Comfortable cruising was aided by a watertight cargo hatch and a wooden seat with back. The wooden cockpit cover kept spray off the canoeist's legs. Copper air tanks in bow and stern turned the boat into what Rushton would

have called an "unsinkable life-boat." In the photo Charles M. and Saidee Sweet Nichols take this boat for a cruise on Chautauqua Lake about 1895.

Museum purchase　　　63.166.1

50. DECKED SAILING CANOE *Wasp*

L: 16'　　B: 30"　　wt: 87 lbs

Designed by Paul Butler, built by William F. Stevens, Lowell, Massachusetts, 1888

Wasp is the best-known canoe of designer and sailor Paul Butler. With the help of W. F. Stevens, who trained as a builder of shells, Butler strove for ever more speed. He favored a great deal of freeboard so the canoe could be sailed so far heeled over that the sails almost dragged in the water. His passion for light weight resulted in masts and spars made of spirally-wound laminations of spruce and deck fittings of aluminum. Gadgets he developed to give better control and safety under sail include the cross-sliding seat, quick-release cleats for the sheets, and the modified Norwegian tiller seen on this boat. Butler's developments made possible enormous increases in sail area and speed. "Sixteen by thirty" boats like this carried anywhere from 130 to 180 square feet of sail and could reach fifteen miles per hour under favorable conditions. *Wasp* had several rigs during her career, but she came with little rig of any sort when acquired by the museum.

Wasp is equipped with a single-bladed paddle for emergencies, but there is no pretense that this is a cruising canoe. She won the American Canoe Association championship sailing trophy in 1892 and 1893 sailed by Butler, and in 1895 and 1901 with other skippers. She also successfully defended the ACA International Challenge Cup in 1895.

DONOR: Francis Russell Hart Nautical Museum　　　65.9.1

51. Decked Sailing Canoe *Folly*

L: 15'   B: 37"   wt: 170 lbs

Built by an unknown builder, ca. 1900

This nicely-built canoe is substantial enough to sail in heavy weather; she was probably designed for the large bays and estuaries along the coast, rather than inland waters like those of the Adirondacks. She has a thirty-seven-pound bronze centerboard, a sliding seat, and a cross-head tiller to help the skipper stay upright in strong winds. The masts are hollow for lightness and wrapped with line for strength.

DONOR: Robert E. Henry, Jr.   65.1.1

52. Princess Model Decked Cruising Canoe *Diana*

L: 14'   B: 32"   wt: 134 lbs

Built by J. H. Rushton, Canton, 1882

Cincinnati judge Nicholas Longworth, an early canoeist, designed the Princess model with J. H. Rushton. His aim was to make a better sailing boat out of the early Rob Roy type cruising canoes. The Princess was considered one of the larger canoes in the 1880s, with full lines and more sheer than a Rob Roy. Simple lateen sails, a roomy cockpit, foot steering gear, backboards and cushions, and copper flotation tanks made it a comfortable and safe cruiser. Dr. Charles Neide, an Albany dentist and charter member of the American Canoe Association, cruised his Princess *Aurora* 3,300 miles from the 1884 meet on Lake George to the Gulf of Mexico, sleeping in a tent erected over the cockpit. The tent photographed with *Diana* is an original Rushton canoe tent made between 1883 and 1906, probably by Leah Pflaum Rushton (gift of Nathaniel Wells).

Lucien Wulsin purchased this boat as a seasoned canoeist. His first craft had been a second-hand Rushton

American Traveling Canoe, in which he cruised to the headwaters of the Mississippi in 1879. By the turn of the nineteenth century he was a partner in the Baldwin Piano and Organ Company, and a prominent industrialist and philanthropist.

DONOR: Lucien Wulsin II   64.211.1

53. Decked Cruising Canoe, Modified Vesper Model

L: 16'   B: 31"   wt: 90 lbs

Built by J. H. Rushton, Canton, ca. 1900

Although there were many different models of cruising canoes available by the turn of the century, some canoeists preferred to modify existing boats. This boat is a good example. Ralph Rogers, a manufacturer of motorcycle sidecars and an active American Canoe Association member, bought a standard Vesper as a young man. He named her *Seraph* and cruised her down the Mississippi in the winter of 1905, sleeping on cork cushions in a cockpit tent.

Rogers married an eager outdoorswoman in 1907, and with her and their daughter, took family camping trips together. They often combined their interests in canoeing and motorcycling by hauling the canoe on a modified sidecar. "But would the motorcycle pull the load?" wrote a

contemporary. "'Huh!' said the motorcycle—'Huh-huh-huh-huh- h-h-hhhhhhhh!' And away they went, with Mrs. Rogers and the baby" in the sidecar.

About ten years later *Seraph* wore out. Rogers bought another Vesper and modified her as you see here for more comfortable tandem paddling with single blades. The Radix centerboard was replaced with a single leeboard, the rudder removed, the sternpost carved down, a new deck with a longer cockpit installed, and the Bailey rig replaced with a single tiny sail.

DONOR: R. Craig Summers in memory of Ralph Rogers   89.83.1

54. VESPER MODEL DECKED CRUISING CANOE

L: 16'   B: 31"   wt: 110 lbs

Built by J. H. Rushton, Canton, between 1895 and 1900

The Adirondack Museum has two Vesper model canoes. The other one (entry 55) was in excellent shape when acquired, but this one, in poor shape, is important to the collection for some of its metal fittings that are lacking on the better example. The hardware is particularly valuable: turnbuckles which allow adjustments to the rudder gear, the tiller head, rudder, and hardware for the sail. The boat also has a complete set of interlocking cockpit covers, illustrated here. In the days when men of leisure cruised the waterways of the continent in "poor man's yachts," they often traveled to the put-in by rail, packing all their gear and the canoe's rig inside the cargo hatches and the cockpit. The hatches were then locked, and the cockpit closed with a set of covers which slid onto the coaming one at a time, hooking together, until the last one could be secured with a little padlock. The canoe was then checked as baggage and the skipper made the initial stage of his journey in the comfort of a first-class carriage.

DONOR: Frederick Lenning, Jr.   81.24.1

55. VESPER MODEL DECKED CRUISING CANOE

L: 16'   B: 32"   wt: 110 lbs

Built by J. H. Rushton, Canton, between 1903 and 1906

Rushton advertised his Vesper model as the "ultimate cruising canoe." Watertight cargo hatches kept duffel dry and made the boat an "unsinkable life-boat," and the boat

was easily paddled if the wind died. The patented Radix centerboard was constructed of seven sheets of brass which, when raised, telescoped flush with the keel inside a very low centerboard trunk leaving a fairly unobstructed sleeping place for the skipper (see entry 58). The boat's fine lines and great spread of sail also made her fast and fun to race. The boat has no permanent ballast. Instead, the sliding hiking board allowed the sailor to get his weight out to windward to keep the boat upright in a fresh breeze. Rushton marketed this stock model to capitalize on the fame of the original *Vesper*, which he had designed with Robert W. Gibson and which won the 1886 American Canoe Association Challenge Cup Race.

This boat was used by the Pruyn family at their "great camp" Santanoni, near Newcomb. The sails and running rigging are replicas of the originals, but otherwise, except for a few pieces of hardware, the lines, and the tiller, the boat is original.

DONOR: Edward Lansing Pruyn   80.22.1

56. CRUISING CANOE *Nomad*

L: 16'   B: 32"   wt: 107 lbs

Built by J. H. Rushton, Inc., Canton, between 1906 and 1915

Right up to the end of his life J. H. Rushton worked closely with canoeists to come up with new designs. The Nomad model was suggested by D. Perry Frazer, an avid canoeist and noted outdoor writer. Frazer felt that the Ugo, one of Rushton's stock paddling canoes, would make a good cruising canoe for the mouth of the Hudson, where "wind, current and tide often struggle for the mastery." Rushton accordingly built a decked Ugo. Instead of the wide board decks he usually put on sailing canoes, he built the *Nomad* with a strip-built deck, a longer version of decks he usually put on rowboats and paddling canoes.

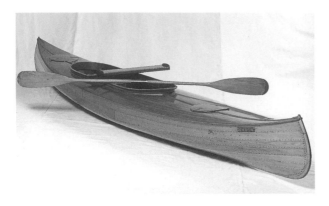

The purchaser of a Nomad from Rushton could choose his own rig. Rushton suggested an "improved Bailey" rig, but Frazer rigged his own boat with two leg-o'-mutton sails. It was paddled with a double-bladed paddle. This boat is missing its rig, but it retains the disappearing Radix centerboard and the sliding seat.

This Nomad model, also named *Nomad*, was purchased for use on Whitney Park near Tupper Lake.

DONOR: Stanley Johnson   60.43.1

(See Appendix for sail plan of *Nomad*.)

57. OPEN SAILING CANOE

L: 13'1"   B: 31"   wt: 57 lbs

Built by J. H. Rushton, Canton, 1883

When Arpad Gerster ordered this boat from J. H. Rushton, the sailing canoes popular with most canoeists had much longer decks, leaving only a five- or six-foot-long cockpit in which the skipper sat. An open boat like this one was lighter. It also has copper flotation tanks fore and aft which helped offset the dangers of swamping. It was paddled with a double-bladed paddle and had two "modified Bailey" sails, a type of rig popular with canoeists. The centerboard may be a later addition to the boat, since open sailing canoes were offered in the Rushton catalogs by 1877, but folding centerboards were not available until 1882.

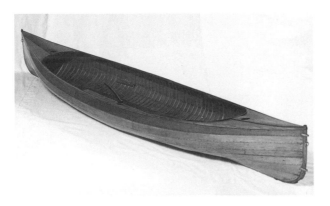

This boat would have been classified by the American Canoe Association as a "paddleable sailing canoe." The tumblehome sides make it easier to paddle. It originally had two mahogany plank seats for two paddlers, both of whom used double-bladed paddles. Gerster sailed and paddled it on trips away from his camp on Raquette Lake until one day a guide, "young, strong and brainless, started to pull water-filled canoe ashore and impact of water tore off planking from stern piece." The boat was repaired, but shortly thereafter Gerster acquired a similar boat in good condition (entry 58).

DONOR: John C. A. Gerster   56.61.4

58. OPEN SAILING CANOE

L: 13'   B: 30"   wt: 69 lbs

Built by J. H. Rushton, Canton, ca. 1894

"IF YOU DO NOT SEE WHAT YOU WANT ASK FOR IT," wrote Rushton in the "greeting" to his 1903 catalog. One of the elements in his success was this willingness to build what the customer wanted. Sometimes such modifications were incorporated into his stock models, and sometimes they simply resulted in a one-of-a-kind customized boat.

In the late 1890s, the entrepreneur William West Durant saw a small open canoe being sailed on Raquette Lake, "smothered in canvas" in light winds, and "in a 'canoe hurricane . . .' under eight square feet of mainsail and a lady's handkerchief for a mizzen." This was another canoe in the museum's collection (entry 57) and was sailed by the New York surgeon Arpad Gerster. Durant liked it so much he ordered a duplicate. By that time the model, a "hunting canoe" with tumblehome, was no longer offered in the catalogs, but Rushton dug out the old forms and built one for Durant, to which he added copper flotation tanks, a sailing rig, and a folding radix centerboard.

Durant used the new boat for a short while and then gave it to Gerster. By then the original had been damaged, and Gerster sailed the new canoe all over Raquette Lake and then on Long Lake, where he moved his camp in 1904. Gerster soon gave up sailing on Long Lake because it "lacked the diversity available at Raquette."

DONOR: John C. A. Gerster   62.67.66

59. OPEN SAILING CANOE

L: 14'8"   B: 28"   wt: 64 lbs

Built by J. H. Rushton, Canton, ca. 1890

Rushton built this on special order for a customer who had very specific ideas about the type of boat he wanted which did not match any of Rushton's stock models. Rushton felt that he learned from his customers in building customized boats, and often incorporated their ideas into his regular offerings.

This is a shorter version of one of Rushton's stock hunting canoes. To build this custom hull, Rushton had only to move the end forms on the jig closer together. The notched risers attached to the inside of the hull are probably for leeboards, which have not survived.

One wonders how well this boat actually sailed. The original owner may have been pleased with Rushton's modifications, but the builder apparently was not, as he did not incorporate them into any of his stock models. The boat was used at a camp near Mountain View in northern Franklin County.

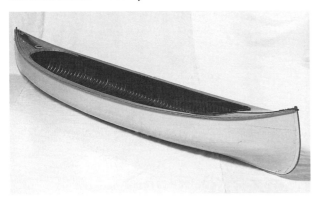

DONOR: John E. Glenn   72.84.1

Rowing Craft

A rowboat is generally distinct from a canoe in its relatively greater width and by the fact that it is propelled by oars, usually two to a person, rather than paddles. The rower faces away from the direction of travel, whereas the paddler faces forward. In other parts of the country the term "pulling boat" is used for these craft, but it is seldom heard in the Adirondacks. Adirondack rowboats range from the Adirondack guideboat to humble flat-bottom skiffs and have been used for all manner of recreation and work.

The Adirondack Museum's guideboat collection is arranged below by geographical location of builder. "Church boats," or "Family boats" are here defined as guideboats longer than eighteen feet.

Adirondack Guideboats

60. SQUARE-STERNED ADIRONDACK GUIDEBOAT

L: 15'   B: 38"   wt: 84 lbs

Built by Reuben Cary, Long Lake, ca. 1870 [?]

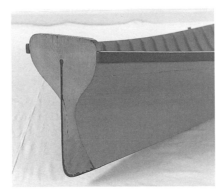

The outstanding feature of this guideboat is the transom-stern carved from a single spruce knee. It gave a more elegant stern than that seen in some other square-sterned boats, such as entry 107, but was more difficult to produce. The narrow planks on this boat are unusual, as well. They average one and one-half inches wide, and there are twelve to a side. The planks on standard guideboats are about three inches wide, with seven or eight to a side.

Reuben Cary continued to build square-sterned models after his neighboring builders had gone to double-enders. While not intended for this use, in this boat's later years the transom provided a place to attach a rudder so a passenger could steer. The hole in the bow deck was probably for a jacklight used for hunting deer.

DONOR: Howard Annin   61.68.1

61. ADIRONDACK GUIDEBOAT *Cub*

L: 17'3"   B: 49"   wt: 92 lbs

Built by Herbert L. Salisbury, Long Lake, about 1880

In the early 1880s, Col. Franklin Brandreth, a summer resident of a large private preserve north of Raquette Lake, had three young daughters who liked to row across Brandreth Lake to a sandy beach for swimming. He worried about their safety in the tippy guideboats that the rest

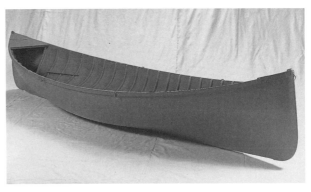

of the Brandreth family used for camping and fishing, so he found a local boatbuilder to build him an especially deep, wide, stable boat for the girls. That he didn't acquire other types of boats that are inherently more stable (a flat-bottomed skiff, for example) is perhaps a testimony of the popularity of the guideboat among sports in the 1880s. It wasn't that the builder was unfamiliar with other types of boatbuilding; Salisbury had only recently moved to the region from Syracuse, and before he left Long Lake a few years later, he built at least two guideboat-like boats with steam-bent frames. (These boats are now at the Mystic Seaport Museum.)

The unusual width of *Cub* was achieved by adding planks and changing the lines, rather than by widening the bottom board. The museum's Blanchard guideboat *Helen*, for example (entry 78), is roughly the same length but six inches narrower. *Cub* is sixteen inches deep at the center; *Helen* is twelve. *Cub* was originally painted dark blue outside and dark green inside, with black wales.

DONOR: Franklin B. Brandreth   63.165.1

62. ADIRONDACK GUIDEBOAT

L: 16'   B: 38"   wt: 83 lbs

Built by an unknown Long Lake builder, ca. 1880

This boat has no yoke cleats and was probably never meant to be carried. It is rather heavier than most guideboats of this length; Floyd and Lewis Grant's *Virginia*, although admittedly built by a master and later than this boat, weighs only fifty-eight pounds.

In any case, this boat was used primarily on a route that has no carries, from the Long Lake Club just downstream from the foot of Long Lake, up into Long Lake and to the village. Long Lake is fifteen miles long, so there were many places to go without carrying. The boat came to the museum with pads cut from a rubber hose protecting the gunwales, probably for transportation overland on a wagon or car.

DONORS: Mr. and Mrs. P. R. Nielson   56.69.1

63. ADIRONDACK GUIDEBOAT

L: 14'2"   B: 37"   wt: 58 lbs

Built by Mitchell Sabattis, Long Lake, before 1890[?]

Mitchell Sabattis was an Abenaki Indian who settled at Long Lake and became one of the most famous Adirondack guides. He certainly built bark canoes, as one might suspect, and Alfred Donaldson, the 1920s historian of the Adirondacks, credited him with inventing the guideboat. The guideboat did not spring full-blown from the forehead of Mitchell Sabattis, or anyone else for that matter, but Sabattis, living in the center of early guideboat development, may well have had a hand in its evolution. This one is nicely built, and if Sabattis did build it, it indicates that he had learned well the technology of his adopted culture. The boat is pictured at Saranac Inn in 1922.

DONORS: Edward L. Richards, Jr., Ernest C. Richards,   82.132.1
and Mrs. Stephen Ells

64. ADIRONDACK GUIDEBOAT

L: 13'3"   B: 36"   wt: 49 lbs

Built by Lewis Austin, Long Lake, 1894

By the end of the nineteenth century many guideboats were built for the use of city sports. This boat, however, was built by a guide for his own use. Lewis Austin knew first-hand the rigors of the carry and built his boat unusually short and light to make his overland travels easier. The cambered deck helps keep water out of the boat.

DeWitt Clinton Flanagan, a sport, persuaded Austin to part with the boat for $55 not long after it was built and used it extensively in the Long Lake region for twenty-five years. The seats are not original.

DONOR:) Thomas T. Bissell   56.67.1

65. ADIRONDACK GUIDEBOAT

L: 14'6"   B: 38"   wt: 54 lbs

Built by George W. Smith, Long Lake, ca. 1895

This is a classic "sport's boat." It was purchased new by Alfred B. Thacher, a New York lawyer who summered on Blue Mountain Lake around the turn of the century. Thacher and two of his fishing cronies bought boats together from local builders.

The finish of this boat has always been "bright," and the owner's monogram is carved in the deck and on the yoke. The workmanship is of the very finest. The stem is the classic Long Lake profile. The oar pins pivot on ball bearings for smoother rowing. The beam is slightly greater forward of amidships, a "cod-headed" shape which some builders felt made the boat faster.

DONOR: Mrs. Alfred B. Thacher   60.37.1

66. ADIRONDACK GUIDEBOAT

L: 16'½"   B: 38¾"   wt: 67 lbs

Built by George W. Smith, Long Lake, 1908

Several fashions in guideboat repair are evident in this boat. Holes are repaired with plastic wood and pieces of wood tacked onto the inside of the hull. In some spots sections of planking have been replaced. Some splits are covered with sheets of brass or flattened tin can. Guides typically carried a little white lead and a handful of tacks to make this type of repair in the woods. This boat was built for the Durand Camp on Long Lake.

George Smith was one of the finest builders of Adirondack guideboats. His boats are characterized by rib feet which run clear across the bottom board and are fitted to the garboard. Most builders cut them off considerably

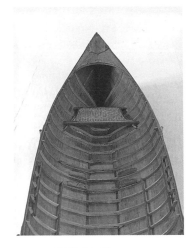

shorter, and many were content to cut them off wherever convenient, regardless of whether or not they resulted in a fair line along the bottom. Smith's boats are also noticeably cod-headed. This one retains its maximum beam for thirty inches forward of the center before it begins to narrow.

DONOR: Waldo M. Allen   70.141.1

67. ADIRONDACK GUIDEBOAT

L: 16'   B: 39"   wt: 93 lbs

Built by George W. Smith, Long Lake, before 1926

This is a well used and crudely repaired example of the work of a high-quality builder. Like most of Smith's boats, this one is cod-headed. Its last home was Camp St. Mary's on Long Lake, and for use there it was painted in the camp color scheme of grey and red.

DONOR: Elliott K. Verner   66.248.1

68. MODIFIED ADIRONDACK GUIDEBOAT

L: 11'4"   B: 38"   wt: 70 lbs

Built by Warren W. Cole, Long Lake, ca. 1900

As outboard motors became available, boaters tried them on whatever craft they had at hand. The Adirondack Museum has two guideboats which were modified for use with outboards, even though a guideboat is not very well suited for use with a motor (the other one is also a Cole boat, entry 72). The fine lines at the stern of an ordinary guideboat give little buoyancy to support the weight of the motor, so the boat would have to be ballasted forward.

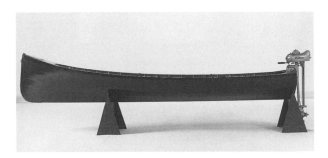

Support for the motor can be increased, however, by cutting off the stern and installing a broad transom, as in this boat. Even so, a guideboat has a displacement hull and a given hull speed faster than which it is difficult to force the boat. A small motor which pushes the boat about rowing speed works best.

This boat was built as a standard guideboat but was damaged when being cartopped to Massachusetts in the late 1920s. In repairing it the owner put in the substantial transom and the seats to "true up the hull and make it sturdier" and also to outfit it for fishing with an outboard. It has a compartment under the center seat.

DONOR: Priscilla H. Noyes   77.191.1

69. ADIRONDACK GUIDEBOAT

L: 16'2"   B: 38"   wt: 53 lbs

Built by Warren W. Cole, Long Lake, ca. 1905

Guideboats were rated cranky or steady—qualities primarily due to the behavior of the occupants but also dependent on the design of the boat. Warren Cole's standard boats were reckoned capacious and steady but not fast because of their relatively round bottoms. He built this boat for his own use, however, and made it sleeker and faster than usual.

Guideboat scholar Kenneth Durant saw Cole in this boat around 1912 and talked him out of it for $70. Durant replaced the conventional fixed pins on the oars with the then-new style pins with ball bearings in them. These were quieter than the old-style oarlocks, which had to be greased regularly and just as regularly spread blackened grease on the rower's clothes and duffel.

Donated in tribute to the guideboat builders of the Adirondacks   57.192.2

(See Appendix for lines drawing of Cole boat.)

70. RACING GUIDEBOAT

L: 15'11"   B: 38"   wt: 62 lbs

Built by Warren W. Cole [?], Long Lake, before 1910

Long Lake native Howard Seaman (1916–1986) was a great promoter of guideboat racing. He encouraged and taught young racers and entered scores of races himself, winning most of them. In 1977, at the age of sixty-one, he won the grueling forty-four-mile solo marathon from Long Lake down the Raquette River to Tupper Lake. Seaman had a short, sharp stroke. He was once measured in a sprint at fifty-six strokes per minute. A passenger remarked, "every time Howard pulled on the oars he would snatch the boat out from under me and the stern deck would fetch up on the knobs of my spine in the small of my back and take off a little hide there."

Seaman's winning record was probably due to his strength, build, stroke, and knowledge of racing strategy. Adirondack guides adopted an easy stroke they could keep up for days on end. They sat up straight and rowed primarily with their arms, their feet braced for comfort against one of the ribs. Racers like Seaman, however, used their backs. He added the broomstick foot stretcher for better leverage. He also reduced friction on the oarlocks by inserting a neoprene sleeve into the strap and by greasing the pins before each race. He replaced the original brass oar pins with stainless steel pins for strength. His boat probably was not built specifically for racing, but its narrow bottom board may have contributed to its speed: 6⅞" wide as contrasted to the 8" or wider bottom boards of H. D. Grant.

Seaman's oars were made by Lyman Beers for Seaman about 1950. They were used only for long-distance races and are lighter and more delicate than Seaman's sprint oars. Made of soft maple, they have a great deal of spring in them. They are also well balanced because of their long overlap of 15". The boat is pictured as if prepared for a racing carry, with the oars shipped with their blades towards the bow, held in place with rubber straps and by the padded yoke.

Howard Seaman raced this boat in one-man competition from the 1940s until his death.

DONOR: Frances Boone Seaman   87.27.1

71. ADIRONDACK GUIDEBOAT

L: 16'   B: 38"   wt: 76 lbs

Built by Warren W. Cole, Long Lake, between 1892 and 1922 [?]

This boat has seen hard use. Many repairs, including fiberglassing, have been made to keep it in service.

DONOR: Thomas I. King, II   72.21.4

72. ADIRONDACK GUIDEBOAT

L: 15'7"   B: 40"   wt: 59 lbs

Built by Warren W. Cole, Long Lake, before 1922

The donor purchased this boat for use at a camp on Raquette Lake in 1950. Shortly thereafter he bought a three-quarter h.p. British Anzani outboard to save the trouble of rowing around the large, often choppy, lake. He attached the motor to the stern of the boat with a standard outboard bracket. These brackets were mostly used for motorizing canoes. There were several models available commercially, or one could use a homemade version like the one on the boat in the photograph. The little Anzani didn't drive the boat much faster than a person could row, so the boat probably performed well with it, although the skipper had to compensate for the weight of the motor and himself in the stern by ballasting the boat forward.

Museum purchase   69.154.1

73. ADIRONDACK GUIDEBOAT

L: 16'8"   B: 47"   wt: 78 lbs

Built by Wallace F. Emerson, Long Lake, about 1917

Guideboats are notoriously tippy. In an attempt to build a boat stable enough for comfortable fly-fishing, Wallace Emerson widened his design. A cousin of the builder called this result "the safest of all guideboats." Although it

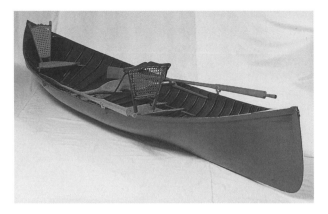

has a yoke, this boat was probably not intended to be carried much. It is relatively heavy and was used primarily on a single lake.

It should be mentioned in the guideboat's defense that while they have little primary stability (they are tippy when lightly loaded), they have a great deal of secondary stability. They may tip alarmingly to a certain point, but at that point they become stable and are reluctant to go over.

DONOR: A. W. Allison   69.166.1

74. ADIRONDACK GUIDEBOAT

L: 13'5"   B: 37"   wt: 57 lbs

Built by an unknown builder in Newcomb[?], 1878

The builder of this boat is unknown, but its date and history are published. In 1883 its owner, a young Philadelphian named Moses Brown, no doubt caught up in the enthusiasm for long voyages in cruising canoes popularized by "Rob Roy" MacGregor, started on a series of trips in this guideboat, which his father had purchased for him in Newcomb. In 1883 he took his sister cross-country from Philadelphia to Harrisburg and returned alone, a trip of 550 miles in twenty days. The following spring he made a trial trip on Delaware Bay for his proposed fall trip: a cruise of fifty-two days and 1,500 miles, in which he

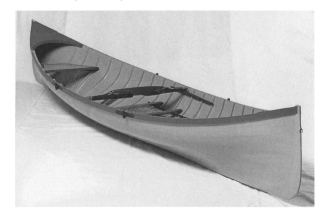

rowed and paddled from Albany down the Erie Canal to Lake Ontario, along the south shore for most of its length, across the lake (out of sight of land), down the St. Lawrence, including running the Long Sault Rapids, and down the Richelieu, Lakes Champlain and George, and the Champlain Canal to Albany. Most nights he slept in his boat under a canvas deck he had rigged up to keep spray and waves out of the boat. Brown also modified his boat with copper air tanks for the longer voyages, and often paddled with a double-bladed paddle. Unfortunately, an unsympathetic restoration has destroyed evidence of the wear and modifications Brown put on his boat.

DONOR: John Brown and Family   62.8.1

75. ADIRONDACK GUIDEBOAT

L: 16'   B: 41"   wt: 91 lbs

Built by Caleb J. or Edmund Chase, Newcomb, between 1850 and 1920

The Chases, father and son, are known as prolific and fine builders, but in this boat they did not achieve the light weight for which the guideboat is famous. It is thirty-three pounds heavier than Floyd and Lewis Grant's *Virginia*, another sixteen-foot boat (entry 101). The boat was probably used at the Tahawus Club, a private preserve established in 1876 near Newcomb; the Chases built a number of boats for the Club.

DONOR: Morris Douw Ferris   57.250.1

76. ADIRONDACK GUIDEBOAT

L: 15'4"   B: 40"   wt: 70 lbs

Built by Caleb J. or Edmund Chase, Newcomb, between 1888 and 1927

Camp Santanoni, the "great camp" of Albany's Pruyn family near Newcomb, boasted a large fleet of pleasure boats including a Rushton Vesper model decked sailing canoe (entry 55), a St. Lawrence skiff, and several guideboats. All were used chiefly as yachts on Newcomb Lake and, like this boat in particular, were built with style and appearance in mind rather than for long hunting or cruis-

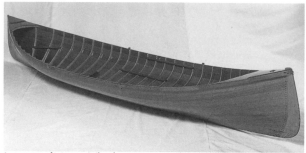

ing expeditions. The boat is entirely planked in Spanish cedar, Rushton's trademark wood for his sheer strakes. A hole in the bow deck with a decorative brass plate was probably for a flagstaff rather than a jacklight. Different footplates accommodate people with different length legs.

The last ribs aft with carved-in "ears" to support the stern seat are Chase characteristics.

DONOR: Thomas I. King II   72.21.1

77. ADIRONDACK GUIDEBOAT

L: 14'6"   B: 39"   wt: 60 lbs

Built by Caleb J. or Edmund Chase, Newcomb, between 1888 and 1921

Although in poor shape, this boat has the classic Chase characteristics of seat-supporting "ears" and the rounded shape of the foot of the stem where it lands on the bottom board inside.

DONOR: Thomas I. King II   72.21.3

78. ADIRONDACK GUIDEBOAT *Helen*

L: 16'11"   B: 43"   wt: 71 lbs

Built by Arthur Blanchard[?], Raquette Lake, 1890

The builder felt that this was his masterpiece, and it is a fine example of the work of a fine builder. The donors used it "much but carefully," and the planks have been skillfully repaired, probably by the builder. It is a bit short

skillfully repaired, probably by the builder. It is a bit short to be considered for a "family boat" or "church boat," but originally had seats for eight. Possibly the "extra" passengers were children. The museum's sixteen-and-a-half-foot Grant guideboat *Ghost* also has an extra, small seat.

The donors modified *Helen* by adding a rudder and adopting feathering, spoon-bladed oars in place of the pinned guideboat oars.

Writing in 1957, the donors remembered that the boat had been built by Arthur Blanchard, one of "two Blanchards who built boats." No other evidence has turned up to indicate that Arthur Blanchard built guideboats, however. It was John Blanchard, Arthur's younger brother, who was well-known as an excellent builder.

DONORS: The Love Family of Philadelphia   57.251.1

79. ADIRONDACK GUIDEBOAT

L: 13'6"   B: 38"   wt: 53 lbs

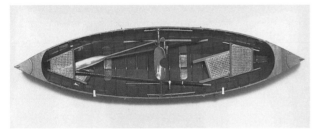

Built by John Blanchard, Raquette Lake, 1935

Willard Hanmer held the opinion that an Adirondack guideboat was most efficient at around sixteen feet in length. His view was shared by most other guideboat builders, which is why the standard boat of the working guide is in that range. As Hanmer put it in 1960, "the twelve, thirteen, and fourteen foot models I build today are nice, light boats to get back where the trout are supposed to be, but you can't make the speed in them. People are not looking for that. Nobody rows any distance anymore."

Many fishermen valued speed less than the ability to reach remote fishing holes. Several builders obliged them. H. D. Grant developed a thirteen-and-one-half-foot model he called a Raider. This is John Blanchard's short boat. It was one of his last and was sold to G. W. and H. M. Alexander of North Creek for $75. When acquired by the museum it retained the original leather thongs used to tie the accessories into the hull for the carry, as shown here.

DONOR: Mrs. Howard Alexander   57.122.1

80. ADIRONDACK GUIDEBOAT

L: 16'1"   B: 39"   wt: 55 lbs

Built by Harold Austin, Blue Mountain Lake, 1975

This boat was built by Harold Austin at the Adirondack Museum when Austin was superintendent of buildings and grounds. Austin used the patterns of his grandfather, Merlin, or Merle Austin of Long Lake.

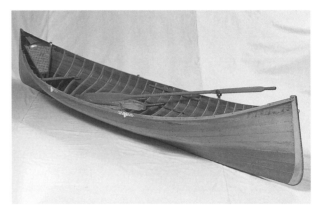

Museum purchase   75.235.1

81. ADIRONDACK GUIDEBOAT

L: 17'4"   B: 44"   wt: 120 lbs

Built by William McLenathan, Saranac Lake[?], ca. 1870

This boat has no yoke cleats and is not quite smooth skinned, but in every other particular it is a guideboat—probably a very early one. It may have been built for the hotel of Benjamin Brewster, the first on Mirror Lake.

Boats like this one, relatively long and heavy, were used in the 1870s to take two or three tourists at a time on sightseeing tours of Lake Placid. The seats no longer exist in this boat, but there were probably at least four. Two guides rowed at the same time, and a circuit of the lake could be made in a morning or an afternoon. This may account for the heavy construction, since classic guideboats are considered too fragile for the stress of tandem

rowing. In 1882 this boat was used to freight building materials to Camp Piney Nook, which was under construction on the shore of Lake Placid, six miles from the nearest road. Much later the boat's owners used an outboard motor on it.

DONOR: Dr. Leroy Wardner   56.74.1

82. ADIRONDACK GUIDEBOAT

L: 15'11"   B: 39"   wt: 65 lbs

Built by William Allen Martin, Saranac Lake, between 1865 and 1886

Willie Martin was one of the earliest and best known of the Saranac Lake guideboat builders. The historian Alfred Donaldson, writing in the 1920s, gave him credit for building the first truly light boats. He probably wasn't the only one, but "Willie Martin's eggshells" became well-known in the Saranac region.

DONOR: Frederick Sutton   64.125.1

83. ADIRONDACK GUIDEBOAT

L: 12'4"   B: 35"   wt: 38 lbs

Built by Theodore Hanmer, Saranac Lake[?], 1890

Guideboat builders were always conscious of the weight of their boats. Many made modifications during their careers in attempts to build ever-lighter boats, but efforts to lighten this boat were extreme. The builder started with a very short length. Then he placed his ribs eight inches apart (instead of the more common five to six) and made them very fine. The widely-spaced ribs were inadequate for support of the gunwale, however, so he added the partial inwale—but not before cutting away all excess

wood. The holes in this inwale also allowed water to drain when the boat was hauled out and tipped over.

The boat was purchased between 1890 and 1895 for use on Osgood Pond near Paul Smiths. The probable builder was Theodore Hanmer, who moved to the Saranac Lake area from Black Brook in 1890 and worked with William Allen Martin before starting his own shop on Lake Street. Theodore Hanmer built over 200 boats before he died at the age of ninety-seven, just five years before his son, Willard.

DONOR: Eleanor V. Salter   70.161.1

84. ADIRONDACK GUIDEBOAT

L: 14'   B: 38"   wt: 60 lbs

Built by an unknown builder, Saranac Lake region, ca. 1900

Most guideboats are fifteen to sixteen feet long because that is the length at which the boat reaches its maximum hull speed. Neither shorter nor longer boats will go faster with a corresponding amount of energy put into rowing. All other things being equal, a longer boat would be faster. All things aren't equal, however; for a guideboat, fifteen–sixteen feet is the optimum balance between length, which allows a boat to go faster if the power is available, and weight and greater wetted surface, which slow a boat down. Shorter and longer boats were built; longer ones that were slower but carried more, and shorter ones that were slower but easier to maneuver and carry. This short boat has half-length ribs in the ends to further cut down on weight.

Edward Livingston Trudeau, the pioneer in the tuberculosis cure of the nineteenth century, was the original owner of this boat. The photograph shows the split planks repaired with sawtoothed metal splines.

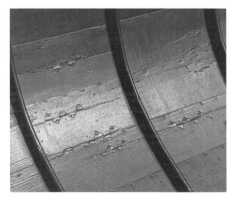

DONOR: Mrs. Henry Garrison   73.89.1

85. ADIRONDACK GUIDEBOAT

L: 16'   B: 41"   wt: 59 lbs

Built by Henry Kilburn Martin, Saranac Lake, about 1905

Henry K. Martin, son of William Allen Martin, also built boats under the name of The Adirondack Boat Building Company. The father had become famous for "eggshell-light" boats; the son carried on the tradition of fine building. This example has a particularly fancy deck which is strip-built of alternating colors of wood. The covering board is beveled on its outer edges, and the coaming is notched where it crosses it.

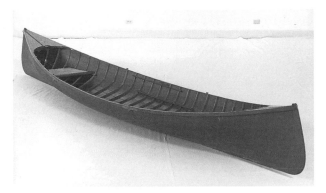

Museum purchase   71.24.1

86. ADIRONDACK GUIDEBOAT

L: 16'   B: 40"   wt: 57 lbs

Built by Willard J. Hanmer, Saranac Lake, 1950

This boat was built around 1950 for use in the Saranac Lake region. The owners' initials are stamped in Hanmer's trademark deck.

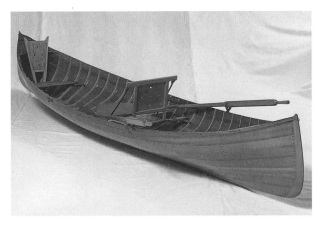

DONOR: Mr. and Mrs. George Skivington and Sons   69.195.1

87. ADIRONDACK GUIDEBOAT

L: 16'1"   B: 40"   wt: 82 lbs

Built by E. G. Ricketson, Bloomingdale, ca. 1900[?]

Like William Vassar, another Bloomingdale builder, Ricketson came late on the scene, and primarily produced boats for use by sports rather than guides. The deck beams on this boat are elegant but heavy. The steam-bent partial ribs between the sawn frames are unusual in that they extend from the top of the sheer strake down, while most so-called half-ribs cross the bottom of the boat and go only part way up the sides. These are so uniformly made and spaced that they are probably original. Varnish was the original finish. The boat has been repeatedly and messily painted, somewhat obscuring its fine lines.

Museum purchase   58.284.2

88. ADIRONDACK GUIDEBOAT

L: 16'   B: 38"   wt: 67 lbs

Built by Ed Harvey, Colton[?], ca. 1880

The Childwold Park Hotel, built on Massawepie Lake in the mid-1880s, had a boat livery stocked with an assortment of rowing craft, including this guideboat. This can be identified as a livery boat by the number on the deck and "C P H Co." stamped into the bottom board. The decks are the distinguishing feature. They look original but are of considerably different sizes. The distinctive heart-shaped covering board matches that on entry 89.

DONOR: Emporium Lumber Company   60.22.28

89. ADIRONDACK GUIDEBOAT

L: 14'3"   B: 36"   wt: 66 lbs

Built by Ed Harvey, Colton, ca. 1880[?]

This boat's hull had been canvased, probably as a repair, when the museum acquired it. It came from Colton, supposedly constructed by a livery owner about whom nothing else is known.

DONOR: Philip Price
68.148.1

90. ADIRONDACK GUIDEBOAT

L: 16'4"   B: 40"   wt: 85 lbs

Built by Bub Stowe, South Colton[?], between 1884 and 1909

The boat livery at the Childwold Park Hotel was at one time run by J. H. Rushton's half-brother, Judd. This boat, a heavily-built livery model, has Rushton-style strip-built decks, deck beams, rounded outwales, and round-headed screws on the coaming but is attributed to Bub Stowe, reportedly the boatbuilder for the hotel. It is four inches longer and three inches wider than Rushton's Saranac Laker.

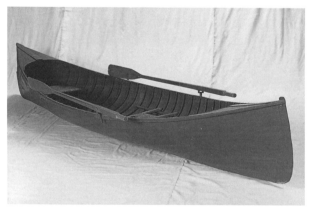

DONOR: Priscilla D. Reich   82.111.1

91. SARANAC LAKER MODEL ADIRONDACK GUIDEBOAT

L: 14'10"   B: 37½"   wt: 62 lbs

Built by J. H. Rushton, Canton, between 1888 and 1890

This is the earliest Rushton guideboat in the museum's

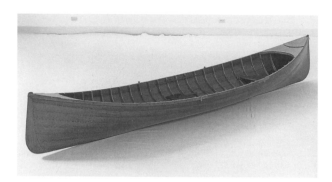

collection. It differs from Rushton's later boats with its relatively plain deck and pie-piece-shaped covering board, squared outwales, and plank seats. The framing is also different, and different from most other guideboat builders. Until 1890 Rushton used ribs ½" x ⅞" on six to seven-inch centers. In 1891 he began offering two grades of Saranac Laker: Grade A had finer ribs spaced closer together. These ⅜" x ¾" ribs were more like what most guideboat builders used, but while they placed them five to seven inches apart, Rushton put his only four inches apart in the Grade A boat.

In the early 1890s, as part of his attempts to reach larger markets, Rushton started selling boats through an agent. This one was purchased through H. C. Squires and Co. in New York, probably for use on Long Island.

DONOR: Thomas R. Wilcox   71.39.1

92. SARANAC LAKER MODEL ADIRONDACK GUIDEBOAT

L: 16'1"   B: 37"   wt: 65 lbs

Built by J. H. Rushton, Canton, between 1888 and 1903

Judd W. Rushton, J. H. Rushton's half-brother, ran the boat livery at the Childwold Park Hotel for a few years in the mid-1890s, so it is perhaps not surprising that this boat was part of the fleet. Its bottom board is stamped with the initials of the Childwold Park Hotel Company. A Rushton guideboat, with its fuller, more stable shape

and heavier construction, probably made a better choice for a livery guideboat than a lighter guide's model.

DONOR: Emporium Lumber Company 60.22.29

93. SARANAC LAKER MODEL ADIRONDACK GUIDEBOAT

L: 16'   B: 38½"   wt: 70 lbs

Built by J. H. Rushton, Canton, between 1888 and 1903

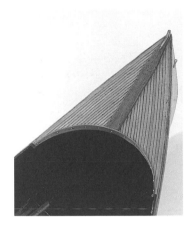

Rushton guideboats are easily distinguished by their finish and trim as well as by their shape. This one shows the fancy strip-built decks supported by scalloped deck beams, the rounded outwales, fancy oarlocks, and round-headed screws in the coaming typical of Rushton guideboats. The center seat backrest is held up by leather straps that could be detached if someone wanted to row from the center without a back. The seats, oars, and yoke are stamped with the owner's name.

DONOR: Beatrice A. Noble 66.161.1

94. SARANAC LAKER MODEL ADIRONDACK GUIDEBOAT

L: 15'10"   B: 38"   wt: 68 lbs

Built by J. H. Rushton, Canton, between 1891 and 1908

"This craft, so familiar to frequenters of the Saranac region, is a very light, swift, and somewhat cranky boat," wrote J. H. Rushton in his 1888 catalog. He was introducing his version of the Adirondack guideboat. One of the elements that contributed to his success as a builder was his knowledge of the market, and in 1888 he knew people wanted guideboats, cranky though they might be. He did not recommend the boat for women and children.

The Rushton boat shop offered an "Adirondack or Saranac Lake Boat" until 1908. Rushton described the boat as "both a pleasure and a hunting boat . . . a connecting link between the two." Rushton guideboats were probably used primarily as pleasure boats and not intended to be carried far. They are heavier than the guideboats built by most other builders, having decorative deck beams and decks, and thick ribs and planking that were

scorned by builders striving for a boat that could be carried a mile or two through the woods. Their shape is also fuller, for greater stability.

This guideboat was fitted with a strongback for a canvas cover to keep out rain and leaves between uses. It was used on Brant Lake.

DONOR: Mrs. Harry Longmire 69.180

95. CANVAS-COVERED GUIDEBOAT

L: 13'   B: 38"   wt: 62 lbs

Built by Myron Augustus Nickerson, Canton, ca. 1898

Myron Nickerson was a farmer of forty-three when he went to work for Rushton to learn a new trade. He worked in the Rushton shop for a while and then went into business with Isaac Hurst, another of Rushton's workmen. Within a few years he was sole proprietor. There was plenty of business to go around; at one time Nickerson had eight men working for him. He built guideboats, skiffs, canoes (both all-wood and canvas-covered), and two motorboats, and at one time he ran a boat livery in Canton. When he needed more business he would load up a wagon with boats he had built over the winter, drive up into the Adirondacks and rent them by the season. He retired around 1907.

Nickerson's designs and many of his details, not surprisingly, look like Rushton's. The strip-built deck and deck beams in this boat are good examples. Nickerson seems to have been more interested in canvas-covered boats than was his mentor, however, and he developed a way of stretching canvas over a guideboat so that the fabric followed the hollow curve at the ends. He might have used this technique to repair leaky boats; this one was skillfully planked and probably held water out when it was new.

DONOR: Mrs. D. A. Blodgett, II 76.97.1

96. Adirondack Guideboat

L: 12'   B: 37"   wt: 61 lbs

Built by an unknown builder, probably in the Indian Lake area, ca. 1880

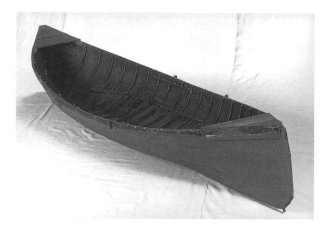

This is somewhat heavy for a boat this short, which is perhaps explained by the fact that it is quite early. It was used in the 1880s by Oliver St. Marie, then storekeeper and later postmaster of Indian Lake. In other respects besides its weight and length, it is of standard construction in rib size and spacing.

DONOR: Gilbert Spring   58.287.1

97. Adirondack Guideboat

L: 16'   B: 38½"   wt: 82 lbs

Built by William Bartlett Kerst, Sabael, between 1895 and 1940

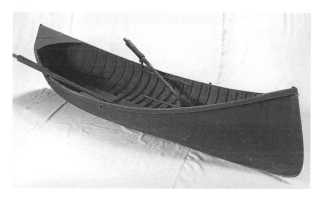

Kerst moved to Sabael in 1895 and began building boats. He built from the patterns of his father-in-law Elijah Fish, with some modifications. One of these was probably the two-piece stem of this boat, used in preference to the rabbetted stem of a standard guideboat. This boat was used at Camp Sabael on Indian Lake. Like many Adirondack boatbuilders of his generation, Kerst soon branched out to build a variety of boat types and, in 1898, to start a livery. He was the first in the area to sell and service outboards. Kerst was also a lumberman, farmer, trapper, and guide. Kerst guideboats were built heavier than most because they were probably not carried but used on Indian Lake.

DONORS: Howard Bullard and E. J. Dikeman   60.23.1

98. Adirondack Guideboat *Ghost*

L: 16'2"   B: 38"   wt: 64 lbs

Built by H. Dwight Grant, Boonville, 1882

Ghost was built for H. D. Grant's son, Sidney, and was exhibited at the New York State Fair in Utica in 1882. The *Boonville Herald* wrote of Grant's exhibit, "these boats are lightly built, tastily painted, and for a speedy pleasure boat cannot be surpassed." *Ghost's* paint scheme, white on the outside and pink on the inside, has been a matter of much comment ever since it came to the museum, but it is close to the original—at least to that used by the boat's second owner. Sidney died of pneumonia in 1884, and the boat was sold to the family on Bisby Lake who gave it to the museum.

Ghost is the earliest Grant boat in the museum. It has the classic tumblehome Long Lake stem profile instead of the later Brown's Tract profile (see Appendix for comparison of stem profiles). It also has feather-edged laps on the planking and heavier ribs, decks, and planking than those used in later Grant boats, and iron screws rather than brass. The seat back is made of four pieces, rather than in the bentwood style used in later Grant boats like *Virginia* (entry 101). The shaped seat pieces and the construction of the deck indicate that Grant was already working towards lightening up his boats. The two pieces of the main part of the deck do not meet; the covering board covers the gap. The decks are oak. The small plank seat was added for a young passenger.

DONOR: Charles F. Maurice   71.141.1

99. ADIRONDACK GUIDEBOAT

L: 15'   B: 38"   wt: 65 lbs

Built by H. Dwight Grant, Boonville, between 1882 and 1886

It is obvious that this early Grant boat was well used. The multiple kick plates indicate that it was regularly rowed by at least three people of varying sizes. It has had many repairs, including wooden patches which sometimes replace a piece of planking and sometimes cover a lap. Other holes were repaired more hastily with the common woodsman's patch of a flattened piece of tin can sealed to the planking with white lead and tacked down with copper tacks.

This guideboat comes in the evolution of Grant's style between *Ghost* (entry 98) and *Virginia* (entry 101). It has better proportioned decks, a more elegant coaming, and a generally less heavy look than the earlier boat, but it does not have the ultimate Grant refinements seen in *Virginia*, nor is it as light. The tacks and screws in this boat are iron; copper and brass fastenings had not yet become common in the Brown's Tract. The planks are fitted together with the feather-edged lap Grant learned from his teacher Henry Stanton, instead of the ship-lapped Grant lap. It also has the slightly tumblehome Long Lake stem profile of Grant's earlier boats.

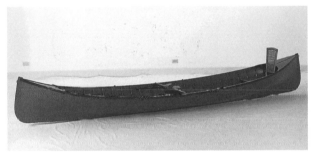

Museum purchase   91.42.1

100. ADIRONDACK GUIDEBOAT

L: 14'   B: 40"   wt: 65 lbs

Built by H. Dwight Grant, Boonville, 1904

Most of Grant's boats were painted—some with the traditional forest colors for guides, and some with more colorful schemes, like the museum's white *Ghost* (entry 98) and orange and blue *Virginia* (entry 101). This one is unusual in being varnished, a finish which was becoming quite popular for boats built for sports at the time. It has an oak "rack," or set of floorboards to protect the bottom of the boat from sharp shoe heels, another feature characteristic of guideboats not intended for cross-country travel and

carrying. Grant typically used high-quality oak for his decks; this boat also has oak outwales. In immaculate condition, it has the classic slightly outward-tipping Grant stem profile. It is the eleventh boat Grant built in 1904, and was for the camp of the owners of the Kingsford Cornstarch Company on Big Moose Lake.

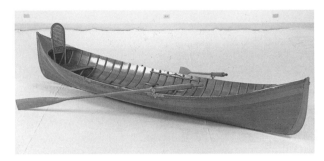

DONOR: Celia A. Hubbell in memory of Orville W. Hubbell   73.113.1

101. ADIRONDACK GUIDEBOAT *Virginia*

L: 16'   B: 40"   wt: 58 lbs

Built by Lewis and Floyd Grant, Boonville, 1905

Virginia was the first Adirondack guideboat to have her lines published. Small-craft historian John Gardner measured and drew her in the summer of 1959, and his subsequent articles in *Outdoor Maine* brought the guideboat to the attention of an international audience. The articles revealed the variation in planking thickness from the ¼" garboard to the ³⁄₁₆" sheer plank and a ½" thick bottom board.

Virginia has a typical Grant stem profile. Grant learned to build the slightly tumblehome Long Lake stem profile, but around 1894 he tipped the top of the stem slightly outward, creating the distinctive Brown's Tract profile. This was done to eliminate the "podgy" look which resulted from increasing the beam in the ends for more buoyancy. It also made bending the sheer plank easier because it eliminated a tight spot near the ends of the boat. Other Grant characteristics include the drain hole in the deck, used when the boat was turned upside down, and the construction of the seats. The steam-bent seat back is

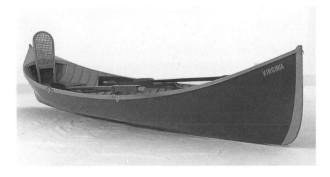

lighter than a mortised one, and the stretchers for the seats themselves have been molded to eliminate excess wood.

Virginia was built as a pleasure boat rather than a guide's boat, the third guideboat from the Grant shop in 1905. She was rarely carried and used mostly on Big Moose Lake. She has always been painted in the colors of the University of Virginia, the *alma mater* of the young man for whom she was built. His monogram appears on the stern.

DONOR: Mr. and Mrs. Robert Jeffress   57.229.1

DONOR: Brigadier General J. T. Bissell   64.170.1

(See Appendix for lines drawing of Parsons boat.)

102. ADIRONDACK GUIDEBOAT

L: 14'3"   B: 39½"   wt: 57 lbs

Built by Parsons and Roberts, Old Forge, 1905

When Riley Parsons died in 1904 his sons Ben and Ira continued the business with the financial backing of John E. Roberts.* This is a typical product of their shop, except that its length fits between their two most common sizes, 15–16' and 13'. This and one of the museum's other Parsons boats (entry 103) have the unusual characteristic of partial ribs fore and aft that do not extend all the way down to the bottom board.

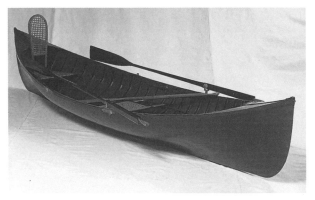

DONOR: Paul J. Thut   77.27.1

*Comstock, ed. *The Adirondack League Club*, 193, contains a useful chronology of the Grant and Parsons numbering systems.

103. ADIRONDACK GUIDEBOAT

L: 13'   B: 38½"   wt: 57 lbs

Built by Parsons Brothers, Old Forge, 1926

This is an unusually short boat for the Parsons shop, built as their twenty-first boat after starting a new numbering system for their boats as "Parsons Brothers" in 1924. It has been hardly used and probably has the original finish.

104. ADIRONDACK GUIDEBOAT

L: 17'   B: 41"   wt: 72 lbs

Built by Riley, Ben, or Ira Parsons, Old Forge, between 1890 and 1945

Attributing boats to the Grant and Parsons shops is easier than it is for many builders because of the distinctive Brown's Tract stem profile. Distinguishing the two from each other is a bit more difficult. Both used metal bands over the tops of their stems, separate from the metal bang strips which protect the edges of the stems, but Parsons's stem caps are slightly heavier than Grant's. Also, the Parsons stem tips outward a bit more than that of Grant. This boat was attributed primarily on the evidence of its length. Grant production records survive, pencil notations on a series of pine boards recording construction date, several dimensions, and purchaser. There is no boat listed on them the length of this one.

The Grant and Parsons shops were the only guideboat builders to have used for their craft a numbering system that has been deciphered. The Grants stamped their boats with both the year and a sequential number starting over each year; the Parsonses used the year and a sequential number which started over again with each new business partnership, of which there were seven. These numbering

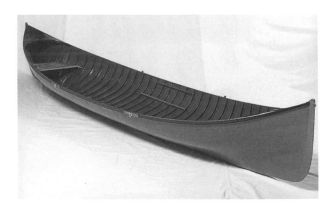

systems normally make dating a Grant or Parsons boat easy. This boat, however, is a puzzle. There is only a "1" stamped in the stems, and on the inside of the yoke cleats, where one normally finds numbers, there is an "L" on the left side of the boat and an "R" on the right side. It was owned by Earl Covey (1876–1952), a guide and hotel-owner on Big Moose Lake. He used the boat in the Big Moose area.

DONOR: Mrs. Earl Covey   57.260.1

105. ADIRONDACK GUIDEBOAT

L: 16'4"   B: 39"   wt: 65 lbs

Built by an unknown builder

The significant amount of rocker in the bottom of this boat suggests that it was built for use on winding water-ways where the rower needed to turn frequently, rather than on a large lake where he would be rowing mostly in a straight line. Its interesting repairs include a patch that is double the width of the planks, probably to fix a puncture.

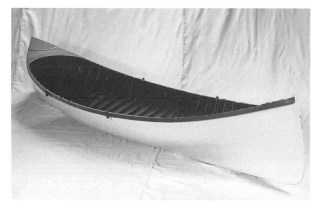

DONOR: Richard Collins   56.90.1

106. ADIRONDACK GUIDEBOAT

L: 11'9"   B: 31"   wt: 41 lbs

Built by an unknown builder

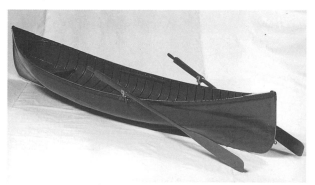

This is the smallest guideboat in the museum's collection. Kenneth Durant, a great admirer of the working guides and their guideboats, felt it was merely "a delicate and charming toy, of no practical use."

Museum purchase   58.284.1

107. "CHASE LAKE" GUIDEBOAT

L: 13'5"   B: 37"   wt: 75 lbs

Built by an unknown builder; found at Black River Flats

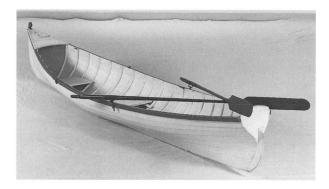

Guideboat scholar Kenneth Durant called this boat "an archaeological gem" because it corresponds to sketches and descriptions of guideboats in their beginnings in the 1830s and 1840s. It seems not to have been carried (there is no evidence of a yoke), but it has all the characteristics of the early portable boats: flat bottom board, lapstrake planking, and sawn frames.

There is no direct evidence that this is a truly ancient boat (Durant thought it was only "a crude effort to make a type of boat in common use at one time"), but some construction details suggest that it is early. The ribs have been gotten out by hand—they are hand-sawn and then spokeshaved. The planks are fastened only from the out-side in, as in normal lapstrake construction, rather than the lap fastenings alternating from the inside out, as well, as in true guideboat construction. There are no screws, which either points to a poor, isolated boatbuilder or a date prior to the 1850s. Construction of guideboats be-came much easier after development of the finely-pointed wood-screw in 1846.*

The knob on the stem, handy for pulling the boat ashore, may be a feature common in the eastern Adiron-dacks; there is one in a Samuel Griggs painting of Schroon Lake from 1871, and it also shows up in photographs of the region. What looks like a piece of stem protruding through the transom is probably an awkward attempt to build a boat with a transom by a builder accustomed to building double-ended boats.

Museum purchase   58.338.1

*Durant, *The Adirondack Guide-Boat*, 133.

108. ADIRONDACK GUIDEBOAT

L: 15'2"   B: 42"   wt: 110 lbs

Built by an unknown builder

A heavily-built boat with no documentation.

DONOR: Atwood Manley   59.32.1

109. ADIRONDACK GUIDEBOAT RELIC

L: 13'4"   B: 38"   wt: 53 lbs

Built by an unknown builder

Acquired for study purposes only, this boat is notable for its unusually wide bottom board. Most guideboats have bottom boards around eight inches wide; this one is twelve.

DONOR: Charles L. Bailey, Sr.   76.106.1

110. ADIRONDACK GUIDEBOAT

L: 15'11"   B: 38"   wt: 89 lbs

Built by an unknown builder

This boat is credited with a rather fantastic history. It is supposed to have gone over Raquette Falls and survived (the only boat to have done so) and to have been used to tow log booms on Tupper Lake. Both stories are suspect, the first because of the violence of the rapids and the second because of the weight and drag of a log boom. As Paul Jamieson reports in a modern canoeing guide, many canoes have been wrecked trying to run Raquette Falls and at least one life lost in the attempts.*

DONOR: Mrs. Alice Bichsel in memory of Henry LaVoy   78.103.1

*Paul Jamieson, *Adirondack Canoe Waters: North Flow*, 69.

111. "LAKE CLEAR" GUIDEBOAT

L: 15'5"   B: 44"   wt: 117 lbs

Built by an unknown builder, Lake Clear area

The builder of this boat was familiar with guideboat construction techniques and stuck to them even though he

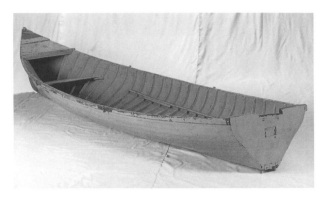

was building a boat that was probably not intended for carrying. This big boat is heavily built all around, has long seat risers for multiple center seats, a wide bottom board, and no yoke cleats. It was built double-ended and then sawn off to accommodate an outboard. The date of its construction is problematical; the simple, transverse deck suggests an early boat, but the transom was probably added some time in the first two decades of the twentieth century.

DONORS: Mr. and Mrs. Edward Comstock, Jr.   84.44.1

112. SWALLOW MODEL FIBERGLASS ADIRONDACK GUIDEBOAT

L: 15'8"   B: 41"   wt: 85 lbs

Built by the Allcock Manufacturing Co., Ossining, 1960

In the 1950s Fox Conner, whose family had been summering at Brandreth Park north of Raquette Lake for a hundred years, began building guideboats in fiberglass, the recently-developed material which was sweeping the boatbuilding industry. He took as his model an especially wide boat on the family's preserve that had been built by Wallace Emerson for fishing. Conner felt that the extra stability would be important in

marketing the boat to a public unfamiliar with guideboats. The fiberglass guideboat was a success; Conner developed three models and was soon making fifty to sixty boats per year in the family's Hav-a-hart trap factory in Ossining. By 1962, however, more factory space was needed for traps, and Conner sold the business to Tom Bissell of Long Lake, who continued to produce the boats until 1967.

The extra width of this guideboat is the same as the original on which it was modeled, but in other respects it lacks some useful guideboat characteristics. There is no yoke for carrying, which reflects the extra weight of the craft; the Emerson guideboat in the museum's collection which is six inches wider and a foot longer than this one weighs eight pounds less. The fiberglass version has no foot brace or even ribs to push against, which reduces its effectiveness as a pulling boat.

DONOR: Fox B. Conner 60.39.1

113. ADIRONDACK GUIDEBOAT

L: 15'4"　　B: 38"　　wt: 96 lbs

Built by an unknown builder, ca. 1880[?]

That this is an early boat is suggested by the fact that it is fastened with iron screws. The hole in the deck was meant for a jacklight for deer hunting at night.

John K. Brown was a Keene Valley guide, builder of camps, and superintendent of the Adirondack Mountain Reserve in 1887 and 1888. He used this boat himself and then sold it to the Weston family before 1900. The boat was probably built some years earlier, possibly in Newcomb. There are only three known nineteenth-century Keene Valley builders, Mason and Legrand Hale, and Horace Braman. The donor, Harold Weston (1894–1972), was an artist who painted in the Adirondacks.

DONORS: Mr. and Mrs. Harold Weston 56.76.10

114. SQUARE-STERNED CHURCH BOAT

L: 18'11"　　B: 42½"　　wt: 113 lbs

Built by an unknown builder, Saranac Lake area[?]

Although square-sterned guideboats are generally thought of as earlier than double-ended ones, this one was probably built after double-ended guideboats became common in the late 1870s. Instead of the one-piece transom-stern of some craft (like the museum's Reuben Cary boat, entry 60) or the smooth run of transom into stem seen in the 1870s sketches of Frederick B. Allen (see narrative p. 000), the shortened but otherwise standard stem of this boat is notched into the transom, which is attached to its upper end. A similar stern is seen in the museum's "Chase Lake" guideboat (entry 107).

This boat was used on the St. Regis Lakes. Everything about its construction speaks capacity, the extra-wide bottom board as well as the length. The nearly full-length seat cleats originally supported three center seats. The boat originally had an awning, and two awning sockets on either side remain. Apparently, when the awning was no

longer used, a new pair of oars was purchased with pins large enough for the awning sockets, which are larger in diameter than the original oarlock sockets.

DONORS: Mr. and Mrs. N. V. V. F. Munson 63.71.1

115. CHURCH BOAT

L: 20'10"　　B: 45"　　wt: 170 lbs

Built by William Vassar, Bloomingdale, ca. 1890 [?]

On Sunday mornings around the turn of the nineteenth century, guests at the Mitchell camp on Spitfire Lake were taken in this boat to St. John's in the Wilderness at Paul Smiths or the Presbyterian Church at Keese's Mills. As many as six could travel together, a number sufficient for lively commentary on the sermon on the way home.

William Vassar was known for the extreme ram bows which made his boats easy to spot from a distance. He also commonly made elaborate decks of alternating strips of light and dark woods which were fastened to an under layer, rather than being nailed together like the classic strip-built decks of J. H. Rushton.

DONOR: Mrs. Robert Hawkins 63.128.1

116. FREIGHT BOAT

L: 19'6"　　B: 42"　　wt: 120 lbs

Built in the Grant shop, Boonville, 1903

This is the fifth boat to come from the Grant shop in 1903, a period in which H. D. Grant's sons Floyd and Lewis were working alongside their father. It was originally sold to Richard Crego, a Boonville guide. Many guides sold their boats to sports every few years and

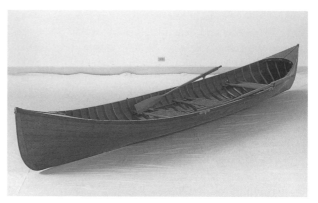

bought new ones; Crego seems to have done that with this one, as the initials "W.S." are on it. It was perhaps this later owner who added the rudder (now missing).

117. CHURCH BOAT OR FAMILY BOAT

L: 18'   B: 46"   wt: 80 lbs

Built by Parsons Brothers, Old Forge, 1914

This is the forty-second boat built by Ben and Ira Parsons after they began labeling their boats "Parsons Brothers" in 1910. Based on existing numbered boats, their total output from 1890 to 1945 was 282 boats.

118. FAMILY BOAT

L: 19'11"   B: 45"   wt: 110 lbs

Built by Parsons Brothers, Old Forge, 1920

This boat is the seventy-seventh built after Ben and Ira Parsons went into business for themselves in 1910. It was originally used on the waters of the Adirondack League Club, where well equipped camps had several standard-length guideboats for experienced adults to use, a scow for the children, and a family boat to take everyone visiting or to the other end of the lake for a picnic.

Guideboat-Influenced Boats

119. GUIDEBOAT-BUILT ROWBOAT

L: 17'   B: 42"   wt: 104 lbs

Built by an unknown builder, possibly in Raquette Lake, before 1912

The sawn frames and provenance suggest that this skiff was built by a guideboat builder. It is not a true guideboat, however, because of the lapstrake construction and lack of a carrying yoke. It was built for pleasure use on Raquette Lake and is equipped with upholstered seats with back cushions and a rudder. Like several boats in our collection, the bottom was canvased below the waterline when the boat began to leak.

120. GUIDEBOAT-BUILT PLEASURE ROWBOAT

L: 14'5½"   B: 42½"   wt: 97 lbs

Built by the Old Forge Boat Company, Old Forge, between 1896 and 1910

Just as guideboat builders built canoes with guideboat construction techniques, so they also built other types of boats. Guideboat-built rowing boats, like this one, were typically heavier and beamier than classic guideboats and used in areas where light weight for carrying was not a concern. This boat has the guideboat's smooth skin and sawn ribs, with elegant, but heavy, decks and decorative deck beams. The builders borrowed the differently-painted sheer strake and splash rail below it from the St. Lawrence skiff. Skiffs were very popular at the time this boat was built in the same area for the same uses.

The Old Forge Boat Company was run by Theodore Seeber, who had worked with the Parsonses. Ben and Ira Parsons built boats in Old Forge from 1890 to 1945 under several different names and with other partners.

This boat was built for use on Fourth Lake.

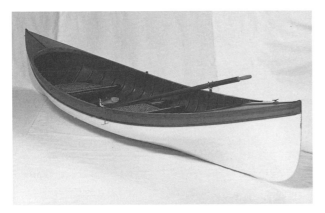

121. GUIDEBOAT-STYLE PLEASURE ROWBOAT

L: 14'10"   B: 44"   wt: 109 lbs

Built by William Bartlett Kerst, Sabael, between 1910 and 1920

In most respects this boat is like a guideboat: flush-lapped planking, sheerline, and general set-up. The ribs have no feet, however, but are placed opposite each other and fastened across the bottom board to floor timbers. Kerst never intended it to be carried and provided no yoke. It was probably built for the Kerst livery in Sabael on Indian Lake.

122. BUYCE BOAT

L: 15'2"   B: 43"   wt: 100 lbs

Built by John F. Buyce, Speculator, 1910

John F. Buyce took up boatbuilding when the demand for guideboats was diminishing. Like other Adirondack builders, however, guideboat construction—flat bottom board and sawn frames—was what he was familiar with and what he liked to use. This is an example of what has become known as a "Buyce boat": a heavy, lapstrake rowing boat built of pine with the framing of a guideboat. Because of their weight, Buyce boats are not meant to be carried and have no yokes, but they row well and became great favorites in the Speculator–Lake Pleasant area.

123. BUYCE BOAT

L: 15'   B: 47"   wt: 160 lbs

Built by John F. Buyce, Speculator, ca. 1920[?]

Buyce built a variety of craft to suit his customers' needs. His transom-sterned boats were good for use with an outboard motor. A selection of Buyce boats is pictured in the photograph around 1920.

124. BUYCE BOAT

L: 15'3½"   B: 41½"
wt: 86 lbs

Built by John F. Buyce, Speculator, ca. 1920

Buyce's sturdy, easy-going boats were well suited for livery use. This was one of five built for Charles S. Brown's boat livery in Speculator.

125. WOOD-CANVAS PLEASURE ROWBOAT

L: 15'5"   B: 38½"   wt: 113 lbs

Built by an unknown builder, before 1923

This skiff may have been an attempt to reproduce a guide-boat-like craft using wood-canvas technology so popular after 1900. The canvas covering may also be a repair; the boat is planked like an ordinary smooth-skinned boat. Its oarlocks and general shape resemble a guideboat, as do the decks; the decks, in fact, look like the work of the elusive Ed Harvey of Colton. The hull is quite fine in the ends, and the canvas there does not follow the reverse curve but bridges across the hollow.

DONOR: Adela E. Smith   68.139.1

126. GUIDEBOAT-LIKE ROWING BOAT

L: 14'5"   B: 38"   wt: 75 lbs

Built by Canton Boat Works, Canton, ca. 1900[?]

By the turn of the century the Adirondack guideboat was popular enough that some builders tried to sell cheaper or "improved" versions. This boat, which has a shape similar to a guideboat, seems to be one of them. Although it does have the guideboat's smooth skin and oarlocks for pinned oars, it has no yoke cleats, indicating that it was not meant to be carried. Instead of the sawn frames of a true guideboat, it is built with steam-bent ribs, easier, and

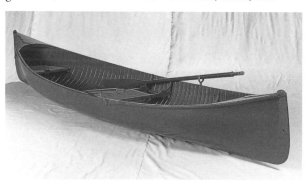

therefore cheaper, to produce. J. H. Rushton offered a true guideboat for $100 in 1900, and a version with bent ribs for $90.

A suspiciously modern-looking plate identifies the builder as the "Canton Boat Works," but no information about that firm has ever been discovered. The name may be one popularly ascribed to a North Country builder by later generations. Possibly he was one of the workmen trained by Rushton who went out on his own when Rushton's shop fell on hard times in the 1890s.

Museum purchase   88.3.1

Whitehalls and Whitehall-Influenced Boats

127. WHITEHALL *Grey Bonnet*

L: 15'1"   B: 47"   wt: 172 lbs

Built by James Everson, Williamsburgh, between 1850 and 1890

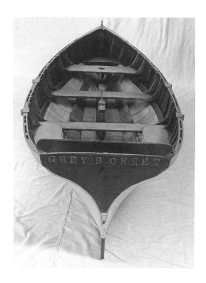

This is a classic example of the popular Whitehall rowboat built during the Whitehall's heyday as a pleasure craft. It substantiates Everson's reputation for fine craftsmanship and light construction in the elegant way in which the framing is notched to meet the keel and the beading on the sheer strake. Knees inset into the seats and the open gunwales are unusual in a Whitehall. Most boats as old as this have been extensively repaired; this one has been heavily scraped and there are several new pieces.

Dr. Frank F. Durand, son of the distinguished American painter Asher B. Durand, purchased this Whitehall for sailing and rowing on Lake George. The rig has not survived.

James Everson originally built boats for working New York watermen, principally the Whitehall boats that they used as water taxis around the busy harbor. As the pleasure boat market developed, he began to produce small sloop and yawl yachts as well as continuing to build Whitehalls for commercial and pleasure use. He was a competitor of Rushton, and in the late 1860s built W. L.

Alden his first canoe. Alden was the first commodore of the American Canoe Association.

DONOR: George H. Danforth   60.41.1

128. WHITEHALL

L: 16'   B: 49"   wt: 164 lbs

Built by an unknown builder, probably in Yonkers, ca. 1895

In the early 1880s, Phineas C. Lounsbury, a New York City banker and later governor of Connecticut, built Camp Echo on the south shore of Long Point, Raquette Lake. He loved to fish but was afraid of the water, so he wanted a boat more stable than a guideboat.

He bought a boat that is a true Whitehall in its general construction but shows guideboat influence in the fact that it has a bottom board instead of a keel. It is unusually lightly built for a Whitehall. Family tradition has it that the boat was built in Yonkers on special order for Lounsbury; he wanted light construction and may have specified the guideboat-like features, too. It was originally painted dark green outside and light blue-green inside.

DONOR: Maxwell Griffith   66.168.1

129. PLEASURE ROWBOAT *Kinder*

L: 15'7"   B: 49"   wt: 185 lbs

Built by an unknown builder, Long Lake, 1884 or 1885

This boat was built in Long Lake in the heyday of guideboat construction there, but its builder was heavily influenced by outside traditions. It has a "built-down stern," which is a boatbuilding term for a stern in which the skeg is formed by part of the hull planking instead of being part of the boat's backbone. The stem is in two pieces, instead of the usual one-piece rabbetted stem of a guideboat, and there was once a rudder. The ribs are sawn from naturally-curving spruce roots, as are guideboat ribs, but do not have feet. Like Whitehall frames, they have two-piece heels. The actual floor timbers are later additions to

the boat, as are some of the heavier ribs. Guideboat traditions seem to have influenced the backbone arrangement of bottom board and sawn ribs.

The donor's father had three of these boats built for his family. The two smaller ones were named for, and used by, the father and mother. This boat, appropriately named, was used by the children. The boat names were painted in black on the inside of each transom in Gothic script. All three boats were painted red with black trim and pale green interiors. The oars were red with pale green tips.

DONORS: Charles E. Keppler, Clara K. French, Richard R. Keppler, Constance K. Millard, and Max P. Keppler   70.187.1

130. LAKE GEORGE ROWBOAT

L: 15'5"   B: 49"   wt: 122 lbs

Built by Henry Durrin, Bolton Landing, about 1905

Most Lake George rowboats have transoms, but some, like this one, are double-ended. It was built by "Hank" Durrin, a hunter and trapper who lived at the Narrows and sometimes worked for F. R. Smith & Sons of Bolton Landing, who were the best-known builders of the type. The construction of this boat, which was built by Durrin on his own, is typical of the Smith shop. The planking is carvel riveted to steam-bent frames. The foot braces are missing but were of the standard adjustable type: dowels

that fit into brackets fixed to the floorboards. The breast-hook is a particularly nice bit of boatbuilding. It is a natural crook into which are mortised the inwales. This boat was used at Diamond Point on Lake George.

DONORS: The Gerald Thornell Family   75.154.1

131. LAKE GEORGE ROWBOAT *Helen*

L: 15'8"   B: 41"   wt: 130 lbs

Built by F. R. Smith & Sons, Bolton Landing, 1908

Miss Helen Simpson, daughter of the Commodore of the Lake George Yacht Club, received this deluxe model of the locally famous Lake George rowboat on her eighteenth birthday. In *Helen* she was turned out nicely for a favorite pastime of the young summer folks of the time who decorated flotillas with lights and engaged a small steamer to tow a string of boats out into the evening calm for singing.

F. R. Smith & Sons of Bolton Landing were the best-known builders of Lake George rowboats. Three men took seven days to complete one. More than two hundred rowboats went to the Sagamore Hotel on Lake George; between 1885 and 1926 Smith's built over six hundred.

The use of the Lake George rowboat evolved similarly to that of the Adirondack guideboat in being first a guide's boat and then a yacht, but it differs from its mountain relations in not being portable. Greater weight and fuller lines give greater stability and seaworthiness for a large lake. Its general shape is similar to a Whitehall, but guideboat influence is more significant. Unlike the Whitehall, which has a normal keel, the Lake George rowboat has a plank bottom board like a guideboat. It was also probably built in the same manner as a guideboat with every other frame fastened to the bottom board and secured with molds, then planked, and then the final alternate frames put in.

DONOR: Mrs. Granville Beals   65.26.1

132. LAKE GEORGE ROWBOAT

L: 15'6"   B: 46"   wt: 128 lbs

Built by F. R. Smith & Sons, Bolton Landing, between 1910 and 1915

This is a fine example of the work of the Smith shop. The oarlocks are offset to allow the use of longer oars. Dowels fit into adjustable brackets to provide an adjustable foot brace. The builders at Smith's favored the use of natural crooks, and they have used two as seat knees. The framing is typical of the Smith shop, having limber holes in the floors to allow water to drain the length of the boat.

DONOR: William G. Wait   65.68.1

St. Lawrence Skiffs and Skiff-Influenced Boats

133. ST. LAWRENCE SKIFF

L: 18'6"   B: 44"   wt: 215 lbs

Built by an unknown builder, about 1895

This is a classic St. Lawrence skiff as it appeared for pleasure use and use by professional guides of the St. Lawrence River. It has a rabbetted keel, unlike the bottom board of a guideboat. Its shape is typical: slightly outward tipping stems and cod-headed. It is built with steam-bent frames and lapstrake planking, with full floorboards and metal seat hangers. It is on the small side; skiffs are typically eighteen to twenty-two feet long. It has a mast step, probably for a spritsail. There is no centerboard, however,

suggesting it was only sailed downwind. The oars are missing, but they were rowed against tholepins, as were most St. Lawrence skiffs.

DONOR: Thousand Islands Shipyard Museum   72.60.1

134. ST. LAWRENCE SKIFF

L: 18'5¾"   B: 42"   wt: 144 lbs

Built by Moses Sauve and Son, Brockville, Ontario, ca. 1890

By the late 1880s the skiffs on the St. Lawrence River had evolved into several distinct types. Many of the builders in the Clayton and Alexandria Bay areas kept producing skiffs for professional fishing guides even though their business in skiffs for pleasure use increased. These boats were generally equipped with spritsails but no rudders. While sailing, the boat is made to change direction by shifting the weight of the crew.

On the other side of the river, the builders of Brockville became famous for their racing skiffs. Moses Sauve was the best-known of these Brockville builders. Most of his skiffs were of smooth-skinned construction, and he equipped them with ordinary spoon-bladed feathering oars, rudders, and sails of any description. Skiff sailors who wished to race could pick from a great variety of sails being developed by sailing canoeists, sails with names like the Mohican Rig or the Modified Bailey.* Guideboat scholar Kenneth Durant felt that Sauve had adopted smooth-skinned construction from guideboat builders across the river and to the south; it is perhaps more likely that the feather-edged lap was adopted from the practices of contemporary competitive canoeists. They, in turn, may have learned from guideboat builders.

This skiff has a smooth skin, but unlike a guideboat it is nailed only from the outside in, not from the inside out as well. It was used in the Adirondacks near North Creek.

DONOR: Anthony Deepe   63.122.1

*"The Brockville (St. Lawrence) Racing Skiff," *The American Canoeist* 5, no. 5 (May 1886): 66–68.

135. ST. LAWRENCE SKIFF

L: 16'   B: 42"   wt: 178 lbs

Built by the St. Lawrence River Skiff, Canoe and Steam Launch Company, Clayton, ca. 1890

The builders of this boat claimed to be the original designers and builders of the St. Lawrence skiff—by descent through two previous owners. They built four different grades of skiffs, in four lengths, and their "Number Four," which is this boat, was "highly recommended for first-class liveries."* This one was part of the livery at the Pontiac Hotel on the north shore of Fourth Lake in the Fulton Chain. It has seen hard use, as have many livery boats, and has gained weight in consequence. The livery manager inserted sister ribs between the original ribs throughout the length of the boat and painted the boat every couple of seasons. As originally built, the Number Four weighed 110 pounds. The livery-grade skiffs produced by the "St. Lawrence Etc." had conventional oarlocks in place of the tholepins of classic skiffs.

DONOR: William G. Wark   74.226.18

* *The St. Lawrence River Skiff, Canoe and Steam Launch Company*, 1895 catalog, 3.

(See Appendix for plans for a St. Lawrence skiff.)

136. PLEASURE ROWBOAT *Eva*

L: 13'3"   B: 36"   wt: 59 lbs

Built by J. H. Rushton, Canton, between 1873 and 1887

Rushton's earliest catalogs describe the advantages of his trademark half-oval ribs. "They have all the strength with half the weight of the old fashioned, broad, flat rib, and are smooth and even. No hand-made rib can equal them in beauty." The mast step and upholstery on the stern seat are probably later additions. This is the oldest Rushton pleasure rowboat in our collection. Instead of a metal

plate or embossed trademark, Rushton painted his name on the stern seat brace. The upholstered seat, which once had a seat back, is probably not original to the boat.

Eva was purchased by a Massachusetts textile manufacturer for his wife, Eva, who died in 1887. It remained in the family until coming to the museum.

DONORS: Dorothy R. and Wilfred A. LePage   69.99.1

137. RUSHTON PLEASURE ROWBOAT MODEL #107

L: 15'1"   B: 42¾"   wt: 97 lbs

Built by J. H. Rushton, Canton, between 1885 and 1893

By the late 1880s, the #107 was, according to Rushton's catalog, "very popular, as it combines to a marked degree the qualities necessary for both rowing and sailing." The boat came with oars and rudder for $70 in Grade C, and for $28.75 more one could have a patent folding brass centerboard, simple lateen rig, and two copper air tanks capable of floating seven people at 150 pounds each, "with their clothing on, keeping their heads above water."*

This is either an early boat or a low-grade one; by 1888 the decks on Rushton's rowboats were 2½" to 3" long; by 1892 the top four grades had long decks made of alternately colored strips of wood, and only grade E had a short, solid deck.

DONOR: Ernest Walker   60.40.1

Rushton's Portable Sporting Boats, 1888 catalog, 9.

138. ROW AND SAILBOAT *Wanderer*

L: 17'   B: 42"   wt: 203 lbs

Built by J. H. Rushton, Canton, 1889

"Rows remarkably well, & sails *finely*," wrote Owen Vincent Coffin in 1889, "even dead against the wind. Com-

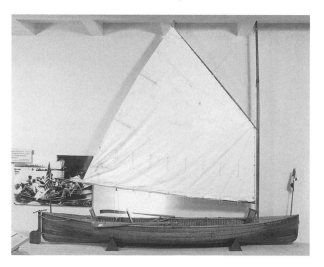

partments make her a regular life-boat, while they are fitted with hatches & can thus be used for storing luggage & tools." Coffin had just taken possession of his new yacht *Wanderer* at Paul Smiths Station, whence it had come from the factory by rail.

Coffin rowed and sailed *Wanderer* fifty miles on her maiden voyage back to the Sagamore Hotel on Long Lake, leaving at 5:00 a.m. and arriving at 9:00 p.m. He and his crew of one carried the boat across the carries on two rectangular yokes. In all, *Wanderer* was rowed 196 miles and sailed 28 in her first year.

Wanderer is J. H. Rushton's pleasure rowboat #105, Grade A, ordered with options of rig, watertight compartments, striped canvas awning (now missing), and two pair of Lyman's patent bow-facing oars at a cost of $177.75. She was rowed and sailed for sixty-four years in the Adirondacks on Long Lake, Blue Mountain Lake, and Lake Pleasant and occasionally accompanied her skipper home to Hartford. O. V. Coffin was governor of Connecticut from 1895 to 1897.

DONOR: William L. Wessels   57.184.1

139. INDIANA #6 MODEL PLEASURE ROWBOAT

L: 14'10½"   B: 38½"   wt: 108 lbs

Built by J. H. Rushton, Canton, between 1895 and 1902

One of the narrower models in Rushton's wide array of pleasure rowboats was the Indiana. This one was purchased for livery use at the Mirror Lake Inn in Lake Placid and has seen rough use. It has been patched on the outside near the keel with canvas, and wooden skids were added to protect the bottom when the boat was drawn up on a dock or shore. It has two center seats and originally had three rowing stations.

The Mirror Lake Inn burned in 1988. It was then the oldest structure in Lake Placid, having been built in 1883. The Wycoff family, from whom the museum purchased this boat, ran that hotel for fifty years.

Museum purchase   56.75.1

140. Iowa Pleasure Rowboat

L: 13'1"   B: 37"   wt: 89 lbs

Built by J. H. Rushton, Canton, between 1895 and 1906

Rushton built his Iowa model "for a small, light, fast rowing skiff . . . well suited to the use of ladies and children who have obtained some proficiency on the water." This example was purchased for the use of Governor Seymour's family at Camp Penwood on Fourth Lake.

DONOR: Alan S. Burstein   76.122.1

(See Appendix for lines drawing of a boat similar to this one.)

141. Rushton Pleasure Rowboat

L: 15'11"   B: 42"   wt: 100 lbs

Built by J. H. Rushton, Canton, between 1895 and 1907

The lapstrake "Pleasure Rowboat" was the mainstay of the Rushton shop until Rushton introduced his wood-canvas canoe in 1901. This one is probably Florida #5 or Delaware #5 model. The earliest provenance we have for it is Lake George, where it was kept in the 1950s.

Lake George resident Frank Schneider restored this boat in the 1960s. He modified the deck, replaced coamings and covering boards with plywood, and added modern oarlocks, floorboards, and seats.

DONOR: Frank Schneider   65.25.1

142. Florida Model Pleasure Rowboat

L: 16'   B: 43"   wt: 108 lbs

Built by J. H. Rushton, Inc., Canton, between 1906 and 1916

The Florida was the most popular model pleasure rowboat built by the Rushton shop in the years following the death of its founder. According to the catalog, it had "all the good qualities of the St. Lawrence River skiff, but is by no means as heavy although stronger. Plumb stems and flatter floor give longer waterline, more floating capacity, and greater safety, while the easy lines give a perfect running boat." The number of pleasure rowboats offered by J. H. Rushton, Inc. had been reduced since the 1890s; by this time the only other stock model was the lighter Iowa, six inches narrower.

DONOR: Richard Jagels   75.254.1

143. Lapstrake Pleasure Rowboat

L: 13'   B: 36"   wt: 80 lbs

Built by L. D. Rogers & Co., Brasher Falls, ca. 1890

Lorenzo D. Rogers operated a woodworking shop in Brasher Falls from about 1870 until 1919. He advertised carriages, sleighs, and general repairs, with fine boats "a speciality." No record remains of how many boats he built, but the two extant ones are evidence that he knew what he was doing. This one is very similar to the pleasure rowboats of his better-known competitor in the North Country, J. H. Rushton. Unlike Rushton, Rogers rounded the inside corners of the keel.

Museum purchase   74.214.1

144. Skaneateles Skiff

L: 14'9"   B: 40"   wt: 105 lbs

Built by the Skaneateles Boat and Canoe Co., Skaneateles, ca. 1910

The popular St. Lawrence skiff was imitated by many builders in the late nineteenth century, including the Skaneateles Boat and Canoe Co. This is their least elaborate model, smaller than most skiffs, and without an armchair-like stern seat. It does have the skiff's general lines and construction, as well as nickel-plated seat hangers and rub rails below the sheer strakes. It is a classic factory-built boat. No particular effort has been made by its builders to make it lighter or finish parts like the seats and breasthook elegantly. It was purchased for use at Kamp Kill Kare, a large private preserve south of Raquette Lake then owned by the Garvan family of Philadelphia.

The Skaneateles Boat and Canoe Co. was the successor to the Bowdish Manufacturing Company, which dated to 1886. The original company ran into financial difficulties in 1893, and in the reorganization, two of the workers, George Smith and James Ruth, purchased it and renamed it. Smith was a Scottish immigrant and Ruth hailed from Peterborough, Ontario; Ruth was given credit in a 1930 Syracuse newspaper article for having introduced rib and batten construction to America.* The company built small boats like sailing canoes, skiffs, and a fourteen-foot "Adirondacks Hunting Canoe" as well as large power yachts in the fifty-foot range. James Ruth lost his life trying to save the company's patterns when the boatshop burned in 1930. Smith sold his interest shortly afterwards, but the business continued into the 1950s.

DONOR: Francis P. Garvan, Jr.   67.132.1

*"Boat Building Joy and Work for 42 Years," *Syracuse Post-Standard*, November 20, 1932.

145. PLEASURE ROWBOAT

L: 15'7"   B: 42"   wt: 108 lbs

Built by Herbert M. Sprague, Parishville, 1922

Sprague kept his eye on the market and studied successful models offered by other builders. On this model he added some features of the popular St. Lawrence skiff. The tholepins mounted on the gunwales, which take oars with slots in them, are one such example. (The present oars themselves seem to have been made too light for this boat

to begin with and have been strengthened.) There is also a fixture to hold the butt of a trolling rod on the inside near the stern, a feature often added to skiffs for muskellunge fishing in the St. Lawrence. The seats are supported with metal seat hangers like St. Lawrence skiffs—at least in places.

Sprague's work was not as fine as that of his more famous competitor, J. H. Rushton. His ribs are heavier and cruder (in this boat they are not all the same) and his nails coarser. He was innovative, however; he applied for a patent in 1889 on a method of producing watertight seams by inserting a strip of treated rubber between the planking, and, as on this boat, he placed a tiny strip of tin between nail heads and wood when making scarf joints to join lengthwise pieces of planking, to reduce splitting.

This skiff was built by Sprague near the end of his life and purchased by the donor's mother for her husband's birthday. It was originally varnished inside and out and spent its life at a camp on Cranberry Lake.

DONOR: Donald A. Spotswood   79.83.1

146. PLEASURE ROWBOAT *Norma*

L: 13'5"   B: 42"   wt: 110 lbs

Built by an unknown builder

The St. Lawrence skiff influenced a number of pleasure rowboats in the North Country in the late nineteenth century, including this little boat. *Norma* is smaller than the classic skiff and does not have the skiff shape. She does

have skiff features of lapstrake construction, tholepin oars, and brass seat hangers. The skiff-like chair seat is not original to the boat. *Norma* was one of a dozen similar boats on West Canada Lake.

DONOR: L. F. Sliter   61.59.1

Flat-Bottomed Rowboats

147. BRANT LAKE FISHING BOAT

L: 15'4"   B: 43½"   wt: 144 lbs

Designed by Charlie Duell and built by Willis Kingsley, Brant Lake, 1914

Duell, a guide and livery-owner, specified that this boat be put together in a manner both simple and purposeful. It is dory-built; that is, a bottom of lengthwise planks is set up, the sawn-to-shape frames are fastened to it, and then the sides are planked. It has seam battens on the *outside*, which not only give protection to the hull but, in the case of the sides, act as spray rails. The boat also has guideboat-like features of natural crook stems and knees. A correspondent of *Forest and Stream* wrote in 1908 that "it is the best all-around fishing boat I ever sat in, and I have sat in a few." In particular he cited the high stern seat, which avoided "the cramped position of the legs which is so tiresome to a person not accustomed to sitting in a low seat. I am convinced," he continued, "that three-quarters of the fatigue of a day's fishing is caused by the posture caused by the low seats in most boats."* He also appreciated the steadiness of the boat when standing up to cast and her seaworthiness.

Museum purchase   71.140.1

*N. E. Spaulding, "Brant Lake Fishing Boats," *Forest and Stream* 71, no. 20 (Nov. 14, 1908): 781.

148. FLAT-BOTTOMED ROWBOAT

L: 12'   B: 41"   wt: 115 lbs

Built by Lewis Grant, Boonville, 1951

Although this is very much a utilitarian working boat, Lewis Grant's care and high-level craftsmanship are evident in details like the beveled chine log and outwales

which taper up into the stem and are beveled so that the oarlock stands up straight.

Lewis Grant continued to build guideboats after taking over his father's shop in 1916, but increasingly the demand was not for those elegant craft but for something more utilitarian. Grant built 116 of these rowboats of his own design of pine and marine plywood before he stopped working in 1957. The Adirondack League Club and its members bought most of them, distributing them at remote ponds so members wouldn't have to carry in a guideboat for every fishing trip. Members used their personal Grant rowboats for hauling freight and for children to row. Old-style guides jokingly referred to these boats as "Bisby guideboats."* Grant charged $125 for this type of boat in 1952. In the early 1920s he charged $155–$207 for guideboats, according to size and finish.

DONOR: Stuart Gillespie   72.93.1

*Lewis L. Grant, excerpts from letters in Kenneth Durant, ed., *Guide-Boat Days and Ways* (Blue Mtn. Lake, N.Y.: The Adirondack Museum, 1963), 230.

Miscellaneous Types

149. "FRENCH LOUIE" ROWBOAT

L: 12'6"   B: 40"   wt: 82 lbs

Built by Hiram Wilson[?], Oneida, ca. 1870

Not all Adirondack guides rowed and "toted" Adirondack guideboats as they took their clients from fishing hole to deer run. "French Louie" Seymour, a renowned guide, trapper, and hermit of the West Canada Lakes area, spread boats throughout his working territory after he built his sporting camp in 1885 so that he had a boat at every lake or stillwater. Among the thirty-eight boats he had hidden in the woods were several "sturdy, well-made, round-bottom boats," made by the Wilson brothers of Oneida, who regularly visited a lean-to on the big West Canada Lake.* This boat is probably one of them. It was originally brought into the woods by one of the Wilsons when he came hunting with Andrew Shepardson of Smyrna in the 1870s, hiring French Louie as guide. When John Shepard-

son built a camp on Limekiln Lake around 1910, he had Seymour bring the boat the twenty-six miles through the woods to the new Camp Wilmajo.

This is a lightly-built boat which originally had a carrying yoke. The carvel planking is riveted to the frames and caulked with strands of cotton wicking.

DONORS: Rebecca Conklin, Alice Per Lee Taylor,   56.78.1
    and Alice McGovern

*Harvey Dunham, *Adirondack French Louie: Early Life in the North Woods* (Saranac Lake, N. Y.: North Country Books, 1970), 95–96.

150. PLEASURE ROWBOAT

L: 14'4"   B: 36"   wt: 98 lbs

Built by Harry Green, Hermon, ca. 1890

Harry Green used a strip method of planking similar to that made famous by the canoe builders of the Peterborough area. Instead of shiplapped edges to the planks, however, he rounded the edge of one plank and hollowed the matching one. The planks are fastened to the ribs but not to each other.

Green built many boats for the Cranberry Lake region, in the hills near his home. This one belonged to Bill Rasbeck (1840–1917), a popular Cranberry Lake guide.

Museum purchase   74.214.2

151. PLEASURE ROWBOAT *Uncas*

L: 13'3"   B: 39"   wt: 63 lbs

Built by an unknown builder, about 1893

When he returned from the Chicago World's Fair, twelve-year-old Ernest H. Webb, a summer resident near Speculator, found this little skiff awaiting him and his playmates. It is strip-planked. The planks are fastened only to the closely-spaced half-oval ribs. The boat was in the care of John Buyce of Speculator for years. Like many camps and boats in the Adirondacks, it is named for a James Fenimore Cooper character.

DONOR: Kate C. S. Cornell   73.112.1

152. PLEASURE ROWBOAT OF PAPER

L: 14'   B: 45"   wt: 250 lbs

Built by Waters Paper Boat Co., Troy, 1900

The design of this boat dates from at least the mid-1870s when it appears in the Waters catalog as a "14-Ft. Gig." Waters claimed it was "a very safe, comfortable family Boat, for fishing or pleasure rowing" for two to six people. The hull sold then for $95—not cheap, even when compared with the competition's all-cedar boats.

Elisha Waters went out of business in 1901. This boat was built to the old design during the company's final year. In addition to oars, however, it had a new method of propulsion: a foot-powered propeller manufactured by the Durand Manufacturing Company which operated in Rochester from 1900 to 1904. The "power plant" weighs seventy-eight pounds. The propeller shaft runs out through a wooden skeg; the paper hull ends at the top of the deadwood.

This boat was received by the museum in poor condition, but it is invaluable as a study specimen. It is the only known paper boat that has a Waters builder's plate. Although punctures in the hull make it appear to have been built from laminations of paper, as were Waters's shells, Waters's rowboats were built from a single thickness of unsized paper. After a solid mold was prepared by fitting keel and gunwales over it, the damp paper was laid over

the mold and tacked in place. It was dried in a heated drying room, then removed from the mold for water-proofing and finishing with hardware and additional woodwork. The waterproofing mixture was a proprietary secret.* The boat was purchased new for use on a lake near Pottersville.

DONOR: Joel Zimmerman   73.79.1

*Kenneth Cupery, "Nineteenth Century Paper Boat Technology: Pasting Together Shreds of Evidence," (unpublished paper, 1990), 9–15, curatorial research files, Adirondack Museum.

153. PLEASURE ROWBOAT

L: 16'   B: 46"   wt: 144 lbs

Built by Harry Green, Hermon, ca. 1900[?]

This is a strip-planked boat from a livery at the Childwold Park Hotel on Massawepie Lake.

DONOR: Emporium Lumber Co.   60.22.30

154. FOLDING ROWBOAT

L: 10'9"   B: 41"   wt: 53 lbs

Built by an unknown builder, early twentieth century

This square-sterned model of the popular folding canvas boat could take a small outboard as well as oars. The potential problem of the sides flexing while rowing is solved by the unusual oarlock arrangement.

Museum purchase   70.203.1

155. "TIN ROWBOAT" RELIC

L: 13'10"   B: 45"   wt: 180 lbs

Built by W. H. Mullins, Salem, Ohio, ca. 1910[?]

In the days before aluminum and modern synthetics, boatbuilders sought an alternative to wood that would be cheaper, or lighter, or require less maintenance. Pressed steel was a fairly successful material, especially as marketed by Ohio's Mullins Company.

From what can be deduced from this rusted relic, this is probably *The Prince*, Mullins's popular family and plea-sure boat. This example was brought up off the bottom of a lake near Gloversville in the southern Adirondacks. When new, it had a long wooden deck, wooden outwales and plank seats, a wooden floor grate, and a Whitehall-style stern seat. It had air chambers fore and aft, and was painted with aluminum paint outside and light blue inside.

DONOR: Mrs. Robert W. Burton   75.262.1

(See Appendix for lines drawing of this boat.)

156. PLEASURE ROWBOAT

L: 11'5"   B: 44"   wt: 80 lbs

Built by John H. Cornwall, North Creek, about 1910

Although John Cornwall was not a regular boatbuilder in the Adirondacks, he must have had some training on Long Island, where he lived before moving to North Creek. This little lapstrake skiff has nice details such as White-hall-like stern "sheets" (or stern "seat" as it's called in the Adirondacks), hand-forged bangstrip, and natural crook breasthook, quarter-knees, and seat braces. The planks are riveted to each other and to the frames, which are steam-bent. The boat originally had a rudder, which had a lengthwise metal strip running along its forward edge that slid down into a receiving fixture on the stern of the boat.

DONOR: Ken Cornwall   73.62.1

157. Wood-Canvas Rowboat

L: 16'1"   B: 45"   wt: 141 lbs

Built by the Old Town Canoe Company, Old Town, Maine, 1926

The Old Town Company made its name in canoes, but also built small rowboats and outboard motorboats using the same wood-canvas construction as in the canoes. "Here are the good qualities of a wooden boat without the disadvantages of a wooden boat," they claimed in their catalog. The museum has two of their rowboats, this one and entry 158. Two grades were available; this one was CS grade, "for general use where superior finish is not desired . . . a common-sense canoe of guaranteed dependability." It originally had a rudder, four seats, two backrests, two pair of oarlocks, and keel and stems outside the canvas. It cost $79.

Harry Parsons, a World War I veteran, annually spent the summers in a tent on Indian Lake for more than twenty-seven consecutive years starting in 1923. For the first few years he rented a guideboat from Kerst's livery in Sabael, but in 1926 he purchased this boat. Four years later he beefed up the inwales and outwales, added an outboard bracket, and bought a four-horsepower Johnson Light-Twin outboard motor. Because he generally camped alone, he rigged up a rope-steering arrangement so he could sit amidships while motoring. For trolling he shut down the motor and used the oars.

DONOR: Mr. and Mrs. Henry G. Parsons   63.204

158. Wood-Canvas Rowboat

L: 16'1"   B: 51"   wt: 182 lbs

Built by the Old Town Canoe Company, Old Town, Maine, 1929

The owners of this boat must have been looking for a good boat for children. It is so heavily built that little skippers could hardly damage its structure, and its spon-

sons make it practically untippable—at least according to the manufacturer. Sponsons, a $22 option, are the separately-canvased longitudinal air chambers attached to each side just below the outwales; they became popular on wood-canvas canoes and rowboats like this one. "The shallow draft offers exceedingly slight resistance to the water, making it an easy boat for women and children to handle. It's an ideal boat for fishing," claimed the catalog.

Judging from the condition in which this boat came to the museum, it did see hard use. Like the museum's other wood-canvas rowboat, it is CS grade. It came from Big Wolf Lake, a private association that had a fleet of Old Town canoes fitted with brass centerboards and lateen sails for racing.

DONOR: Lucia Meigs Andrews   70.177.9

159. Pleasure Rowboat

L: 11'6"   B: 33"   wt: 45 lbs

Built by John F. Buyce, Speculator, ca. 1935

Buyce was best known for his heavy guideboat-built rowboats, but like most other Adirondack builders he built to order. When customers wanted something finer, he gave it to them. He built some guideboats (planked with exotic woods like cypress) and occasionally light lapstrake skiffs like this one. It had a guideboat-style yoke for carrying into remote ponds.

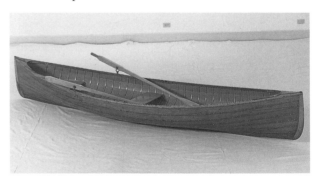

Museum purchase   70.21.1

160. PLEASURE ROWBOAT

L: 15'11"   B: 48"   wt: 150 lbs

Built by Atherton Farr, East DeKalb, ca. 1940

Atherton Farr took up woodworking after he had retired from his dairy farm in the late 1920s. He built sleighs, wagons, furniture, and boats. His rowboats were strip-planked, with the planks concave on one edge and convex on the mating edge. He planked the hull over forms which were temporarily attached to the keel, laying the planks on the forms and fastening them to each other through their edges. The ribs were then bent into the hull and fastened to the planking. In form, this example would make a good outboard boat, with its broad, flat after end, but there is no evidence that it ever had a motor.

DONORS: Steve and Mary Jo Potter   86.41.1

161. PLEASURE ROWBOAT

L: 15'5"   B: 44"   wt: 145 lbs

Built by an unknown builder, possibly in Tupper Lake

This is a carefully-built lapstrake skiff possibly from the shop of a builder named Dyke about whom little is known.

DONOR: Mrs. Earl Owens   66.149.1

162. RANGELEY BOAT *Wood Thrush*

L: 17'1"   B: 46"   wt: 126 lbs

Built by an unknown builder

Rangeley boats are to the lake region of southern and western Maine what guideboats are to the Adirondacks. Developed around 1870 for use on the five large lakes of the Rangeley chain, they were used by professional fishing guides as well as sports who rowed themselves for angling or pleasure. They may be descended from the early skiffs of the St. Lawrence valley. They are typically double-ended, lapstrake boats with half-round steam-bent ribs. They have two-piece keels and two-piece stems. The

planks are thin (generally around $\frac{5}{16}$") and narrow; nine to eleven per side. Classic Rangeley oarlocks are "round socket oarlocks" which consist of a circular oarlock that remains on the oar permanently and has a pin which slips into a socket in the gunwale. As with guideboat oarlocks and St. Lawrence skiff oarlocks, this allows the skipper to drop the oars to fight or land a fish without worrying about their floating away.*

This boat was used in New Hampshire at a private club established in 1883 by people who had summered on the Rangeley Lakes and brought their favorite fishing boats with them. The name of the boat and the club, White Birch Lodge, are on brass plaques on either side of the bow. *Wood Thrush* is a fine boat that has fallen on hard times. Instead of classic Rangeley-style oarlocks, there is a tholepin mounted on the gunwale and an ordinary eyebolt screwed into the oars.

DONOR: John M. Kauffmann   71.134.1

*John Gardner, "The Rangeley Boat," *Building Classic Small Craft*, 165–179.

163. CANVAS ROWBOAT

L: 9'   B: 35"   wt: 20 lbs

Built by Brooksby Gray, Palatine Bridge, 1950

The Adirondack tradition of building light hunting boats continued into the twentieth century. This one was designed and built by an amateur builder for his own use.

He liked the initial stability of the flat bottom better than the rounded bottoms of Rushton's light canoes—and it was also easier to build.

This boat is equipped with crude but lightweight broomstick-and-plywood oars. The rower sits on a large block of styrofoam on the bottom. The skin of the craft is waterproofed canvas stapled over a wooden frame of ribs and battens in much the same style as the canvas canoes of the late nineteenth century; see the museum's canoe model *Dot* (p. 145).

DONOR: Austin W. Hogan, Jr.   78.086.1

164. "COXSWAIN'S GIG" OF PAPER

L: 20'4"   B: 20"   wt: 61 lbs

Built by Elisha Waters and Sons, Troy, ca. 1880

In 1896 *Outing* magazine observed that the chief difference between rowing in the U.S. and in the U.K. was "the universal use of cedar boats by Englishmen and almost equally universal use of paper boats by us." Nineteenth-century small boat enthusiasts were constantly searching for ways to build lighter boats. Paper was substantially lighter than wood, could be molded more easily, and was practical: an impact created a puncture rather than a long crack. Around 1900, however, paper was abandoned because with time hulls built of it became waterlogged and sluggish.

The hull of this boat is made of paper, with wooden ribs and a mahogany sheerstrake. This sheerstrake is a tricky piece of boatbuilding in itself; it was partially steamed and partially molded to produce the outward-curving shape, with a decorative molding along the lower edge.

Elisha Waters, formerly a druggist and paper-box manufacturer, was the country's foremost paper boatbuilder, receiving patents for the process in 1868. For his shells he

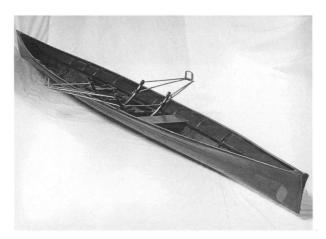

used the best Manila paper, layering it in single sheets over a solid wooden mold. Each layer was coated with adhesive to receive the next; a proprietary waterproofing process gave a piano-like finish to the hull.

A flyer for the Waters Company, ca. 1878, calls this boat a "single scull and coxn., or ladies' gig." In the photograph it is set up for a single rower. By moving the seat and outriggers forward, it can carry a passenger. It is an exercise and pleasure boat, not a racing shell. It is one of the earliest sliding-seat boats extant and, among historic paper boats, the one in best condition.*

DONOR: Richard A. Hughes, Sr.   91.80

*George Balch, *Annual Illustrated Catalog and Oarsman's Manual for 1871* (Troy, N. Y.: Waters, Balch and Co., 1871), and Cupery, "Nineteenth-Century Paper Boat Technology."

165. SINGLE GIG

L: 23'2"   B: 21"   wt: 72 lbs

Built by unknown builder, ca. 1900

Competitive rowing was a very popular sport in the late nineteenth century, and most major cities that were on the water boasted rowing clubs and crews. Around the turn of the century the Lone Star Boat Club on the Harlem River in New York City sold this boat, one of its practice fleet, to John C. A. Gerster, who took it to his family's camp in the Adirondacks. He rowed it on Raquette Lake, and when his family moved the camp to be farther from civilization, on Long Lake.

This is a training craft, of a type sometimes called a wherry (because of its form) or a working boat. It is built heavier and beamier than a racing shell. The builder took pains with the details, such as the sculpted cross-bracing. During the time it was used on the Harlem River it soaked up enough salt water that it became attractive to salt-loving porcupines. One winter, after its move to the Adirondacks, its gunwales were thoroughly gnawed.

DONOR: John C. A. Gerster   63.173.3

166. Competition Single Shell

L: 27'4"   B: 12"   wt: 45 lbs

Built by George Pocock, Seattle, Washington, ca. 1960

George Pocock, who built this boat, was for over fifty years one of the country's foremost builders of racing shells. A third-generation rower and boatbuilder, he emigrated from England in 1911 and settled on the West Coast to take advantage of the tremendous supply of prime softwood lumber. By the 1920s, Pocock was furnishing eighty percent of all shells used by collegiate teams. His innovations included new methods for building lightweight sculls, new types of oarlocks and sliding seats, and steering devices for shells with multiple rowers.

Pocock warned that this "jewel of the boatbuilder's art" was designed and built to be raced only by experienced scullers. All parts of the hull and fittings are as light as practicable. After a racing career downstate, this single was used for pleasure rowing on Blue Mountain Lake.

DONOR: Margaret Setton   79.66.1

Power Boats

The museum's collection of engine-propelled craft is arranged below in chronological order from steam to gasoline.

167. Steam Launch *Osprey*

L: 42'7"   B: 10'5"   wt: unknown

Hull built by an unknown builder, about 1881
Engine built by Clute Bros. & Co., Schenectady, 1881

Osprey is typical of the small steamboats that changed the character of tourism in the Adirondacks. Like most of her sisters, her hull was probably built in the mountains by local boatbuilders. Her engine and boiler were built outside the region. Unlike commercial steamers like *Buttercup*, *Irocosia*, *Killoquah*, and *Toowarloondah*, *Osprey* was built as a private launch. Her first owner was Charles W. Durant,

who purchased Osprey Island in Raquette Lake in 1881. Durant named his boat *Stella*; she was renamed when she and the island were sold to J. Harvey Ladew in the late 1880s. *Osprey* is pictured here, on the left, about 1900.

Museum purchase   57.109.1

168. Gasoline Launch *Camp Katia* (*Carafa*)

L: 20'3"   B: 5'   wt: unknown

Hull built by H. Rasmussen, Essington, Pennsylvania, 1900
Engine built by the Universal Motor Company, Oshkosh, Wisconsin, 1938

Camp Katia is typical of the small launches that became popular after 1900. As she exists today she shows evidence of much cruising and modification. Purchased in 1900 by George H. Earle, Jr., and named *Carafa*, she ran on her original engine until 1938. In 1938 Earle's son Ralph completely re-framed the hull, spliced the keel, replanked the bottom, and replaced the old engine with an up-to-date "Blue Jacket Twin." The rebuilt boat was named after the camp she served on Upper St. Regis Lake.

DONOR: Mary Clayton Earle   65.47.6

169. Gasoline Launch *Eagle Nest*

L: 24'10"   B: 6'   wt: 1,500 lbs

Designed by Frederick Milo Miller[?]
Built by the Lozier Motor Company, Plattsburgh, 1905

The Lozier Company described this model, its Lake Special, as "a splendid little cruiser for small parties, at a moderate cost." By "small parties," the company meant up to twenty-two people. By "moderate cost," the company meant $829. The Hochschild family, which owned *Eagle*

Nest, used her for their small parties and cruises from 1905 until 1928, on the Eckford Chain of Lakes. She was named after the family's camp.

Lozier was proud of its boats. The torpedo stern of this boat, which they claimed to have developed, they felt was superior to the then-common fantail stern, since it was broader on the waterline and therefore more seaworthy. *Eagle Nest*'s single-cylinder, five-horsepower, two-cycle engine they claimed as particularly safe and reliable. The engine ran in only one direction; reversing was accomplished while underway by means of a reversible-pitch propeller.

After her days as a pleasure launch ended, *Eagle Nest* was used by lumbermen for towing booms of logs across the lakes. The lumbermen installed two successive power plants. The engine now in the boat is a Lozier like the original that has been reconstructed from parts.

DONOR: Harold K. Hochschild   67.87.1

170. Gasoline-Powered Inboard Speedboat *Skeeter*

L: 45'   B: 4'5"   wt: 4,658 lbs

Built by Gas Engine & Power Company and Charles L. Seabury & Company, Consolidated, Morris Heights, New York City, 1905

Skeeter had a short racing career, competing only three times in the summer of 1905. She was retired not because she was unreliable or slow, but because she couldn't win races. The early Gold Cup races were governed by a set of handicapping rules intended to equalize competition between large and small boats. Because of her length, *Skeeter* was heavily penalized, having been designed according to classic rules of naval architecture that equated length with speed. In her only Gold Cup race she turned laps of twenty-seven m.p.h., making her one of the fastest speedboats of her day, but she was beaten by the twenty-seven-foot-long *Chip* traveling nine m.p.h. slower. Her owner,

E. J. Schroeder, "traded up" to *Dixie II*, with which he had better luck.

Skeeter's original and only engine, a Model F, Serial No. 3 Speedway, was built in 1905. It was rated at sixty-one horsepower, about the same as the Volkswagen "Bug" of the late 1960s. The engine was started by means of a hand crank; ignition was provided by a magneto. The crankshaft and six cylinders were lubricated by individual oil lines from a box-like brass oil tank mounted on the engine. Each oil line had its own metering orifice with an adjustable drip system. The engine displacement is 1018 cubic inches. The cylinders have a 6" bore and the pistons a 6" stroke. *Skeeter*'s propeller has a 23" diameter and a 34" pitch. She is pictured here ca. 1910 on Raquette Lake with Robert Collier at the wheel.

DONOR: Belle Thompson   57.107.1

171. Naphtha Launch

L: 21'9"   B: 5'4"   wt: unknown

Built by the Gas Engine & Power Company and Charles L. Seabury & Company, Consolidated, Morris Heights, New York City, 1906

Alfred Gwynne Vanderbilt and his family used the hull of

this boat in the Adirondacks. Like many naphtha launches, she was converted to gasoline power in the early twentieth century. The engine now in the boat is from another naphtha launch used in the Adirondacks. It developed two horsepower and propelled the boat at a top speed of seven m.p.h.

DONOR: Bernard Ross   60.42.1

172. GASOLINE LAUNCH *Madge*

L: 22'   B: 5'4"   wt: unknown

Built by the Fay and Bowen Engine Company, Geneva, 1906

Madge was purchased for use on West Canada Lake in the southwestern Adirondacks. She originally cost $800. Fay and Bowens were known for reliability and conservative design. The company claimed that "our stock outfits will be found *safe* for women and children, *faster* than other boats of corresponding size and rated horsepower, *roomy* enough for any reasonable party, and of a *beauty* to satisfy the most fastidious."

She is original in all respects except finish; the donor gave her to the museum in 1961 because he felt he was getting too old to crank the original two-cycle engine by hand to get it started.

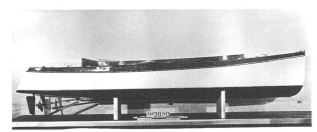

DONORS: Mr. and Mrs. Clay B. O'Dell   61.60.1

173. GLASS CABIN LAUNCH *Whileaway*

L: 28'   B: 6'3"   wt: 3,500 lbs

Built by the Gas Engine & Power Company and Charles L. Seabury & Co., Consolidated, Morris Heights, New York City, 1915

In 1915 the millionaire socialite Harry Payne Whitney and his teenaged son Cornelius Vanderbilt Whitney watched their new 177-foot steam yacht *Whileaway* slide down the ways at the Cramp shipbuilding yard in Philadelphia. The hull was steel and rather like a houseboat in style, with plate-glass windows instead of portholes, and light, airy staterooms. Soon to hang from her davits was what the builders called a wooden "Coupe Yacht Tender," hull #2443, built by the New York firm which had made its name in naphtha launches. The tender had the same name as her mother ship. She was powered by a forty-horsepower Speedway gasoline engine that could drive her about sixteen m.p.h. About 1925 the Consolidated Shipbuilding Company (the same firm that had built the original boat with a shortened name) built a larger and faster coupe yacht tender for Mr. Whitney, and the smaller *Whileaway* was sent up to his Adirondack estate.

The tender *Whileaway* has survived in remarkably

untouched shape. It is not hard to imagine C. V. Whitney cruising around Little Tupper Lake, sitting comfortably in the glass-enclosed owner's cockpit with its varnished mahogany wainscoting, leather cushions, and cut and frosted glass electric lights. He could signal to the skipper in his unprotected forward cockpit by means of an electric bell. His guests sitting aft, on the bench seat with *Whileaway* painted on the backrest, were protected from the Adirondack weather by an awning.

Whileaway's hull below the waterline has been sheathed in a rubberized cloth, probably in the 1950s. Her original power plant has been replaced with an eight-cylinder Universal engine. The historic photograph shows Harry Payne Whitney and his party visiting the yacht *Vanitie* from the tender *Whileaway*. The photograph is courtesy of the Mariners Museum, Newport News, Virginia.

DONOR: Cornelius Vanderbilt Whitney   56.16.1

174. GASOLINE EXCURSION LAUNCH *Fulton*

L: 38'6"   B: 5'10"   wt: unknown

Built by Jack Rivett, Old Forge, between 1915 and 1925

The design for *Fulton* and her sister launches *Mountaineer* and *Adirondack* was Rivett's own and suggests that he was not greatly familiar with the construction of large boats. There is very little lengthwise support to this launch, nor are there any substantial thwartships bulkheads. The engine is at the extreme forward end of the boat, which gave a long, open cockpit and kept the weight well forward to help the boat avoid squatting while underway. She was originally powered by a six-cylinder, 100-horsepower Kermath engine.

Rivett's three vessels had long careers as excursion launches. They could be rented for fishing, and moonlight

trips were especially popular. *Fulton* ran between Inlet and Old Forge until 1973.

DONOR: John F. Prendergast   75.259.1

175. INBOARD LAUNCH *Tadpole*

L: 16'   B: 4'2"   wt: unknown

Built by the Mullins Boat Co., Salem, Ohio, 1919

Tadpole was purchased new for use on Fourth Lake. With her flat bottom, shallow draft, and protected propeller, she was ideal for exploring its bays and inlets. The hull is well built, with a cross-planked, tongue-and-groove bottom having a tunnel in it for the propeller. Mullins, a company that made its name primarily in the manufacture of steel boats, did not build the power plant; it is a three-horsepower Ferro two-stroke, single-cylinder engine.

About running the boat one of *Tadpole's* early skippers wrote: "I learned to start and operate the boat when I was nine, and remember particularly the tricks on starting. The single cylinder engine would run in either direction, of course, and the crank would turn it correctly but was slow and laborious (and a little dangerous). If you primed it just right, however, and set the spark advance properly, you could grasp the flywheel directly and with a smart twist backwards cause a 'backfire' which would set the engine off in the right direction. Of course, if the twist was too smart, the engine would run in the wrong direction and you would have to start all over again."

DONOR: Sherman Skinner   64.104.1

176. GASOLINE-POWERED INBOARD SPEEDBOAT *El Lagarto*

L: 25'10"   B: 5'1"   wt: 3,440 lbs

Designed and built by John L. Hacker, Detroit, Michigan, 1922; modified by F. R. Smith and Sons, Bolton Landing, under the direction of George Reis, 1929–1937

"The Leaping Lizard of Lake George" was one of the most successful raceboats in America. Initially named *Miss Mary* and powered by a Peerless engine, she was built in 1922 to meet the new, restricted rules of the Gold Cup. She had an undistinguished career until George Reis purchased her in 1925 and re-christened her *El Lagarto*. In 1928 he installed a Packard Gold Cup engine which enabled her to achieve competitive speeds. In 1931 "The Lizard" started winning, and over the next six years garnered three President's Cup victories, one National Sweepstakes victory, and three consecutive Gold Cup victories. In 1935 she was clocked at 72.727 m.p.h. in a mile trial, the fastest straightaway speed ever attained by a boat of the restricted Gold Cup class. Her propeller has a 17" diameter and a 27" pitch.

El Lagarto's brilliant record can be attributed to Reis's consummate driving skill and to constant alterations by Reis and his mechanics. The most significant modification to the hull was putting steps on the bottom. The steps, with air introduced through tubes through the hull, broke the suction of the water and enabled the boat to leap across the surface, gaining speed by staying off the water.

The minor modifications Reis and his crew made to ignition, fuel consumption, and handling were innumerable. The list of major modifications is headed by engine changes. *Miss Mary* was purchased with a 200-horsepower Peerless engine (her third); *El Lagarto* won all of her victories with one of two interchangeable 275-horsepower Packard Gold Cup engines. In the final two years of her career she raced with a D12 Curtiss aircraft engine Reis had modified by the Menasco Motor Works. The reliable Packard was modified, too, including installation of new pistons in 1933, which boosted compression ratio from 7.6:1 to 9.5:1.

The original Packard Gold Cup engines Reis used for racing between 1929 and 1935 had displacements of 621 cubic inches, bores of 5⅜", and strokes of 4⁹⁄₁₆". They developed 275 horsepower at 2,500 r.p.m. Until 1935 Reis used eighty-six-octane aviation fuel in his engines, blended with twenty-eight cc. of tetra-ethyl of lead per gallon. Forty to fifty gallons were burned in each of the three heats of a Gold Cup race. The Packard engine now in the boat is a replacement installed by Reis after a fire in the 1950s destroyed his racing engines.

George Reis retired from competition in 1937. *El Lagarto* spent the next quarter-century as a runabout on

May You and the Lizzard keep on winning
Bill Anderson.

Lake George, averaging 2,000 miles per year. Reis enjoyed speeding under the two-bay bridge from Bolton Landing to the Sagamore island at sixty m.p.h. and reminding his breathless passenger *afterwards* that he was blind in one eye. *El Lagarto* comes from behind *Delphine IV* in this photo of the 1935 Gold Cup on Lake George. Photograph courtesy of William Morgan.

DONOR: George C. Reis   63.174.1

177. GUIDEBOAT-BUILT OUTBOARD BOAT *Gull*

L: 17'9"   B: 43"   wt: 219 lbs

Built by Fred M. Rice, Saranac Lake, 1926

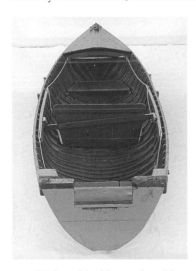

In 1931, a twenty-five-year-old woman named Martha Rebentisch, weakened by a long bout with tuberculosis, answered an unusual advertisement in the Saranac Lake newspaper. "WANTED," it read, "to get in touch with some invalid who is not improving, and who would like to go into the woods for the Summer." The ad had been placed by a fifty-five-year-old guide and boatbuilder, Fred Rice. Rice installed Rebentisch on a mattress in the bow of his boat and motored her into an *al fresco* life in which she was to find health and an author's inspiration for thirty-three years. She published her books under the name Martha Reben.

Fred M. Rice learned boatbuilding from his father, a builder of small sailboats from Willsboro. Most of his boats were probably ordinary guideboats whose chief characteristic was light weight for portability. By the mid-1920s, however, most of Rice's business was for trips on the Saranacs where he didn't have to carry the boat. When he built *Gull* he used guideboat-building techniques of sawn frames and smooth skin but abandoned light weight and added a crude transom for an outboard motor. He also lengthened the boat; in his words, "the extra length was added to make the boat faster with a motor and was added to the middle of the boat to make it carry a bigger load." When Rice took Reben into camp in 1931 he used a four-horsepower Johnson outboard on *Gull* and towed a canoe full of supplies. Rice was typical of many of his contemporaries throughout the country who tried to adapt their long, narrow displacement boats to outboard motors.

Museum purchase   64.27.1

178. WOOD-CANVAS STEP PLANE MODEL OUTBOARD HYDROPLANE

L: 13'11"   B: 4'   wt: unknown

Built by the Old Town Canoe Company, Old Town, Maine, 1928

For Adirondackers who couldn't afford to race a boat like *Skeeter* or *El Lagarto* there was outboard racing. Races for stock boats like this one were held as part of regattas throughout the region and provided excitement between the heats of the Lake George Gold Cup races of the 1930s.

Though not as big or as fast as the Gold Cup boats, outboard craft were exciting enough for many. An advertisement contemporary with this boat claimed, "THE OUTBOARD HYDROPLANE IS THE FASTEST DETACHABLE MOTOR CRAFT EVER BUILT. If you want all the thrill of flying without the expense or danger, this boat will give it to you."

The design of outboard hulls mirrored advances in inboard racing hulls. "Steps" on hull bottoms were in use by 1906; they break the suction of the water on the boat and

help it plane. A fin on the bottom just forward of the single step helps with steering.

This is Old Town's version of Penn Yan's Baby Buzz model, which set the world's outboard speed record of fifteen m.p.h. in 1925. Norman J. Martin bought it second-hand, and in 1933 he took it for a spin off his camp on Lake Champlain. A sudden gust of wind tipped the boat on its stern and nearly sent Martin to the bottom. The experience so unsettled him that he never used the boat again. "It went so fast it was scary," Martin remembered. The motor used with the boat was a 1928 stock model Johnson K-40 twin cylinder outboard which developed 7.15 horsepower at 3,500 r.p.m. It sold for $165 when new and weighed sixty-one pounds.

Museum purchase   88.114.1

179. ELECTRIC LAUNCH

L: 15'   B: 49"   wt: 535 lbs

Built by the Electri-Craft Corporation, Syracuse, 1934

"AS REVOLUTIONARY AS THE FIRST ELECTRIC LIGHT," claimed the Electri-Craft Company of Syracuse of this launch. Its four six-volt batteries developed three to four horsepower, which would speed you to your fishing grounds at four to seven m.p.h., and once there you could troll at one to two m.p.h. The electric power plant was clean, comfortable, and simple enough for amateurs to operate. Silence was perhaps its most attractive feature. "Picture yourself on a moonlight night with some congenial companion—lolling back in ELECTRI-CRAFT's restful cushions—listening to your favorite radio programme . . . and you have the answer to small boat luxury." The original owners of this boat practiced humane deer jacking in it; they would cruise up the Miami River at night with a flashlight looking for deer to observe but not shoot.

The Elco Company had successfully marketed electric boats during the 1890s, but times had changed when Electri-Craft introduced this model in the 1930s. By then,

you could outfit yourself with an outboard boat and motor of the same size and horsepower for little more than half the $375 price of this one. While the outboard was noisier, it had a much greater range than the eight-mile maximum of the Electri-Craft.

This boat was purchased from the Kerst boat livery in Sabael in 1935. After World War II the owner found that recharging was a problem on a lake as large as Indian Lake and converted it to an outboard. He wasn't a very large man, and he would sit in the former engine compartment to operate the outboard, which he attached to the stern.

DONOR: Revs. Frank H. Stroup and William A. Guenther   67.120.1

180. SECTIONAL METAL OUTBOARD BOAT

L: 12'4"   B: 3'6¼"   wt: 172 lbs

Built by an unknown builder, ca. 1940

Boatbuilders in search of portability came up with some curious results. The sections of this boat are held together with bolts and can be nested one inside the other. The resulting 40" x 42" x 18" package was probably intended to be transported by car from home to fishing grounds. It is very heavy for its size. It was found under water in Raquette Lake.

DONOR: Bernon K. Tourtelot   56.80.1

Special Purpose Boats

In this section are boats which do not readily fit into the other categories of the collection, either because the museum owns few examples (such as the sailboats), because they can be used with varying means of propulsion (duck boats), because they were designed for very particular circumstances (logging boats and iceboats), or just because they are whimsical oddities.

Sailboats

181. IDEM CLASS RACING SLOOP *Water Witch*

L: 32'3"   B: 8'2"   wt: unknown

Designed by Clinton Crane, 1897
Built by the Spalding St. Lawrence Boat Company, Ogdensburg, 1900

The Idem class for the St. Regis Yacht Club was one of Clinton Crane's first design commissions. He had the light and fluky winds of the mountain lakes in mind, and, as he wrote in his autobiography, decided "that a one-design class, to be a success, must be relatively fast as compared to other boats of similar size and must be fun to sail. Otherwise, although the racing may be even between different members of the class, the class is doomed to failure."* The fact that all twelve boats built in the class have survived nearly a century, and most are still racing, suggests that he was right.

    The hull of *Water Witch* is supported by two longitudinal interior trusses intended to keep the boat in shape despite her long overhanging bow and stern, yearly hauling, and the stresses put on it by capricious mountain winds. In place of a fixed keel having lead ballast at its lower edge, she has a ballasted centerboard that can be pulled up into a trunk, somewhat reducing her draft.

DONOR: Mrs. Ogden Reid   61.10.1

*Clinton Crane, *Clinton Crane's Yachting Memories* (New York: D. Van Nostrand and Co., 1952), 20.

(See Appendix for plans of an Idem.)

182. RUSHTON CRUISER #3 MODEL SAILBOAT

L: 16'   B: 5'   wt: unknown

Built by J. H. Rushton, Canton, between 1888 and 1892

While best known for his canoes, J. H. Rushton of Canton built many other types of small boats, especially during the height of his business in the 1880s and 1890s. Some, like this cruising sailboat, were a far cry from the

"portable boats" with which he made his fame. In 1895 Rushton wrote, "As a beautiful little sail boat, capable of being rowed, these CRUISERS have no equal. Thousands saw and admired the one we exhibited at the WORLD'S FAIR and many have since been sold."

    This boat was used originally on Lake Champlain. The rig has been changed at least once. Rushton probably built few boats this size.

DONOR: Robert Spring   79.53.1

183. SWAMPSCOTT DORY

L: 21'3"   B: 68"   wt: unknown

Built by Elbridge Gerry Emmons, Swampscott, Mass., ca. 1900

"Around 1900 the Swampscott sailing dories were about the hottest thing in small racing craft afloat," writes John Gardner. "For the next two decades the Swampscott dory was easily the most popular small-craft type in the Northeast." E. Gerry Emmons was the country's largest dory builder at the time, going out of the business before 1920.*

    Swampscott dories were the "aristocrats of the dory clan," not to be confused with classic, slab-sided dories

best known as the working boats of the Grand Banks fishermen. Instead of the broad bottoms of the fishing dories, the dory-yacht has a narrow bottom and rounded sides. The museum's dory was purchased by New York surgeon Arpad Gerster and sailed by him and his son on Long Lake. The son, also a doctor, bought a three-horsepower Johnson OA 60 motor for the boat in the early 1930s and built a little chock for the slanting transom to mount the outboard vertically on the dory. Maynard E. Bray photograph, courtesy Mystic Seaport, Mystic, Connecticut.

DONOR: John C. A Gerster   63.173.1

*John Gardner, *Building Classic Small Craft*, vol. 2 (Camden, Maine: International Marine Publishing Company, 1984), 206; and vol. 1 of the above (1977), 85.

Iceboats

184. ICE PUNT

L: 12'2"   B: 36"   wt: unknown

Built by an unknown builder, in the Raquette Lake area

Builders developed this craft for travel over Adirondack waterways in the spring and fall when the ice was unreliable. It was a sledge as the skipper pushed it over the ice; if the ice gave way it became a punt and he jumped aboard and rowed. It is probably a home-made boat, with handles borrowed from a plow or cultivator. The builder cleverly used the sheer strake as a seat riser.

The ice punt was also known in the Thousand Islands region to the north of the Adirondacks. This one was found at William West Durant's Camp Pine Knot, where it was used to navigate Raquette Lake. Pine Knot stands on a point with no road access, and all supplies must still come across the water.

DONOR: Arthur Howe   57.115.1

185. STERN-STEERING ICE YACHT *Hornet*

L: 28'   B: 16'   wt: unknown

Built by G. L. Courville, Burlington, Vermont, ca. 1930

In the days before the internal combustion engine, iceboats were the fastest vehicles in the world, sometimes achieving speeds up to 100 m.p.h. The earliest were simply sailboats mounted on runner planks, but by the 1870s specialized iceboats were being built of a timber framework mounted on a thwartships runner plank. In 1879 Catskill builder H. Relyea designed a radical new hull composed of a lengthwise center timber crossing a runner plank, and stepped the mast several feet forward of the intersection. This new design was immensely successful and became the standard into the 1930s.

Because of heavy snowfall in the Adirondacks, conditions are seldom good for "hard water sailing," which accounts for iceboats being rare here. Iceboat sailors have tried to pursue their hobby on Lakes George and Champlain, however. *Hornet* was built for use on Lake Champlain and then purchased by a sailor on Diamond Point on Lake George. She was built to the 1870s era design by a Burlington man who was probably not a production builder. She has a cockpit lined with cushions for the crew aft of the mast instead of the narrow fore-and-aft beam popular between 1880 and 1930. *Hornet* is in very good condition, missing only her tiller and some hardware. Iceboats typically "age" more gracefully than "soft-water boats" since they are used much less often, and when they are, they are not in the water.

DONOR: Marie Bergh Collins   75.22.1

Logging Boats

186. JAM BOATS

L: 11'10"   B: 47"   wt: unknown

Built by the Cape Cod Shipbuilding Corp., Wareham, Massachusetts, ca. 1920

Finch, Pruyn and Co. had some of their river-drive boats locally built (entries 188 and 189) but these two were products of a nationally-known boatbuilding factory. They are cleverly built. The garboards are thickened at the bottom to form chine logs, and the same thing in reverse on the sheer strake provides a hefty outwale. This is a classic skiff in that it has a flat, cross-planked bottom with a sharp bow and a transom stern. The term "skiff" is often used loosely in the Adirondacks, referring historically to such diverse boats as this one, the round-bottomed St. Lawrence skiff, and the Adirondack guideboat.

These boats are quite short and were probably used more in boom-tending around Glens Falls than in running logs down the Hudson. One has been used with an outboard motor.

DONOR: Finch, Pruyn and Co.   71.11.1 and 2

187. RIVER-DRIVE BATEAU

L: 23'4"   B: 5'5"   wt: unknown

Built by the J & J Rogers Company, Ausable Forks

The Penobscot River bateau probably influenced the shape of this river-drive boat, either through lumbermen who had worked in Maine or through the tourist industry; in the 1870s the owners of Ausable Chasm built several Penobscot bateaux to carry tourists through the gorge. There is no indication of rowlocks on the boat, suggesting that the river drivers used poles or paddles.

This bateau is an elegant, well-made boat. The overhang fore and aft helps river drivers leap ashore or onto log jams dry-shod. The hull is not symmetrical, being wider and higher towards the bow, which keeps the bow

from burying when going over a drop. The planks speak of an impressive forest on the Rogers land. They run the full length of the boat, and four of the six are twenty inches wide.

The ironwork on this bateau, consisting of sheathing at the bow and stern, painter rings, and an unusual system of metal splines between the planks, was manufactured by Gilson Melvin Slater, a blacksmith in Ausable Forks who also made repairs to logging harness. In the spring he closed up shop and joined the river drive.

DONOR: Henry Rogers   57.157.1

188. RIVER DRIVE BOAT

L: 15'1"   B: 4'   wt: unknown

Built by an unknown builder

While not as elegant in looks as the classic Penobscot-style river-driving bateau, this boat is well designed for its job, which was driving logs down the Hudson for the Finch, Pruyn and Co. of Glens Falls. It has great rocker fore and aft which aids in quick turning. It is a punt in form, with a cross-planked bottom, and was handily built of dimension lumber. It was probably little used before it came to the museum; the edges of the planks are still crisp, and there are no marks on the bottom from the river-driver's caulked shoes. Finch, Pruyn and Co. in the mid-twentieth century changed river transport for road transport, but they retained their color scheme. Finch, Pruyn logging trucks were still painted the same powder-blue as these boats in the early 1990s.

DONOR: Finch, Pruyn and Co.   57.120.1

189. RIVER-DRIVE BOAT

L: 15'7"   B: 5'5½"   wt: unknown

Built by an unknown builder

Square-sterned, broad-transomed boats like this one were commonly used in Adirondack river drives. Similar craft were known as "North River Boats" in the West Canada Lakes country; the Hudson was known sometimes as the North River. Like entry 188, it was used by the Glens Falls firm Finch, Pruyn on the Hudson and has a great degree of rocker.

DONORS: Finch, Pruyn and Company   57.120.2

Duck Boats

190. METAL DUCK BOAT

L: 13'7½"   B: 37"   wt: 102 lbs

Built by W. H. Mullins, Salem, Ohio, ca. 1900[?]

"Wooden Boats Crack Open when exposed to the weather. Become water logged when in use," advertised W. H. Mullins in 1896. "Mullins' Metal Boats are the best on the market. Made of Stamped and Embossed Manganized Steel. Most durable, lightest, nobbiest and artistic boats ever made." This is probably Mullins's "Get There" Ducking Boat, which could be purchased from the New York sporting goods dealers Abercrombie and Fitch for $22 or $29, depending on the style. It came from North Creek, the same "home port" of one of the museum's other two duck boats. It had a low stool amidships for the hunter and

one set of oarlocks. The embossed planking laps and rope trim not only add to the boat's nobbiness, but strengthened the hull as well.

DONOR: Mr. and Mrs. Ray Waddell   69.164.1

191. DUCK BOAT

L: 15'10"   B: 28"   wt: 153 lbs

Built by C. Albert Jacob, Jr., Chestertown, 1914

A low profile for camouflage and stability for a shooting platform were more important in many duck boats designed for use in sheltered waters than seakeeping qualities or speed. This one was used for duck hunting on Loon Lake and the Schroon River.

The builder was a piano manufacturer who summered in Chestertown. He was not a professional boatbuilder, but he did a nice job on his duck boat. Jacob probably got his design from plans or by looking at the cuts in a catalog. He used natural crooks in the framing, perhaps obtained from a local guideboat builder. The hull of this boat is covered with canvas. The tiny bumps are a result of ageing paint.

DONOR: C. Albert Jacob, Jr.   66.145.1

192. DUCK BOAT

L: 12'   B: 37½"   wt: 138 lbs

Built by Claude Straight, North Creek, ca. 1945

Most duck boats are characterized by stability for shooting and wide, flat bottoms for navigating in shallow waters where ducks are found. The shallows and marshes of the central Adirondacks are not prime duck habitat, but they do support muskrat populations worth harvesting. Claude Straight built this boat to set muskrat traps. Trapping furnished only a part of his income. Like many natives, he was a jack-of-all-trades. He also ran a small hotel, operated a ski tow, and raised beagles for fox hunting. He built this boat one winter in his kitchen; his wife was probably glad when the project was finished in the spring.

The bottom of this boat is made of whatever random

width boards Straight could find. The crude paddle looks hardly used.

Paddle Boats

193. WATER BICYCLE

L: 10'   B: 48"   wt: unknown

Designed by Stuart J. Baird, built by "Monty" of Sickler's Garage, Whitesboro, ca. 1930

Pedal- and paddle-boats have perennial appeal to both amateur and professional builders. The design of this amateur-built boat is not unique; it is simply a safety bicycle on pontoons. It took good balance and a calm lake to ride it without getting a dunking. Nevertheless, the Baird family used it for over thirty years at their camp on First Lake in the Fulton Chain. The snapshot catches Eunice Baird Whittlesey riding the waterbike at the age of fifteen in 1937.

194. CHILD'S MODEL STERN-WHEEL CATAMARAN

L: 8'   B: 28"   wt: 69 lbs

Built by Freeman Baker, Saranac Lake, about 1940

The photograph shows Baker's paddleboats at the Mirror Lake Inn on Lake Placid; they were also particularly popu-

lar on Lake Flower in the 1930s and 1940s. Special races were held for them with classes for the single, tandem, and child's models. They differ from most paddle-boats in that the skipper does all the work with his arms, leaving only the steering to the stronger legs. The editors at *Everyday Science and Mechanics* in 1936 hailed the boat as a light, speedy craft, and felt it would "make an interesting racer if extended, with seats for a whole rowing crew."*

Museum purchase   77.101.1

*"Stern-Wheel Racing Catamarans," *Everyday Science and Mechanics* (August, 1936), 320.

195. PADDLEBOARD *Pilikia*

L: 12'5"   B: 20"   wt: 43 lbs

Built by an unknown builder, before 1945

English Channel swimmer Charles M. Daniels had this built as an exercise craft that he could also use to enjoy the waters of Bear Pond on his estate near Long Lake. To use it he lay prone on the board and paddled with his arms; a little coaming kept the water from running up his nose.

Pilikia is professionally built and of a high degree of craftsmanship. There is not a flat panel in it, and the wood is of the highest quality. It may be the product of a Long Lake shop; certainly someone like George Smith or Warren Cole had the necessary skill.

Boatbuilders

Represented in the Adirondack Museum collection or active in the North Country before 1975. Slight changes in corporate names have not been noted.

Most of the boatbuilders in this list did not run big businesses. Indeed, with the exception of J. H. Rushton, those who built guideboats probably did so only seasonally. Information on them is scarce. The list below summarizes what is recorded on builders known to have built boats for the Adirondacks contained in Adirondack Museum files: boatbuilders files in the curatorial office, library vertical files, and the Kenneth and Helen Durant manuscript collection. Doubtless, more information on them could be found with extensive research into local records. What is recorded here is what is known, even if vague. In a few cases, we know only that a certain boatbuilder existed.

In this context "North Country" means that region of New York State north of the Mohawk and south of the St. Lawrence rivers, east of Lake Ontario and west of Lake Champlain. Most of this region is taken up by the Adirondack mountains; most of its population, including businesses like boatbuilding, is around the edges.

The list is arranged as follows:

—Name of builder or corporate name of boatshop

—Dates: Ideally birth and death dates followed by active dates ("w."); sometimes only one or the other or partial entry for one.

—Place of business

—Product

—Brief comments

Abercrombie & Fitch
ND
New York
Dealers only; carried William English canoes

Adirondack Boat Building Co.
1906–[?]
Saranac Lake
Guideboats
Successor to Martin's Boat Shop

Albany Boat Corp.
1909–1932
Watervliet
Runabouts and raceboats

Alden, William M.
w. ca. 1880 [?]
Newcomb
Guideboats
Son-in-law of Caleb Chase

Allcock Manufacturing Co.
1957–1962
Ossining
Fiberglass guideboats; see entry 112

Allen, Henry
w. ca. 1890–1900
Hermon
Rowboats and canoes
Worked with Harry Green

Anderson, Leonard
1873–1941; w. 1899[?]
Tupper Lake
Guideboats
Worked with Alaric Moody

Austin, Hank
1835–1925
Long Lake
Guideboats

Austin, Hiram
B. 1852; w. ca. 1880
Long Lake
Guideboats

Austin, Lewis
1866–1901; w. ca. 1890
Long Lake
Guideboats; see entry 64

Austin, Merlin or Merle
1875–1951; w. ca. 1910
Long Lake
Canoes, guideboats; see entry 20

Austin, William
w. 1850[?]
Long Lake
Guideboats[?]

Bailey, Alonzo
w. ca. 1850
Schroon Lake
Stern-wheel steamboat

Bain, A. & Co.
1885–1888
Clayton
Skiffs, canoes; see entry 17
Successor to X. Colon, succeeded by St. Lawrence River Skiff, Canoe & Steam Launch Co.

Baird, Stuart J.
w. ca. 1930
Whitesboro
Amateur builder; waterbicycle; see entry 193

Baker, Freeman J.
w. 1920s and 1930s
Saranac Lake
Paddlewheel boats, runabouts, excursion launches
See entry 194

Barlow, William
1854–1933; w. ca. 1880–1920
Horicon
Flat-bottomed fishing boat

Barnum, Ed
D. 1926; w. 1880–1915
Malone
Guideboats

Bates Brothers (C. J. and George)
w. ca. 1900
Lake George
Sayonara steam launch

Bellows, Cassius ("Cash")
w. 1890s
Chateaugay Lake
"Bellows boats"

Bellows, Millard
w. 1890
Chateaugay Lake
"Bellows boats"

Bernard, Matthew
w. ca. 1926
Golden Lake, Ontario
Birchbark canoes; see entry 6

Billings, Albert Henry
1853–1903; w. ca. 1880–1903
Lake Placid
Canoes, guideboats; see entry 24

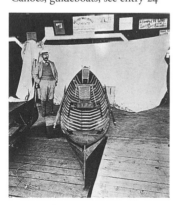

A. H. Billings with one of his boats.
P. 20098.

Bissell, Daniel
w. 1870
Newcomb
Guideboats[?]

Bissel, Harvey
w. 1853
Newcomb
Guideboats[?]

Blanchard, Arthur
w. ca. 1890
Raquette Lake
Guideboats; see entry 78

Blanchard, Charles
w. ca. 1900[?]
Blue Mountain Lake
Guideboats

Blanchard, John
1878–1948
Raquette Lake
Guideboats; see entry 79

Bliss, C. Herman
1890–1927
Lake Placid
Guideboats, canoes; see entry 25
With Tom George bought business
    of A. H. Billings to form
    George & Bliss

Boardway, Charles
w. 1890–1920
Malone
Guideboats and rowboats

Bolton, William
1872–1967; w. ca. 1890–1920
Horicon
Flat-bottomed boats

Bonney, Harve
ND
Indian Lake
Guideboats

Bowdish, Edward
1856–1938; w. 1880s–1893
Skaneateles
Racing and sailing canoes

Bowdish Mfg. Co. (1888) was reor-
    ganized under new manage-
    ment in 1893 as the Skaneateles
    Boat and Canoe Co.

Bowdish, Nelson S.
1831–1916; w. 1886–1893
Skaneateles
Canoes
Also an artist; father of Edward

Braman, Horace
D. 1903
Keene
Guideboats

Brasher Boat Company
w. ca. 1890
Brasher Falls
Pleasure rowboats

Breen, William
w. ca. 1870
Boonville
Guideboats

Brown, A. C. and Sons
w. ca. 1880s–1900
Tottenville, Staten Island
Steamboats on the Eckford Chain
    built on-site

Brown, C. J.
w. ca. 1930
Canton
Indian Girl canoes after Rushton
    shop closed; may be same per-
    son as Everett Brown

Brown, Everett "Cyclone"
1916–1930s
Dekalb
Indian Girl canoes; see C. J.
    Brown

Brown, Nelson
w. for Rushton 1878–1916
Canton

All Rushton models
May have worked for J. R. Robinson for a short time

Brush, Melvin
w. ca. 1930
Fulton Chain
Power boats

Buyce, Alvah
w. ca. 1890[?]
Speculator, Lake Pleasant
Guideboats[?]

Buyce, John F.
1870–1947; w. 1890–1947
Speculator
Guideboats, rowboats; see entries 122, 123, 124, 159

Canton Boat Works
w. 1890[?]
Canton
Rowboat; see entry 126

Cantwell, Joseph J.
w. 1902
Saranac Lake
Rowboats[?]

Cape Cod Shipbuilding Corp.
ND
Wareham, Mass.
Rowboats; see entry 186

Carey [or Cary], Reuben
1847–1933; w. ca. 1870–1900
Long Lake, Raquette Lake, Brandreth Lake
Guideboats; see entry 60

Carlton, Charles
w. 1880
Lake Placid
Square-sterned guideboats, sailboat

Case, W. L.
ND
Indian Lake
Guideboats[?]

Chapman, Earl B.
w. 1927
Lowville
Guideboats

Chase, Caleb Judson
1830–1911; w. 1851
Newcomb
Guideboats; see entries 75, 76, 77

Chase, Edmund Judson
D. 1927
Newcomb
Guideboats

Son of Caleb; see Caleb for boats built

Clark, Daniel
w. 1850
Westport
Ships for Lake Champlain

Clark, David
w. 1850
Westport
Ships for Lake Champlain

Clute Brothers & Co.
w. 1881
Schenectady
Steamboat engines; see entry 167

Cole, Charles
w. ca. 1890–1898
Long Lake
Guideboats
Brother of Warren Cole

Cole, Simon
B. 1846; w. 1870
Long Lake
Guideboats[?]

Cole, Warren W.
1854–1922; w. 1892
Long Lake
Guideboats; see entries 68, 69, 70, 71, 72

Warren Cole (right) with one of his boats at the Sportsmen's Show, Madison Square Garden, New York City, 1899. P. 10894.

Colon, Xavier
w. 1868 – ca. 1908
Clayton
St. Lawrence Skiffs
Becomes A. Bain & Co., 1885

Cornwall, John H.
w. ca. 1910
North River
Amateur builder; see entry 156

Cossey, Stephen, James, Henry, and William
w. 1880
Ticonderoga
Boats & ships for Lake Champlain

Courville, G. I.
w. ca. 1930
Burlington, Vt.
Ice Yacht; see entry 185

Crandall, Will
ND
Lake George
Pleasure rowboats[?]

Crane, Clinton
w. 1897 in the Adirondacks
New York City
Designer of Idem class as well as other sailing yachts and speedboats; see entry 181

Dean, Walter A.
w. 1883–1918
Toronto, Ontario
Canoes; see entry 27

Denner, E. T.
ND
Chippewa Bay
St. Lawrence skiffs[?]

Duell, Charles
1842–1907; w. ca. 1880–1907
Horicon
Flat-bottomed fishing boats

Durand Mfg. Co.
w. 1890
Rochester
Canoes; foot-powered propellers; see entry 152

Durrin, Henry
w. 1905
Bolton Landing
Lake George rowboats; see entry 130

Durrin, Sherm
w. 1920s
Lake George
Rowboats

Duso, Harry
w. 1930s
Saranac Lake
Outboard raceboats

Dyke, [?]
ND
Tupper Lake
Guideboats[?]

Electri-Craft Corp.
w. 1933–1940
Syracuse

Small electric launches; see entry
179

Emerson, Wallace F.
1874–1953; w. 1905
Long Lake
Guideboats; see entry 73

Wallace Emerson cutting ribs in his shop, ca. 1920. P. 8058.

Emmett, Dan
w. ca. 1910–1950
Corey's
Birchbark canoes
See entry 7

English, William, Canoe Co.
w. 1861–1920s
Peterborough, Ontario
Canoes; see entry 30

Everson, James
w. ca. 1850–1890
Williamsburgh
Whitehalls; see entry 127

Farr, Atherton W.
1864–1957; w. ca. 1920s–1945
East Dekalb
Rowboats; see entry 160

Fay and Bowen Engine Co.
1900–1937
Auburn, Geneva
Motor launches; see entry 172

Fenton, Charles
w. ca. 1880
Beaver Lake
Dugout; see entry 10
Son of Orrin

Fenton, Orrin
w. 1826–1870
Beaver Lake
Guideboats

Fish, Elijah
B. 1842
Sabael
Guideboats, rowboats

Fish, Ernest
1877–1910; w. ca. 1890–1910
Sabael
Guideboats, rowboats

Fish, Lee
w. 1925–1960
Sabael
Dories, mahogany speedboat,
cruisers

Flagg, Arlo C.
ND
Saranac Lake
Guideboat

Flanders, A. B.
ND
Tupper Lake
Unknown

H. & D. Folsom Arms Co.
ca. 1900
New York City
Dealer only; Rushton and Morris
canoes

Freeman, Mahlon C.
1849–1920; w. ca. 1898–1919
Fulton
Launches and strip-built canoes,
rowboats; see entry 33

Fulton Pleasure Boat Co.
1892
Fulton
Canoes, skiffs, rowboats, sailboats,
combinations

**Gas Engine & Power Company and
Charles L. Seabury & Co.,
Consolidated**
1896–1918
Morris Hts., New York City
Naphtha and gasoline launches;
see entries 170, 171, 173
The Gas Engine & Power Co.
joined with Charles L. Seabury
in 1896; in 1918 the company
became the Consolidated Shipbuilding Corp.

George, Tom
w. ca. 1890–1949
Lake Placid
Guideboats, canoes, launches; see
entry 25
Worked for A. H. Billings, bought
shop with C. H. Bliss 1906, ran

George & Bliss alone
1927–1949

Gerrish, E. H.
w. 1875–1909
Bangor, Maine
Wood-canvas canoes; see entry 38

Gordon, Thomas
w. 1860–1904
Lakefield, Ontario
Canoes
Later became Lakefield Boat Mfg.
Co.

Grant, Floyd D.
1866–1941; w. 1880–1934
Boonville
Guideboats; see entry 101
Son of H. D. Grant

Grant, Henry Dwight
1833–1911; w. 1879–1911
Boonville
Guideboats; see entries 98, 99, 100

Grant, Lewis L.
1878–1960; w. 1895–1934
Boonville
Guideboats, canoes, and flat-
bottomed rowboats; see entries
21, 101, 116, 148

Grant, William
1833 1918; w. 1870 1900
Edwards
Rowboats, sailboats

Graves, Frederick D.
w. 1875
Boston, Mass.
Guideboats; at least one designed
to sail

Graves, Nathaniel S.
w. 1903
Blue Mountain Lake
Guideboats

Gray, Brooksby
w. 1950
Palatine Bridge
Amateur builder; see entry 163

Green, Harry
1833–1903; w. ca. 1890–1900
Hermon
Strip-built rowboats and canoes;
see entries 16, 19, 150, 153

Grisdale, Frank
w. 1933
Lake Placid
Power boats

Harry Green in his shop, ca. 1890. P. 11748.

Hacker, John L.
w. ca. 1908–1956
Detroit and Mt. Clemens, Mich.
Runabouts, speedboats; see entry 176
Operated Hacker Boat Co. in Watervliet about 1916. See Albany Boat Corp.

Hale, Mason
w. ca. 1910
Keene Valley
Guideboats

Hale, LeGrand
w. ca. 1890
Keene Valley
Guideboats

Hall, Frank
w. ca. 1890
White Lake Corners
Guideboats[?]

Hamner, Charles
1882–1956
Long Lake
Guideboats[?]

Hamner, Ed
w. ca. 1910
Long Lake
Canoe; see entry 20

Hanmer, Henry
D. 1939
Lake Placid
Guideboats[?]

Hanmer, Theodore
1860–1957; w. ca. 1890–1948
Saranac Lake
Guideboats; see entry 83
Father of Willard

Hanmer, Willard J.
1902–1962
Saranac Lake
Guideboats, outboard boats, flat-bottomed boats, canoes; see entries 26, 86

Harvey, Ed
w. 1890[?]
Colton
Guideboats

Hathaway, Carl
B. 1929
Saranac Lake
Guideboats
Worked with Willard Hanmer in the 1950s

Havens, Alex and Carlos
w. 1886
Port Henry
Unknown

Hayes, Dennis
ND
Westport
Unknown

Hayes, Ellsworth
B. 1848; w. 1880
Newcomb
Guideboats[?]

Haynor, Jake
w. ca. 1900
Old Forge
Guideboats
Worked in Parsons's shop

Hegeman, John
w. 1874
Ballston Spa
Portable boats

Henderson, Scott
w. 1906
Cleverdale on Lake George
Row and motor boats

Hinkson, Daniel
1861–1946
Tupper Lake
Guideboats[?]

Hitchcock, John
ND
Beaver Lake, Number Four
Guideboats

Huntington, Henry E.
w. 1892
Tupper Lake
Guideboats[?]

Hurst, Isaac A.
w. 1890s

Canton
Guideboats
Worked with Myron Nickerson

Jackson, Alfred
w. 1880–1912
Brushton
Lapstrake pleasure rowboats

Jacob, C. Albert, Jr.
1893–1969; w. 1914
Chestertown
Duck boat; see entry 191

Joyner, Fletcher
w. ca. 1880–1900
Glens Falls, Schenectady
Canoes and pleasure rowboats
Son Edgar ran the business after Fletcher's death

Kenyon, Fred, George, and Merit
w. 1897–1901
Saranac Lake
21' Truscott gasoline launch (kit boat)

Kerst, William Bartlett
1874–1950; w. 1895–1940
Sabael
Guideboats, launches, rowboats; see entries 97, 121

King Canvas Boat Co.
1880s–1920s
Kalamazoo, Mich.
Portable boats; see entry 47

Kingsley, Willis
w. 1914
Chestertown and Brant Lake
Flat-bottomed fishing boats; see entry 147

Kip, Benjamin F.
w. ca. 1880–1900 for Rushton
Canton
Designed some Rushton boats; see entries 35, 36

Kip, William F.
w. ca. 1880–1900 for Rushton
Canton
Rushton boats

Krumbholz, [?]
w. 1886
Saranac Lake
Guideboats
Worked for Adirondack Boatbuilding Co.

Lakefield Canoe Company
1913–ca. 1960

Lakefield, Ontario
Strip-built canoes; see entry 31

Lake George Boat Company
1930s
Lake George
Production runabouts
See Clarence Livingston

Leonard, John T.
w. 1873
Morley
Canoes[?]

Leyare, Joseph (Leyare Boat Works)
1905 – ca. 1927
Ogdensburg
Launches, skiffs, and sloops[?]
Successor to Spalding St. Lawrence
Boat Co.

Link, Edwin
w. 1945–1958
Binghamton
Sectional canoes and rowboats; see
entry 48

Livingston, Clarence
1912–1988; w. 1930s
Lake George
Runabouts (Lake George Boat
Co.)

Lozier Motor Co.
w. ca. 1898–1905
Plattsburgh
Launches; see entry 169

McCaffery, William
w. ca. 1910
Bloomingdale
Guideboats

McCormick, James
w. 1920
Potsdam
Wood/canvas canoes; see entry 46

**McLenathan, William (McLenathan
Brothers)**
w. 1850–1870
Lake Placid, Saranac Lake
Guideboats; see entry 81

Marsha, C. H.
w. 1890
Long Lake, Tupper Lake
Adirondack boats, oars, paddles,
rowlocks
Successor to H. L. Salisbury

Martin, Henry Kilburn
w. 1902–1906
Saranac Lake

Guideboats, canoes, "St. Lawrence
boats"; see entry 85

Martin, William Allen
1849–1907
Saranac Lake
Guideboat; see entry 82
Father of H. K. Martin

Maurice, Charles F., Sr.
w. ca. 1908
Bisby Lake
Amateur builder; see entry 40

Mead, George
w. 1920s
Lake George
Lake George rowboats[?]

Miller, Edward
1877–1962; w. ca. 1900–1925
Fort Covington
Launches

Miller, Frederick Milo
w. ca. 1890–1903
Morris Heights, Plattsburgh
Launches
Designer; worked for Charles
Seabury and Lozier

Miller, George
w. 1904–1928
Clayton
St. Lawrence skiffs

Moody, Alaric B.
b. 1854
Tupper Lake
Guideboats

Morris, B. N.
w. 1882–1920
Veazie, Maine
Wood and canvas canoes; see entries 39, 41

Mullins, W. H., (Mullins Boat Co.)
1919
Salem, Ohio
Pressed steel boats and small
wooden launches; see entries
155, 175, 190

Nickerson, Myron Augustus
1843–1926; w. ca. 1887–1907
Canton
Rowboats, canoes, guideboats; see
entries 23, 95
Worked with Rushton before
working with Isaac Hurst, then
alone

Old Forge Boat Company
1896–1910
Old Forge
Guideboat-built rowboats, guide-
boats; see entry 120
See Theodore Seeber, Ben and Ira
Parsons

Old Town Canoe Co.
1900–
Old Town, Maine
Canoes, rowboats, outboard boats;
see entries 22, 157, 158, 178

Owen, Dyton
b. 1908
Tupper Lake
Guideboats[?]
Son of Earl Owen

Owen, Earl
1881–1943; w. 1895–1940
Tupper Lake
Guideboats[?]
Worked in Rushton's shop before
going independent. Son of
Luther Owen

Owen, Luther W.
w. ca. 1890s
Potsdam, Tupper Lake
Guideboats[?]
Founded Owen Boat and Motor
Co. in Tupper Lake, 1890

Palmer, Cyrus H.
1845–1897
Long Lake
Guideboats

Palmer, Ransom
Before 1898
Long Lake
Guideboats

Parsons, Ben
1868–1945; w. 1890–1941
Old Forge
Guideboats

*The Seeber and Parsons boat shop, 1892. Left to
right: Ira Parsons, Len Ingersoll, Theodore Seeber,
Riley Parsons, Ben Parsons.* P. 20704

Son of Riley with brother Ira:
 1890–1896 Seeber & Parsons;
 1897–1904 Parsons & Co.;
 1904–1909 Parsons & Roberts;
 1910–1945 Parsons Brothers
See entries 102, 103, 104, 117, 118

Parsons, Ira
1860–1949; w. 1890–1941
Old Forge
Guideboats

Parsons, Riley
1839–1904; w. 1880s–1904
Old Forge
Guideboats
Father of Ben and Ira, worked with
 H. D. Grant

Peacock, Thomas
ND
Saranac Lake
Unknown

Peck, Chet (Charles A.)
B. 1828; w. 1890
Saranac Lake
Unknown

Peck, Robert J.
w. 1887
Long Lake
Guideboat accessories and repairs

Perkins, C. E.
w. 1900–1920
Malone
Guideboats[?]

Peterborough Canoe Co., Ltd.
1892–1962
Peterborough, Ontario
Canoes; see entries 28, 29

Philbrick, J. A.
B. 1836; w. 1870–1880
Harrietstown
Guideboats[?]

Plumley, John
w. 1872
Long Lake
Guideboats[?]

Pocock, George
w. 1911–1960s
Seattle, Wash.
Racing shells; see entry 166

Poillon, C & R
w. ca. 1842–1900
New York City
Steamboat *Effingham* for Schroon
 Lake

Rarick, Art
w. 1916
Fourth Lake
Custom launches, guideboats

Rasmussen, H.
w. 1900
Essington, Penn.
Motor launches; see entry 168

Ricc, Fred M.
1876–1966; w. ca. 1900
Saranac Lake
Guideboats; see entry 177
Son of Fred W. Rice

Rice, Fred W.
1852–1934; w. 1879–1904
Saranac Lake
Guideboats

Rice, George
w. 1902
Saranac Lake
Unknown

Rice, Herbert
w. ca. 1910
Canton, Dekalb Jct.
Worked for Rushton before going
 independent

Ricketson, E. G.
w. ca. 1889–1900
Bloomingdale
Guideboats; see entry 87

Rivett, Jack
1869–1949; w. 1920s
Old Forge
Gasoline excursion launches; see
 entry 174

Roberts, John
w. 1904–1909
Old Forge
In partnership with Parsons Brothers

Rogers, J. H.
w. 1875
Ogdensburg
Skiffs, hunting, fishing boats

Rogers, L. D. & Co.
1853–1926; w. ca. 1880–1919
Brasher Falls
Pleasure rowboats; see entry 143

Rushton, John Henry
1843–1906; w. 1873–1906
Canton
Pleasure rowboats, canoes, duck

boats, small launches,
 guideboats
Shop continued under son Joseph
 Henry (Harry) and then half-
 brother Judd W., until 1915 or
 1916. See entries 14, 15, 34–37,
 42, 43, 52–59, 91–94, 136–142,
 182

Ruth, James
1868–1930
Skaneateles
Canoes, pleasure rowboats;
 see Skaneateles Boat and
 Canoe Co.

Sabattis, Isaac
D. 1912
Long Lake
Guideboats[?]

Sabattis, Mitchell
1817–1906
Long Lake
Guideboats[?]; see entry 63

**St. Lawrence River Skiff, Canoe and
 Steam Launch Co.**
1888–1895
Clayton
Cedar canoes; see entry 135
Successor to A. Bain & Co.;
 became Spalding St. Lawrence
 Boat Co.

Salisbury, Herbert L.
w. 1870s–1881
Long Lake, Saranac Lake
Adirondack boats and oars, paddles, supplies; See entry 61

Sauve, Moses & Son
w. ca. 1890
Brockville, Ontario
Skiff; see entry 134

Seeber, Theodore
D. 1898; w. 1888–1896
Old Forge
Guideboats
Worked with Riley Parsons

Sexton, Jesse
1869–1928; w. 1895–1925
Hague
Launches: *Ella, Gypsey, Uncas*

Shaw, Charles E.
w. 1890s
Saranac Lake
Guideboats

Sheldon Lumber Yard
1930s
Fort Ann
"Sea Sleds"

Sherman, Jehaziel
w. 1824
Lake Champlain
Steamboats

Shumway, [?]
ND
Lake Placid
Guideboats

Skaneateles Boat and Canoe Co.
1893–1940s
Skaneateles
Pleasure skiffs, rowboats, and
canoes; see entry 144

Slater, Warren J.
1849–1921
Moody-on-Big Tupper
Guideboats
Worked with Alaric Moody

Smith, F. R. & Sons
w. 1908–1920
Bolton Landing
Lake George rowboats; see entries
131, 132

Smith, George
w. 1890–1932
Skaneateles
Canoes, rowboats, sailboats
Partner with James Ruth in
Skaneateles Boat and
Canoe Co.

Smith, George W.
1866–1926; w. 1907–1926
Long Lake
Guideboats; see entries 65, 66, 67

Smith, Olie
w. 1912
Lake George
Unknown

Spalding St. Lawrence Boat Co.
1895–1905
Ogdensburg
Sailboats, sailing yachts, dinghies,
skiffs, canoes, and launches; see
entry 181
Successor to St. Lawrence River
Skiff, Canoe and Steam
Launch Co. Became Leyare
Boat Works

Sprague, Herbert M.
1856–1929; w. 1869–1920s
Parishville
Guideboats, rowboats, and canoes;
see entries 18, 145

Stanton, George B.
1847–1935; w. 1876
Long Lake
Guideboats
Brother of Henry Stanton

Stanton, Henry
1844–1881; w. 1880
Long Lake
Guideboats

Stanton, William
1818–1890
Long Lake
Guideboats[?]

Stephens, William Picard
1854–1946
New York City
Canoes
1873–1883 built boats, then
designed yachts and wrote
about yachting

Stevens, William F.
B. 1850; w. 1866–1918
Lowell, Mass., and Bath, Maine
Racing canoes; see entry 50

Stowe, Bub
w. ca. 1884
Colton
Guideboat; see entry 90

Straight, Claude
w. 1945
North Creek
Amateur builder; see entry 192

Streeter, Asa
1830–1900
Horicon
Flat-bottomed fishing boats

Streeter, Elmer
1860–1940
Horicon
Brant Lake fishing boats

Thomas, Willard
ND
West Bangor
Rowing/outboard boats

Thompson, Albert
ND
Cranberry Lake
Unknown

Thompson, George L.
ND
Cranberry Lake
Unknown

Thompson, Louis
w. 1905
Inlet
Bark canoes

Vassar, William
w. ca. 1890–1920s
Bloomingdale
Guideboats; see entry 115

Villeneuve, Joseph
ND
Tupper Lake
Unknown

Vincent, [?]
ND
Lake Placid
Guideboats[?]

Waters, E. & Sons
w. 1867–1901
Troy
Paper boats; see entries 152, 164
Also Waters & Balch

Watertown Boat & Canoe Co.
w. 1881
Watertown
Pleasure boats and canoes

Watson, Benjamin
w. 1840
West Troy
Steamboat for Piseco Lake

White, E. M.
1889–1947
Veazie, Maine
Canoes; see entry 45

Wilbur & Wheelock Co.
w. 1897
Clayton
St. Lawrence skiffs, canoes

Wilson, Hiram
w. 1870–1902
Oneida
Pleasure rowboats; see entry 149

Williams, [?]
w. ca. 1890
Malone
Guideboats

Wood, Jerome
1840–1923
Raquette Lake, Pottersville, Long
Lake
Guideboats

Appendix

This appendix contains plans for nine types of boats discussed in the text. Complete plans for all these boats, except the tin rowboat and the St. Lawrence skiff, are available for sale by the Adirondack Museum.

The plans are of three types: lines plans, construction plans, and sail plans. The lines show the shape of the boat and the hull seen broadside on. The half-breadth plan is one half of the hull as seen from above. The body plan is transverse or cross-sections of the hull as seen from the end. This plan is divided in half down the middle, with the shape of the boat from midships forward on one side and the shape of the boat from midships aft on the other.

A classic text useful for understanding the basics of reading plans and for boat construction generally is Howard I. Chapelle's *Boatbuilding: A Complete Handbook of Wooden Boat Construction* (1941).

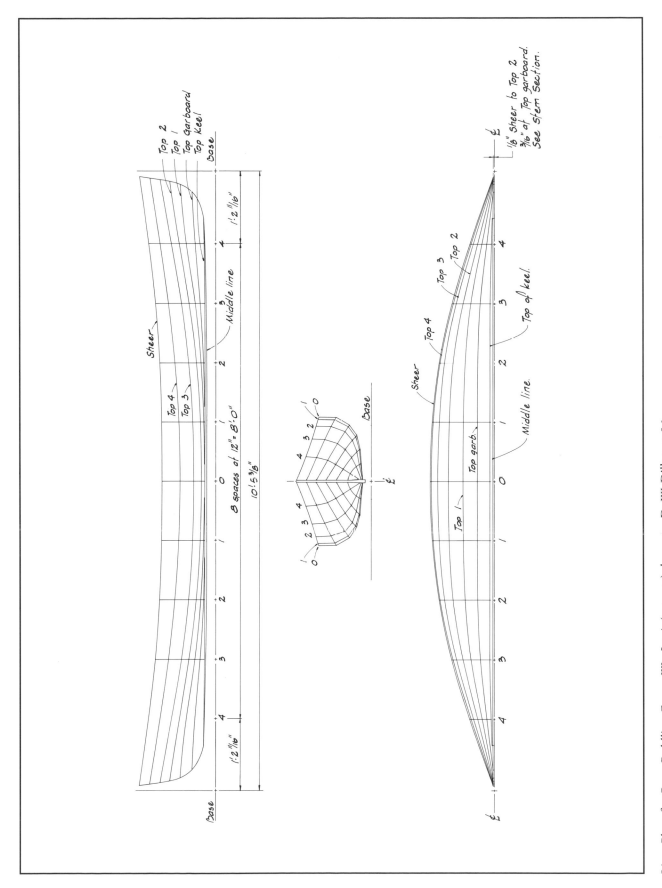

Lines Plans for Open Paddling Canoe *Wee Lassie* (entry 15) drawn by D. W. Dillon, 1986.

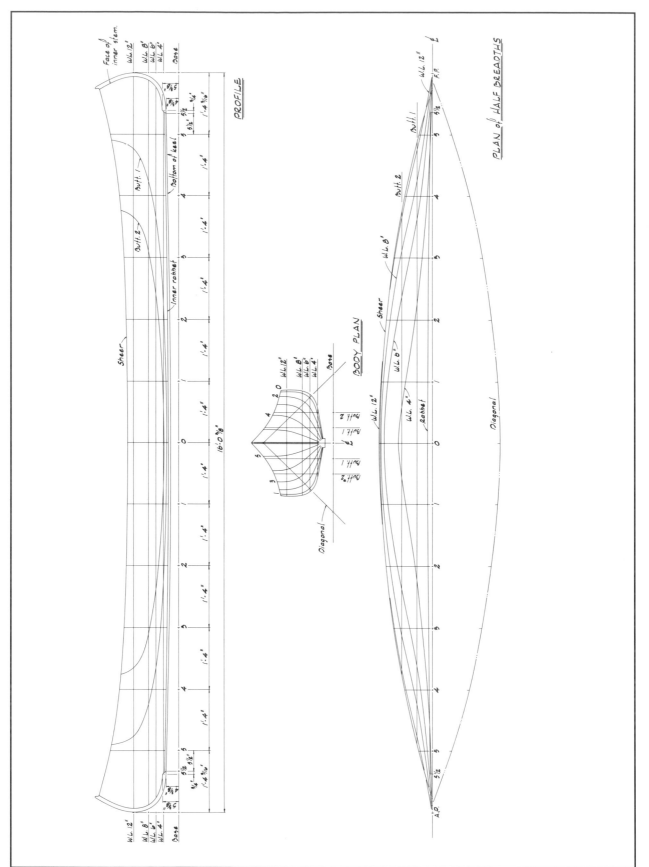

Lines Plans for Arkansaw Traveler Model Open Paddling Canoe (entry 36) drawn by D. W. Dillon, 1984.

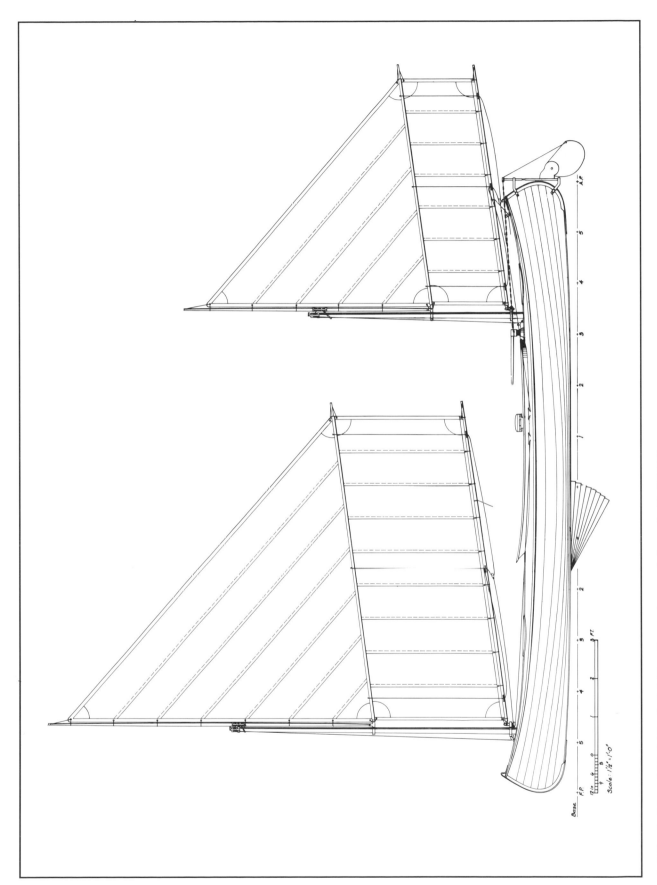

Sail Plan for Nomad Model Decked Sailing Canoe (entry 56) drawn by D. W. Dillon, 1994.

THE ST. LAWRENCE RIVER SKIFF.

LIKE the sneakbox, the ducker and the tuckup, the St. Lawrence River skiff, so highly praised by all who have used it, is the outgrowth of certain conditions and local surrounding , and like each of the others it is specially good for its destined use. The exact origin of the boat is not quite clear; it is practically but a large canoe, and so it might be considered as an enlargement of the ordinary open canoe so common on the St. Lawrence; but as the drawings show, it resembles much more closely the decked canoe of the States in model and construction.

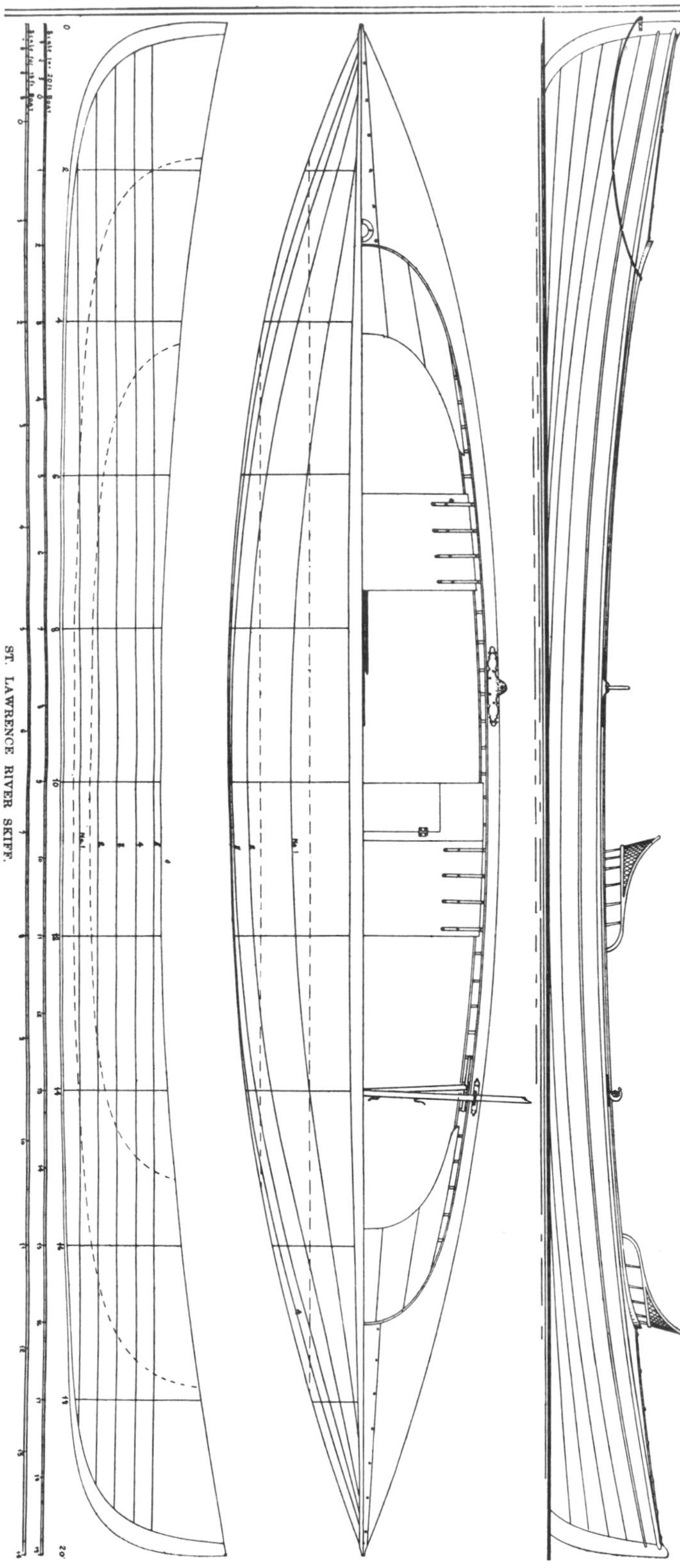

The boats are used everywhere about the Thousand Islands for fishing, rowing and sailing, to the exclusion of all other small boats. They are handled by professional boatmen, who show the greatest skill in their handling. The accompanying design, for which we are indebted to Dr. A. Bain, of the St. Lawrence River Skiff, Canoe and Steam Launch Co., was made to send to Switzerland, the boat being built there. Dr. Bain has used and studied the St. Lawrence skiff for many years, and has probably done more to improve and develop it than any one else.

But little explanation of the drawings is needed. the dimensions being given below. the ordinary size is 20 to 22ft. long and 3ft. 6in. beam, but a scale is given for a 15ft. boat as well, which would be a very good 15×31½ canoe. The boat is rowed in either direction, and is provided with chair seats for the passengers. In the center is the fish box, the top of which forms a seat. In

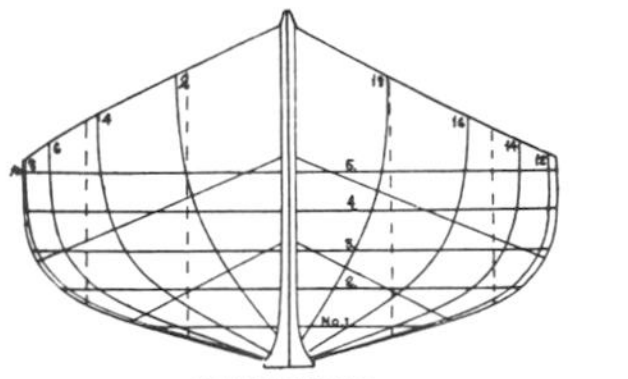

MIDSHIP SECTION.

addition to the rowlocks the gunwale is provided with a folding metal hook on each side, with a socket on the opposite side of the boat, to hold a trolling rod, as shown. The hull is lapstrake, with timbers small and closely spaced, there being a small deck at each end. A folding board and one sprit sail is used.

The chief peculiarity of the boat is the absence of a rudder, even in sailing, the steering being done by trimming the sheet and changing the balance of the boat. The boatman brings her up into the wind by moving into the bow, and causes her to fall off by moving aft, handling her as perfectly as could be done by a rudder. The shifting position of the center of lateral resistance is shown in the sail plan, the after center being when trimmed by the stern for running, and the forward one when going to windward. The measurements are as follows:

	20ft. boat.	15ft. boat.
Length over all	20ft.	15ft.
L. W. L.	19ft. 1 in.	14ft. 3⅜in.
Beam, extreme	3ft. 6 in.	2ft. 7½in.
Draft	8 in.	6 in.
Least freeboard	8 in.	5½in.
Sheer { Bow	10¼in.	8in.
{ Stern	10⁹in.	8⅛in.
Fore side of stem to mast tube	2ft. 9 in.	2ft. 0⁶in.
Coaming { Fore end	3ft. 11in.	2ft. 2⁸in.
{ After end	17ft.	12ft. 9 in.
Rowlocks {	8ft. 9⁴in.	6ft. 7⁴in.
Slot { Fore end	6ft. 10in.	5ft. 1½in.
{ After end	9ft. 5 in.	7ft. 0⁶in.
Mast, deck to truck	8ft. 7 in.	6ft. 5 in.
Diameter { Deck	2⁶in.	2 in.
{ Truck	1 in.	0⁶in.
Boom, length	12ft. 2 in.	9ft. 1⁸in.
diameter	1⁸in.	1 in.
Sprit, length	10ft. 6 in.	7ft. 11in.
diameter	1 in.	0⁶in.
Sail, foot	11ft. 10in.	9ft. 10⁶in.
luff	7ft. 1 in.	5ft. 4 in.
head	5ft. 6 in.	4ft. 1⁸in.
leech	12ft. 9 in.	9ft. 7 in.
tack to peak	12ft.	9ft.
clew to throat	12ft. 8 in.	9ft. 6 in.
area	.76sq. ft.	43sq. ft.

TABLE OF OFFSETS, 20FT. BOAT.

Stations.	HEIGHTS.		HALF-BREADTHS.					
	Deck.	Rabbet.	Deck.	No. 5.	No. 4.	No. 3.	No. 2.	No. 1.	Rabbet.
0...	2 2⁴			0¹						0⁴
2...	1 10²	2³	8⁷	8¹	7¹	1 5⁴	3⁴	1	0⁴
4...	1 7²	0³	1 3⁴	1 2⁷	1 2³	1 1	10	5	1⁴
6...	1 5²	0¹	1 7¹	1 6⁷	1 6⁴	1 5²	1 2⁷	8⁴	1⁷
8...	1 4		1 8⁷	1 8⁴	1 8⁴	1 7²	1 5⁴	10⁵	2
10...	1 3⁴		1 9	1 8⁴	1 8⁷	1 8⁴	1 6	11⁴	2
12...	1 4		1 8³	1 8²	1 8²	1 7⁴	1 5¹	10⁴	2
14...	1 5	0¹	1 6⁴	1 6²	1 6	1 4⁴	1 2²	8²	1⁷
16...	1 7¹	0⁴	1 2⁶	1 1⁷	1 1²	11⁴	9¹	4⁷	1³
18...	1 10⁵	2³	8	7³	6⁴	5¹	3⁴	1	0⁴
20.	2 2⁴		0¹						0⁴

TABLE OF OFFSETS, 15FT. BOAT.

Stations.	HEIGHTS.		HALF-BREADTHS.					
	Deck.	Rabbet.	Deck.	No. 5.	No. 4.	No. 3.	No. 2.	No. 1.	Rabbet.
0...	1 5		0⁷						0²
2...	1 4⁴	1⁶	6⁵	6¹	5³	4¹	2⁶	0⁴	0⁴
4...	1 2²	0⁴	11⁴	11³	10⁵	9⁵	7³	3⁴	1¹
6...	1 0⁴	0¹	1 2³	1 2²	1 1⁴	1 1²	11⁹	6²	1³
8...	11⁷		1 3⁴	1 3⁴	1 3²	1 2⁷	1 1	7⁷	1⁴
10...	11⁴		1 3⁴	1 2⁴	1 3⁵	1 3²	1 1⁴	8³	1⁴
12...	11⁷		1 3²	1 3³	1 3	1 2³	1 0⁶	7⁷	1⁴
14...	1 0⁴	0¹	1 1⁴	1 1³	1 1⁵	1 0⁴	10⁵	6²	1²
16...	1 2³	0⁴	10⁴	10⁵	9⁶	8⁷	5⁶	3²	
18...	1 4⁶	1⁶	6	5⁴	4²	3²	1		
20...	1 8		0¹						0²

ST. LAWRENCE RIVER SKIFF.

MOHICAN C. C.—The last camp-fire of the season was held on the evening of April 6 at the Windsor. Plans for the summer work were arranged, and there is every appearance of an active and successful season. After the meeting we were entertained in regal style with eating, drinking and smoking, interspersed with delightful music, excellent singing and stories old and new. We gathered around the bowl of glorious punch, determined to make this the closing of our winter camp-fires a grand success.—PURSER.

Lines Plans for St. Lawrence skiff by the St. Lawrence River Skiff, Canoe and Steam Launch Company (similar to entry 135). Plans appeared in *Forest and Stream* April 25, 1889.

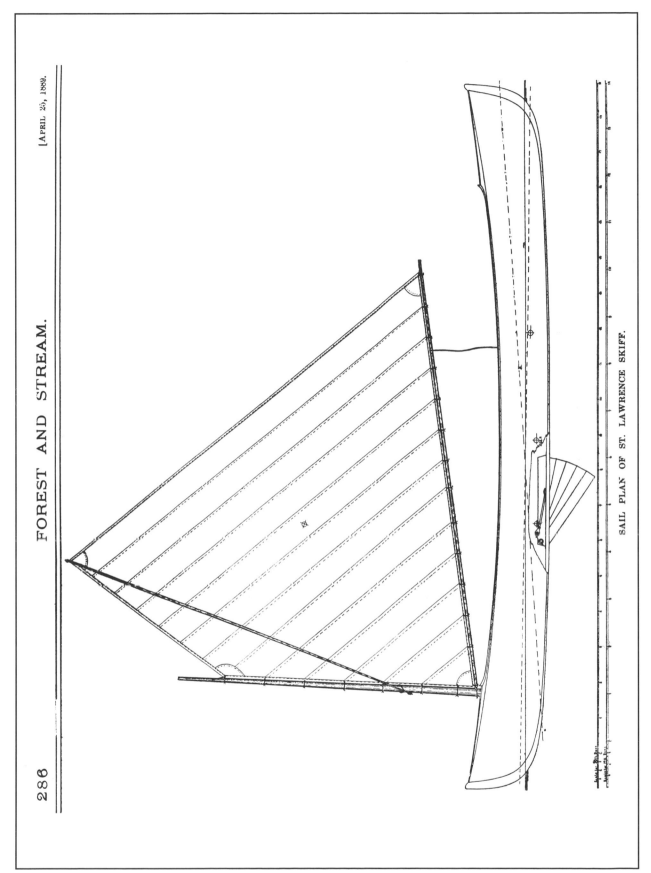

FOREST AND STREAM.

286

[APRIL 25, 1889.

SAIL PLAN OF ST. LAWRENCE SKIFF.

Sail Plan for St. Lawrence skiff by the St. Lawrence River Skiff, Canoe and Steam Launch Company (similar to entry 135). Plans appeared in *Forest and Stream* April 25, 1889.

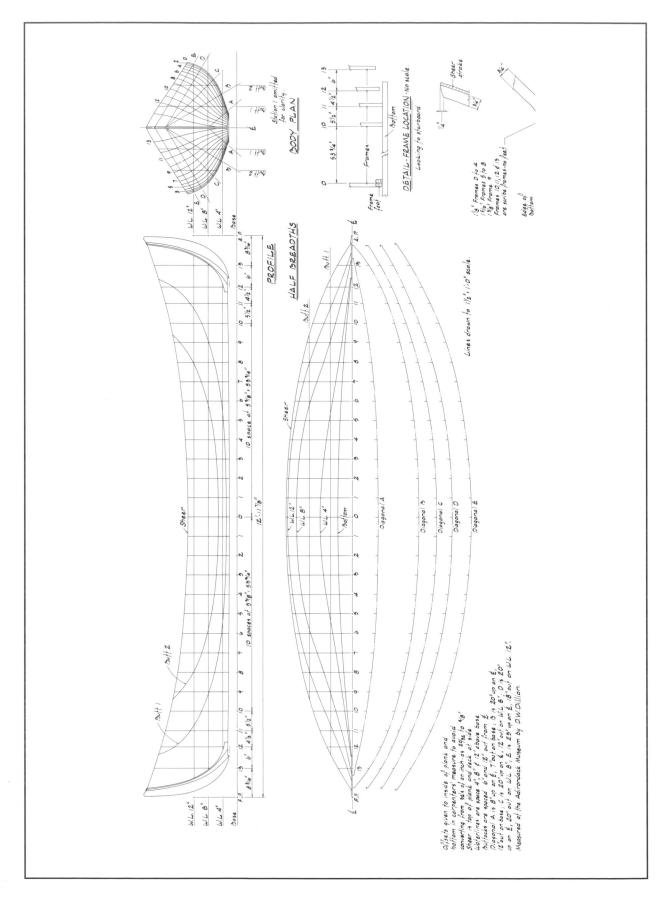

Lines Plans for an Adirondack Guidboat by Parsons (entry 103) drawn by D. W. Dillon, 1984.

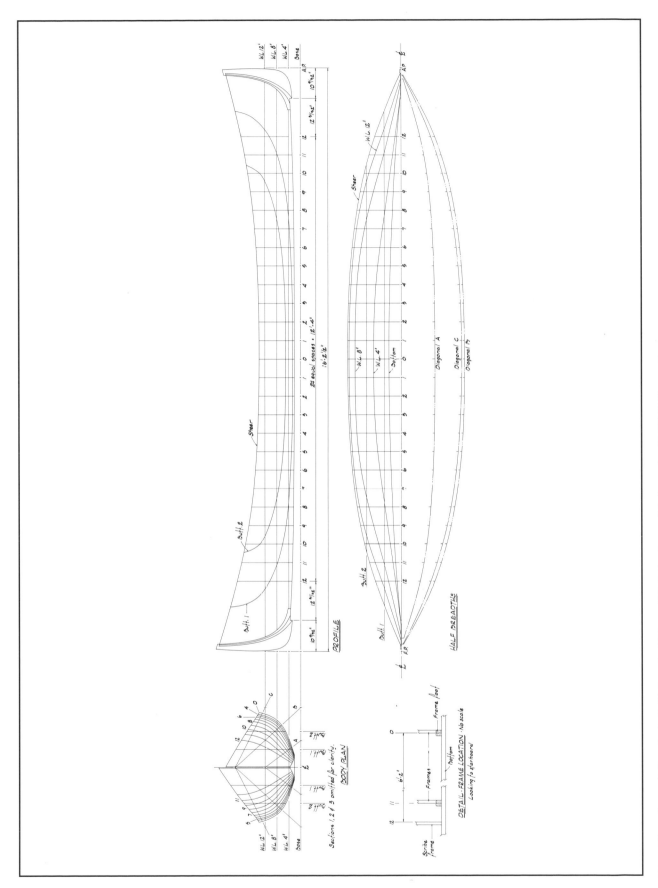

Lines Plans for an Adirondack Guideboat by Warren W. Cole (entry 69) drawn by D. W. Dillon, 1984.

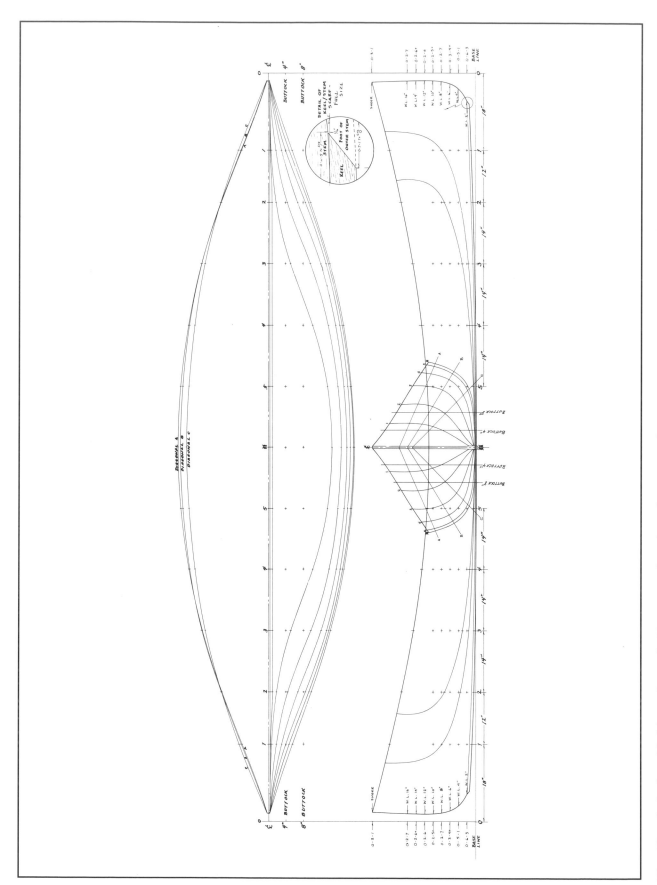

Lines Plans for Rushton Model #109 Lapstrake Pleasure Rowboat (an earlier version of entry 140) drawn by W. E. Mills, 1984, from a boat at Mystic Seaport Museum.

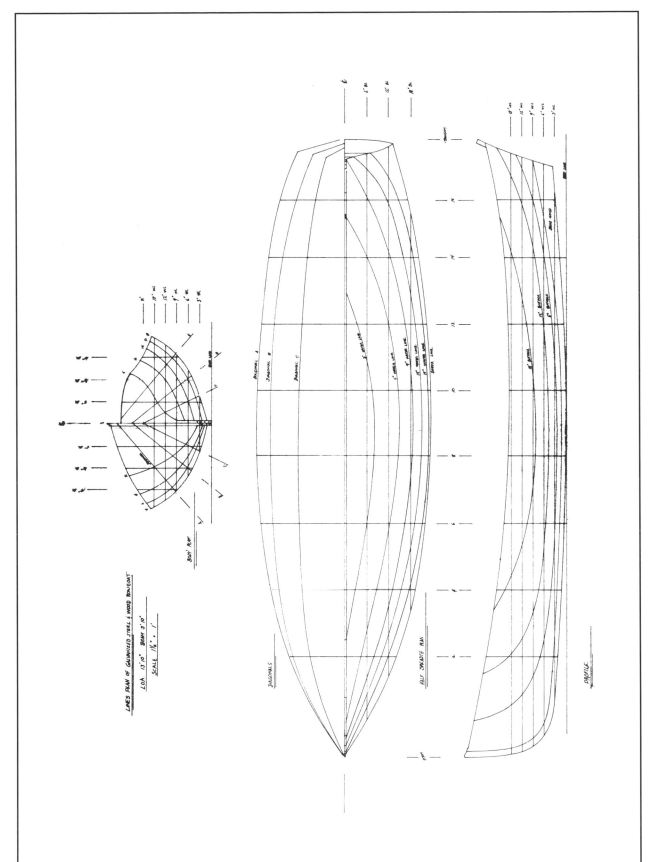

Lines Plans for "Tin Rowboat" (entry 155) drawn by F. Everett Smith, 1988.

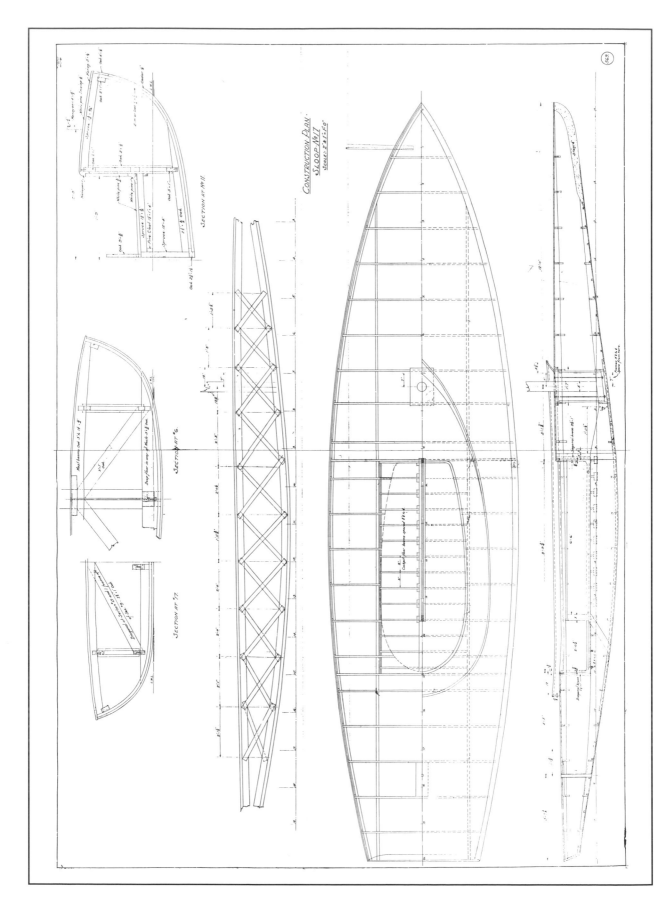

Construction Plan for Idem Class Racing Sloop *Water Witch* (entry 181) drawn by Clinton Crane between 1897 and 1900.

Sail Plan for Idem Class Racing Sloop *Water Witch* (entry 181) drawn by Clinton Crane between 1897 and 1900.

Glossary

aft, after
toward the back end of the boat, in that direction.

amidships, midships
in the middle of the boat.

ballast
weight placed low in the boat to increase stability. "Live ballast" is people, placed where they do the most good.

battens
in sails, wooden slats inserted in pockets to keep trailing edge of sail flat; in boat construction, thin strips of wood covering the seams between planks, inside the hull.

beam
in boats, the measurement of greatest width.

bilge, bilges
of hulls, the area where bottom meets side, described as "slack" or "hard" depending on the curvature.

boom
the spar attached to the foot (or bottom edge) of a sail.

bottom board
the central structural part of a guideboat. A single wide board, tapered to narrow ends, laid flat. Ribs and stems are fastened to it before the guideboat is planked.

bow
forward end of a boat in its usual direction of travel.

breasthook
in a boat without a deck, a pointed piece of wood fit between gunwales at the bow, reinforcing their convergence; traditionally made from wood with very sharply curving (or hooking) grain.

camber
the thwartships curvature of decks, causing them to shed water.

canoe
a small boat of long and narrow proportions, sharp at both ends and light in weight, usually propelled by paddle.

caulking
material such as cotton or oakum driven into the seams of a carvel planked boat to make them tight.

carry
the Adirondack word for *portage*; a path overland from one body of water to another, or the task of carrying a boat over it.

carvel, caravel
type of boat construction in which planks are fitted flush, edge to edge, and fastened to the frames. The seams between planks are then usually caulked.

catboat
a decked centerboard sailboat of shallow draft and broad beam, with a single sail.

cat rig
sail rig typical of catboats: a single sail, often gaff-rigged, with the mast stepped well forward in the bow. Many two-masted decked sailing canoes are said to be cat ketch rigged, because their masts carry only one sail each, mainmasts are stepped way forward, and the second masts (mizzen masts) are shorter.

centerboard
a metal or wooden plate, housed in a longitudinal "trunk" over a "slot" in the keel of a sailboat. Pivoting on a pin in the keel, it is lowered into the water to provide resistance to lateral motion (side-way) in sailing.

chine
the line of intersection between sides and bottom of a flat or V-bottom boat.

chine log
longitudinal timber connecting frames at the chine, to which side and bottom planking are fastened.

cleat
a piece of wood fastened into a boat to support or fasten something else, as in "yoke cleat" or "seat cleat"; also a piece of hardware for fastening lines.

clinker-built
see lapstrake.

clinch-nailing
a method of fastening, especially of lapstrake boats, with malleable nails or tacks which are driven clear through the two parts and a "clinching iron" is held against the further side to turn the points back into the wood, so that they tighten and hold.

Nomenclature for Small Craft

The terms used for the parts of inland boats are often different from those used on salt water.

Here are the basic parts of a 1903 rowboat *hull*—or body.

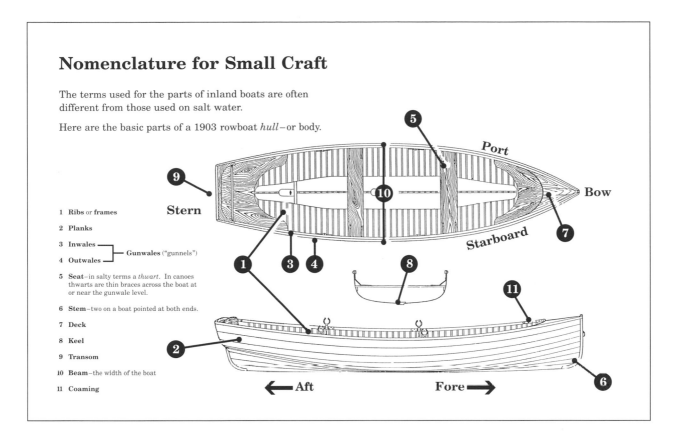

1 **Ribs** or frames

2 **Planks**

3 **Inwales** ⎤
4 **Outwales** ⎦ — **Gunwales** ("gunnels")

5 **Seat**—in salty terms a *thwart*. In canoes thwarts are thin braces across the boat at or near the gunwale level.

6 **Stem**—two on a boat pointed at both ends.

7 **Deck**

8 **Keel**

9 **Transom**

10 **Beam**—the width of the boat

11 **Coaming**

Stern · **Port** · **Bow** · **Starboard** · ← **Aft** · **Fore** →

---

closed gunwale
of wood/canvas canoes, a type of construction in which the top ends of the ribs and the spaces between ribs are covered.

coaming
the trim around the edge of decking as it opens into cockpit or open hull; usually raised to deflect water.

cockpit
of decked boats, an area left open for seating.

covering board
in small-boat decks, a piece of trim covering the centerline joint; used also of the fan-shaped forward part of typical guideboat decks, which overlaps the main deck piece.

crank, cranky
of a boat, "tippy" or "tender." That is, unstable, difficult to keep level.

daggerboard
as distinguished from a centerboard, which serves the same purpose, a daggerboard slides upward or downward through its trunk and slot, and comes completely out of its trunk when not in use.

deadrise
A measure of how far a boat is (at any point in its length) from being flat bottomed. A boat that has deadrise is not flat bottomed. A boat might have more deadrise forward than aft, or at both ends than amidships.

deck beam
thwartships piece of wood which supports the deck.

displacement
as an adjective, of a boat, displacing as much water when moving as when at rest; designed to move very easily at low speeds and therefore usually sharp at both ends under water. (See pages 176 177.)

double-bladed paddle
a paddle having a blade at each end, used alternately on each side of the craft.

double-ended
of boats, sharp or pointed at both ends.

fair
of curving lines, such as those of gunwales, or curved surfaces, such as the sides of boats: pleasingly smooth and even, gradual in any changes of their curvature; having no bulges, depressions, or wiggles, large or small.

feather-lapped planking
see guideboat lap.

fitting
generic term for specialized boat hardware, such as oarlocks, cleats, painter rings.

form
see mold.

forward
toward the bow; in that direction.

frames
transverse structural parts of a hull, defining its cross-sectional shape. (*see also;* Ribs)

freeboard
the amount of a boat's side that is above the water, normally or under a given load; thus, a way to speak of the boat's margin

of safety against water coming in from waves or changes in trim.

gaff rig
sail rig in which main sail is four-sided, with forward (vertical) edge attached to mast (usually by hoops) and upper (slanting) edge to a spar called the gaff.

garboard
on either side of a boat, the plank next to the keel or bottom board.

gore
triangular piece cut out of birch bark to make it fit the desired form, or, as in "gored planking," the horizontally tapered section of planking in the bilge area of a wood-canvas canoe. Tapering the planks in this section makes possible planking the rest of the canoe with straight planks of uniform width.

gudgeons
the "female" parts of the hinge-like hardware on which a rudder turns; see pintles.

guideboat lap
a type of planking in which the planks overlap as in lapstrake planking, but each is beveled to a thin edge in the area of the overlap, so that there is no clapboard effect; the boat is instead "smooth-skinned."

gunwale
the upper edge of a boat's side, including its reinforcement or trim, which may include an inner part (inwale), an outer part (outwale), and a gunwale cap.

hatch
an opening in a deck, giving access to space underneath; usually provided with watertight cover.

hull
the body of a boat exclusive of its hardware and equipment, sail rig, etc.

inboard
boat with a motor installed inside the hull; such a motor.

inwale
longitudinal part reinforcing the inner, upper edge of a boat's side; see gunwale.

kayak
as derived from the skin-covered boats of Arctic peoples, a very shallow double-ended boat, usually fully decked, paddled from amidships with a double-bladed paddle.

keel
the main center-line structural member of a boat's bottom, often projecting below the planking (not necessarily present in flat-bottomed boats); in certain sailboats, a deep, downward extension of this structural member providing resistance to lateral movement and often carrying ballast; the keel of a wood-canvas canoe, not integral to its construction and often omitted, is fastened on outside the canvas, mainly for the bottom's protection.

keelson
longitudinal timber inside a boat, running over the frames above the keel and fastened through them to it.

knees
pieces of wood used in bracing structures coming together at an angle: decks to sides, seats to planking, gunwales to tran-

som; also, the naturally curved raw material or "root-stock" for such parts as well as the ribs of guideboats.

lapstrake, lapstreak
a type of boat construction in which the planks overlap like clapboards and are fastened to each other as well as to the frames with rivets or clinch-nails.

lateen
a single-sail rig common on canoes (and Sunfish and Sailfish); the sail is triangular, with spars on two sides, linked together at their forward ends, the upper one (yard) hung from the (relatively short) mast.

launch
displacement powerboat, often with a roof or canopy over the passenger seating area.

leeboard
the usual means of providing resistance to lateral movement in open canoes being sailed; related to centerboard and daggerboard, but mounted outside the hull (often one on each side) and thus requiring no trunk or opening in the bottom.

leeward
to or on the side away from the pressure of the wind. The "lee" of a boat or a land-mass is the area it shelters from the wind; but a "lee shore" is a shore to leeward, against which a disabled boat could be blown.

limber holes
openings in the under edges of frames, permitting water inside a boat to pass through them.

lug sail
a four-sided sail suspended from a spar (called a yard) which hangs obliquely on the mast. Unlike a gaff sail's, its leading edge, or luff, is not attached to the mast but forward of it.

mast
an upright pole of some sort, supporting a sail.

mast partner
thwartships part with a hole in it, directly above mast step; a mast is "stepped" by sliding its foot through the partner and into the step.

mold
a structure over which a wooden boat is built, defining the boat's shape. A solid mold gives the whole hull's shape, as in a wood-canvas canoe mold; a set of differing sectional molds, spaced apart on a strongback, gives the shape of a small lapstrake boat.

naphtha
a volatile, flammable petroleum distillate used as both fuel and expansive liquid in boat engines around the end of the nineteenth century.

oar
a pole with a blade at one end and an in-line handle at the other; used in pairs in rowing, one hand for each oar, and pivoting on some kind of fulcrum (such as oarlocks or tholepins) on the gunwales.

oarlock
a metal swivel crutch for holding an oar in rowing; may be open, so that the oar drops into it from above; closed, so that it remains loosely on the oar; or pinned to the oar in one location; in all cases it has a shank which fits into a socket mounted on the gunwale and pivots there.

offsets
    loosely, a set of measurements which describe the particular shape of a hull.

outboard
    boat designed to have a removable motor attached to the transom; or, such a motor.

outrigger
    a structure for supporting oarlocks outboard of the gunwales, as in rowing shells or, less extremely, in some fixed-seat rowing boats of narrow beam; also, rarely in the Adirondacks, a secondary, parallel hull attached to a narrow boat to stabilize it, usually in sailing.

outwale
    longitudinal piece reinforcing the upper outer edge of a boat's side; see gunwale.

paddle
    an implement for propulsion using two hands; has a cross-handle at the upper end, a shaft which can be gripped lower down, and a blade.

pintles
    mounted on the forward edge of the rudder, these are the "male" parts of the rudder hardware; see gudgeons.

planing
    of hulls, designed to be supported, when running at normal speeds, by the inertia of the water, rather than by displacement as when floating at rest; thus, rising and "skimming over the water." (See pages 176–177.)

planking
    the wooden covering on a boat's ribs or frames, comprised of planks (also called strakes or streaks) or strips, and having various kinds of seams according to the type of construction. See clinker, lapstrake, carvel, guideboat lap, shiplap, and strip-building.

plumb stem
    a stem that is perpendicular to the water's surface.

rabbet
    a recess cut out of the face of a surface; a keel can be rabbetted to receive the garboard, and guideboat stems are rabbetted to receive the ends of the planks.

rake
    slant, or inclination away from the vertical; used of masts and transoms, commonly, and of stems. Reverse-raked stems, as in most guideboats, are often called tumblehome stems.

ribs
    transverse structural members in small wooden boats where there are many such parts, of small scantlings; would be called frames in larger boats or where they are heavier and fewer; of two basic types: steamed and bent, or sawn to shape, often from naturally curved timber.

rig
    as a noun, the arrangement of sail(s), spar(s) and lines, etc., of any sailing boat; as a verb, of a boat, to put its sails and spars, etc., or other accessories in readiness for immediate use.

rocker
    the greater or lesser convexity of a boat's bottom profile. If the profile is flat from end to end, the boat has no rocker.

rowlocks
    for the fussy, distinguished from oarlocks as including the oarlocks and the sockets in which they pivot.

rudder
    an underwater blade affixed to a boat, usually at the stern, for steering; distinct from the mechanism for turning it, which may be a simple tiller or yoke with steering lines.

runabout
    a planing inboard boat with open cockpit(s); typically mahogany, v-bottomed, with cushioned seats, windshield, and forward steering.

sawn frames
    ribs or frames sawn from naturally curved wood (in guideboats, usually spruce roots); distinguished from bent frames.

scantlings
    specifications for the width and thickness of the parts of a boat, particularly the frames (ribs) and planking; generally, an index of the weight and strength of the boat.

scarf, scarph
    a joint by which the ends of two pieces of wood are united in matching bevels so as to form a continuous piece.

sheer
    the top line of a hull as seen in profile; also, the amount of curvature in this line, or the difference in height between the ends and the middle of the hull.

sheerstrake
    the top plank on the side of a hull.

shiplap
    a type of planking in which the plank edges are rabbetted to half their thickness and the rabbets overlapped.

skeg
    a downward extension of the keel, at the stern, usually of a boat whose bottom rounds upward in that area; improves tracking and may support propeller shaft or rudder.

skiff
    often in other regions, a flat-bottomed boat with a transom, or any handy small workboat; in the Adirondacks, a guideboat or other double-ended rowing boat.

sloop
    single-masted sailing boat carrying a mainsail and a foresail (jib).

spar
    simply put: the "sticks" in a rig; long timbers, round in section, used for masts, booms, etc.

spiling
    the process of determining the actual shape or curvature a flat plank must have in order to fit its place on a boat.

sponsons
    longitudinal flotation chambers fitted outside and just beneath the gunwales of some canoes and rowboats, to increase stability.

stem
    the upright (in end-view) structural member forming the pointed end or ends of a boat, to which the ends of the planks are fastened.

stern
    the after or back end of a boat.

strake
    a single width of planking running the full length of a carvel or lapstrake boat; may be of one piece, or two or more pieces joined end-to-end. See planking.

strip-building
or strip-planking; a type of construction in which the planks are so narrow that they can be sprung edgewise as necessary to fit against each other over the complex curvature of the hull, and therefore do not need to be individually spiled.

strut
a fixture supporting the outboard end of a propeller shaft.

tiller
lever attached to a rudder, by which it is turned to steer a boat.

thole pin, tholepin
wooden or metal pin mounted vertically on the gunwale, on which or against which an oar is rotated in rowing.

thwart
in a small boat or canoe, a piece of wood extending from one gunwale to the other. Elsewhere the term may include seats, but in the Adirondacks, seats are called seats.

thwartships, athwartships
across the boat, versus lengthwise.

transom
the stern of a square-sterned boat, or either end of a pram or punt.

trim
of a boat's position in the water: how close it is to floating along its designated waterline. A canoe otherwise empty but for one person in the stern is out of trim.

tumblehome
the inward curving or slanting of the sides of a boat, so that in cross-section the widest beam is below the gunwales; common in canoes and at the sterns of runabouts and outboards; similarly, the inward rake of the stem or stems, as in many guideboats.

waterline(s)
the height of the water's surface all around a boat at its normal level of immersion; in a drawing of a boat's "lines," the waterlines show the boat's shape at several such horizontal planes, under and above the water.

windward
toward or against the wind; to or on the side against which the wind is blowing. Leeward is the sheltered, downwind side.

wineglass transom
a transom which, curving downward into a skeg, resembles the basin and stem of a wineglass.

yacht
strictly speaking, any boat built or used mainly for pleasure, regardless of the size or type.

yoke
in guideboats, a shaped wooden accessory for carrying the boat on one's shoulders; a simpler form replaces the straight middle thwart in some canoes.

Selected Bibliography

Most of the work for this book was done in the superb collections of the Adirondack Museum library. It is not within the scope of this bibliography to cite all the ephemera, periodicals, and manuscripts used herein. Any serious student of Adirondack boats and boating—and indeed, the history of inland pleasure boating in general—should explore the following major resources, all of which are in the library collections:

Kenneth and Helen Durant Collection: forty-three linear feet of manuscript material, exhaustively indexed, which is the result of Kenneth Durant's sixteen-year study of the Adirondack guideboat.

Contemporary guidebooks: the most widely-read of which were published by Seneca Ray Stoddard (generally titled *The Adirondacks Illustrated*) and E. R. Wallace.

Boatbuilders' catalogs: published only by some of the larger, full-time builders (only two guideboat builders issued circulars or catalogs). Several are widely available in reprint form, and an almost complete series of Rushton catalogs is available on microfilm.

Government reports: particularly those issued by the Adirondack Survey (Verplanck Colvin) and the Conservation Department.

Periodicals: for contemporary commentary, *Forest and Stream* and *The American Canoeist* are particularly valuable; for a modern perspective see *WoodenBoat*, *Wooden Canoe*, *Adirondack Life*, and *The New York State Conservationist*.

Two other major types of sources which are not at the Adirondack Museum should be mentioned here: the American Canoe Association collection at the New York State Historical Association in Cooperstown, New York, and twentieth-century boating periodicals such as *Motor-Boating*, *MotorBoat*, *Yachting*, and *Rudder*.

Below are listed the most useful and generally available works referred to in preparation of *Boats and Boating in the Adirondacks*. For a complete listing of all works cited the reader should consult the footnotes.

GENERAL WORKS ON AMERICAN HISTORY AND CULTURE

Belasco, Warren. *Americans on the Road: From Autocamp to Motel, 1910–1945*. Cambridge, Mass.: M.I.T. Press, 1979.

Braden, Donna. *Leisure and Entertainment in America*. Dearborn, Mich.: Henry Ford Museum and Greenfield Village, 1988.

Jakle, John. *The Tourist: Travel in Twentieth Century North America*. Lincoln, Neb.: University of Nebraska Press, 1985.

Lewis, David L., and Laurence Goldstein, eds. *The Automobile and American Culture*. Ann Arbor, Mich.: University of Michigan Press, 1983.

Nash, Roderick. *Wilderness and the American Mind*. New Haven: Yale University Press, 1967.

Schmitt, Peter J. *Back to Nature: The Arcadian Myth in Urban America*. New York: Oxford University Press, 1969.

Sears, John F. *Sacred Places: American Tourist Attractions in the Nineteenth Century*. New York: Oxford University Press, 1989.

Spectre, Peter H. *Different Waterfronts: Stories from the Wooden Boat Revival*. Gardiner, Maine: Harpswell Press, 1989.

Wiebe, Robert. *The Search for Order, 1877–1920*. New York: Hill and Wang, 1967.

GENERAL SECONDARY WORKS ON ADIRONDACK HISTORY AND CULTURE

Ackerman, David H., ed. *Placid Lake: A Centennial History, 1893–1993*. Lake Placid, N.Y.: The Shore Owners Association of Lake Placid, Inc., 1993.

Aber, Ted, and Stella King. *History of Hamilton County*. Lake Pleasant, N.Y.: Great Wilderness Books, 1965.

Bellico, Russell. *Sails and Steam in the Mountains: A Maritime and*

Military History of Lake George and Lake Champlain. Fleischmanns, N.Y.: Purple Mountain Press, 1992.

Comstock, Edward Jr., ed. *The Adirondack League Club, 1890–1990*. Old Forge, N.Y.: The Adirondack League Club, 1990.

Donaldson, Alfred. *A History of the Adirondacks*. 2 vols. 1921. Reprint, Harrison, N.Y.: Harbor Hill Books, 1977.

Graham, Frank. *The Adirondack Park: A Political History*. New York: Knopf, 1978.

Hochschild, Harold K. *Township 34: A History with Digressions of an Adirondack Township in Hamilton County in the State of New York*. New York: privately printed, 1952.

Jamieson, Paul, and Donald Morris. *Adirondack Canoe Waters, North Flow*. Lake George, N.Y.: Adirondack Mountain Club, 1991.

Manley, Atwood. *Rushton and His Times in American Canoeing*. Blue Mountain Lake, N.Y.: The Adirondack Museum; Syracuse, N.Y.: Syracuse University Press, 1968.

Pilcher, Edith. *Up the Lake Road: The First Hundred Years of the Adirondack Mountain Reserve*. Keene Valley, N.Y.: The Adirondack Mountain Reserve, 1987.

Terrie, Philip G. *Forever Wild: Environmental Aesthetics and the Adirondack Forest Preserve*. Philadelphia: Temple University Press, 1985.

———. *Wildlife and Wilderness: A History of Adirondack Mammals*. Fleischmanns, N.Y.: Purple Mountain Press, 1993.

SOME PRIMARY SOURCES FOR ADIRONDACK HISTORY

Bishop, Nathaniel Holmes. *The Voyage of the Paper Canoe*. Boston: Lee and Shepard Publishers, 1878.

Brenan, Dan, ed. *Canoeing the Adirondacks with Nessmuk: The Adirondack Letters of George Washington Sears* (1962) with revisions by Robert L. Lyon and Hallie E. Bond. Reprint, Blue Mountain Lake, N.Y.: The Adirondack Museum; Syracuse, N.Y.: Syracuse University Press, 1992.

Durant, Kenneth. *Guide-Boat Days and Ways*. Blue Mountain Lake, N.Y.: The Adirondack Museum, 1963.

Emerson, Ralph Waldo. "The Adirondacs, A Journal," in *Poems*. Boston: Houghton Mifflin and Co.; Cambridge, Mass.: The Riverside Press, 1892.

Hammond, Samuel H. *Hills, Lakes, and Forest Streams, Or, A Tramp in the Chateaugay Woods*. New York: J. C. Derby, 1854.

———. *Wild Northern Scenes: Or, Sporting Adventures With the Rifle and the Rod*. New York: Derby and Jackson, 1857.

Headley, Joel Tyler. *The Adirondack; Or Life in the Woods* (1849) with an introduction by Philip G. Terrie. Reprint, Harrison, N.Y.: Harbor Hill Books, 1982.

Murray, William Henry Harrison. *Adventures in the Wilderness, Or, Camp Life in the Adirondacks* (1869) with preface by William K. Verner and introduction and notes by Warder H. Cadbury. 1869. Blue Mountain Lake, N.Y.: The Adirondack Museum; Syracuse, N.Y.: Syracuse University Press, 1970.

Sears, George Washington. *Woodcraft*. 1920. Reprint, New York: Dover Publications, 1963.

Street, Alfred Billings. *Woods and Waters, Or, The Saranacs and Racket*. New York: M. Doolady, 1860.

Todd, John. *Long Lake*. Pittsfield, Mass.: E. P. Little, 1845.

WORKS ON BOATING AND BOAT TYPES

Adney, Edwin Tappan, and Howard I. Chapelle. *The Bark Canoes and Skin Boats of North America*. Washington, D.C.: Smithsonian Institution, 1964.

Alden, W. L. *The Canoe and the Flying Proa, Or, Cheap Cruising and Safe Sailing*. New York: Harper and Brothers, 1878.

Bray, Maynard. *Mystic Seaport Museum Watercraft*. Mystic, Conn.: Mystic Seaport Museum, Inc., 1979.

Chapelle, Howard I. *American Small Sailing Craft: Their Design, Development and Construction*. New York: W. W. Norton, 1951.

Durant, Kenneth and Helen. *The Adirondack Guide-Boat*. Blue Mountain Lake, N.Y.: The Adirondack Museum; Camden, Maine: International Marine Publishing Company, 1980.

Durant, Kenneth. *The Naphtha Launch*. Blue Mountain Lake, N.Y.: The Adirondack Museum, 1976.

Fenton, William N., and Ernest Stanley Dodge. "An Elm Bark Canoe in the Peabody Museum of Salem." *The American Neptune* 9, no. 3 (July 1949).

Fostle, D. W. *Speedboat*. Mystic, Conn.: Mystic Seaport Museum Stores, 1988.

Fuller, Benjamin A. G. "The Coming of the Explosive Engine." *The Log of Mystic Seaport* (Autumn 1993).

Gardner, John. *Building Classic Small Craft*. 2 vols. Camden, Maine: International Marine Publishing Co., 1977 and 1984.

———. *The Dory Book*. Mystic, Conn.: Mystic Seaport Museum, 1987.

Hunn, Peter. *The Old Outboard Book*. Camden, Maine: International Marine Publishing Co., 1991.

Mitchell, Richard K. *The Steam Launch*. Camden, Maine: International Marine Publishing Co., 1982.

Museum Small Craft Association. *Boats: A Manual for their Documentation*. Nashville, Tenn.: American Association for State and Local History, 1993.

Stelmok, Jerry, and Rollin Thurlow. *The Wood and Canvas Canoe: A Complete Guide to its History, Construction, and Maintenance*. Gardiner, Maine: Harpswell Press, 1987.

Webb, W. J., and Robert W. Carrick. *The Pictorial History of Outboard Motors*. New York: Renaissance Editions, Inc., 1967.

Index